THE NEW ENGLAND KNIGHT:
SIR WILLIAM PHIPS, 1651–1695

Born in 1651 in what is now Maine, William Phips became a sea captain out of Boston, an adventurer in search of Spanish treasure in the Caribbean. He captured and plundered Port-Royal in Acadia, now Nova Scotia, and led an unsuccessful expedition against Quebec in 1690. He became the first royal governor of Massachusetts in 1692, put an end to the Salem witchcraft trials, and negotiated a treaty with the native Wabanaki.

This biography presents a well-rounded picture of Phips, one that looks at all phases of his colourful career. He was an unusual figure among colonial governors, and his very uniqueness, as well as his difficulties as governor, help us to understand the politics and society of New England during his era. Helped and hindered by his obscure origins, Phips struggled for advancement, and his struggle illustrates the fluid nature of the British Empire in the late seventeenth century.

Phips's life was left unexplored by scholars for the past seventy years. *The New England Knight* reconstructs his career using contemporary material that brings life and immediacy to the narrative. It interacts with recent studies in colonial, imperial, aboriginal, and marine history to set Phips's eventful life in context.

EMERSON W. BAKER is an assistant professor in the Department of History at Salem State College and an editor of *American Beginnings: Exploration, Culture and Cartography in the Land of Norumbega.*

JOHN G. REID is a professor in the Department of History at St Mary's University and author of *Acadia, Maine, and New Scotland: Marginal Colonies in the Seventeenth Century.*

EMERSON W. BAKER AND JOHN G. REID

The New England Knight:
Sir William Phips, 1651–1695

UNIVERSITY OF TORONTO PRESS

Toronto Buffalo London

© University of Toronto Press Incorporated 1998
Toronto Buffalo London

Printed in Canada

ISBN 0-8020-0925-5 (cloth)
ISBN 0-8020-8171-1 (paper)

∞

Printed on acid-free paper

Canadian Cataloguing in Publication Data

Baker, Emerson W.
  The New England knight: Sir William Phips, 1651–1695

  Includes bibliographical references and index.
  ISBN 0-8020-0925-5 (bound)   ISBN 0-8020-8171-1 (pbk.)

  I. Phips, William, Sir, 1651–1695.   2. Massachusetts – History – Colonial
  period, ca. 1600–1775.   3. Adventure and adventurers – Massachusetts –
  Biography.   I. Reid, John G. (John Graham), 1948–   .   II. Title.

  F67.B24 1998   974.4'02'092   C97-932687-7

University of Toronto Press acknowledges the financial assistance to its
publishing program of the Canada Council for the Arts and the Ontario Arts
Council.

This book has been published with the help of a grant from the Humanities
and Social Sciences Federation of Canada, using funds provided by the Social
Sciences and Humanities Research Council of Canada.

For Jackie, Peggy, Jane,
Megan, Robert, and Sarah

Contents

A genealogy of the Phips family appears on page 6.

Illustrations follow page 104.

List of Maps

Preface

Sir William Phips had an unlikely career. On that much there has been agreement among virtually all the historians who have written about this treasure seeker and early royal governor of Massachusetts Bay. Our biography will not challenge the consensus on this point, but it will be our contention that there are precious few other areas of interpretation in which Phips has received due attention. Without attempting to portray Phips as a heroic character, or even necessarily – depending on one's taste in historical figures – an attractive one, we will argue that the significance of his life has been overlooked in the many simplistic references made to him by historians who have been disinclined to probe more deeply. Some have seen Phips as a braggart and bully, hopelessly out of his depth when thrust into governorship. Others have regarded him as a simpleton whose proximity to major processes and prominent individuals entitles him to be regarded at best as the Forrest Gump of Anglo-America in the 1690s, caught up in events he could not understand, or at worst as a clown whose freakish rise through the social ranks made him ultimately a ludicrous figure. Our contention will be that new questions need to be asked about Phips and his career, and new answers reached.

William Phips was born in 1651 to a family that lived by farming, and by trade with Wabanaki inhabitants of the area, in a small English community in the Kennebec region of northern New England in what is now Woolwich, Maine. Moving to Boston as a ship's carpenter in young adulthood, he married a merchant's widow and became a sea captain. During the 1680s, with support from wealthy English patrons, Phips headed a series of expeditions searching for sunken Spanish treasure ships in the Caribbean. Although he operated at first on the notoriously ill-defined margins that separated legal activity from piracy, a spectacularly successful expedition in 1686–7 brought him not only wealth but also respectability in the form of a knighthood. His career was then temporarily thrown into confusion by a series of events that began with a further and unsuccessful voyage, continued with a brief and unhappy sojourn as a patronage-appointed royal official in New England, and finally merged into the era of the English Revolution of 1688–9.

The pattern for the later phases of Phips's life was set by a nascent alliance with the political faction of the Puritan divines Increase and Cotton Mather, which was consolidated by Phips's religious conversion in early 1690. Among the immediate results were his successive appointments to command military expeditions against the French colonies of Acadia and Canada later that year. Unsuccessful as these ventures were in important respects – disastrous, in the case of the Canada expedition – Phips emerged personally unscathed and with political wounds that proved to be superficial. In London for most of 1691 and early 1692, he played a significant role in the discussions that led to the issuing of a new charter for Massachusetts, and he was then appointed as the colony's first royal governor. In that office, Phips claimed successes in putting an end to the Salem witchcraft trials and in negotiating a treaty with the Wabanaki in 1693. He also encountered serious setbacks, which arose from his conflicts with neighbouring colonial governors, customs officials, a naval captain stationed in Boston, and significant sections of the Massachusetts political elite. Although he had strong supporters, drawn from a wide social spectrum, Phips's crucial goal of using his governorship to assert English control over northern New England, Acadia, and Canada – and to enrich himself further while doing so – remained unfulfilled. Recalled to England to answer the charges of his critics, he died of a fever in London in early 1695.

The first biography of Phips was written in 1697 by Cotton Mather. Mather, who had regarded Phips as 'one of my own Flock, and one of my dearest Friends,' had both personal and political reasons for portraying the late governor in a favourable light.[1] Hence his account of Phips's heroic journey through life, beginning in the 'despicable Plantation' of his birth and ending with the accumulation of enough laudable deeds to justify the title 'PHIPPIUS MAXIMUS.' According to Mather, Phips was characterized by 'undaunted Fortitude' and by a 'Humble and Modest Carriage' that complemented his 'Hatred of Dirty or Little Tricks.' He was a kind neighbour, a faithful husband, and a conscientious church member, though not given to 'any mighty show of Devotion.' In his service to New England, stated Mather, Phips turned 'the old *Heathen* Virtue of PIETAS IN PATRIAM, or, *LOVE TO ONES COUNTRY* ... into *Christian;* and so notably exemplified it ... that it will be an Essential *Thread* which is now to be interwoven into all that remains of his *History*, and his *Character.'*[2]

All of this was controversial enough even in Mather's lifetime. Phips had many critics, including Mather's fellow divine, Samuel Willard, who had publicly indicated, in the election sermon he delivered in Boston in 1694, his distress at what he regarded as Phips's arbitrary uses of power. Mather's biography of Phips came under attack in 1700 by the Boston polemicist Robert Calef, who considered it an egregious self-justification on the part of Mather.[3] Later biographers have differed about the weight to be given to Mather's work. The laudatory account delivered by William Goold in 1879 to the Maine Historical Society – celebrating the achievements of a native son of Maine – used Mather's work extensively and chided another author, Francis Bowen, for expressing caution about some of Mather's more extravagant assertions. Bowen's biography of 1854 had taken Mather's word for Phips's personal virtues, but it had offered the judgment that Phips's lack of education had made him 'unfit to lead an army, or to govern a province, and the chance, which placed him in such situations, was an unlucky one.'[4] Another biography that drew heavily on Mather – filling in the gaps with an odd mixture of inference and invention – was Alice Lounsberry's *Sir William Phips: Treasure Fisherman and Governor of Massachusetts Bay* (1941). In Lounsberry's, view, Cotton Mather was 'the most eminent scholar of his day, a gentleman whose word should not be doubted,' while Phips was 'a stalwart, adventurous Colonist.'[5] To be fair, Lounsberry did consult a variety of other sources, but the book's methodology is dubious, and the long shadow of Mather is all too visible in its contentions.

Insofar as there was a real golden age of scholarly biography of Sir William Phips, it came long after Bowen and Goold and several years before Lounsberry. The late 1920s saw the appearance of two works of genuine substance and lasting value. In 1927 the Maine Historical Society published Henry O. Thayer's biography of Phips as 'adventurer and statesman.' The ninety-four-year-old Thayer had served for several years at Woolwich as a member of the clergy, and his generally favourable assessment of Phips bore some of the marks of local filiopietism. Distinguishing Thayer's work, however, was the care with which the author handled evidence – notably in matters of detail – and his recognition that Mather was a 'friendly biographer' from whose judgments dissent was necessary at times. For Thayer, Phips was undoubtedly a brave and vigorous patriot, but he was also an uneducated and undisciplined individual whose outbursts of violent temper 'cast spots of deep blemish' on his character.[6]

In 1928 Phips finally gained the sustained attention of a professional historian. Viola Florence Barnes was one of the most distinguished members of the 'imperial school' of historians, which was developed at Yale by Charles McLean Andrews. Her definitive study of the Dominion of New England was published in 1923, and in later years she presided over the Berkshire Conference of Women Historians.[7] Unfortunately, Barnes's study of Phips appeared only in the form of two linked articles in the first volume of *New England Quarterly*. Even so, she succeeded in just forty-six pages in situating Phips in imperial context while also setting earlier biographies in the mythological tradition of self-made heroes. For all that, she was not immune to the myth. She concluded that the evidence revealed 'the very human, likeable, and essentially modern adventurer that was William Phips.' Short as Barnes's study is, and although its arguments are debatable in places, it continues to represent the inauguration of detached scholarly examination of Phips.[8]

The legacy of all this biographical work on Sir William Phips has been decidedly mixed. Apart from brief though insightful sketches by C.P. Stacey and Richard R. Johnson in encyclopedic works, there has been no scholarly biography written since Barnes.[9] Much of the most effective writing, surprisingly perhaps, has focused on Phips's treasure-hunting activities. The *New England Quarterly* followed up on Barnes's works by publishing substantial articles in the early 1930s by Cyrus H. Karraker and Robert H. George, both of whom explored aspects of Phips's Caribbean voyages. Karraker's book on the search for sunken treasure off the coast of Hispaniola appeared in 1934.[10] Then came a lengthy gap until the publication in 1979 of Peter Earle's book, *The Treasure of the Concepción: The Wreck of the Almiranta*. Earle traced the fate of the treasure galleon *Nuestra Señora de la Concepción* from its final voyage in 1641 through successive searches and salvage attempts, until the 1970s. He firmly identified for the first time the vessel's identity and used both Spanish and English sources, including a crucial ship's journal he had located in the county archives of Kent, to shed new light on Phips's voyages. Although the book focuses on other searchers as well as Phips and covers a much longer period than just the 1680s, the sophistication of Earle's approach to such matters as patronage relationships and his

sureness of touch on navigational questions combine to make his work
an indispensable source on this phase of Phips's life.[11]

Other elements of Phips's career have fared very differently in much
of the scholarship of recent decades. The incompetence of his general-
ship during the expeditions of 1690 has largely been taken for granted,
and as a figure in the London of the post-revolution era Phips has been
portrayed – if at all – as nothing more than the creature of Increase
Mather.[12] As governor of Massachusetts, Phips's main historiographical
distinction has rested securely in his having been contemptuously dismissed by almost all the historians of colonial New England who
referred to him. More than one author has found in Phips a welcome
opportunity to enliven a political narrative with a touch of wit at the
expense of the 'fat, choleric hero,' as David Levin referred to him.
Michael G. Hall commented, 'Phips did try to carry on the traditional
pattern of a weak governor. But an ungoverned temper and a swash-
buckling personality were fatal flaws.'[13] Others have taken a more serious view. Perry Miller obviously did not see in Phips an embodiment of
the New England mind: 'Phips (bewildered in a dignity that was none
of his choosing) was anything but a [John] Winthrop; after him, the
governorship was foreseeably bound to degenerate from the pinnacle
of ultimate adjudication into a merely administrative office, and so to
be at the mercy of conflicting interests.' The harshest verdict was that of
J.M. Sosin, who condemned Phips as 'a crude, outspoken man with a
violent temper and poor judgment,' whose administration was 'disastrous' and whose death was the termination of a 'short, sordid tenure'
as governor.[14]

Like all stereotypes, these portrayals have elements of truth. But they
owe much to a willingness to accept at face value the contentions of
Phips's critics, notably in the superficial paralleling of Phips's violent
confrontation with the naval captain Richard Short and his entirely different dispute with the customs collector Jahleel Brenton. In many of the
historical treatments there are also strong hints of a visceral sense that
Phips's obscure origins made him fitter to wear the ass's head of the
rude mechanical with ideas above his station than to be compared – as
by Cotton Mather – to 'the Renowned *Fabius Maximus*, who ... did,
through a Zeal for his Country, overcome the greatest Contempts that
any Person of Quality could have received.'[15] Phips has often been portrayed in caricatures, and if the professional historians have not quite
reached the flights of fancy that enabled an author to inform young British readers in 1947 of the delight with which this 'attractive rascal' led

his crews of 'merry scamps' and 'cheerful scallywags,' it has not been for want of trying.[16]

New historiographies, however, raise new questions. For us, there have been at least four strands of recent interpretation that have been influential in our efforts to provide a fresh perspective on Sir William Phips and his times. The first has been the history of the non-English peoples of northeastern North America. Phips grew up with the Wabanaki as his everyday companions and with a close awareness of the proximity of the French settlements of Acadia. He had a lifelong interest in the northeastern areas that were included in the Massachusetts charter of 1691, especially their resources and thus their capacity to enrich both the empire and himself. In our view, this preoccupation and its reflection in the negotiations conducted by Phips with Wabanaki and Acadians is central to any understanding not only of his personal motivations but also of his career as governor. In exploring this theme, we draw in part on our own earlier studies but also on those of other major authors such as Jean Daigle and Kenneth M. Morrison.[17] Richard R. Johnson's biography of John Nelson, whose career as a merchant trading to Acadia overlapped at crucial times with that of Phips, has been invaluable, as has Johnson's earlier work on the empire and New England. While our view of Phips differs in certain respects from that of Johnson, his examination is unmistakably based on evidence rather than stereotype. The Nelson biography, along with William Godfrey's study of John Bradstreet, exemplifies the successful portrayal of individual lives pursued in the shifting contexts of early modern empires in northeastern North America.[18]

A second area of reinterpretation that has informed our understanding, particularly of the seagoing phases of Phips's life, can be placed under the general heading of marine history. Marcus Rediker's justifiably acclaimed study of the experience of seamen travelling the Atlantic on merchant and pirate vessels has assisted us in placing Phips's voyages on the continuum between legality and illegality, and in explaining behaviour – such as Phips's use of abusive language – that had social as well as purely personal origins. Recent historians of the later Stuart navy, notably Sari R. Hornstein and J.D. Davies, have illuminated for us the background to Phips's success in finding patrons for his treasure-seeking voyages, as well as setting a context for rapid social mobility – as enjoyed by successful 'tarpaulin' naval officers – within which Phips's experience can be more accurately assessed.[19] Phips's upward mobility was conspicuous, yet his critics were fond of observing that he did not noticeably refine his manners. The harsh language that he frequently used on those who incurred his displeasure, especially if their social origins were higher than his own, created a partially accurate impression that Phips was rude and unlettered. On the other hand, it contributed to his ability to gain and hold the support (whether of a crew sailing for virtually equal shares or of a crowd being roused to action on the wharves of Boston) of those who admired his repeated and often calculated lack of due respect for his betters.

Thirdly, we owe much to historians of the monied interests that were wielding increasing influence in the empire of the early 1690s. The insights of P.G.M. Dickson – a wise and influential teacher of one of us – were published in 1967 in *The Financial Revolution in England: A Study in the Development of Public Credit, 1688–1756*. Later studies by D.W. Jones and Gary Stuart De Krey further explored trade patterns and the role of City of London merchants of the era; a complementary North American dimension was added by Alison Gilbert Olson.[20] For the English empire as a whole, the financial implications of the Revolution of 1688–9 and the expensive wars that followed it have been explored by John Brewer in *The Sinews of Power* and in the extended analysis of the role of 'gentlemanly capitalism' advanced by P.J. Cain and A.G. Hopkins.[21] Phips's career was ending just as the outlines of Brewer's 'fiscal-military state' were beginning to be defined. Yet his experience during the 1680s as a projector (using this term in the sense conveyed in Daniel Defoe's *Essay upon Projects*, to mean a poor but ambitious individual intent on pursuing lucrative schemes), together with the access to Dissenting merchant networks that he gained from his close association with Increase Mather, caused Phips to set a high value on his ability to attract significant monied interests to potential trade opportunities in New England, Acadia/Nova Scotia, and Canada. In Phips's career, the apparently separate worlds of, on the one hand, Whitehall and the City of London and, on the other, the Wabanaki and Acadian communities of northeastern North America were brought into close juxtaposition.[22]

The fourth influence on our study has been the ongoing re-examination of the social history of seventeenth-century New England, which gathered much of its initial force from the publication in 1970 of works by Kenneth Lockridge, John Demos, and Philip J. Greven.[23] The community studies of these authors and the diverse trains of inquiry that followed them have tended to be highly interdisciplinary, drawing on such cognate fields as anthropology, demography, psychology, historical geography, and historical archaeology. In our study, works of this kind have been particularly influential in our understanding of Phips's early life and kinship ties and his role in the Essex County witchcraft outbreak of 1692. The analysis of Salem witchcraft by Paul Boyer and Stephen Nissenbaum, and the broader contexts provided by authors such as Demos and David D. Hall have led to a new and more subtle appreciation of the complexities of witchcraft, which in turn has produced a substantial corpus of new interpretations.[24] We have drawn on this material in delineating the social, political, and military aspects of Phips's involvement. We have benefited too from recent studies of the work cultures of early New England. In particular, Stephen Innes's *Creating the Commonwealth: The Economic Culture of Puritan New England* has been indispensable in our efforts to gauge the significance of Phips's suddenly acquired wealth and the unorthodoxy of its provenance, as he attempted to move in Puritan circles that were socially and geographically distant from his own origins on the periphery of New England.[25]

Although much of the renewal in the early history of New England has been manifested in works dealing with southern New England, a reexamination of early northern New England was also begun in 1970 when Charles E. Clark published his innovative study, *The Eastern Frontier*. In this work, Clark expressed the hope that further insight would be gained from collaboration between historians and archaeologists. This proved to be a realistic goal and an accurate prediction. Following the work of Helen Camp at Pemaquid in the mid-1960s, a series of scholars have combined historical analysis with archaeological field data to reveal much about early colonial settlement in the territories that later became the State of Maine. In particular, Robert Bradley's ongoing excavations of the house in which Phips was born and raised and Frank White's related genealogical research on the family have provided important evidence regarding an otherwise little-known phase of Phips's life.[26]

Sir William Phips's story is vivid and dramatic, with the themes of treasure seeking, witchcraft, frontier warfare and diplomacy, transatlantic trade, and imperial and colonial politics all woven into a life that lasted only forty-four years. We hope that this biography will do justice to such a colourful career as well as painting a broader picture. As all historical biographers must, we grappled with the question of whether to take a strictly focused approach to an individual life or to attempt a wider portrayal of a 'life and times.' The decision to lean more towards the latter approach and write a long book was not lightly taken. It was influenced by our historiographical inclinations. In the era of the new imperial history, it is high time in our view that imperial, colonial, and aboriginal historiographies entered into a new and dynamic three-way relationship. While we do not pretend that our work can make any more than a modest contribution to such a grand scheme, we believe that a study of Phips's career provides an unusual opportunity to link seemingly disparate lines of inquiry.

In part, we see our study as a contribution to English imperial history in a crucial transitional period. Phips's ascent from obscure origins provides a striking illustration of the fluidity of the empire in this period and its potential to be used as a means of social mobility for individuals who had the skill, luck, and lack of scruples to do so effectively. The transition from the fringes of piracy to high office has been more familiar to historians of the Caribbean than to those of mainland North America, but it is powerfully illustrated in Phips's career. Patronage was crucial, as was access to the monarch, either in person or through an intermediary. Phips was able to mobilize these advantages successfully. Nevertheless, his obscure social origins carried a price – in the contempt of influential figures, who regarded him as rude and unlettered, and in his lack of personal resources to be used for the patronage of others. Thus, Phips's career offers an insight into the way in which the empire worked in the late seventeenth century and reflects the complexities of class relations during his lifetime.

We believe that our work also bears on certain significant aspects of New England history. Phips played a role in most of the important sociopolitical issues in Massachusetts from 1689 to 1694, including the aftermath of the Revolution of 1688–9, the charter negotiations, the Salem trials, and the conflicts accompanying charter government and tighter imperial control of trade. More generally, his career offers a caution against the historiographical tendency to consider the history of the more heavily populated areas of Massachusetts Bay in isolation from that of northern New England. Phips understood well the interdependence of northern and southern New England, and his Maine origins were reflected in the social and political networks that he forged prior to and during his governorship.

These preoccupations also influenced Phips's relations with non-English peoples. He grew up in a society – situated in Wabanaki territory, on the borders of the English and French spheres of influence – which gave him close personal experience of the Wabanaki and probably also of the French. There was nothing fixed or foreordained at this time about the future direction in which English-Native-French relationships would evolve. Phips was consistently committed to diplomatic understandings with the Wabanaki, preceded by military hostilities if necessary, and to expeditions of conquest against the French. That he failed on both counts does not alter the reminder his career offers historians that most of what the English were presumptuous enough to call 'New England' was contested terrain in the late seventeenth century.

Beyond the historiographical, the decision to take a life-and-times approach was grounded in our belief that only this kind of study could do biographical justice to Phips. Not only did his life intersect with key events and processes in the history both of New England and of the empire, but it was characterized by a central paradox that stemmed from the tension between his colonial and imperial roles. Sir William Phips began life as an outsider to the Puritan elite of Massachusetts. His rough manners and language remained conspicuous even when he became governor. That he had rejected the slow but worthy route to social advancement by incremental steps from sea captain to merchant, and had opted instead for the rakish and possibly diabolical attractions of treasure seeking did not help. But in the London of the 1680s and 1690s, Phips was much less of a kenspeckle figure. Although he had his detractors, notably in Whitehall, his pursuit of rapid social advancement was ordinary enough in the naval offices where he first sought patronage. Nor was his social background as unimpressive in England as in North America, for he could muster respectable family connections, even though he himself was a poor cousin. His success as a projector and his seeming ability to promise new trade opportunities made him an attractive figure to City merchants in the era immediately following the Revolution of 1688–9, when the merchants wielded considerable political power in their role as suppliers of credit to the fiscally stretched English state. That his knowledge of northern New England gave him the ability to negotiate effectively with the Wabanaki and Acadian inhabitants was a further recommendation in an empire where commercial ambition was rapidly outstripping the limitations of territorial control.

Thus, if there is a central theme to Phips's career, it lies in his continuing attempt to reconcile his rapid ascent to imperial office with the shakiness of whatever respectability he enjoyed in New England. Among members of his erstwhile social class, he remained popular. Those who were offended by his rough manners and unabashed acquisitiveness and by the unorthodox company he kept granted approval less easily. Similarly, Phips's wealth impressed some, while the manner of its attainment repelled others. His alliance with the Mathers brought with it enmities as well as friendships. Most promising of all was the political accommodation he eventually reached with the rural deputies of the House of Representatives, although death intervened before he could build on this foundation. Phips's search for simultaneous acceptance in both of his transatlantic milieux thus ended indeterminately. Even so, we believe that when his various roles are explored in a way that removes the overlay of caricature to reveal a three-dimensional figure, some worthwhile inferences can be drawn that bear on – and may even change – our understanding of the interaction of imperial, colonial, and Native influences in New England and the rest of northeastern North America in this period.

There are three further matters on which preliminary comments should be addressed to the reader. First, most of the characters who appear in this book are male. This reflects in part the reality that Phips – whether at sea, in London to gather political and merchant support, or in Massachusetts as governor – operated mainly in small, all-male circles. Also, his limited literacy precluded the generation of any substantial amount of evidence regarding his private life. As far as we know, he kept no journal and wrote few if any letters to friends or relatives. Any family papers that did survive were probably lost with the rest of the family's estate when Phips's principal descendants fled Boston as Loyalists during the American Revolution. Hence, such important matters as his relationship with his wife and other female relatives or with his wife's family are effectively closed from view. We hope that our work is sensitive to gender in our recognition that Phips's public career represented an overwhelmingly male experience and in our interpretation of specific episodes such as the Salem trials, but we acknowledge a limitation in the evidence and thus in our portrayal.

Secondly, because of the diversity of the individuals Phips encountered during his career, we have provided introductions for the main personages dealt with in the book to an extent that some readers may find superfluous. That the marquis of Carmarthen, for example, was a Tory peer and a former chief minister of Charles II would not come as a surprise to any reader familiar with English political history of the era of the Revolution of 1688–9, but that reader might need the information that Madockawando was a Penobscot chief and the father-in-law of the baron de Saint-Castin. A reader knowledgeable in the social and diplomatic history of the Wabanaki might well be in the opposite position. Thus, at the risk of cluttering the narrative in places, we have not assumed extensive prior knowledge on the part of every reader.

A third issue has to do with the Wabanaki themselves. Ongoing research by scholars and a new activism among Native people during the late decades of the twentieth century have made this an interesting but often confusing time to be portraying the history of the Native groups of the areas now known as northern New England and the Maritime provinces. The structuring of these peoples and the appropriate distinctions to be drawn among them have been interpreted in a variety of ways. For clarity, we have chosen to use the generalized term Wabanaki as a broad definition of ethnic identity among the groups from the Saco to the Penobscot rivers, adding specific geographical descriptors wherever possible, and to refer separately to the Wuastukwiuk (Maliseet) and Mi'kmaq peoples who lived farther to the northeast.[27]

Acknowledgments

This book has been in the making for almost a decade. During those years we have benefited from the assistance of numerous individuals, who have encouraged our work in a variety of ways, and from financial and institutional support. The library staff at Saint Mary's University and Salem State College have been unfailingly and unstintingly cooperative. We have been graciously and efficiently received at other libraries and archives, notably during extended visits to the Bodleian Library, the British Library, the Henry E. Huntington Library, the Maine Historical Society Library, the Massachusetts Historical Society, the Massachusetts State Archives, the National Maritime Museum of Great Britain, and the Public Record Office. For hospitality during research trips we thank Ian and Diana Dethridge and Iain L. Kennedy Reid.

Scholars who have responded generously to our requests for advice and assistance have included Nicholas Dean, Peter Dickson, Anthony Farrell, D.W. Jones, James Kences, and William C. Wicken. Robert Bradley, Peter Earle, and Frank White were kind enough to share with us important references and data from their research. We have also received ongoing intellectual sustenance from conversations with members of our own departments, notably Colin Howell, Paul Marsella, Dane Morrison, Richard Twomey, Michael Vance, and Donna Vinson. Derek Barr provided computer graphics assistance. When the manuscript was in draft, it was read in whole or in part by a number of scholars whose comments were crucial not only in saving us from errors but in prompting us to refine our arguments: Barry M. Gough, Richard R. Johnson, Elizabeth Mancke, Daniel Vickers, and the readers consulted by the University of Toronto Press and the Humanities and Social Sciences Federation of Canada. We are greatly indebted to all those named here, although they are in no way responsible for whatever errors and infelicities may persist in our work.

The research for this book was funded by grants from the Social Sciences and Humanities Research Council of Canada, the Senate Research Committee of Saint Mary's University, and a faculty research grant from Salem State College. Publication was assisted by a subvention from the Aid to Scholarly Publications Program of the Humanities and Social Sciences Federation of Canada. We are grateful for all of this support and for the more general institutional facilities provided by Saint Mary's University and Salem State College. At Saint Mary's, Marlene Singer repeatedly supervised the assembling and shipping of an unwieldy manuscript. We also extend warm thanks to our editors and other staff members of the University of Toronto Press, notably Gerry Hallowell, Emily Andrew, and our copy-editor, Carlotta Lemieux.

Finally, we have the difficult task of adequately thanking the members of our families. Our respective spouses have had to put up with nearly ten years of this project, and only one of our children has any recollection of a time when Sir William was absent from our lives. Our acknowledgment to all of them is expressed on another page.

THE NEW ENGLAND KNIGHT

1

Early Life, 1651–1682

Cotton Mather's biography of Sir William Phips was designed to leave no doubt about the obscurity of the origins from which Phips rose. Assuring his readers that 'a Person's being *Obscure* in his *Original* is not always a Just Prejudice to an Expectation of *Considerable Matters* from him,' Mather described Phips as being born 'at a despicable Plantation on the River of *Kennebeck*, and almost the furthest Village of the Eastern Settlement of *New-England*.' For good measure, Mather also related how Phips as governor later sailed in sight of the Kennebec and would address the young soldiers and sailors under his command in pious vein: *'Young Men, It was upon that Hill that I kept Sheep a few Years ago; and since you see that Almighty God has brought me to something, do you learn to fear God, and be Honest, and mind your Business, and follow no bad Courses, and you don't know what you may come to!'*[1] Mather had his own reasons, both political and intellectual, for portraying Phips in this way. The reality was more complex than he allowed, yet the task of sifting the reliable from the unreliable in Mather's account is not a simple one.[2] Relatively little is known from other sources about Phips's early life in an area of unstable colonial settlement from which few records survive for this period. A low literacy rate, combined with a lack of regular government, minimized the number of both official and personal papers. The series of wars that affected the region in the late seventeenth and early eighteenth centuries destroyed many papers and scattered others. As a result, only an imperfect narrative of the early years of William Phips and his family can be essayed. Nevertheless, with Mather's biography cautiously used and with comparative evidence added for the entire region, the experience of the young William Phips can be reconstructed in general terms. This broad picture

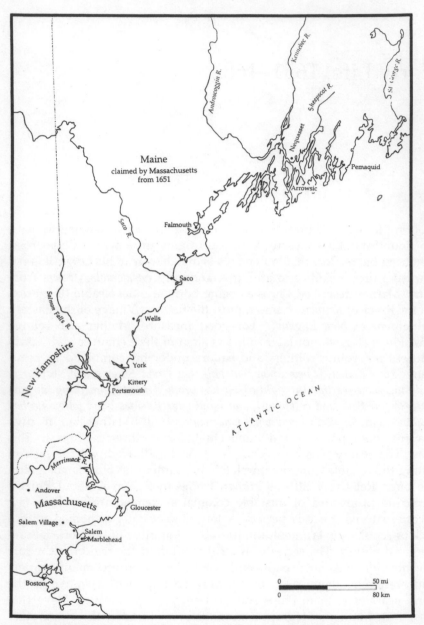

MAP 1 Atlantic coast from Massachusetts Bay to St George River, mid-seventeenth century

reveals influences that exerted a lifelong influence on Phips's attitudes and goals.

Phips was born on 2 February 1651 on his father James's farmstead at Jeremisquam Neck, overlooking the Sheepscot River at Nequasset, in what is now Woolwich, Maine. As a young man, James Phips had been one of the first wave of English settlers to move to coastal Maine. He had been raised in Mangotsfield, one of the four parishes of the hundred of Barton Regis, several miles east of Bristol. Apprenticed to John Brown, a Bristol blacksmith and probably a gunsmith, Phips migrated with Brown at some time in the late 1620s or early 1630s.[3] Following Mather, and considering James Phips's indentureship, historians have traditionally viewed the Phips family as being poor folk with humble West Country antecedents, but in fact the family's principal connections were neither humble nor centred in the west of England. Robert Phips of Nottingham had received the family's coat of arms in the mid-sixteenth century, a mark of at least technical gentility. Robert had three sons. The oldest, George, belonged to 'Walton hall neere Nottingham,' but George's only surviving son, Francis Phips, moved to Reading in Berkshire. While little is known of his social status there, he was certainly able to offer educational opportunities to at least two of his five sons. The oldest, Francis, attended King's College, Cambridge. The youngest, Constantine, was admitted to Gray's Inn in 1678, and later became a leading London attorney, a prominent Tory, and for a time lord chancellor of Ireland. In the 1690s he also served as a London agent for Massachusetts, a post he received through his second cousin, Sir William Phips.[4]

The connection between William Phips and the Robert Phips family is established in part by a letter written in 1693 by Sir Henry Ashurst, who was well acquainted with both Sir William Phips and Constantine Phips. Constantine, Ashurst mentioned, was Sir William's 'Coszen.'[5] The relationship is also demonstrated by the use of the same coat of arms by the two branches of the family. A family pedigree was compiled by Elias Ashmole in 1664 for Constantine's oldest brother, Francis Phips Jr, who was then a student at Cambridge. It included the family coat of arms granted to Robert Phips, and this same coat of arms appears on the marble monument to Sir William Phips in the London church where he was buried, on the family tomb in Charlestown, and on the wax seal attached to his will.[6] The pedigree is incomplete, failing to include the offspring of either William or Anthony, the younger sons of Robert Phips of Nottingham. William was almost certainly the William who was the father of

GENEALOGY OF THE PHIPS FAMILY

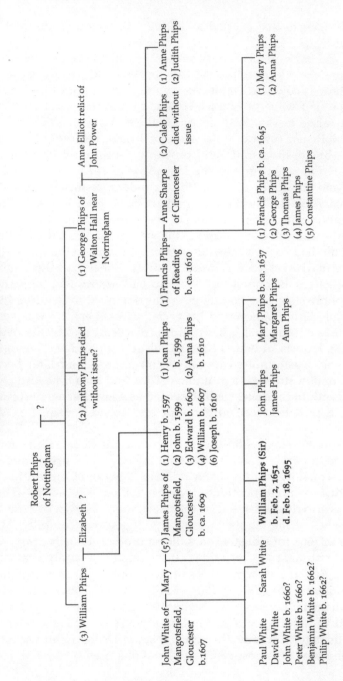

James Phips of Mangotsfield and grandfather of Sir William. The most likely sequence of events would have Robert Phips's youngest son, William, leaving home to seek his fortune near the growing city of Bristol. The birth of seven of William's children was recorded at Mangotsfield between 1597 and 1614. James is not among them, but he was probably born in 1608 or 1609 (when there is a gap both in the parish registers and in the dates of birth of the seven children). A James Phips, son of William Phips, was baptized in Nottingham on 29 August 1610, presumably during a family visit. After his father's death, James left England for the fishing and trading post of Pemaquid.[7]

Situated a few miles east of the Sheepscot River, Pemaquid was among the first New England settlements and was the easternmost English outpost. In the 1620s, Pemaquid harbour became a haven for English fishers and a focus of the Anglo-Wabanaki fur trade. During this period, it came to be largely controlled by two proprietors, the partners Robert Aldworth and Gyles Elbridge, who were successful Bristol merchants. Five years after their initial purchase of the fishing station at Monhegan Island in 1626, Aldworth and Elbridge obtained the 12,000-acre Pemaquid patent from the Council for New England. This title legalized their existing operations at Pemaquid, which had begun sometime in the late 1620s. The proprietors never ventured to New England, although they were responsible for sending many settlers there, including their agent Abraham Shurt. This connection meant that Pemaquid rapidly became, in effect, a colony of Bristol.[8]

Among those who moved from Bristol to Pemaquid were John Brown and James Phips. On 1 March 1626, James (described as the 'son of William Phippes, formerly of Mangotsfield, county of Gloucester, tyler, deceased') was apprenticed to Brown for a term of eight years. Brown's family was from Barton Regis, so the men may have known each other well before the apprenticeship. There is no record of James Phips becoming a freeman of Bristol, which would have been likely to occur after completion of his apprenticeship if he had still been in the city, and the presumption is that he and Brown migrated before 1634.[9] In 1639 Brown and one Edward Bateman purchased all of Nequasset (present-day Woolwich, Maine) from the local Wabanaki sachem, who was known to the English as Robinhood. In 1646 Brown and Bateman sold Jeremisquam Neck, a large tract on the eastern side of Nequasset, to James Phips and John White. This was apparently the same John White who had served an apprenticeship as a sugar refiner under Robert Aldworth. Aldworth had established the first sugar house in Bristol in 1609, processing cane sugar from Madeira, the Azores, and Brazil. The venture flourished until the mid-1630s, when Aldworth's death, combined with competition and a decline in prices, seriously damaged the refinery business. It is likely that White then found himself unemployed and migrated to Maine to work on another Aldworth enterprise.[10]

The Phips-White plantation was one of a series of large tracts occupied by English colonists in a ribbonlike thread of settlement that extended along the mouth of the Kennebec River and adjacent coastal areas. In this regard, the property was quite isolated, but numerous vessels sailed past it on their way upriver to Sheepscot or up the Back River to reach the Kennebec. Most important, the plantation was well positioned to attract local Native travellers as well as Englishmen, for it was conveniently situated for Native traders who were coming downriver from the Sheepscot, Kennebec, or Androscoggin rivers. Archaeological excavations indicate that Phips and White built their homestead on land that had been occupied by Native people off and on for over three thousand years. For a trading post, it was a perfect location.[11] Although records do not survive to provide details of the trading operations by James Phips and John White, there is no reason to doubt that, like their neighbours, they were actively involved in this profitable business. The three other contemporary residents of Nequasset, Francis Knight, Edward Bateman, and the Smith-Hammond family, all participated in the fur trade. None of their trade accounts survive, save for a single tantalizing page of Knight's ledger from 1647, which refers to beaver, moose, otter, and even bear skins.[12]

Phips and White had a distinct advantage over other fur traders in that James Phips was a gunsmith. Armourers and gunsmiths were in short supply on the Wabanaki coast and in great demand to repair firearms, which were easily broken and difficult to mend without a forge. The Council for New England succeeded in 1622 in prompting the English crown to prohibit the trading of firearms to Native inhabitants, but enforcement was notoriously lax.[13] Although Christopher Levett saw only a few guns among the Natives during his 1623–4 visit to Maine, the Native ownership of guns grew during the following decades. For example, when the Jesuit missionary Gabriel Druillettes arrived at a Kennebec Wabanaki village in 1646, the inhabitants saluted him with 'a salvo of arquebus shots.'[14] In 1668 the Massachusetts General Court legalized the arms trade, having realized that it could no longer be prevented. Four years later, the traveller John Josselyn noted, 'Of late he is a poor Indian that is not master of two guns.'[15]

For Wabanaki hunters and warriors, two guns were desirable because one of them was likely to be out of order. The earliest surviving reference to the repair of firearms belonging to the native inhabitants of this region dates from 1631, when the gunsmith at the Plymouth Colony's Penobscot trading post testified – during proceedings against the firearms trader Edward Ashley – that 'he would have put a loke on an Indians peece which he tooke of his owne for the purpose but finding he could not make it fitt notwithstanding with some pin or parte thereof he mended the Indians peece.'[16] The gunsmith was James Phips's brother William. At the time he was under indenture to Plymouth Colony, although by 1639 he had returned to become a burgess of Bristol. James Phips's work must have resembled that of his brother William. With few smiths available who were capable of repairing firearms, James's plantation must have been a frequent resort of Natives who came both to trade furs and to have their guns fixed. Thus, Cotton Mather remarked of Sir William that 'his *Birth* and *Youth* in the *East* had rendred him well known to the *Indians* there,' with whom he had 'Hunted and Fished many a weary Day in his Childhood.'[17]

Mather's description of the Phips-White holdings as 'a despicable Plantation' is more questionable.[18] Recent archaeological excavations at the site by Robert Bradley have provided an opportunity to determine just how despicable it really was. The house, built sometime between 1639 and 1646, was a substantial structure. The core (structure 1) consisted of a 15 by 72 ft longhouse, probably divided into four rooms, with the southernmost 12 by 15 ft section possibly serving as a byre. The longhouse was a fairly common type of building in the Bristol area and throughout the West Country, its origin being medieval. A second episode of construction (structure 2) made the building L-shaped, perhaps providing an attached second home so that both Phips and White would have their own discrete living spaces. This 20 by 60 ft addition appears to have been more substantially built than the core, for its 14 by 5 ft hearth was constructed on a carefully laid fieldstone footing, whereas the hearth of the first structure had amounted to thin flagstones laid on grade. A 29.5 by 14.5 ft outbuilding (structure 3) stood about 20 ft south of the longhouse. A drainage ditch outside the uphill two sides of the building diverted water from it. Structure 3 may have served as a small barn or storage building.[19]

The excavations have produced a large assemblage of artifacts, ranging from ceramic shards to clay tobacco pipes. Generally they suggest that the Phips and White families had household possessions similar to those found at other sites of this period in the region. The one clear indication that the family was not well off is the absence of window glass at the site. In the mid-seventeenth century glazed windows were expensive. Not only was the technology quite new, but the fragile windows had to survive the long crossing from England. Nevertheless, the majority of nearby contemporary archaeological sites do show evidence of glass windows, which suggests that the Phips family was of less than average wealth.[20]

Aside from the absence of glazed windows, the plantation was impressive. Indeed, the principal structure is the largest yet excavated in Maine, though its method of construction was far from elaborate. The main house, additional wing, and outbuilding were all built with a technique known as post-in-ground construction. Rather than having a stone foundation or footing, the building's chief structural posts were anchored directly into the ground in post holes. This was a relatively cheap and easy method of construction, popular in northern New England and on the Chesapeake in that period, for it saved the precious time and money that would have been expended in building a foundation. The problem with this type of construction was that eventually the posts rotted, and unless they were repaired, the house collapsed. It appears that the Phips homestead survived for forty years with very little repair work. While this method of construction was crude, it was in widespread use at the time by people of all ranks of society. Overall, the building seems to have been typical, and although the lack of windows hints at limited wealth, the plantation was hardly as 'despicable' as Cotton Mather declared. Presumably, Mather used the term to exaggerate the humbleness of Phips's origins and thus make the future governor's rise seem all the more remarkable.[21]

Mather may also have been exaggerating when he stated that William Phips's 'fruitful *Mother*' had 'no less than *Twenty-Six* Children, whereof *Twenty-One* were Sons.'[22] Only six Phips children can be counted, three boys and three girls. The girls were Mary, Margaret, and Anne; the boys, John, James, and William. However, like many New Englanders of the time, Phips was part of an extended family. Sometime after his birth in 1651 and before 1655, his father died, for by the latter date his mother had married John White, her deceased husband's partner. This probably was White's first marriage, for his eight surviving children were all born after this point. Only six of the children are known by name: John Jr, Philip, David, Benjamin, Sarah, and Peter.[23] Therefore, in Phips's extended family fourteen children reached adulthood. Others may have been stillborn or have died young, but considering the low rate of infant and childhood mortality in early New England, it is difficult to believe that Phips was one of twenty-six children born to one mother.[24]

Few of the family birth dates are known, but limited evidence suggests that William was one of the youngest of the Phips children. Mary was born about 1637, making her some fourteen years older than William. His half-brother Philip White was about ten years younger than he. Most of the Phips and White children led obscure lives by comparison with William, several of them dying before or just about the time of his success. His brothers John and James and his sister Anne all predeceased him. In later years, when the childless Sir William and Lady Mary sought an heir, they chose to adopt her nephew, even though there were suitable nephews and half-nephews on the Phips-White side of the family. Overall, the evidence hints that William Phips and the Phips-White clan may have grown apart, although William remained in close touch with a few of his siblings. In seventeenth-century New England, kinship ties played a crucial role in society, not just between brothers and sisters but among more distant relations as well. With a small population recently spread out over a sizable area, the importance of kin – and even the kin of friends and neighbours – was accentuated, representing important links to a wider world.[25]

Although 'despicable' is not the *mot juste* for the Phips-White plantation, there is no denying that William Phips and his siblings were born to a life of limited material comfort and considerable insecurity. Like its neighbours, the Phips homestead was seated by the water, clinging to a rocky shore. In both a literal and a figurative sense, the English presence was marginal. The small settlements existed among a sizable Wabanaki population and on Wabanaki sufferance. As far as European spheres of influence were concerned, Pemaquid represented the eastern extreme of any realistic English claim. Beyond were the equally marginal French settlements, their western limit marked at the time of William's birth by Pentagoet, at the mouth of the Penobscot River. In 1654 Robert Sedgwick, a Massachusetts merchant and militia officer, led an English naval squadron against the French colony of Acadia and easily seized the principal French posts, which remained in English hands until 1670. William Phips no doubt grew up with the story of Sedgwick's feat. What effect all this had on him cannot be gauged precisely, though naval and military action against the French in both Acadia and Canada, accompanied by diplomatic overtures to the Wabanaki, were to form the cornerstone of his later aspirations for the salvaging of English influence in the region and for the consolidation of an enlarged colony of Massachusetts Bay.[26]

If the neighbouring French and resident Wabanaki added an element of uncertainty to the English presence in the region, so did a lack of established government. For much of the seventeenth century, the English settlements between Pemaquid and the Kennebec had no organized governing structures. In 1623 the Council for New England had granted the region between the Kennebec and St Croix rivers severally to six council members, but they developed no settlements. In 1635 the council regranted the region to Sir William Alexander, who did nothing to encourage settlement in this territory that was fleetingly designated 'the county of Canada.'[27] In 1628 and 1630 Plymouth Colony received patents for lands on the Kennebec, but it made only sporadic efforts to assert its authority. Plymouth was more interested in the fur trade than in any administrative burdens.[28]

During the 1650s and 1660s, a large group of Massachusetts merchants began to enter this power vacuum as they moved into the area to capitalize on its wealth of furs, timber, and fish – the principal exports of New England. In 1654, for example, Thomas Lake and Thomas Clarke began their operations along the Kennebec, combining fishing, trading, timbering, and shipbuilding with speculation in thousands of acres of land.[29] To safeguard their substantial investments, they favoured firm control of the region by Massachusetts. Between 1651 and 1658, the Massachusetts Bay Colony asserted and consolidated its control of the English settlements of the Province of Maine as far as the west bank of the Kennebec. The situation was complicated, however, by a new interest taken in the region by the Restoration monarchy of Charles II. In 1664 the crown granted the territory east of the Kennebec to James, duke of York, the king's brother. At the same time, a royal commission was dispatched to examine governmental and boundary issues in New England. The commissioners visited the Province of Maine to deliberate on the claims of Massachusetts but did not venture east of the Kennebec. Instead, they appointed justices to go to the area, gather the English settlers to take an oath of loyalty, and establish the duke's government. At the time, the fourteen-year-old William Phips was too young to participate, but his stepfather, John White, took the oath.[30] Once the royal commission had departed, no further initiatives came from the duke of York, and Massachusetts soon moved again to expand its jurisdiction. In 1674 the Bay Colony incorporated the region between the Kennebec and Pemaquid as its new County of Devon.[31]

Even though Massachusetts Bay had won the contest to administer the area, the colonists did not necessarily conform to the religious and social norms of the corporate communities of southern New England. By social class and in some cases by religious inclination, fishers were differentiated from any Puritan ideal of community.[32] Yet even in the absence of any formal structures of government, this did not imply a state of chaos or anarchy. Like the ungoverned Acadian settlements to the east between 1654 and 1670, the English communities in the Kennebec-Pemaquid region were fully capable of keeping the peace and maintaining a necessary level of coherence and collaboration. In each case, harmonious relations with Native inhabitants and a pragmatic bent when dealing with colonial authorities of whatever nationality were crucial (as can be seen from the fact that the Pemaquid and Kennebec settlers were said to have welcomed a French military expedition in 1671 with a *joye sensible*).[33] With a small population scattered throughout a large area over which English control had never been asserted in any practical terms, settlers had little option but to work cooperatively in trading, fishing, and farming – and or in defence during threatening times. As well, because of the small population there was a tendency to intermarry, thereby strengthening the bonds of cooperation with kinship ties. These factors reduced the need for formal governance.

The region's stability was also a result of the presence of leading Massachusetts merchants such as Thomas Clarke and Thomas Lake. Although these men lacked any secure legal authority, their political and military offices in Massachusetts, combined with their wealth and social standing, gave them power and influence. So, most importantly, did their role as creditors. What effect this political climate had on young William Phips is largely a matter for speculation, but during his childhood he would rarely have seen any formal political rules or authority; those who enjoyed the greatest individual prestige were wealthy merchants who had made large profits and attained power in the community without any real clothing of legitimacy. Phips's combativeness in later life and his frequent disregard for the constraints of social or political conventions may have owed something to their example.

Similarly, his acquisitiveness may have had its origins in an appreciation of the commercial value of the resources of the Kennebec region. In addition to the fur trade, there were active fishing stations on various islands and rocky peninsulas. Fishing was not confined to the ocean. The Pejebscot was famous for its sturgeon, and fishers journeyed up the Kennebec to Nequasset each spring to harvest migrating alewives, the best bait for their deep-sea operations.[34] The rivers also harnessed water power in tide mills that processed timber. Rapid deforestation along the Massachusetts coast meant that by the 1650s the Kennebec region was a centre of the industry, exporting pipe staves, barrel staves, and lumber.[35] The prime timberland and the numerous tide mill locations combined with extensive mudflats for ships' ways to create attractive conditions for ship construction. The royal commissioners observed, that 'these parts' had 'the best white Oakes for Ship Timber.'[36] By the third quarter of the seventeenth century, shipbuilding had become firmly established in the region.[37] Farming was also important to the local economy. Hay growing on the abundant salt marshes supported cattle raising on a considerable scale. Cattle and other livestock were shipped to Massachusetts to feed the growing urban population, as well as to the Caribbean. In his *History of the Indian Wars*, William Hubbard referred to the 'considerable River called Ships-coat, upon the Banks of which were many scattered Planters, who lately flying from their Dwellings, for Fear of the *Indians*, left, as was judged, a thousand head of Neat Cattel.'[38] This prosperous farming community included the Phips-White plantation at Nequasset.

Few residents had the wealth to enter commercial farming on the scale of merchants such as Thomas Clarke and Thomas Lake. Most of them, including the Phips and White families, probably planted some food crops and supplemented them with fishing, timbering, or fur trading. The Phips family would have farmed actively in addition to its gunsmithing and trading. Cotton Mather has the young William *'keeping of Sheep in the Wilderness*, until he was Eighteen Years Old.' This statement, laced with biblical allusion, goes on to imply that Phips was like David in that he was taken by divine intervention *'from the Sheepfolds, from following the Ewes great with Young ... to feed his People.'*[39] The Phips family probably did have a significant number of sheep as well as cows and pigs. But this may not have been sufficient for their needs. A rare surviving court record shows that the family purchased a barrel of beef from the Hammonds, who owned a nearby plantation. When William failed to pay for the beef, the court awarded the Hammonds the sum of three pounds and costs.[40] Clearly, the scale of the family's farming was not sufficient to free it from the necessity of purchasing food on occasion.

William Phips would certainly have spent much of his childhood carrying out chores on the farm. Feeding and caring for livestock, chopping wood, and planting and harvesting crops would all have been part of his daily routine. The evidence suggests that little or none of his time was spent on formal education. Only later in life did he learn to read and write, and then with great difficulty, according to his detractors. He did not become a church member until he joined Boston's North Church in 1690. Even so he was well in advance of his stepbrother Peter White, who was not baptized until he was caught up in the Great Awakening. When Peter and his wife Rachel were baptized, both were over seventy. William's lack of literacy and the fragmentary evidence of the family's late age of baptism and church membership indicate that the Phips-White children did not have a rigorous religious upbringing.[41] This would partly have been because of the absence of clergy for much of the time. A lay preacher, Robert Gooch, served the Kennebec region from 1660 to 1665, and so for a while in the 1670s did the Harvard-educated minister Ichabod Wiswell. Nevertheless, regular church attendance and religious education do not appear to have been among the early influences on William Phips.[42]

Mather records that when Phips was eighteen he apprenticed himself to a shipbuilder, signing a four-year indenture. The name of the shipbuilder is unknown, but all evidence suggests that Phips apprenticed with the Clarke and Lake company. Not only was the Clarke and Lake shipyard the largest in the Kennebec region, but it was the closest to Phips's home. Lying just across the bay from Phips's Point, it was part of the company's main settlement at Spring Cove on Arrowsic Island. So although no documents specifically place Phips at Clarke and Lake, geographical proximity suggests this, as does the connection with Increase and Cotton Mather. Thomas Clarke and Thomas Lake were prominent Boston merchants, and Lake had moved into Boston's North End, where he had joined Increase Mather's North Church, thus virtually assuring its financial well-being. Moreover, Lake's daughter Ann married the Reverend John Cotton, and after his death she married Increase Mather. Mather's first wife had been Maria Cotton, John Cotton's aunt. Hence, the Mathers, Cottons, and Lakes were all closely bound by marriage as well as friendship. The Lakes are the clearest connection between William Phips and the Mather family. In the conversion statement that preceded Phips's baptism in 1690, he mentioned having heard Increase Mather preach in 1674, when he was 'some time under ... [his] Ministry.'[43]

Phips completed his apprenticeship in 1673 and promptly moved to Boston to work as a shipwright. Not long afterwards he married Mary Spencer Hull, the widow of John Hull of Boston. Apparently unrelated to his contemporary and namesake (the wealthy Boston goldsmith and mint-master), Hull was described by Mather as a 'well-bred merchant.' He left his young and childless widow with a modest estate of eighty-one pounds.[44] Mary was the daughter of Captain Roger Spencer, a Charlestown merchant who had extensive ties to Maine. In 1647 he was listed, along with other Pemaquid-area merchants, in the account book of Francis Knight – a trader at Nequasset, who was living in Pemaquid at the time (and was probably Shurt's successor as agent for the patentees). Interestingly, the account refers to Knight's operations at Nequasset, which may well have been tied into the Phips-White establishment. Spencer continued to have some interests in the Pemaquid area, for he was doing business with Knight there as late as 1655.[45] Described as a 'seaman' in 1654, Spencer might more accurately be labelled a merchant or land speculator. In 1653 he joined Thomas Lake in the effort to purchase Wabanaki lands along the Kennebec. At the time, political events in England had left open to question the validity of Plymouth Colony's title to extensive Kennebec lands, for during the interregnum of 1649–60 it seemed possible that Plymouth's royal charter might lose its value in favour of locally held deeds. Spencer purchased three tracts from Wabanaki vendors, in partnership with Lake and several other men, but within a year he had sold his interests in the deeds to Thomas Clarke.[46]

Spencer took a more lasting interest in the development of the lower Saco River. In 1653 the town of Saco granted him the right to build a sawmill on the river's great falls, although it is unclear whether this mill was ever built.[47] Spencer later moved to the Saco area, and in 1658 he and Brian Pendleton bought a neck of land at nearby Winter Harbour, where he remained at least long enough for his daughter Lydia to marry Freegrace Norton in 1662. However, he also developed interests on Casco Bay, and by 1669 he was living in Boston, where in 1672 he was indicted for selling strong drink. When he died in 1675, his estate had been greatly diminished by mortgages and debts. Mather states that Spencer had 'suffer'd much damage in his Estate, by some unkind and unjust Actions, which he bore with such Patience, that for fear of thereby injuring the Publick, he would not seek Satisfaction.' His widow Gertrude apparently died between 1678 and 1681.[48]

Roger Spencer's ties to Francis Knight and Thomas Lake, as well as his presence at Pemaquid and on the Kennebec, indicate that he must have known James Phips and his family long before his daughter married William. It is not beyond possibility that Mary and William met as chil-

dren and that a childhood relationship formed the basis for their marriage. The Spencers and Hulls enjoyed higher social status in New
England than the Phips-White family, but neither was wealthy, so
although William Phips may have taken a modest step upwards through
his marriage, he gained no great family fortune. Fragmentary evidence,
including the diarist Samuel Sewall's description of Mary Spencer
Phips's grief at the death of her husband in 1695, suggests that a genuine
affection bound the two, and this impression is confirmed by the absence
of any suggestion of sexual impropriety during Phips's lengthy absences
from home, despite the keen attention of his critics to any personal flaws
they could identify.[49]

It is impossible to get a close sense of Mary's personality because she
left such a slender historical record, but she was clearly a strong and
intelligent woman who was a partner to her husband in every sense of
the word. She often assumed the role of what Laurel Ulrich has called
the 'deputy husband,' managing the family affairs during William's
long absences. As both the daughter and the widow of a merchant, she
made the most of this role and pushed its limits. Of ten transactions
recorded for William Phips in the Suffolk County registry of deeds, fully
half took place when he was not even in New England. Mary is mentioned specifically in only one of these, when 'Lady Mary Phips, attorney of Sir William Phips,' purchased land in 1687 adjacent to their brick
mansion, but in the other four cases she must also have been acting
independently of any bidding from her husband. Most of her contemporaries merely co-signed deeds with their husbands or administered their
estates, but Mary negotiated the purchase of the family mansion on her
own. While William was in England during the charter negotiations of
1691–2, she executed several mortgages that earned a healthy 6 per cent
return, as well as purchasing a mortgage from the merchant John Foster.
Close associates and family friends such as Foster and John Phillips (the
father-in-law of Cotton Mather whom Mather described as Sir William
Phips's 'Fidus Achates, and very dear Friend, Kinsman, and Neighbour')
usually witnessed these instruments, thus supporting Mary's right to
this activity.[50]

That Mary Spencer Phips's opinion carried weight with her husband
on other crucial occasions is indicated by the evidence surrounding at
least two episodes: in 1683, when she reportedly persuaded him to consider shanghaiing the hostile royal agent John Knepp from Boston to the
Caribbean; and in 1690, when Sir William hesitated to assume command
of the Port-Royal expedition because he thought she might disapprove.

After his death, her business activities became more visible. She bought shares of ships, made loans, and even sued when payments were missed. She also remarried well – after a long enough delay that again showed her independent character – choosing Peter Sargeant, a kinsman of Sir William's powerful erstwhile ally Sir Henry Ashurst. Given Mary's family background and William's limited literacy, she emerges from the surviving evidence not merely as her husband's close political and financial adviser but as the financial mind of the family and an intriguing historical persona in her own right.[51]

Not long after the Phipses' marriage in 1673, William contracted with several Bostonians, principally Thomas Joles, to build a ship of 117 tons, which was to be delivered to Joles with a full lading of cargo, presumably foodstuffs and timber. Soon afterwards, Phips returned to the family homestead at Jeremisquam Neck to begin construction of the ship. On the basis of an investigation of what appear to be the boat ways of the shipyard in the mudflats adjacent to the Phips homestead, maritime historian Nicholas Dean has suggested that the ship was similar to one built in 1639 not far to the south at the Trelawney Station on Richmond Island. John Winter reported that the Trelawney vessel was 'betwixt 49 and 50 foot by the keel, 18½ foot to the beam,' and that he proposed 'to bring her to two decks with a forecastle and a quarter-deck, nine foot in hold and 4½ foot betwixt the decks.'[52] This was a sizable ship and was an ambitious undertaking for a young shipbuilder who was working during an ominous time. In 1675 southern New England became embroiled in the conflict known to the English as King Philip's War. Maine remained largely peaceful in 1675, but growing Anglo-Wabanaki tensions led to a separate but related war there in the summer of 1676.[53]

The armed conflict began on the Kennebec on 14 August 1676, when a Wabanaki force mounted a surprise attack on the Clarke and Lake fortified compound on Arrowsic, killing or capturing about fifty settlers, seizing much-needed supplies, and burning the settlement. Thomas Lake was killed while trying to flee.[54] The gunfire and smoke would have been immediately noted at the Phips homestead, a short distance across Hockomock Bay. The 117-ton ship had been launched and was virtually complete, but its lading of lumber was still on shore. Not having the luxury of time to load, Phips gathered his family and neighbours and departed for Boston in the barely finished ship. The destruction of his house, along with those on neighbouring lands, soon followed. Mather's account praised Phips's role in the escape and com-

pared him to Noah launching the ark, but he also noted the dire financial cost of abandoning the cargo: 'The *first Action* that he did, after he
was his own Man, was to *save his Father's House*, with the rest of the
Neighbourhood, from Ruin; but the Disappointment which befel him
from the Loss of his other *Lading*, plunged his Affairs into greater
Embarasments with such as had employ'd him.'[55]

The depth of Phips's loss can be measured by the series of lawsuits he
faced during the eighteen months following his hurried departure from
Maine. Although many New Englanders, particularly ships' captains
and aspiring merchants like Phips, were frequently in court fighting
civil cases, Phips had rarely been involved in such proceedings.[56] His
avoidance of them suggests that he had managed on the whole to meet
his obligations and had dealt with people who did likewise. All of this
changed with his reversal of fortune in 1676. First, Francis Dodson successfully sued for payment of twenty-three pounds that Phips owed
him for stoning a cellar. The contract had been signed in March 1676,
when Phips was still solvent and had apparently decided to build a
house in Boston. Elizabeth Hammond then sued Phips for three pounds
that was owed from a sale of beef on the Kennebec the previous year,
and Daniel Turell Jr sued Phips for the sum of thirteen pounds, nine
shillings; the nature of the latter debt was not stated, but it may have
been for hardware for the ship Phips had built, because Turell was an
anchorsmith.

Finally, Phips was involved in a suit and countersuit with Thomas
Joles over settlement of the contract to build the ship. When Phips lost
the case and was ordered to pay eighty-five pounds, he became
enraged. 'In a deceitfull and felonious way,' alleged his opponents, he
seized the award from the hands of Joles's attorney, John Walley, 'and
threw it into the fire and burnt it.'[57] In January 1678 the court sentenced
Phips to pay the eighty-five pounds to Walley and a five-pound fine to
boot. By the time he appeared before the court, Phips had regained his
composure, and when he apologized for his behaviour the court cut his
fine in half. Phips's earlier avoidance of lawsuits provides an interesting
contrast with his combative behaviour on this occasion. The episode
suggests that in his business life he did not seek trouble but that when a
conflict arose he did not like to lose. His reaction also hints at the stress
arising from his financial straits.

Unfortunately, at this time of personal setback, Phips fades temporarily from the historical record. Neither William nor Mary Spencer
Phips appears in a single document in Boston for four years following

the 1678 incident with John Walley.The couple are not listed as property owners, though they may have rented accommodation, or perhaps they lived with members of Mary's family in Charlestown. William apparently continued to ply his trade, but he soon expanded his horizons to the sea as well. He must soon have put disappointment behind him and begun to rebuild. By Mather's account, his physical presence was imposing in young adulthood, cutting the figure of an individual who would not be kept down for long: 'For his *Exterior*, he was one *Tall*, beyond the common Set of Men, and *Thick* as well as *Tall*, and *Strong* as well as *Thick*: He was, in all respects, exceedingly *Robust*, and able to Conquer such Difficulties of *Diet* and *Travel*, as would have kill'd most Men alive: Nor did the *Fat*, whereinto he grew very much in his later Years, take away the Vigour of his Motions.'[58]

For all that, the events of August 1676 represented a turning point in Phips's life. They marked in a sense the end of his youth, at the age of twenty-five. They certainly brought an end to his residence in the Kennebec region, even though he visited Pemaquid frequently when he was governor during the 1690s. Furthermore, the personal traits and abilities of a lifetime must largely have been moulded by this time. The crucial ability that Phips lacked as yet – crucial both to his own lived experience and to the opportunity of the historian to follow his personal development – was full literacy. Even Cotton Mather admitted that it was not until just before his marriage that Phips 'learn'd, first of all, to *Read* and *Write*.' The anonymous writer of a pamphlet of 1694 entitled 'A Letter from New England' put the matter in a harsher light: 'It is an unlucky thing the want of Education, in a Man ... who (as they say) Learned to read since he was Married, and cannot yet read a Letter, much less write one, and there being no Carpenter's Work in the Government they expect he will not serve them Long.'[59] Phips could, of course, sign his name. He did so with distinctively elaborate capital letters, 'W' and 'P,' the 'P' requiring two separate strokes of the pen. The capitals are never replicated in the written texts of the documents he signed, which suggests that the signature represented the limit of his writing ability, or at least that it did at one time. Many of the official letters issued in Phips's name while he was governor were written in a hand that resembled the signature, but with differences that raise the possibility that his personal secretary, Benjamin Jackson, was trying to make it appear that the signatory was also the writer.[60]

While there was nothing disgraceful in a governor's use of a secretary as a scribe, other evidence indicates that Jackson also covered for his employer's difficulty in reading. Two independent accounts exist of an episode in early 1693 that formed part of an ongoing quarrel between Phips, who by then was governor of Massachusetts, and the governor of New York, Benjamin Fletcher. Fletcher had been enraged by statements reportedly made by Phips in a conversation with a New York political fugitive, Abraham Gouverneur, which Gouverneur had mentioned in a letter that was intercepted by Fletcher. Fletcher sent a messenger to Boston who met with Phips on the morning of 17 January 1693. One account of this meeting was given by an anonymous letter writer who either was present or received a first-hand description of the incident: 'Sir William unluckily at the Messengers arrivall opens before him the packquet his Clerk not looking over the papers reads him only the Coppy of a Letter sent to [New] York upon which the quarrel was founded and not Coll Fletchers Letter and enters himself into a great rage.' The other account was given by the messenger himself, who identified the clerk as Jackson and added a few more details: 'Sir William opened the Letter, and gave his Clerke Governours [Gouverneur's] Letter which being in Dutch, Sir William Phips said there was need of an Interpreter, I acquainted him it was translated into English, after the Letter was read I demanded about Governour ...'[61] Both accounts thus make Phips seem dependent on Jackson in his efforts to make sense of the papers before him.

In sum, all direct evidence indicates that Phips's degree of literacy, even as governor, was very limited. Confirmation of this is provided by the negative evidence that no private letters by Phips are known to exist or indeed any documents that he can be shown to have written. Given his geographical as well as social origins (for the West Country from which his father had migrated was an area of relatively low literacy in England, as was the Kennebec region in New England), this situation is not surprising. But for an aspirant to wealth and position in a colony in which Puritan religious sensibilities had made formal schooling relatively widespread, the lack of literacy was a serious matter. It was not necessarily disastrous if the assistance of others – Jackson, the Mathers, Mary Spencer Phips – could easily and quickly be enlisted; but in seventeenth-century New England, which has been described by Kenneth Lockridge as 'a half-literate society in which literacy correlated with cosmopolitan status and with wealth,' it was a characteristic not to be widely advertised by an ambitious individual or one with status to protect.[62]

A further legacy of Phips's upbringing that was remarked on by his critics was his lack of social graces. Most of these references are closely connected with his use of harsh and abusive language. In 1694, for example, the aged minister John Higginson headed a list of complaints about Phips's governorship by identifying 'the lowness of his Education and parts' and 'his Natural passionateness.'[63] That Phips frequently resorted to profanity and threat is documented so consistently and pervasively that it is beyond doubt. These incidents range from the occasion in November 1683 when he was reported to have invited two Boston constables to 'kiss his Arse and called him [sic] shit breech and threatned them what he would doe,' to the episode towards the end of his life when he engaged in what the diarist Sewall discreetly called 'very warm discourse' with the lieutenant-governor of Massachusetts, William Stoughton, over the refusal of a sheriff to release a protégé of Phips from jail.

At least once, when corresponding with his long-standing political foe, John Usher, this tendency was reflected even in official correspondence. In a short-lived gesture of conciliation in October 1692 the New Hampshire lieutenant-governor appealed to Phips to ignore 'what ever ill minded prejudiced persons may buz in your Ears.' He was rewarded by Phips's sarcastic assurance that 'their Majesties affaires shall not suffer ... by my being bussed [kissed] in the ears (as you terme itt) by evill minded and prejudiced persons.' For his part, Cotton Mather handled his biographical subject's blunt disposition by commenting blandly – in a phrase beloved of those historians who have seen crudeness and violence as central to Phips's character – that he was 'of an Inclination, cutting rather like a *Hatchet* than like a *Razor*.'[64]

The evidence suggests that there was an element of calculation in Phips's boorishness. His displays of anger and loud contempt were frequently used for clearly discernible purposes: to ridicule social superiors by publicly making them lose their composure; to gain support by this means among members of his own social class, whether a ship's crew or a dockside crowd; and at least once, in the case of the naval captain Richard Short, to humiliate a disloyal client. Only on the rarest of recorded occasions did verbal threat lead to personal violence, and again this was with definable if not necessarily praiseworthy goals: to quell a mutiny aboard ship; to induce an Acadian to reveal the whereabouts of a concealed cash box during the plundering of Port-Royal in 1690; and to punish Short. Furthermore, Phips could be made presentable enough to meet productively between 1683 and 1692 with four English monarchs (not that the quality of their manners should be taken for granted either) as well as with leading City of London merchants and a variety of Whig and Tory politicians. An especially revealing episode occurred at the capitulation of Port-Royal in May 1690. According to a French eyewitness, Phips met the surrendering governor, Louis-Alexandre Des Friches de Meneval, with courtesy and military correctness, but as soon as Phips reached the Port-Royal fort for the act of surrender, his manner changed abruptly, and his display of anger at the reported pilfering of stores by undisciplined soldiers of the French garrison was the signal for the prolonged and systematic pillaging of the fort and town. Both politeness and loutishness had their uses at the appropriate times; what makes this incident significant is the fact that · the appropriate times occurred so closely together.[65]

To be sure, there were occasions when Phips had difficulty controlling his temper even when calculation might have dictated that he do so, as when he seized the award from John Walley and threw it into the fire. At times a vigorous and enthusiastic person, Phips could also be moody. A New York envoy, immediately after a stormy session with Phips in August 1693, was approached by an unnamed Massachusetts council member who 'seemd ashamed' of the governor's behaviour and commented (more about the heat of Phips's passion than about the summer weather), 'Sir you must pardon him his dogg-days, he cannot help it.'[66] There is evidence too that Phips did lack social sophistication, and perhaps social confidence as well, to an extent that must have been politically detrimental while he was governor. As far as the records show, he did not entertain often, and on at least one occasion when he accepted an invitation to visit Samuel Sewall for a glass of brandy, he does not appear to have returned the courtesy. Even his close political ally Increase Mather only rarely made a diary entry mentioning a visit to the governor's mansion.[67]

Nevertheless, any simple equation of Phips's demeanour in later life with the nature of his rural upbringing is misleading. No doubt he learned the uses of harsh language in the fishing harbours of the Kennebec region and studied them further while at sea in young adulthood, but the charge of boorishness that was so often levelled at him was not always sustainable – and when it was made openly, he was fully prepared to offer a vigorous response. When Governor Fletcher informed him, in the context of the Gouverneur affair, 'You have forgott ... your manners to gentlemen,' Phips responded, 'If (as you say) I have forgott my manners to Gentlemen I have forgott what you never had.'[68] Sir William Phips's life did proceed from humble beginnings, though not as humble as Cotton Mather would have had his readers believe; and beyond doubt, his origins in a farmer-fisher community, at both a geographical and a cultural distance from the urban centres of southern New England, affected his relationships with members of all social classes in his later life. He remained, however, an active participant in the shaping of those relationships and in his own search for advancement.

2

The Making of a Projector

As William Phips approached thirty years of age, his efforts at self-advancement had brought real but limited progress. Ambitious and acquisitive, drawing constantly on the network of family and other associates whose northeastern connections matched his own, Phips the sea captain was well established in Boston. His, however, was not the Boston that formed the social and political centre for the agricultural towns lying farther inland. Phips's environment was the port, where his peripheral origins and colourful language smoothed rather than hindered his path to acceptance and a modest prosperity. However, the conventional pattern of coastal and Caribbean trading voyages offered restricted scope to an individual whose aspirations ran to larger possibilities. 'He would frequently tell the Gentlewoman his Wife,' wrote Cotton Mather, 'That he should yet be *Captain of a King's Ship*; That he should come to have the *Command of better Men* than he was now accounted himself; and, That he should be Owner of a *Fair Brick-House* in the *Green-Lane* of *North-Boston*; and, That, it may be, this would not be all that the Providence of God would bring him to.'[1]

A sea captain of ability, even one like Phips who had begun with limited resources, could realistically hope to build enough capital over the years to emerge as a merchant on a substantial scale. The path, however, was arduous and slippery and unlikely to yield acceptance into the colonial elite in the first generation.[2] To ascend with greater speed and certainty would require mercantile connections at a level far removed from Phips's current circle, or an infusion of wealth from some other source: the kind of riches, perhaps, that reputedly lay in wrecked Spanish treasure galleons in the Caribbean. Voyages to the Bahama Banks and elsewhere were talked about on the Boston wharves, although no treasure seeker had yet returned wealthy. Phips eventually succeeded where others had failed. His success was the product of a dynamic that was to exert a continuing influence on his career: the harnessing of his acquisitiveness and commercial ambitions to the demands of English patrons and to the needs of an empire in the throes of redefinition through changing relationships with Spain, France, and the Native inhabitants of claimed territories.

It was through English patronage, as well as his own efforts in the Caribbean, that Phips found his role as a 'projector' – a role that fitted his seagoing background as satisfactorily as it promised a chance of fulfilling his seemingly unlikely aspirations. A projector, as defined in Daniel Defoe's *Essay upon Projects* (1697), was a penurious individual who sought wealth and advancement through money-making schemes financed by others. In the development of 'the Projecting Humour that now reigns,' Defoe attributed crucial significance to Phips's arrival in England in 1687 with more than £200,000 in salvaged Spanish treasure. The projecting spirit, according to Defoe, 'had hardly any Hand to own it, till the Wreck-Voyage ... performed so happily by Captain *Phips*, afterwards Sir *William*; whose strange Performance set a great many Heads on work to contrive something for themselves.'[3] As a would-be projector in the early 1680s, Phips certainly had the necessary ambition to make his way in the world. By the time he reached England to seek patronage, as Mather briefly recorded, he also had some experience of treasure seeking:

Being thus of the *True Temper*, for doing of *Great Things*, he betakes himself to the *Sea*, the Right *Scene* for such Things; and upon Advice of a *Spanish Wreck* about the *Bahama's*, he took a Voyage thither; but with little more success, than what just served him a little to furnish him for a Voyage to *England* ... Having first informed himself that there was another *Spanish Wreck*, wherein was lost a mighty Treasure, hitherto undiscovered, he had a strong Impression upon his Mind that *He* must be the Discoverer; and he made ... Representations of his design at *White-Hall*.[4]

Other evidence indicates that, inadvertently or by design, Mather may have underestimated the proceeds from Phips's little-known first treasure-seeking voyage. The only solid evidence of the episode comes in a court case of 1682, in which four of Phips's former crew members sued him and the two quartermasters of the *Resolution* for nonpayment of half of their share in a recent venture that was almost certainly the

Bahamian voyage. The Massachusetts Court of Assistants, sitting as a court of admiralty, ordered the four to receive the half-shares of twenty-seven pounds each.[5] A voyage in which a full share was worth fifty-four pounds would certainly qualify as a profitable enterprise. It was enough to prompt the royal customs official Edward Randolph to mention, in August 1683, Phips's 'late successfull returnes' as a treasure seeker, while a Spanish narrative of 1687 recalled that Phips had 'for some years followed the art of discovering shipwrecked vessels, not without considerable success.'[6]

Be that as it may, Phips obviously needed solid patronage if he was to follow up on these early activities. His representations in London attained success in the summer of 1683 for reasons that no doubt owed something to his powers of persuasion but also fitted into a more general context. Accounts of unusually rich wrecked treasure galleons had been as common in London as in Boston. Sir John Narbrough, a leading admiral of the 1670s and since 1680 one of the navy commissioners, had long taken an interest in these rumours, and he now became Phips's chief patron. According to the Spanish ambassador in England, Don Pedro Ronquillo, Narbrough's interest stemmed from the period in the 1650s when he had served in the Caribbean in the navy of the Protectorate; Narbrough was said to have gained his information indirectly from the pilot who had sailed on board the wrecked *Nuestra Señora de la Concepción* during the 1640s.[7] One John Farmer, a Bermudian, reported meeting an Englishman who, while being held captive in Hispaniola, had heard of a galleon wrecked on the coast of that island. Potential Spanish searchers for the wreck had been discouraged, the informant had added, by 'a kind of Demonical prophites who said it should never be brout away except by sum of the English nation.'[8] More generally, the salvaging of Spanish wrecks had already emerged in the English Caribbean as a recognized way of attaining wealth, though as yet only on a modest scale. In 1682 the governor of Jamaica, Sir Thomas Lynch, complained to his counterpart in the Bahamas that the English inhabitants of the Bahamian islands were preoccupied more with 'pillaging the Spanish wrecks' than with building stable settlements.[9]

Lynch's disdainful view of treasure-hunting activity was an indication of the conflict in Jamaica between the freebooting approach of buccaneers such as Sir Henry Morgan, who saw the future of Jamaica in terms of privateering and illicit trade, and the planter class. Lynch and his planter supporters associated the salvaging of treasure with preying on Spanish ships and settlements, which lay close to the blurred and disputed boundary between privateering and piracy. For them, all these activities threatened to undermine the fragile basis of an English-Spanish coexistence, which alone could provide the necessary stability in the region.[10] The controversy resonated in London also. William Blathwayt, the influential secretary to the Privy Council committee known as the Lords of Trade, observed in May 1682 to his close friend and colleague Sir Robert Southwell, 'I should be exceeding glad you could gett a Narrative of Our South Sea Buckaniers for though some of them be up and down london yet their apprehension of the Spanish Ambassador (who intends to prosecute them) is such that they cannot be easily mett withall.' Blathwayt's interest in buccaneering exploits notwithstanding, his considered view was made clear a few weeks later when he received word of Lynch's arrival as governor to take over from the temporary administration of Morgan: 'Sir Thomas finds the Island extreamly out of order and 'tis no wonder considering the hands it has been in.'[11] Blathwayt mistrusted those whose approach to empire openly embraced the possibility of private gain by violent or adventurous means, and the Caribbean offered no shortage of archetypal subjects for his disapproval.

The navy commissioners took a different view, following the lead of Narbrough and Sir Richard Haddock (who in 1683 was the first to be appointed the navy's commissioner of victualling).[12] Narbrough's personal experience included conflict with Spanish authorities while in command of an expedition to the west coast of South America in 1670–1. Although both of the expedition's ships were naval, their mission had been commercial: to trade with aboriginal inhabitants in the private interest of Charles II, and to explore any further opportunities for English trade in the South Pacific. The opposition of the Spanish in Chile blocked these goals, but Narbrough succeeded in bringing the vessels back unharmed and the expedition provided a clear example of the use of naval resources for the private commercial interest of the monarch.[13]

More recently, an English freebooting vessel commanded by Bartholomew Sharpe had spent much of 1680 and all of 1681 in often chaotic efforts to find gold mines and Spanish plunder in Central America and on the west coast of South America.[14] When Sharpe finally arrived in England, he faced charges of piracy at the behest of the Spanish ambassador, but he was given a more friendly reception by the navy commissioners. In November 1682, having been acquitted by a jury, Sharpe received a commission to command the naval sloop *Bonetta* on a voyage to search for a Spanish wreck off the Hispaniola coast – the same wreck that Phips would later seek.[15] For reasons that are not entirely clear from the surviving evidence, Sharpe's command of the expedition was then revoked in favour of Edward Stanley, but the *Bonetta* departed in April 1683 on a lengthy though fruitless search.[16] Thus, when Phips arrived in London to seek patronage for a treasure-salvaging voyage to the Bahama Banks, his project was not considered outlandish by Narbrough, Haddock, and their colleagues. By the same token, it was unlikely to make a favourable impression in Blathwayt's Plantations Office.

Phips's success in making the necessary contacts has traditionally been viewed as one of the more remarkable parts of his story. How could a carpenter from a 'despicable plantation' on the fringe of empire gain the backing of high-ranking naval officers and the crown itself? However, now that Phips's family tree is known, an explanation is not so difficult. To wealthy New Englanders, Phips may have been an outsider of humble origins, but in England his family connections were sufficiently respectable to enable even a poor cousin to muster introductions that would smooth his entry into an official culture in which connections of family and locality were crucial to success. It is uncertain how long it took Phips to achieve his goal, for Mather did not record when Phips arrived in London, but by 19 June 1683 his efforts had borne fruit. The Admiralty commissioners wrote on that day to the Navy Board to direct that 'his Majesties prize Ship the Rose of Argiere ... be forthwith fitted to Sea, and that all possible dispatch be used therein.' The vessel, provided with supplies for nine months, was to be lent to Phips. By 19 August, Edward Randolph – travelling to New England as a royal emissary – was reporting to Southwell on the passage he was about to take: 'The Rose frigott of 20 gunns an Algereen prize is fitted out to sea and bound to the Spanish wreck off the Bahama Islands under the conduct of one Phips ... He is to call at Boston to take in his diving Tubs and other necessaryes.' The fitting-out records of Phips's vessel were dated the next day, and Phips's signatures on them show that he took possession on 3 September.[17]

The active role of Narbrough and Haddock in lending the *Rose* is established by a later document recalling that those two had been 'Privy to the Designe upon which the said shipp was sent abroad.'[18] Yet two navy commissioners alone – or the entire Navy Board, for that matter – would not have had the power to lend a naval vessel. The first of the four signatures on the Admiralty commissioners' order for fitting out the *Rose* was that of Daniel Finch, second earl of Nottingham, who was first lord of the Admiralty. This rising Tory politician, who was to have interactions with Phips while secretary of state in the 1690s, did not personally sign all such orders. The likelihood is, however, that Charles II was directly involved in lending the *Rose*, at the instance of Narbrough – who, as a contemporary later observed, had 'a great and well deserved Interest with the Court' and the ear of both the duke of York and the king.[19] Certainly, the king had the largest interest in any proceeds from the voyage. In addition to the royalty of one-tenth that would formally be due to the crown, Charles II was to be personally entitled to one-quarter of all the treasure recovered.[20]

Of the *Rose* itself, there are conflicting descriptions. Variously referred to in contemporary sources as the *Golden Rose* and the *Rose of Algiers*, the vessel was by all accounts an Algerian prize. In naval listings the *Golden Rose* appears in 1682 as a 163-ton, six-gun fireship with a maximum complement of thirty-five, captured in 1681. According to the *London Gazette*, however, the *Rose of Argier* carried twenty-four guns when captured and had a crew of 220.[21] That the same vessel would have different uses and crew sizes in the English and Algerian navies is not implausible, though the possibility of confusion between two vessels is raised both by Randolph's reference to a frigate of twenty guns and by the fact that the English consul in Tripoli had recorded the capture in 1677 by Narbrough (who at the time was commanding the English fleet in the Mediterranean) of a substantial Algerian warship named the *Golden Rose of Algiers*.[22] Furthermore, the fitting-out record of 1683 was unequivocal in describing Phips's vessel as 'his Majesties ... Frigat the Rose Prize.'[23]

Even though Phips was thus entrusted with a moderately powerful naval vessel, the limits to the trust were indicated by the placing of two royal agents on board, John Knepp and Charles Salmon.[24] The entries in Knepp's journal of the early months of the voyage suggest a naval background, and he was probably the same John Knepp who was listed some three years later as purser on board the fourth-rate warship *Assurance*. Salmon has survived on record chiefly as the artist who drew an elaborate colour map of the Bahama Banks while on board the *Rose*.[25] What view Salmon took of Phips's role as commander is unknown, but Knepp's verdict was scathing. His portrait of Phips as a lax disciplinarian and a gratuitous aggressor towards other ships, which he sent to England in early 1684, was undoubtedly the major factor prompting a secret royal instruction to the Massachusetts magistrates William Stoughton and Joseph Dudley in late February that they were to seize the *Rose* 'in case you shall be informed or suspect that the said William Phips or his Seamen may endeavour to defraud Us of Our said ship, or of the Benefit of that Undertaking.'[26] Although sending Phips to the Bahamas with a prize vessel offered the crown the possibility of substantial returns for a relatively small outlay, it carried an element of risk that depended in large part on the performance of an untested commander.

Knepp's journal and the documents preserved with it provide essential evidence on the crewing of the ship and the organization of the voyage. When Knepp went aboard the *Rose* at its moorings on the Thames on 3 September 1683, he had the first of his many disputes with crew members – over the articles of agreement to be signed before departure. Knepp's citation of the authority of Narbrough and Haddock did nothing to persuade the chief mate and other seamen to sign, until Phips intervened when he arrived the following day. The signing took place immediately before to the ship's departure on 5 September, with Narbrough and Haddock present to witness the first eight of the forty-two signatures, including that of Phips, and with Randolph witnessing all of them. The articles, as well as asserting the primacy of royal commands in determining the movements of the *Rose* and prescribing the royal one-quarter share, provided for the organization of the voyage on a basis of shares. Each crew member was responsible for supplying his own arms and ammunition and for paying for one share of the ship's provisions. The only wages paid, to the surgeon and the cook, were to be borne by the crew. Of the proceeds of the voyage after deduction of the royal tenth and one-quarter, each 'Foremast or common man' was to have one share. Phips was to have three – defined as one for himself, one for his commission, and one for his supplying all necessary equipment – and each boy was to have one-half. The mate was to have only one-eighth more than a common share. Although all signatories were obliged to obey Phips's lawful commands, the ship's company as a whole had extensive powers in conjunction with Phips to decide by vote whether or not a 'refractory or undeserving person' should continue to be entitled to a full share or any share at all.[27]

After the *Rose* had sailed, Phips and Knepp clashed repeatedly over the extent of the powers that remained to Phips as commander. Knepp, expecting ship's discipline on a naval pattern, complained that Phips responded only mildly to the misdemeanours of the crew. On 6 October 1683 Knepp recorded that he himself had spoken out against drunkenness and swearing: 'They said god damn them they would Swear and be

drunk as often as they pleased and they told me that their captain
would not have said soe much to them which was very trew for let them
doe what mischief they pleased he would say nothing to them for it.'
Two days later, after a crew member had admitted to breaking open a
door to draw off brandy belonging to Knepp, Knepp quoted Phips as
excusing the mildness of his reprimand on the grounds that 'men that
pay for theire owne victualls and received noe wages will not be corrected for every small fault.'[28] A similar argument took place in Boston
on 31 December 1683, shortly after Knepp had been slightly wounded
by a sword cut which he blamed on two of the crew whom he had met
on a dark street. According to Knepp, Phips asserted 'that it could not be
expected that he could carry a strict command where Every man found
his owne Provisions and receives noe wages.' To this, Knepp replied
'that if he had carried but a small command when he came to sea first
hee might have had them under command still, but soe long as he made
every sailor his companion he Must not expect that they will be commanded by him or by any body Else.'[29]

Knepp was undoubtedly a hostile observer. Edward Randolph, not
normally backward as a critic, made no known complaint of his experi-
ences as a passenger on the voyage to Boston. Admittedly, he had not
been told by Phips (as evidently Knepp and Salmon had) 'that we must
be contented to lye upon a chest till we come for new England for all the
cabens and cradles were taken up already.' Yet Salmon stayed on with
the voyage after Knepp left the ship in Boston professing to fear for his
life, and Salmon's later complaint was not against Phips but to the Treasury for arrears of his pay from the crown.[30] But even if allowance is
made for Knepp's naval bias and the animosity he had aroused among
the crew, it is likely that many of his observations were accurate. Phips's
regard for those he considered to be of his own social class and the suggestion that this hindered him from exercising command was a recur-
rent theme even during his later years as governor of Massachusetts.

There was another reason for Phips's attitude to the command of the
Rose: despite the royal involvement in lending the vessel and fitting it
out, the expedition was based on the slenderest of financial footings.
Phips, by Mather's account, had virtually no resources of his own. Questioned by Knepp, he allowed only 'that their was a good many ... he had
received money of but he had forgot their names.'[31] It is not improbable
that Phips had received investments from some individuals whose
names did not appear in any written record of the voyage's business
organization. Haddock and Narbrough are strong possibilities. Both

had been actively involved in the preparations for the expedition to an extent that suggests they were not acting purely as disinterested intermediaries for the crown. Haddock had even intervened personally with the Treasury in July 1683 to expedite the payment of £300 for fitting out the *Rose*.[32] Yet whatever investments Phips had received, they were barely adequate. Eight days out from London, according to Knepp, the *Rose* was found to have provisions only for a month. When Phips put in at Limerick the next day, twenty men apparently went on shore to shoot whatever sheep and poultry could be found. Four months later, again if Knepp is to be believed, the same expedient was adopted during a visit to an island in Boston harbour (which also involved the brutal sexual assault of a female settler by a number of the crew).[33]

Further evidence of improvisation, with its implied loosening of the authority of a commander who could not easily provide even the essentials for the expedition, can be found in Phips's dealings in Boston with the merchant Robert Bronson. As well as signing receipts on behalf of individual crew members to whom Bronson had provided supplies, Phips accepted cash for purposes ranging from 'to Gett his docker out of prison' (£6) to the purchase of a three-sixteenths ownership of the sloop *Rosebud* (£62), which was to accompany the *Rose* to the Bahamas. In all, on 13 December 1683, Bronson presented Phips with an account for £200, and two days later Phips signed a declaration promising that he would deliver to Bronson a quarter share of the proceeds of the voyage.[34] By 11 January 1684, apparently after he and at least five of the crew had received further advances from Bronson, Phips and Bronson concluded articles of agreement by which Bronson would be entitled to a full share. A further document three days later committed Phips to collect and deliver share portions owing to Bronson from crew members. Bronson was still trying to collect on these commitments in early 1691, but their significance in December 1683 and January 1684 was that they demonstrated the weakness of Phips's financial arrangements.[35]

One result of these organizational travails was to accentuate the power of the ship's company to the point where the vessel more closely resembled a pirate ship than one in which the share system was operated along lines congenial to the likes of John Knepp. Another result was that Phips was moved to assert his leadership by deliberately provoking the established authorities ashore. The affinities of the *Rose* to piracy became fully explicit only as the voyage proceeded. According to Mather, Phips was twice threatened in 1684 by mutinous crew members who sought to force him to take the ship 'to drive a Trade of Piracy on the *South Seas.*' But Phips prevailed on both occasions, including the time when the mutineers consisted of the great majority of the crew and threatened to maroon Phips and his 'eight or ten' loyalists if he did not comply; he retained command long enough to make port in Jamaica. The details of these episodes are recorded only by Mather, but their general veracity is corroborated by the later depositions of crew members and by the evidence of Governor Hender Molesworth of Jamaica. Molesworth described the 'notable Mutinye,' though he attributed it not so much to the crew's desire to take over the ship as to their wish for a dividend of what little treasure had been found, 'to the end that upon the first occasion they may Leave his Majesties Ship and betake themselves to that bewiching Trade [of privateering].'[36]

Although 'privateering' was the word Molesworth used, the tone and context of his comment make it clear that the 'bewiching Trade' he had in mind was the form of privateering that was indistinguishable from piracy. The *Rose* had shown tendencies in this direction even before leaving New England. That the share system was so equal that every adult member of the crew was on virtually the same basis – and that even Phips's three shares were justified according to specific responsibilities – was indicative in itself. As Marcus Rediker has observed, such a pay system 'represented a radical departure from practices in the merchant service, Royal Navy, or privateering.'[37] Furthermore, the authority reserved to the majority of the crew in the ship's articles was no mere cipher, as became clear during the arrangements to add the *Rosebud* to the expedition. Initially negotiated by Phips with the Boston owners of the *Rosebud*, the draft agreement was put to a meeting on 8 January 1684 which, according to Knepp, was attended by 'our commander and most of our company' as well as by the owners and crew of the sloop. The crew of the *Rose* rejected the agreement on the grounds that its provisions relating to the eventuality of the *Rosebud*'s loss gave an unfair advantage to its owners and crew by comparison with the lack of safeguards enjoyed by the company of the *Rose*. Only after renegotiation the following day did the mates Michael Coan and William Covell put their names to the agreement as representatives of the ship's company 'by the Consent of the Maj. part of them.' Phips had been overruled and, like a pirate captain, had been 'governed by a Majority.'[38]

The disputes between the crew and Knepp over language and drinking are also indicative of a conflict that depended on social class and set the *Rose* apart from both merchant and naval ships. To cite Rediker, '"rough talk" at sea had distinct social implications'; its endorsement by

Phips, through his refusal to give more than a mild rebuke to those who insulted Knepp on the transatlantic voyage, was striking.[39] By early January 1684, Knepp also had a more serious charge against Phips – and against his wife. In Boston on 3 January, a few days after he had been attacked by the two crew members, Knepp confided to his journal a disturbing conversation he had had with Salmon: 'this day Mr. Salmon being at Capt. Phips house his wife said that she understood that Knepp has given an account home to the [navy] commissioners ... and I here that hee intends to goe home and will not goe the Voyage but I have perswaded my husband to force him to goe, for if he goes home my husband and his company are afraid that the commissioners will send for the ship home before they have made their voyage.'[40] Even though no more is heard of this reported plan to kidnap Knepp, it suggests the extent of Mary's partnership in decisions affecting the treasure-seeking venture and the lengths she was willing to go to see it succeed. Knepp eventually found a passage to England in May 1684 – but not before recording on 21 January that a ship's captain had informed him 'that a great many of the Roses men told him that if Capt. Phips did not make them a Voyage upon the wreck according to their Expectation ... that then they would goe and take the first Spaniard they met withall.'[41]

This last allegation is plausible in the light of the mutinies later that year. Yet the traces of exasperation that Knepp sensed in Phips's crew also hint at another reality – that no matter what took place aboard the *Golden Rose* or ashore, Phips was no pirate captain. All his actions during the voyage of the *Rose* suggest that he was far too aware of the value of the naval patronage links, which he had been able to create in 1683, to jeopardize them by moving too far into the hazy area that separated piracy from legitimate enterprise. Yet he maintained a fine balance between the two. If Salmon's report is accurate, Phips had considered forcibly embarking Knepp – though, paradoxically, his reason for doing so would have been to maintain for a crucial period of time, his good name with the navy commissioners. More generally, Phips was aware of the perils of orthodoxy for a captain whose authority over the crew was as tenuous as his was and as dependent on cutting an impressive figure in disregard of the powers that be. The evidence is clear that this was, for Phips, a congenial task and that – again paradoxically – his chief technique was to flaunt his naval connections and even to claim that 'he had discoursed his Majestie alreadie, [and] he did not question but to discourse with him againe.'[42]

Knepp's journal is the only direct source for Phips's conflicts with the

Massachusetts governor and magistrates while he was in Boston. While no doubt questionable on details (Knepp frequently, for example, makes Phips's critics speak in virtually the same words as one another and in words strikingly similar to those already used by Knepp in his journal), this account portrays Phips's actions in terms that find corroboration in their similarity to those reported by Molesworth from Jamaica. On 1 November 1683, two days after reaching its moorings in Boston, the *Rose* began a sustained campaign of firing across the bows of merchant and fishing vessels to make them strike their colours as they would to a naval vessel. The masters of these ships were then boarded and served with a bill for the cost of the shot. These incidents went apparently unchallenged for some eleven days before an affray on shore brought matters to a head. Starting with a quarrel over whether Phips had the power to impress a carpenter from another vessel, the affair developed into a general brawl between the respective crews. When constables intervened and threatened to report the matter to the governor, Phips reportedly declared in crudely abusive terms that he did not care for the governor's authority. His crew then volubly supported him, adding, according to the testimony of one John Flood, that 'as for the Governour and the Goverment here they did not value a fart and they generally said soe and that they had a better goverment in this harbour of Boston then the Governour ... and that they would ride Admiral in spight of them all, in all their discourse they cursed all that belonged to this country and swore soe much that their oaths were more then their others [*sic*] words of discourse.'[43]

The matter came to a hearing before the governor, Simon Bradstreet, on the Monday following the Saturday on which the brawl had occurred. At the same time, the issue of Phips's right to make other vessels strike their colours was raised. Phips's claim that he had 'private orders from his Majestie for soe doing but these he would show to noe body' and his complaint about the actions of the constables merely caused Bradstreet to deliver a magisterial rebuke. After hearing two days of testimony, Bradstreet found Phips and his company 'much to blame' but dismissed them with a warning because the *Rose* was 'upon his Majesties private interest.' He told Phips (again, according to Knepp's account) 'that every body in Boston Knew very well what he was and from whence he came: therefore desired him not to carry it soe loftily amoung his country men and Likewise told him that he beleived that he had not orders from his Majestie to make all ships strik as he did – and to make them pay for the shot.'[44] Phips reacted angrily and con-

tinued for another month to fire on occasion at passing vessels, until on
13 December he fired no fewer than five shots – including one that hit
the bow – at a vessel commanded by Thomas Jenner.[45]

Jenner may have been deliberately singled out for this treatment.
Knepp's journal records that Jenner claimed to have known Phips in
London, but their relationship likely went back further. Jenner was a
mariner from Charlestown, the home of Mary Spencer Phips and a community that William had frequented during the late 1670s. Even more to
the point, Jenner had been a trader on the Wabanaki coast in earlier
years. In 1657 he had been arrested on the Kennebec for trading with
Native inhabitants without a licence, from a vessel that carried trade
goods that included more than a hogshead of brandy and half a hogshead of sack. Unregulated coastal traders represented a serious threat to
the colonial residents of the region. They competed with resident traders such as the Phips and White families and were known to jeopardize
Anglo-Wabanaki relations because of their sharp practice in trade and
the sale of liquor and firearms. During the tense winter of 1675–6, the
kidnapping of several Wabanaki by a coaster had contributed to the
spread of Anglo-Wabanaki hostilities. Members of the Phips and White
families, having been profoundly damaged by the warfare of that era,
may have had especially long memories with regard to Jenner; though
one of Jenner's partners in 1657, John Phillips, later became a close
friend and political ally of Phips, so Phips clearly bore no general
grudge from those events of his childhood years. Between Phips and
Jenner, however, there was neither friendship nor alliance, as witness
Jenner's formal complaint to Governor Bradstreet.[46]

This time Phips was questioned by a number of magistrates. According to Knepp, William Stoughton, who later served under Phips as lieutenant-governor, demanded to see Phips's orders, observing that if
Phips could not produce any, he would have 'very much affronted' the
royal authority by his pretensions. Stoughton also apparently maintained (albeit in words suspiciously close to Knepp's) that Phips was
'fitted out upon his Majesties private Interest and was noe actuall man
of war.' Ultimately fined five pounds as well as being sentenced to pay
five pounds to Jenner, Phips succeeded by a plea of poverty in having
Bradstreet remit payment until after his voyage to the wreck, but he was
denied permission to appeal to the Admiralty board. A day later,
according to Knepp, he sent ten men with cutlasses to wrest the pennant
from a passing ketch.[47] The issue then faded from Knepp's journal, to be
replaced by Knepp's apprehensions for his personal safety. Three

months later, however, a report reached Boston of a quarrel that had arisen between Phips and Governor Robert Lilburne of the Bahamas after Phips had ordered the governor's ketch to strike its pennant.[48] Later in the year, Governor Molesworth complained to William Blathwayt about Phips's conduct in Jamaica towards one of several Spanish trading vessels currently in port. 'Upon some mistaken punctilio of the Sea,' reported Molesworth, Phips had 'discharged a Shot at one of the Spaniards who upon a festivall day had put out his Penant.' Then, 'with a Crowd of Rabble at his heeles,' Phips had sought out the Spanish captain in the streets of Port Royal and threatened him in an effort to make him pay for the shot. Only when a bystander intervened to pay off the demand had a more serious incident been avoided. Even so, said Molesworth, the matter had led the Spanish factor to threaten withdrawal of Spanish trading ships.[49]

Molesworth was caught in a similar dilemma to that of Bradstreet. Unwilling to risk seriously undermining the success of a voyage that involved the private interest of the king, both governors found themselves in the unfamiliar situation of dealing with a captain who, as Molesworth put it,was 'making use of the King's name to fight against himselfe.' In Jamaica as in Massachusetts, Phips's social origins compounded the affront: 'This man,' complained Molesworth, 'never knew better education than what belongs to a Carpenter, and never pretended before now to the Title of a Captain and cannot yet shew a Commission for it, yet assumes more to him selfe then any of the Kings Captains have done.'

In Jamaica, however, there was another issue at stake, one that was as significant to Blathwayt as to Molesworth. Phips's actions were interpreted by Molesworth as deliberately disrupting commercial relations between the English and Spanish in the Caribbean, 'incouraged under hand by some ill Willers of the Trade.'[50] Phips's motives were probably simpler than this, though he left no direct record of them, and neither did Mather, who preferred to draw a discreet veil over these episodes. Since Phips was still short of cash and was intent on recruiting a new crew to replace the mutineers who had left the *Rose*, it was in his interests to be conspicuous. The limited evidence also indicates that he enjoyed turning the social order upside down by using the king's name and suggesting that he had private royal instructions, which he always refused to display; it gave him the chance to ridicule the established authorities with impunity. In doing so, Phips emulated – or parodied – the customary regard shown by naval captains for the royal honour as expressed in salutes (though regular naval vessels sometimes ignored perceived slights in the interests of avoiding damaging international incidents that might affect trade). Phips was undoubtedly aware that he was on safe ground with a patron such as Narbrough, who had himself come into conflict with the Spanish in the Americas and had no hesitation in employing others who had done so. Blathwayt, however, would inevitably take a very different view, and if Phips's naval contacts were ever to fail him, this might have serious implications for his place in the patronage structures of the empire.[51]

In the meantime, the central purpose of the voyage of the *Golden Rose* was to salvage treasure, and up to the time of the vessel's arrival in Jamaica it had had very little success in doing so. Even before the *Rose* left Boston, the indications were not good. The intended wreck on the Bahama Banks had already been visited by other treasure-seekers, and when Phips arrived in Boston in October 1683 he found that a New England vessel – the *Good Intent*, commanded by William Warren – was about to leave on the same errand. According to Knepp, Phips made a vain attempt to have Bradstreet intervene on the grounds that by stopping Warren, he would avoid bloodshed. 'For,' stated Phips, 'I have an order from his Majestie that noe ship nor vessell shall go to the wreck but my self.' Eventually, Phips came to an agreement to sail in association with Warren, who in return would contribute divers and equipment. Meanwhile, the master of another vessel newly arrived from the wreck described the limited success there of six ships with thirty able divers and declared that he 'would not give five pounds for any mans share that goes to make a voyage now.'[52]

The *Rose* eventually departed from Boston on 19 January 1684. Reports reaching Boston placed it in the Bahamas by 9 February and at the wreck by 16 March. The same reports spoke of smallpox among both Phips's and Warren's crews and of its afflicting the few good divers they had. The reports in May were marginally more favourable. Phips had recruited divers from one of the vessels already at the wreck and had succeeded in persuading the other ships to depart in deference to his royal orders. One of the returning captains, asked by Knepp to appraise Phips's chances, replied 'that he had not got much yet but if there were any silver left they believed that he would get it, for there was noe body there to hinder him.'[53]

This assessment was judicious. The later depositions of two crew members of the *Good Intent*, John Carlile and Edward Pell, indicated that in July there had been a dividend of £11/10/– per share. Treasury corre-

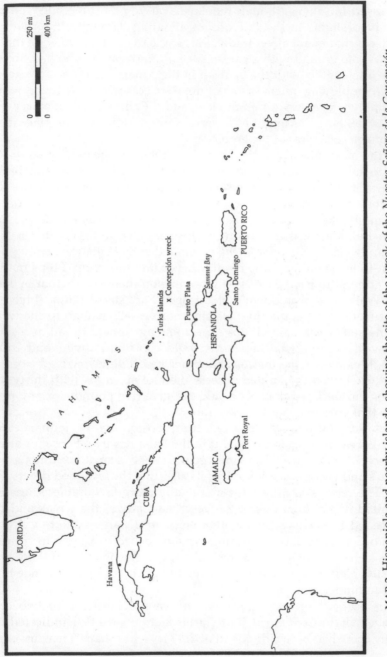

MAP 2 Hispaniola and nearby islands, showing the site of the wreck of the *Nuestra Señora de la Concepción*

spondence after the voyage documents the receipt from Phips of 'a Pig of Silver,' which by early 1687 had been turned into coinage valued at £198/4/–.[54] Silver had been retrieved, but in the context of the expense involved and the large number of seamen aboard the *Rose*, *Rosebud*, and *Good Intent*, the amounts were very small. There was even a suggestion in later depositions that the *Golden Rose* itself had been for some reason excluded from the July dividend. According to the statement of crew member William Bryant, which was corroborated by Henry Dickeson, 'there was some shareing among the vessels there in consortship but no shareing among the ship's company.'[55] This would help explain the mutinies that took place soon afterwards. According to Mather, it was the crew's 'growing weary of their unsuccessful Enterprize' that brought about the first mutiny, which Phips reportedly quashed without delay. 'Captain *Phips*,' wrote Mather, 'though he had not so much of a Weapon as an *Ox-Goad*, or a *Jaw-Bone* in his Hands, yet like another *Shamgar* or *Samson*, with a most undaunted Fortitude, he rush'd in upon them, and with the Blows of his bare Hands, *Fell'd* many of them, and *Quell'd* all the Rest.'[56] Although Mather's account is uncorroborated in its details, it is not implausible. If it is true, it represents one of only three convincingly documented occasions during Phips's life when his actions were personally violent.

The second mutiny was a more elaborate affair, and Mather's account portrays Phips as prevailing by stratagem rather than physical force. He and the few loyal members of his crew stealthily brought their guns to bear on the tent that served as the headquarters of the mutineers, whereupon the mutineers abandoned the articles they had drawn up to govern their prospective pirate voyage and apologized to Phips in terms which, though reported only by Mather, offer an insight into the nature of their relationship with him: '*that they never had any thing against him, except only his unwillingness to go away with the King's Ship upon the* South-Sea *Design: But upon all other Accounts, they would chuse rather to Live and Die with him, than with any Man in the World; however, since they saw how much he was dissatisfied at it, they would insist upon it no more, and humbly begg'd his Pardon.*'[57] The implication of this apology, though Mather used it simply as an example of Phips's sterling character and steadfastness in the face of mutiny, was that from the perspective of a pirate crew Phips had all the right qualifications for leadership if only he had been willing to use them to that end. Despite the apology, the ship's company of the *Rose* did not sail together for much longer. On arriving in Jamaica, Phips and the mutineers made complaints and accusations against one another and then parted ways. Mather states that Phips 'Turn'd them off,' though other crew members later testified that the mutineers deserted.[58] Either way, it was with essentially a new crew that Phips sailed from Port Royal in November 1684.

While in Jamaica, Phips undoubtedly sought further information about the location of potentially lucrative wrecks. One individual who claimed to have been his chief informant was Sir Richard White, although, as Peter Earle has shown, the claim was self-serving and probably spurious. Phips may also have met with Edward Stanley, commander of the *Bonetta*, who was in Jamaica during part of Phips's stay.[59] Whatever clues he gathered, he now steered for Hispaniola. Mather's account of what followed is short and general but suggestive:

[In Hispaniola] by the Policy of his Address, he fished out of a very old *Spaniard*, (or *Portuguese*) a little Advice about the true Spot where lay the *Wreck* which he had been hitherto seeking, as unprosperously, as the *Chymists* have their *Aurifick Stone*: That it was upon a *Reef of Shoals*, a few Leagues to the Northward of *Port de la Plata*, upon *Hispaniola*, a Port so call'd, it seems, from the Landing of some of the *Shipwreck'd* Company, with a Boat full of Plate, saved out of their Sinking Frigot: Nevertheless, when he had searched very narrowly the Spot, whereof the old *Spaniard* had advised him, he had not hitherto exactly lit upon it. Such *Thorns* did vex his Affairs while he was in the *Rose-Frigot*; but none of these things could rotund the Edge of his Expectations to find the *Wreck*.[60]

Mather's account indicates that Phips's purpose in the voyage of the *Rose* had not been purely to make for the Bahama Banks but also to seek richer rewards off Hispaniola – as Stanley was doing at the same time and with no greater success. For the time being, though, Phips decided to abandon the search and return to England. Repeated revictualling – Jamaica, Hispaniola, and finally Bermuda – dissipated most of the silver salvaged on the Bahama Banks.[61] The stop in Bermuda in the spring of 1685, not mentioned by Mather, was eventful. Again, Phips intervened in an internal colonial dispute, having been courted on this occasion both by Governor Richard Coney and by a prominent and imprisoned opposition leader, Henry Bish. According to Coney's report to the Lords of Trade, the critics of his government were 'guided by Mr. Bish, whoe sayth to Captain Phipps, that he doth, or that he would doe well not to meddle betwixt the Governor and the Country. They designed to send me aboard Captain Phipps for England if he would take me uppon this Account vizt: That seing me in danger, and my selfe timorous, I should desert my Commission and desier him to secure me from theyre fury.'[62] Instead, Phips – who declared on his return to England that it was the intent of Bish and his cohorts 'to sett up for a free Common wealth and to follow piracy' – took on board Bish and Sarah Oxford, who was described by Coney as 'a principal Abetter and contriver [with Bish].'[63] During the summer of 1685 Phips and the *Golden Rose* arrived back in the Thames after an absence of almost two years.

New troubles now began for Phips. The most immediate was his imprisonment at the behest of Bish. From the confines of the Tower of London, Phips appealed to the earl of Sunderland, the senior secretary of state, on 3 August 1685, and relief came the next day in the form of an order channelled through Blathwayt 'that Bayl bee given on His Majesty's behalf for Captain Phips for soe much as relates to his bringing over the Prisoner.'[64] A second matter of concern was Molesworth's complaint regarding Phips's conduct in Jamaica, which had been considered by the Lords of Trade on 23 February 1685 and had resulted in an order 'that this matter be laid before the Committee when Captain Phipps shall come into England.'[65] There is no evidence that this inquiry was ever pursued, but although Phips apparently escaped further trouble from this quarter, the Treasury also was interested in the voyage of the *Golden Rose*, and it began its scrutiny in early 1686 with a letter to Haddock and Narbrough to direct them to provide a copy of the 'private Instructions given by the late King to Captain Phipps.' The inquiry continued with the involvement of Samuel Pepys, Admiralty secretary, and with questions directed to Phips himself. The result was a calculation that the wear and tear on the *Golden Rose* had cost in excess of £700, while the total returns to the crown amounted to almost £471.[66] Not by any standard had Phips's voyage proved to be a productive investment.

Phips was now in a familiar predicament, once again the penurious projector. Although he was in possession of what he believed to be more exact information regarding the location of the Hispaniola wreck, his lack of financial success meant that he was unlikely to be allowed to borrow a naval vessel again. During the winter of 1685–6 he apparently had some encouragement from Sir Richard White, who had recently returned from Jamaica.[67] What he needed most, however, was not encouragement but wealthy patronage. In Narbrough, he still had a valuable ally. As close or closer to the new king, James II (who in February 1685 had succeeded on the death of his brother, Charles II) as he had been to the old king, Narbrough offered possible access to highly placed investors. And Phips did have some personal merits: even though he had not brought back the desired treasure in the *Rose*, he had at least resisted the temptations of piracy and had brought back the ship. 'So *proper* was his Behaviour,' recorded Cotton Mather, 'that the best Noble Men in the Kingdom now admitted him into their Conversation.' Notwithstanding Mather's capacity for embellishment, it is clear that Phips's social origins would not represent an insuperable barrier as long as Narbrough retained his interest in the treasure-seeking project.[68]

For all that, the process was not easy or quick. An aristocratic observer recalled that Phips's scheme 'went a begging for a great while, and Lord Sunderland, Lord Portsmouth, and several others, refused to be concerned in it, and to venture any money upon it.'[69] Finally, a successful approach was made to Christopher Monck, the second duke of Albemarle, who later testified that he was first informed about the wreck on or shortly before Lady Day (25 March) 1686.[70] Although Albemarle had enjoyed substantial wealth and influence during the later years of Charles II, he had fallen on difficult times by the mid-1680s. In part, the reason was financial, a result of the way of life that had given him his reputation as a heavy drinker and gambler. He had also quickly lost favour at the court of James II, largely because of his incompetent military performance as lord-lieutenant of Devon during Monmouth's rebellion. In August 1685 Blathwayt reported tersely to Southwell, 'The Duke of Albemarle sensible of what past in the West and his not having any new preferment or Title ... has surrendered to the king all his employments.'[71]

Neither Blathwayt nor Southwell admired Albemarle, whose activities in the Americas, which included investment interests in Carolina and the Bahamas, were accompanied by outspoken support on occasion for Sir Henry Morgan's role as an office holder in Jamaica.[72] To their dismay, in the early months of 1686 Albemarle was beginning to regain his position at court. On the death of Sir Philip Howard, Molesworth's short-lived successor as governor of Jamaica, Albemarle sought the appointment, and in mid-April 1686 Blathwayt informed Southwell with no good grace that he had obtained it. Investment in Phips's proposed voyage to the Hispaniola wreck offered Albemarle a gambler's chance of retrieving his financial situation as well.[73] For Phips and Narborough, Albemarle was an ideal patron. Despite his current difficulties, he could afford to invest considerably, and he had the weight to mobilize other substantial contributors.

Accordingly, the business organization for Phips's voyage beginning in 1686 was much more elaborate than that of 1683. It is well documented, largely because of the later disputes among the investors and their heirs, which resulted in court proceedings and the generation of extensive testimony. Phips's own testimony indicates that the process began when he made Narbrough and Albemarle aware that he had 'credible Information' about the wreck. Narbrough acknowledged that he was 'well acquainted' with Phips at the time.[74] The next two investors were relatively obscure figures: Isaac Foxcroft, a lawyer from the Inner Temple, and Francis Nicholson of Hatton Garden.[75] The four partners now searched, through the agency of Phips, for a suitable ship. The choice was the *Bridgewater*, a 200-ton vessel that was bought by the partners for £860 and renamed the *James and Mary* in honour of the king and queen. Phips then recommended the acquisition of a sloop to be commanded by Francis Rogers, who had been captain of the *Rosebud* on the earlier voyage. The partners purchased the 40-ton *Henry* from John Smith, a London merchant who now became the fifth partner in the syndicate. It is unclear whether Smith was initially invited to join the venture or whether he gained entrance by pestering the others until they relented. Both scenarios were later be put forward in disputed court testimony.[76]

Two more members of the partnership were added later, and they were prominent figures. Albemarle made a vain attempt to interest Lord Dartmouth, who declined to buy a one-eighth share even though Albemarle assured him that the sending of a trade cargo on the *James and Mary* would minimize the risk of an outright loss even if the wreck was not found. More willing to be persuaded were the treasurer of the navy, Lord Falkland, and his stepfather Sir James Hayes, who had close connections at the court as a former secretary to Prince Rupert.[77] Albemarle's share – of the investment and also of the proceeds after deduction of both the king's tenth and the one-sixteenth part of the remainder that was to be the payment to Phips for his role as commander – was one-quarter. Narbrough, Foxcroft, Nicholson, Smith, Falkland, and Hayes each had a one-eighth share, which was valued on paper at £400, although later accounting suggests that the real cash investment of a one-eighth share was about £325.[78] It is probable that in 1686, as in 1683, there were also investors who did not appear in the formal records. Certainly, the Boston merchant Richard Wharton believed himself entitled to 'many hundreds' of pounds from Phips after the voyage was completed, and according to one deposition he did receive £300 'for the service of amataba an Indian diver that Sir William had att the wreck with him which the said Wharton was Interested in.'[79] According to one source, Sir Richard Haddock also had an involvement and 'was so unlucky that he sold his hundred pound share for ninety but a month or two before the thing was found. It would have brought him eight thousand pounds.'[80] In other respects, the organization of the expedition was more formal than had been the case in 1683. It was better provisioned, and the crews sailed for wages not shares. Phips's role, while payable by a share, was essentially that of an employee. The articles of agreement signed during the summer of 1686 bound him to return to London within twelve months with the proceeds of the voyage or stand obliged to the investors 'in the penal sume of twenty thousand pounds.'[81]

The investors also had formal safeguards from the crown, though initially these were slender enough to cause them some concern. The crucial document allowing the expedition to set forth was a royal order of 18 July 1686. Issued through the Admiralty and signed by Pepys, it authorized Albemarle or his substitutes to search for and salvage any wrecked vessels 'to the Windward of the Northside of hispaniola, or about the Islands, or Shoales of Bahama near the Gulf of Florida in America.'[82] Although this was the basis on which the investors entered into their articles of agreement with Phips almost two weeks later, the terms and the provenance of the order brought a polite but sharp admonition to Albemarle from Narbrough and Foxcroft that the royal order was 'but an Authority countermandable as soon as the Shipp is gone out of the River' and that there was 'noe time expressed in itt, whereby it is Defective.'[83] Albemarle apparently took this warning to heart and sought a grant under the Great Seal, or Privy Seal, though Phips had long been in the Caribbean by the time Albemarle obtained it. On 20 February 1687 a further order under the Admiralty seal put a three-year term on Albemarle's authorization, beginning on the original date of 18 July 1686, and this was confirmed by letters patent under the Great Seal twelve days later.[84] All in all, Albemarle and the six other investors had mobilized a small company, as the authoritative W.R. Scott has pointed out when comparing it with other joint-stock ventures of the period, but it had adequate investment for the projected task and, by March 1687, a sound basis in formal royal sanction.[85]

Phips was now free, as Cotton Mather put it, to 'set Sail for the *Fishing-Ground*, which had been so well *baited* half an Hundred Years before.' In reality, it was some forty-five years since the wreck of the *Nuestra Señora de la Concepción*.[86] Those who sailed from the Thames in September 1686 aboard the *James and Mary* and the *Henry* were probably unaware of the exact identity of the wrecked vessel they sought, but Phips and Rogers knew where they proposed to search. They had the added encouragement that they were undoubtedly familiar with the reports that had been reaching London not only of the frustrated efforts of the *Bonetta* but also of Stanley's continuing belief – based in part on a brief recent sighting of the wreck by a passing vessel – that it could and should be found.[87]

The early weeks of Phips's voyage were not altogether encouraging. The two vessels lost contact on 4 October, and in bad weather the *Henry* proceeded slowly to the Azores, which it reached eight days later. By the time Rogers caught up with Phips in Barbados on 11 November, the *James and Mary* had been there for ten days. After taking on water and provisions, the two vessels left Barbados on 16 November and anchored eleven days later in Samana Bay, on the northeast coast of Hispaniola.[88] Although some way east of Puerto Plata, the harbour named for the efforts of the *Concepción*'s survivors to bring ashore silver plate, Samana Bay offered plentiful supplies of good fresh water and what the journal of the *Henry* described as 'all necessary provision fitting for man.'[89]

Phips hoped to do some trading while in Samana Bay but succeeded only in making contact with a group of French hunters, who exchanged a number of wild hogs for liquor from the trade supplies carried by the *James and Mary*.[90] Advised by the hunters that there was no Spanish settlement nearby, Phips decided to sail north to the Ambrosia Bank, but he and Rogers were again separated in bad weather and both eventually put into Puerto Plata. There, Phips repeatedly fired signal guns, and at last on 28 December the ships were approached by 'four Spanyards ... [who] came from the governor of S Iago to know what wee were.'[91] In contrast to his behaviour in Jamaica two years earlier, Phips's welcome to the visitors befitted an expedition that wanted trade both for commercial reasons and as a diversion of any suspicion that treasure salvaging was intended: 'Capt: Phips went a shoare and treated them very Kindly, Likewise sent the Governour a present togeather with a Letter to settisfie him of our aboade in this place.'[92] A further encounter on 4 January, this time with the *alferez* (a minor military official) of the nearby Spanish settlement, went equally well. Trading followed, although the journal of the *James and Mary* admitted that it was 'not at all to answer our Expectation.' Rogers and the *Henry*, meanwhile, had been to the Turks Islands in an unsucccessful attempt to find supplies of salt. He arrived back on 8 January and was then sent to begin the search for the wreck. On 12 January the chief mate of the *James and Mary*, William Covell – who, like Rogers, had been one of those who had signed on with the *Golden Rose* in September 1683 – came on board the *Henry* with three divers and the vessel weighed anchor again.[93]

It took Rogers six days to find his chosen vicinity on the Ambrosia Bank, and then the *Henry* spent a number of uncomfortable and danger-ous hours manoeuvring among the boilers (submerged pieces of coral on which the sea broke and foamed) before it was in a position to start searching. The first day of 'dilligent Inspection,' 19 January, passed without result, but the early afternoon of the twentieth however, brought a dramatic discovery that filled an entire page of the *Henry*'s journal:

The Boate and Cannew went a searching and in 2 hours time our Boate Return'd on Boarde againe, Bringing us happy and Joyfull News of the Cannew's finde-ing the Wrecke, their being in her Mr Covle, Francis and Jona, the 2 dieverrs ... She lyes in the midst of Reife betweene 3 Large boylers that the tops of them are dry att low Water, in some places upon her there is 7: fathoms which is the Larg-est depth, 6: and 5: the Shoalles, Most part of the Timber is consum'd away, and soe over Growne with Currle [coral] that had itt not been for her Guns shee woulde scarce Ever beene founde itt being att Least 45 Yeares since shee was Lost, and the Richest Ship that Ever Went out of the West Indies.[94]

The divers spent the next two days working on the wreck, raising eight bars of gold of assorted sizes as well as almost three thousand coins. On 23 January, with the weather deteriorating, Rogers decided to return to Puerto Plata. It was a lengthy and dangerous undertaking, delayed by weather, near-shipwreck on an uncharted reef, and a diversion to the Turks Islands prompted by the sight of a vessel which Rogers took to be a potentially unfriendly 'great ship.' Only on 7 February did the *Henry* drop anchor by the *James and Mary* at Puerto Plata.[95]

Rogers and Covell, perhaps exercising a prerogative of old shipmates of Phips, now decided to play a trick on their commander. 'This day,' recorded the journal of the *James and Mary* on 7 February, 'towards 4 a Clock Mr. Rogers Came in who gave us to understand that they had been on the Bank and had two or three dayes faire weather they searched the banck and told us they had don as much as any men could doe.' The entry on the eighth had a different tone: 'This morning our Captain sent our longboat on board Mr. Rogers which in a shoart time returne with what made our hearts very Glad to see which was 4 sows

1 barr 1 Champene 2 dow boyes 2000 and odd Dollars by which wee understand that they had found the wreck.' Mather's account confirms this story and adds some details of Phips's reaction to the transformation of disappointment into elation. *'Thanks be to God!'* Mather has Phips exclaiming, *'We are made.'*[96]

Before this declaration could come true, however, there was much to be done in salvaging the treasure and bringing it safely to port; but the five years or so that had led up to the discovery of the wreck of the *Concepción* had indeed seen the making of Phips as a projector. As Defoe pointed out, if Phips's expedition of 1686–7 had failed, it would have been ridiculed: 'Bless us! that Folks should go Three thousand Miles to Angle in the open Sea for Pieces of Eight! why, they wou'd have made Ballads of it, and the Merchants wou'd have said of every unlikely Adventure, 'Twas like *Phips* his Wreck-Voyage.'[97] That the voyage now stood on the verge of success was partly the result of Phips's persistence. Also, to an extent that is difficult to gauge in the absence of clear evidence about how much information he had on the location of the wreck, it was due to his navigational skills and those of Rogers. More generally, it was a consequence of the priorities of influential naval figures such as Narbrough and Haddock and the access to patronage networks which they had been able to provide. For Phips, these connections offered the possibility of wealth and social advancement. Nevertheless, in view of the conspicuous exploits of both himself and his crew during the voyage of the *Golden Rose*, these linkages were unlikely to earn him any credit in the more sober and conventional administrative offices of Whitehall.

3

Treasure Gained and Patrons Lost

Calmness and competence are not virtues that historians have normally associated with William Phips. In some phases of his life, they were qualities he seldom if ever evinced. At Puerto Plata in February 1687, however, as during two subsequent months at the wreck and on the return voyage to London in the spring, Phips was firmly and steadily in command. To convey some thirty tons of silver safely to the Deptford naval yard with a crew hired for wages was arguably the greatest single feat of his improbable career. It was an achievement that brought him considerable wealth and a social respectability of sorts, as well as earning him an opportunity to return to the wreck during the winter of 1687–8 and then have the prospect of holding government office in New England. Yet it did not bring him solid financial security or real social acceptance in Massachusetts. The death of Sir John Narbrough in May 1688 and the duke of Albemarle the following October removed his principal patrons. The contempt of the governor of New England, Sir Edmund Andros, prompted Phips to make a rapid exit from Boston and return to London. There, on the eve of the Revolution of 1688–9, he faced a difficult and uncertain path – either towards rehabilitation as an active projector or towards social and political advancement.

On 8 February 1687, however, there was no uncertainty. After the initial elation, it was down to business for Phips, Rogers, and their crews. Phips's first priority was to careen the two vessels: first the *James and Mary* and then, with a coat of tallow applied 'to make her iff Possible to saile better,' the *Henry*.[1] Enough supplies were taken on to allow what was expected to be a lengthy sojourn at the wreck to pass without interruption. The main food source was a generous supply of hogs bought from Spanish hunters and salted on board ship. Wood and water were also laboriously stocked. Then there was the matter of the trading cargo. Earlier trading efforts had been disappointing, and, now that the wreck had been found, trade was no longer needed as an insurance against a losing voyage. The solution was to sell off most of the remaining goods. Notably, Phips sold a large quantity of liquor to crew members at an attractive price.

With these matters attended to, the *James and Mary* and *Henry* weighed anchor on the evening of 16 February, 'both of us Intending for the Banke.'[2] As before, to get there in the absence of favourable winds proved to be a lengthy task, but by the twenty-first the *James and Mary* rode at anchor by the reef, to be joined the next day by the *Henry*. William Covell was apparently anxious to see the wreck again and went out in the *James and Mary*'s pinnace to salvage some coins late on the twenty-second. On the twenty-third Phips made his final preparations, including a visit to the wreck in the morning. The journal of the *James and Mary* records that 'our Capt went to the wreck with the Divers' but does not specify whether Phips actually went below to inspect it at close quarters. On the same morning, he arranged the positioning of the ships, ordering Rogers 'to come to Anchor between the Wreck and us [*James and Mary*], as neare the Reefe as Conveniently he could without Danger.' The systematic recovery of the *Concepción*'s cargo could now begin.[3]

The daily work of salvage was recorded in the journals of the two vessels. With additional insights drawn from modern divers and visitors to the reef, it has been described fully and well by Peter Earle.[4] The task was gruelling, especially for the divers, and at first progress was relatively slow. The crew devoted six days to salvage, taking only Sundays off. As the journal entry of the *James and Mary* piously noted on 6 March, 'This day being the Lords day wee rested notwithstanding the weather was faire.' A total of nine work days were lost to bad weather and one because 'our Capt. wold not lett the Divers worke by Reason he see that some of them were nott well.'[5] Two factors, as Earle has pointed out, greatly accelerated the process after the first week of work. The first was the arrival of two more vessels, a Jamaican shallop commanded by Abraham Atherley and a Bermudian sloop under the command of William Davis. Both masters had sailed with Phips on the Hispaniola coast during the voyage of the *Golden Rose*, and Atherley later claimed 'that Sir William Phipps had never found this wreck but by him.' Whether this was true and whether or not Phips was expecting them when they arrived on 28 February 1687, Atherley and Davis declared that they had 'come on Purpose to seeke for the Wreck.' They were welcome – if not immediately, then at least as soon as Phips had concluded an agreement for their services – because they brought more divers. There was also the possibility that a vessel as small as Davis's sloop could safely be manoeuvred close enough to the wreck to allow the use of a Bermuda tub, enabling the divers to stay down for half-hour periods rather than coming to the surface frequently to draw breath. However, this strategy was apparently abandoned only a day after it was first attempted, when Davis briefly ran aground on a boiler.[6]

The other reason for the acceleration was that in early March the divers moved into what had been one of the main storerooms of the *Concepción*. Instead of scattered coins and other small silver items, they began to bring up heavy lumps of fused coins, which represented the contents of chests that had rotted away in the water. On 5 March they retrieved one and a half doughboys of gold, though no more gold was found in the succeeding days. Soon it was not unusual for a ton of silver to be salvaged in a single day, though yields were always subject to the fluctuations of the weather. But in mid-April came a sustained decline, the reason for which was recorded in the journal of the *James and Mary* on the fourteenth: 'Our boats went to the Wreck but haveing Clear'd the roome where they work'd before our Dyvers spent this day in finding a new one wherefore they brought aboard but a small quantity.'[7]

Phips now faced a difficult decision. He was aware that he had by no means exhausted the *Concepción*'s treasure, but presumably he also recognized that the wreck's location could not be concealed for long. Oaths of secrecy could not guarantee the silence of either Davis (who had already been dispatched to Jamaica) or Atherley, or of their crews. On the other hand, Phips had enjoyed several undisturbed weeks, had retrieved what was by any standard a huge cargo of silver, had not yet found a new storeroom in the wreck, and was running short of supplies. This was surely the right time to make for home, wealth, and security. Phips decided it was. On 19 April, leaving Atherley to spend a week on further salvage and wait to see if Davis would return, Phips and Rogers sailed for the Turks Islands. There they took on supplies, met as planned with Atherley, and loaded the silver he had retrieved. They then departed, on 2 May, for England.[8]

The voyage home was not, of course, as simple a matter as the sparse observations of the *James and Mary*'s journal might suggest. Mather accurately identified the difficulty: 'His [Phips's] Men were come out with him upon Seamens Wages, at so much *per* Month; and when they saw such vast Litters of Silver *Sows* and *Pigs*, as they call them, come on Board them at the Captain's Call, they knew not how to bear it, that they should not *share* all among themselves, and be gone to lead *a short Life and a merry*, in a Climate where the Arrest of those that had hired them should not reach them.' According to Mather, Phips met the situation with a vow to dedicate himself 'unto the Interests of the Lord *Jesus Christ*, and of his People, especially in the *Country* which he did himself Originally belong unto,' if only he was brought safely back to England with the treasure. More tangibly, he gave an undertaking to the crew 'that besides their *Wages*, they should have ample *Requitals* made unto them; which if the rest of his Employers would not agree unto, he would himself distribute his *own share* among them.' Although Mather was no doubt correct in noting that Phips still kept 'a most careful Eye upon them,' his assurances were apparently accepted and, according to later evidence, were honoured by Albemarle.[9] It was after an uneventful voyage that the *James and Mary* sighted the Scilly Isles on 3 June 1687 and found anchor at the Downs on the sixth. The *Henry* arrived a few days later.[10]

Word of Phips's arrival travelled quickly, and inevitably caused a stir. From Deal, the port closest to the anchorage at the Downs, letters spread the news of what was reported to be a treasure worth £250,000. Sir Roger Strickland, captain of the warship *Bristol*, wasted no time in writing from the Downs to Samuel Pepys, the Admiralty secretary. Pepys in turn was quick to order a naval party to board the *James and Mary* 'to keep a good guard and Strict Watch for preventing the takeing out or other disposale of any part of the said Plate till further Order.' A day later, 9 June, the Treasury ordered customs officials on board to safeguard the king's share and ensure that none of the treasure was 'imbezilled.' On the same day, an admiralty court warrant obtained by the Spanish ambassador, Don Pedro Ronquillo, for an embargo pending establishment of the bullion's ownership was prevented by unfavourable tides from being served and was then promptly revoked by the crown.[11] By the fourteenth, with the ship anchored within the secure confines of Deptford, the Treasury had ordered the principal officers of the Royal Mint to weigh the silver and gold and receive the king's tenth. The silver, including some 3,070 pounds set aside for the two crews, weighed just over 68,511 pounds troy, and the gold came to some 25 pounds troy. Most of the silver, almost 55 per cent, was in pieces of eight; the remainder was chiefly in bars. In sterling, the proceeds of the voyage were worth somewhat less than the figures being popularly reported, probably between £205,000 and £210,000. For an investment of £3,200, not all of which had even been paid over by the adventurers, the return was spectacular.[12]

Phips now enjoyed celebrity. The London Gazette gave prominence to his feat, and a broadsheet was soon published that emphasized the general lack of success of efforts to retrieve sunken treasure 'till the industrious Captain William Phipps, a Native of New-England, bent his Study and Resolution to bring that Art to so great a Perfection, as to anticipate Fame.' Phips was also praised for having 'in this whole Voyage ... lost neither Man nor Boy, although they were in so great hazard.'[13] Letters and diaries duly expressed amazement at the expedition's dramatic success. 'My Lord Duke Albemarle has had a lucky bout,' commented Charles Bertie to his niece, the countess of Rutland, 'in adventuring 800 l. to weigh up a gallion laden with bullion.' Albemarle had had 'extraordinary good fortune,' echoed the duke of Beaufort. 'Mountains are made of the matter,' observed another correspondent, 'but it is certainly a very considerable thing.' The diarists John Evelyn and Narcissus Luttrell used identical words to describe the proceeds of the voyage: 'a vast treasure.'[14]

How vast was it in reality? According to the historian W.R. Scott, who was followed by such eminent authorities as J.H. Clapham and John Maynard Keynes, it was sufficient to alter the course of England's financial history. Phips's treasure, Scott argued, encouraged the formation of many more joint-stock companies and thus contributed substantially to the expansion of the market in stocks in the early 1690s and thereby to the foundation of the Bank of England.[15] Although respectful scepticism may be the most prudent approach to this contention, the fact that it was advanced by a scholar as cautious as Scott is an indication that the value of Phips's cargo was remarkable. While it was considerably less than the treasure brought to England by Sir Francis Drake a century earlier, it was much larger than the proceeds of any one of the most famous exploits of Henry Morgan and the buccaneers.[16]

Phips's share amounted to some £11,000 – one-sixteenth of the total after the royal tenth had been deducted and the sum of a little over £8,000 had been distributed to the crew members. But the monetary gain was only part of Phips's reward. According to Mather, Albemarle recognized his honesty in returning to England with the treasure by sending Mary Phips 'a Present of a Golden Cup, near a Thousand Pound in value.'[17] Towards the end of July came another acknowledgment when the investors gave a dinner at the Swan Tavern in London for all the crew members. A contemporary reported, 'They gave the captain a gold medal and chain, and to every sailor silver ones; the medals have the King and Queen's picture.'[18] According to earlier reports, Phips had received another medal and gold chain around the time he received the principal honour that flowed from his successful voyage. This was in late June (the *London Gazette* gave the date as the twenty-eighth, though Luttrell noted it on the twenty-sixth) when Phips was called to Windsor, presented by Albemarle to James II, and knighted 'in consideration of his Loyalty, and good services in a late Expedition.'[19]

A knighthood, as Phips was to find out on a number of occasions, did not necessarily obscure 'what he was and from whence he came.'[20] When William Blathwayt referred in 1691 to 'this Poor Knight' or when one of Phips's Boston critics alluded sarcastically to 'the New England Knight,' the curl of the lip could not have been conveyed more clearly.[21] Nevertheless, for Phips the knighthood was a symbol of his attainment of the most effective forms of patronage. Although – despite his pretensions of 1683-4 – he had never been a naval captain, he had now made the kind of advance through levels of social preferment that in the later Stuart era was virtually unique to the most successful or fortunate 'tarpaulin' naval officers.[22] It was also impressive in New England, to some if not to all. The diarist Samuel Sewall was struck by the coincidence that the news of Phips's knighthood arrived in Boston on the same day as the wife of Governor Sir Edmund Andros, 'so have two Ladies in Town.' Sewall hoped to make some personal profit from the likelihood that Mary Spencer Phips would now look for a house appropriate to the Phips's changed circumstances. In this he was disappointed, but he did seize the opportunity to deliver a pious admonition and see it graciously received: 'I went to offer my Lady Phipps my house by Mr. Moody's and to congratulate her preferment. As to the former she had bought Samuel Wakefield's House and Ground last night for £350. I gave her a Gazette that related to her husbands knighthood, which she had not seen before and wish'd this success might not hinder her passage to a greater and better estate. She gave me a cup of good Beer and thank'd me for my visit.'[23]

Despite all the celebration and such happy images as that of 'the Duke of Albemarle ... melting his dividend of silver in his garden himself,' there was another side to Phips's triumphant return to London. As Defoe recognized in his *Essay upon Projects*, the success of the expedition of 1686-7 dramatically changed the expectations that projects could create.[24] For some, this was a matter for disapproval. John Povey, assistant to Blathwayt, on 11 June 1687 added to the outflow of news of the *James and Mary*'s arrival by writing to Sir Robert Southwell. Although Povey, like others, marvelled at the profit generated, his letter carried the sour implication that such unorthodox goings-on were inseparable from the appointment of Albemarle to the governorship of Jamaica: 'I doubt not but you have heard much of the many projects on foot by those who are going to Jamaica and amongst others of the Dukes sending a ship to fish for a Wreck which has layn in the Sea ... 40 years and has been searched for by all Nations.'[25]

Another result of Phips's success was continuing friction with Spain. Anglo-Spanish commercial relations were theoretically in good condition during the 1680s, but there were some serious irritants. In the Caribbean, English aggression against Spanish shipping had been barely restrained by governors such as Lynch and Molesworth, and the appointment of Albemarle to Jamaica foreshadowed new depredations. Don Pedro Ronquillo's insistent demand for restitution of the Spanish treasure which had so ostentatiously been imported to London was unlikely to be seriously considered in Whitehall. The expedition, after all, had yielded almost £21,000 to the English crown and there was the prospect of more to come from a further effort in 1687–8. Nevertheless, James II felt constrained in late December 1687 to assure angry English merchants trading to Spain that 'he would be answerable for any damage to them' arising from the quarrel. On Phips, his £11,000 securely in hand, the dispute had little direct effect except that it betokened a hostile diplomatic climate for the voyage he was to begin in the late summer of 1687.[26]

Phips must have had some anxious moments as a result of a conflict that unfolded during the summer of 1687, even though he was not among the principals involved. The merchant John Smith had returned hastily from a sojourn in Flanders when he heard of the arrival of the *James and Mary*, only to discover that the other partners had agreed to disqualify him from his one-eighth share of the treasure on the grounds that his contribution to the cost of the expedition had never been fully paid. Petitioning the Privy Council for redress, Smith found himself referred to what promised to be an expensive and exhausting suit in Chancery court. The case proceeded long enough to provide an invaluable source for historians on details of the expedition's business organization that would otherwise have been lost. Smith maintained not only that his share had been as fully subscribed as those of the others but that he had undertaken virtually the entire burden of organizing the fitting-out. He also claimed to have provided Phips with a letter of credit for £150, without which the expedition could not have proceeded.[27] Phips's testimony was one of the shorter submissions, by comparison with those of Albemarle and Narbrough. He denied having any full knowledge of discussions among the partners but stated that Smith's role in fitting out the two vessels had been less than crucial, and he declared that he had accepted the letter of credit only at Smith's own insistence.[28] In the event, Smith found it impossible to sustain his fight for long. In an affidavit of 21 July 1687 he revealed that Francis Nicholson – self-servingly – had urged him to settle, because 'he might Confide that he had great persons to Contend with and that they had six to one and had the money in their hands and that the Law was Chargeable and he might be kept out twice seaven years.' With Albemarle about to leave for Jamaica, and Narbrough shortly heading for the wreck with Phips, Smith saw the force of these arguments and apparently reached a settlement.[29]

Phips also had to face more directly personal accusations and demands. The least plausible came from Sir Richard White, who claimed to have played a prominent role in facilitating the expedition of the *James and Mary*. To Ronquillo, White now alleged that Phips had found the site of the wreck only by breaking open a letter with which White had entrusted him, in which White had recorded the secret. Peter Earle, whose research uncovered the accusation, has discounted it, though he noted that it may have had some effect on James II; on 9 September 1687 the king ordered the sum of £1,000 to be paid to White out of the royal share of the treasure, 'as of Our free guift and Royall Bounty.'[30] A more likely allegation, though trivial by comparison, was that of a disgruntled cook from the *James and Mary* who said that some small gold items had been retained undeclared by Phips. Serious suggestions of the illegal importation of part of the treasure were made more than a year later, though not against Phips. Five crew members of the *James and Mary*, including William Covell, were arrested in early September 1688 'for being concerned in defrauding his Majesty of about 1000 weight of Silver which was runn privately on Shoar.' They were released without charge some days later. While the five were in custody, Richard Covell (a mariner whose relationship to William Covell, if any, is not clear from surviving evidence) had a petition read by the Privy Council alleging that Phips had withheld five hundredweight of silver that was due to him for provisions and as a reward for services at the wreck. Despite an order to Phips to respond in writing, this matter too disappeared, no doubt in the throes of the Revolution of 1688–9.[31]

Phips also did his best to avoid responding to a demand by the Boston merchant Richard Wharton, who tracked him down in London during the summer of 1687 to demand payment of several hundred pounds from the proceeds of the expedition. The substance of the matter is obscure, especially in view of a later deposition by an apprentice of Wharton, who maintained that he saw Phips give his master – deceased by the date of the deposition – a payment of £300 for the services of an Indian diver.[32] However, there was no obscurity, at least in the mind of Wharton, about Phips's evasiveness shortly before his return voyage to the wreck: 'He semed greatly Rejoyced to see me and for 3 or 4 dayes treated me with great Respect ... [but] at last when I made my demands – and was in Earnest to adjust – he tould me he would only goe to Graves End, and dispatch the Ships – about to the Downes – and in two dayes be at london againe, but Saw not cause, to Returne any more Soe that wee must wayt untill a Second voyage be Ended – and then I hope Soe to provide, that he shall not a Second time have Opertunity to abuse my Respect.'[33]

Phips must have been relieved to sail for the wreck in early September 1687. As well as extricating him from the controversy with Wharton, his departure offered the enticing prospect of adding to the treasure already salvaged and then taking up the office of provost marshal general of New England, which he had been granted in August. According to Mather, he had turned down an offer of membership of the Navy Board – unlikely though not impossible – in favour of a patriotic return to Massachusetts to oppose the authoritarian excesses of Andros.[34] First, though, there was the wreck to attend to. His departure had already been seriously delayed. Detailed planning for the return voyage had begun within five days of the *James and Mary*'s arrival in the Thames, when Albemarle, Narbrough, Falkland, and Hayes had met at Windsor with James II and a small group of advisers. The meeting was productive and resulted in the new expedition having direct royal and naval involvement. The king agreed to contribute the use of a frigate, eventually designated as the *Foresight*. Its captain was to be the same Edward Stanley who had commanded the *Bonetta* in its lengthy and unsuccessful searches of the Hispaniola coast.

Responding to the investors' well-founded fears of competition, the king also agreed to 'hinder as much as by Law hee may, any of his other Subjects to search for Plate ... [at] this Wreck.'[35] The question of the extent to which Albemarle's patent of 4 March 1687 could justify prohibition of other vessels from the wreck, especially if they had been permitted or encouraged to go there by colonial governors, was a difficult one, but the expedition was clearly to be provided with sufficient force to act as a discouragement to others regardless of legal niceties. In return, the crown was to have a substantially larger share of the profits than in the voyage just completed. The king was to have one-fifth of the first £150,000 recovered and one-third of any amount in excess of that sum.[36]

One other matter that was made clear on 14 June 1687 was that Phips would not be the leader of the new expedition. This time, Narbrough was to take command. At least one contemporary observer, writing in late July, took this as an indication of mistrust: 'Sir John Narborough [sic] is going away in three or four days ... as a guard with Sir Phips, in quest of the remainder of the treasure.'[37] It may have been so, although the fragmentary corroborating evidence – the reaction of Narbrough when Phips retreated to port, shortly after the voyage had begun, for repairs to a damaged foremast – suggests that any doubts that existed were over the level of Phips's enthusiasm for a return to the wreck rather than over any fear that he would disappear with the treasure.[38]

There were in fact good reasons for Narbrough to lead, quite apart from his long-standing interest in the wreck and the opportunity it now presented for an old sea captain to make a profitable and impeccably legitimate 'good voyage.'[39] First of all, the wreck would have to be brought under control and policed for unlicensed vessels. When Narbrough arrived at the wreck on 15 December, it proved an easy task to scatter the twenty or so sloops and six larger vessels that he found there. In fact, as Captain Stanley recorded in the journal of the *Foresight*, 'Upon sight of us Severall of the Sloops gott to sail and turn'd to and fro.' Nevertheless, a report by Albemarle in late November of earlier skirmishes, drownings, and killings at the wreck made it clear that the need for conspicuous naval force had not been imaginary.[40] Another concern was what several of the investors defined in retrospect as 'great Apprehensions of Attempts by ffoureigners on the said Wreck.'[41] Ronquillo's protest put the Spanish in the first rank of possible contenders, but reports soon began reaching Narbrough of a Dutch squadron under the command of Charles, Lord Mordaunt. A prominent Whig peer who had found it advisable to leave England for the Netherlands soon after the accession of James II, Mordaunt had served for a time in the Mediterranean fleet under Narbrough. He was not known to have any hostile intentions towards his former commander but was treated with suspicion nevertheless.[42]

The expedition had a strong naval flavour, which had not been characteristic of the voyage of the *Golden Rose* or of that of the *James and Mary* and *Henry* in 1686–7. As well as the *Foresight*, several other frigates visited the wreck: the *Swan* for nine days in April 1688; the *Falcon* from March until early May; and the *Assistance*, which was assigned to give support at the time of Mordaunt's arrival. There was none of the bravado that Phips had shown in 1683–4 in his efforts to substantiate his flimsy credentials as a naval commander. Instead, a wary and professional defensiveness prevailed, which prompted Captain Lawrence Wright of the *Assistance* to prepare himself in Samana Bay for a fight with Mordaunt 'in case those Holland ships should make any Attempt upon us, It being allwayes my Opinion to provide against the worst.'[43] Apart from the naval presence, the expedition's fleet was far larger and more expensive than either of the previous expeditions. The *James and Mary* and *Henry* sailed again, along with a vessel named the *Princess* and Phips's large armed merchantman, the *Good Luck and a Boy*. There were also freight vessels, and a large amount of diving equipment was carried aboard the *Good Luck and a Boy*. For the investors – who now included the master of the Royal Mint, Thomas Neale, as the purchaser of three-quarters of the share formerly held by John Smith, the remainder having been taken by Albemarle – the cost was much greater than that in 1686. The business arrangements called for the sum of £10,500 to be deposited with two disinterested intermediaries for defrayal of the costs 'according to each persons proportion.'[44]

The fleet had been meant to sail in midsummer 1687 in conjunction with Albemarle's voyage to take up his governorship of Jamaica, but he had taken ill, apparently because of overindulgence in the festivities marking his intended departure. It was early September by the time the vessels sailed, and they left without him. By this time, rumours were spreading in London that other ships were already at work on the wreck. The expedition was making an uncertain beginning, especially as Phips's most experienced diver, Jonas, one of the Native divers from the Gulf of Florida (who were reputed the best available) had recently died in London from a fever.[45] Further problems soon emerged. On 15 September, in one of the storms that continually slowed the fleet's progress towards Madeira, the *Good Luck and a Boy* lost part of its foremast and Phips decided to turn back and make towards Plymouth for repairs. Albemarle, meanwhile, having at last recovered sufficiently to depart, was forced into Plymouth by bad weather on the twenty-third, and Phips was still there when he resumed his voyage on 12 October.[46] Narbrough wrote to Hayes from Madeira on 15 October saying that while in Plymouth, Phips proposed 'to refitt' and follow him 'to Barbadoes with all expedition.' In the meantime, Narbrough had lost touch with the *James and Mary* on 28 September. His arrival at Barbados on 16 November brought reunion with *James and Mary* but 'noe Acctt of Sir Wm Phipps.' When Albemarle also arrived there later in the month and could offer no better news of the *Good Luck and a Boy*, Narbrough's concern became acute. Phips was carrying essential diving equipment and four weeks' provisions. 'My Lord Duke ... tells me,' Narbrough informed Hayes, 'he left Sir Wm Phipps at Plymouth, if he should be in England still I am afraid he never designe to proceed further.'[47]

The fact that Phips's mishap with his foremast – which Narbrough clearly regarded as a fairly minor calamity – caused him not only to return to Plymouth but also to linger there for the best part of a month is a curious and unexplained incident. On the face of it, Phips had every reason for haste. Yet his personal stake in this expedition was less than in either of the previous ones. To what extent he stood to gain financially is unclear from the surviving evidence, but this time he did not command. Any glory that came from a further valuable haul of treasure would belong largely to Narbrough, with Albemarle close enough in Jamaica to claim a share of personal credit. It is also likely that Phips was anxious to return to Boston. Even if Cotton Mather exaggerated the idealistic zeal with which he longed to take up his New England office, the fact remains that he had not seen his wife for almost four years, and he must have relished the prospect of setting up house as a wealthy and knighted citizen of the colony he had left in humbler circumstances.[48] Such considerations may or may not have influenced the length of his stay in Plymouth in the autumn of 1687, but as far as the wreck of the *Concepción* was concerned, Phips was no longer the single-minded projector he had been a year earlier.

Nevertheless, on 7 December he caught up with the rest of the expedition in Samana Bay.[49] By mid-month, the fleet had arrived at the wreck and dispersed the vessels found there. What remained to be seen was the extent to which the accessible treasure rooms had been exploited and perhaps exhausted. Narbrough's considered estimate by mid-April was that the unlicensed searchers had taken up, between May and December 1687, silver to the value of some £250,000.[50] But he remained convinced that there was plenty more to be had, suggesting in early May that only one-quarter of the treasure had so far been cleared. While this seems overoptimistic, Narbrough was certainly correct in his belief that the *Concepción*'s cargo had been much larger than what had so far been discovered. How to get at the remaining treasure, though, was the crucial question.[51]

If the number of divers could have made the difference, the expedition would soon have equalled the earlier success of Phips. Even before reaching the wreck, Narbrough had taken on twenty-two additional divers from a sloop that had foundered, setting them to work for a one-twentieth part of whatever they recovered. By early May, with a number of sloop captains enjoying the incentive since March of a one-quarter share of treasure recovered as well as the privilege of dining fortnightly on the *Foresight* when accounts were cleared, the total number of divers had reached two hundred. The returns were still disappointing. Narbrough informed Falkland on 4 May that he had thirty hundredweight of silver in hand – about one-twentieth of what Phips had been carrying on the *James and Mary* a year before. Narbrough's plan was to stay longer if the king could be persuaded to extend the loan of the *Foresight* beyond the original one-year deadline. By 26 May, however, ill with a fever and having recovered only another three hundredweight, he had changed his mind and planned to sail immediately for England.[52]

Phips had already left for Boston. The records of his leave taking on 8 May hint at an abrupt departure. The captain's journal of the *Foresight* had Phips going only 'for port Isabella [just west of Puerto Plata] to wood and watter,' while the lieutenant's journal struck an uncertain note in recording that he had left 'as we Judged for Newengland.' But there was certainly no trace of tension in a letter written to him by Narbrough on the twenty-sixth.[53] The level of Phips's activity at the wreck is difficult to gauge because there is no surviving journal from the *Good Luck and a Boy* and he was rarely mentioned in other journals from mid-December until he sailed on 1 February to take on water at Puerto Plata. He was absent for more than a month, arriving back at the wreck on 7 March.[54] Whether by accident or design, he missed the arrival of Mordaunt's Dutch squadron. He also missed Mordaunt's departure after an oddly uneventful visit, during which Edward Stanley had hospitably taken some of the Dutch officers to see the wreck.[55]

There was still great anxiety over the small returns of treasure when Phips returned to the wreck on 7 March. Continuing efforts to break through the thick coral deposits covering the aft storerooms were unsuccessful; and by 9 April Phips was ready to use gunpowder to make what certainly would have been his most dramatic contribution to the search. The captain's journal of the *Foresight* described concisely what took place: 'Sir Wm Phipps endevord to blow up a Currell rock which hee judged to bee over a Plate room the Divers placed the [powder] chest and Sir Wms Guner Fird the fuse but the Trunck which the fuze was in being made of canes split before it burnt halfe down: soe that the Powder in the chest was damnafied.' Phips tried again five days later, but again 'could not fire itt.' As Peter Earle has observed, this failure was probably merciful for Phips and those who shared the long-boat with him directly above the wreck; but it left the expedition in a precarious position.[56] A week later Narbrough went to the wreck with Stanley and recovered a copper gun. The next day Phips went along with them in a pinnace, and he also salvaged a gun from a nearby location. As far as the evidence reveals, this was the last of Phips's underwater discoveries, just over two weeks before he left for New England. Narbrough never did leave the wreck. His intended departure on 26 May was delayed by a breakage of the *Foresight*'s cable, and he died in the early morning of the twenty-seventh. He was buried at sea later in the day.[57]

Narbrough's death sealed the fate of the expedition of 1687–8. The *Foresight* reached the Downs on 20 July 1688 with silver worth less than £10,000. When it anchored in the Thames in early August, its reception was subdued. Of the investors, only Foxcroft and Nicholson were present, accompanied by John Hill, Narbrough's father-in-law and attorney. Of the visit on the same day of the representatives of the Royal Mint, the lieutenant's journal commented briefly but with an unusual trace of elegy: 'The Kings Officers of the Mint came on Board and took out all the Wrack Silver: Weighed out to them Thirty two Hundred thirteene pound Ten ounces 32:13:10 off which the King had the 5 pt. They went up againe afternoone and our Pinace with the Silver.'[58] Nevertheless, the surviving investors were not doing too badly. Taking the two voyages of 1686–8 together, the failure of 1688 offset only a small proportion of the earlier returns. Ironically, the only outright loser – in his personal capacity – was the master of the Royal Mint, who had purchased three-quarters of John Smith's former share. No doubt Smith was following news of the expedition closely and critically. So was William Blathwayt, who had taken the trouble to add a postscript to a letter to Sir Robert Southwell in May saying, 'We have not as yet any great News from the Wreck.' What Blathwayt no doubt had in mind was not just treasure hunting but also the activities of Mordaunt, about which his clerk John Povey had been keeping Southwell informed in earlier weeks.[59] But the expedition, for Blathwayt, was also closely bound up with the projecting spirit it represented and with what he regarded as the recklessly undisciplined behaviour of Albemarle in Jamaica.

'The D. of Alb.,' Blathwayt had observed in June 1688 in another of his telling postscripts, 'dances upon the High Rope and will soon break his own neck or destroy that Government.'[60] There were several contributing strands to this judgment. It derived in part from accounts reaching London of the dissolute behaviour of Albemarle and his entourage. A report being retailed in early July stated that 'most of his Grace's family have had the good luck to win at play very large sums from several in the island, that had been a-fishing upon the wreck, so that they parted with it freely as they found it.'[61] More serious from a political standpoint were Albemarle's clumsy and self-serving interventions in Jamaican factional disputes, his reliance on Sir Henry Morgan and the old buccaneering faction, and his reported tolerance of piracy.[62] Disorder, piracy, treasure: it was easy to associate them in Jamaica, just as it was in Bermuda, where the collector Henry Hordesnell explained his difficulties in retrieving royal dues on the wreck's treasure by citing a local maxim 'that a man can never gett an estate by being honest.'[63] At least in the minds of Blathwayt and his colleagues, a colonial governor such as Albemarle was in no position to represent sounder values.

Much more promising was Sir Edmund Andros in New England. Blathwayt had made the comparison explicit in April 1686 when, having told Southwell that he would 'wonder to hear' of Albemarle's securing the Jamaica governorship, he added, 'You will like better to hear of Sir Edmund Andros going to New England for whom, tho' his name be not yet declared, We are preparing a Commission and Instructions.'[64] The preparation of these documents had not gone smoothly. The establishment of the Dominion of New England without an elected assembly and with the powers of taxation resting in the hands of governor and council did not sit well with Andros any more than it did with Blathwayt or Povey. Povey had implied as late as 20 May 1686 – Andros's commission was dated 3 June – that the prospective governor might refuse the office: 'The Constitution Intended for that Government being without an Assembly I doubt he finds not that cause to hope for his satisfaction therein as otherwise he might have done, But not having yet kissed the King's hand upon this new promotion it is not to be guessed what meanes he will take.' Two days later, Blathwayt was sure the appointment would proceed, but he informed Southwell that Andros was 'not at all elevated by the honor of this Commission which obliges him to raise money by himself and Councill and so to make all Laws without

an Assembly.' The following week, Povey observed more philosophi-
cally, '[I] find a Plantation Government without an Assembly seems
very Mysterious and wish it may Answer the King's Service in New
England.'[65]

Once Andros had accepted the governorship, he had no alternative
but to work within the procedures enjoined by a constitution that was,
as Richard R. Johnson has shown, not only *sui generis* among forms of
colonial organization but also a product of the personal intervention of
James II.[66] He did so with a vigour that earned for him, soon after his
arrival in Boston in late 1686, equally vigorous opposition from those in
the colony who lamented with Cotton Mather 'the Miseries which were
come, and coming in upon poor *New-England*, by reason of the *Arbitrary
Government* then imposed on them.' Even the interim government
headed by Joseph Dudley had avoided breaking abruptly with practices
that had existed under the old charter, which had been voided in 1684.
But Andros immediately levied direct and indirect taxes, as well as taking other measures such as the imposition of quitrents on landholders,
and he did not hesitate to prosecute those who refused to comply.
According to Mather, 'packt and pickt *Juries* were commonly made use
of, when under a pretended *Form of Law*, the Trouble of some Honest
and Worthy Men was aimed at.'[67]

As for Blathwayt and his colleagues, they were left with no choice but
to support Andros no matter how ill conceived they privately believed
his commission to be. Also a longstanding ally – or client – of Blathwayt
was Edward Randolph, who since his passage to Boston with Phips on
the *Golden Rose* had added a number of offices to his collectorship of
customs, including most notably the position of secretary of the Dominion of New England.[68] By the spring of 1688, when the dominion was
enlarged to include New York and New Jersey in addition to the New
England colonies per se, Blathwayt had evidently abandoned his earlier
reservations, though he could not resist a characteristically sarcastic
flick at the expense of those he sought to advance: 'You see ...,' he wrote
to Southwell on 5 May 1688, 'what alterations have been made on the
continent of America to the advantage of our Friends. The French have
occasioned it by their incursions and I believe this union may make us
more formidable. Mr. Randolph is as great a Secretary as Sir Ed. Andros
a Governor. The latter has lost his Wife and the former wishes he had.'[69]

It was into these factional cross-currents that Sir William Phips was
about to plunge when he sailed from the wreck three days after Blathwayt had thus confided in Southwell. Phips was totally unprepared for

political manoeuvring at this level. Mather's account has him arriving in Boston filled with zeal to make his office of provost marshal general (a legal position involving the supervision of county sheriffs) a centre of resistance to the tyranny of Andros, 'hoping, by his Deputies in that Office, to supply the Country still with Conscientious Juries, which was the only Method that the *New-Englanders* had left them to secure any thing that was Dear unto them.' According to Mather, the regime reacted violently to the threat Phips represented: 'Yea, he was like to have had his *Person* Assassinated in the Face of the Sun, before his own Door.'[70] The notion that Andros or anybody else would have deemed Phips worth assassinating was a ludicrous exaggeration, and it casts doubt on Mather's account of the entire episode. More convincing is the judgment of the historian Viola Florence Barnes, who has suggested that Phips's intention in the late spring of 1688 was much simpler: to establish himself as a member of the ruling elite of the dominion and in the process to enjoy the discomfiture of those magistrates who had treated him with contempt in earlier years and were now excluded from office.[71]

Unfortunately for Phips, he faced serious obstacles. One was that the dominion government – at least as far as New England itself was concerned – had taken form long before Phips's arrival, and the council had already appointed a provost marshal general and sheriffs. The appointment of office holders had become increasingly restrictive and exclusive over the years. The criticism that the dominion represented a clique of outsiders had been difficult to sustain at the beginning when New Englanders such as Dudley and Stoughton had been wielding a strong influence, but by the spring of 1688 the scope of the administration had narrowed, though both Stoughton and Dudley remained as councillors.[72] Phips would now be seen, at best as an unwelcome intruder and at worst, and more likely, as a contemptible upstart. A second problem was that Phips was manifestly unqualified for the position of provost marshal general. He lacked any legal or government experience, and even his literacy was doubtful. Andros's administration had plenty of members whose approach to office was self-seeking, but competence was a virtue worth having, and competence in the management of a treasure-hunting voyage was not the same as competence as a provost marshal general. Finally, Andros was extremely busy. When Phips arrived, the governor had just returned from an extended tour through Wabanaki territory claimed as part of New England as far eastward as the St Croix River. Andros then had to deal with the expansion of his responsibilities to include New York and New Jersey, news of which arrived formally on 5 July but had been reported informally in advance. Thus, it is not surprising that Phips could not secure a meeting to assert his right to office.[73]

Even if Phips was met by contempt and indifference in Boston, rather than by the outright hostility alleged by Mather, it was clearly a bruising experience. He landed from a pinnace on 1 June, having made the short journey from Portsmouth, New Hampshire. Mary Spencer Phips heard of his impending arrival only that day, while returning to Boston from hearing a sermon preached at Watertown. According to Samuel Sewall, she was 'ready to faint' at the news. The arrival itself was well attended: 'Many of the Town ... [went] to complement him.' More praise was to follow, including a Harvard commencement address by William Hubbard – standing in for Increase Mather as president – who 'compared Sir William ... to Jason fetching the Golden Fleece.'[74] Making a political impression, however, was more difficult. Ignored by Andros, Phips finally addressed a letter to the governor in late June, demanding that all sheriffs be dismissed and that 'Deputations from me for the due and Regular Execution of the said Office may take place.'[75] A few days later, when writing to Fitz-John Winthrop, who was in London, Andros stated that Phips had decided to return to England on the *Good Luck and a Boy* but wished 'to have his Marshal's place settled, for which he hath given me a paper.' On 6 July Phips had his wish insofar as he was sworn into office as provost marshal general. But the council apparently refused to dismiss the sheriffs, and this led to an angry confrontation on the seventh in which Phips blamed Randolph for opposing the measure. He threatened to 'sett mee forth in my Colors,' claimed Randolph, 'and was going home and would make it known.'[76] On the same day William Covell, as master of the *Good Luck and a Boy*, received permission to clear from Boston for London. After a few days' delay, they set sail on the sixteenth, and Phips anchored at the Downs exactly one month later.[77]

To sail with Covell aboard the *Good Luck and a Boy* must have seemed like a return to a simpler and more familiar world. Yet there was nothing simple about the predicament in which Phips now found himself. His threat against Randolph had been an empty one, an outburst that only highlighted his lack of any effective influence in London. His principal patron, Narbrough, was dead. Albemarle was unwell and was preoccupied in Jamaica. A rumour of Albemarle's death circulated in London in July, which proved to be unfounded, but he succumbed on 6 October following a serious illness precipitated by his overenthusiastic celebration of the birth of the Prince of Wales.[78] It is uncertain whether, by the time of his death, Albemarle had any knowledge of the arrangements that had been made on his behalf by his attorney in England, the earl of Bath, for a further expedition to the wreck. Narbrough's assurances that a large amount of treasure remained had led James II to agree to continue the loan of the *Foresight* for another voyage. In mid-September 1688 the investors retained the services of two captains, Robinson and Weston, but because of the crisis leading to the revolution, the *Foresight* never left the Downs. Three other vessels did go, including the *James and Mary*. Except that this voyage was a failure, nothing of significance is known about it.[79]

Nor is it known whether Phips refused to participate in this latest venture to the wreck, whether he was unable to reach a new agreement with the investors, or whether he was never approached. One surviving document hints at a last connection with Albemarle, recording a loan of £270 granted by Phips to Albemarle on 1 November 1688. Filed and presumably signed in Boston, the obligation is an oddity in that by this time Phips had long since departed for London and Albemarle had already died. Albemarle's agent in the transaction was Thomas Monck, his illegitimate son and captain of his yacht. Monck must have negotiated the loan with Mary Spencer Phips before learning of his father's death in Jamaica. That the obligation was due to double to £540 if not repaid by 1 July 1689 suggests that a venture of some kind, perhaps a treasure-seeking scheme, was involved. The full context of the matter, however, remains obscure.[80]

What is clear is that the death of Narbrough and Albemarle marked the end of a phase in Sir William Phips's life. From his first arrival in London and his subsequent departure·in the *Golden Rose* at the age of thirty-two, Caribbean treasure-hunting had been his main preoccupation. The evidence suggests some slackening of his commitment in late 1687, and in June and early July 1688 he had begun to move in a new direction. But his sojourn in Boston had been disastrous, and now at the age of thirty-seven he was back in London to face an uncertain future without patrons. Treasure seeking, to be sure, had changed the trajectory of his career; he was much wealthier than he had been before 1687, and he retained at least the nominal trappings of success in his knighthood and his swearing into office in Boston. While good fortune had had some bearing on his advancement, he owed much of his success to his ability as a projector. His willingness to take chances and cut corners, initially nurtured by his efforts to shed the constraints of his obscure and peripheral origins in New England, had been an essential ingredient; and so, despite his doubtful literacy, had his command of different forms of spoken language. Assisted by his better-connected English relations, Phips had been able to present himself convincingly to prospective patrons while retaining the capacity to use a harsher style of address not only at sea but also in purposeful confrontations with his social superiors. Yet the results of it all were far from clear. Just as £11,000 was not enough to keep him permanently in the style appropriate to his knighthood, the knighthood itself had shown little sign of compensating for his lack of the political skills and connections that counted in the Dominion of New England.

There was, however, one important result of his stay in Boston. On 3 June, the first Sunday after his arrival, he had attended the North Church to hear Cotton Mather preach; Samuel Sewall recorded with satisfaction that 'the Whitsuntiders [Church of England] have not his company.'[81] While there is no knowing what this choice signified in terms of Phips's spiritual condition, its more temporal result was to inaugurate a relationship with Mather and his father, Increase Mather, that would eventually help repair the damage done to Phips by the death of his patrons. Not that a friendship with Increase Mather, who had been in England since May 1688 to represent the grievances of the Dominion of New England's critics, would advance Phips in all quarters relevant to whatever his ambitions might be in New England.

About the only point of resemblance between Mather and the duke of Albemarle was the disdain that both evoked from the Plantations Office. 'Increase Mather ... etc.,' wrote Blathwayt in June, 'are come hither with Addresses and have audiences of the Great ones now ... But I hope Sir Ed. Andros has taken such Root in His Majesties good opinion as to withstand some shocks.'[82] Disdain or not, Mather obtained five personal interviews with James II between late May and mid-October 1688, and he was able to gain similar audiences with William III after the Revolution of 1688–9.[83] Given the gains that had accrued to Phips through the occasional access to the court which Narbrough and Albemarle had brought him, Mather's repeated and friendly interaction with successive monarchs would have sufficed in itself to make him an attractive figure. That Mather also provided a possible route towards the discomfiture of Andros, Randolph, and their insufferable cohorts offered Phips the elements of a new allegiance.

4

Respectability and Revolution

The Revolution of 1688–9 dealt surprisingly kindly with Sir William Phips. Between August 1688 and March 1690, he succeeded in overcoming both the humiliation of his brief career as provost marshal general of New England and the loss of his principal patrons. The spring of 1690 saw him admitted to membership of Cotton Mather's North Church and given command of an expedition against Port-Royal, the headquarters of French Acadia. The revolution itself and the overthrow of the Dominion of New England that followed it provided an essential context for these attainments and the new respectability they symbolized. More specifically, Phips's associations with both Cotton and Increase Mather gave him access to influential networks on both sides of the Atlantic which substituted for his earlier relationships with such patrons as Narbrough and Albemarle.

All of this was attained by taking essentially minor and passive roles in the major events affecting New England. For the most part, Phips was carried along by currents that he did not resist. Nevertheless, the revolutionary era did provide him with a political apprenticeship, just as it saw the establishment of new and lasting factional patterns in New England's affairs. The chief purposes of Phips's treasure-seeking expeditions had been material gain and social mobility, with his office of provost marshal general an important but tangential result. The activities in which he increasingly participated with the Mathers were overtly political. Opposition to the dominion and support of the revolutionary regime that replaced it in April 1689 offered new opportunities for social, political, and military advancement. Yet Phips also had to pay a price in the form of enmities that more complex and more lasting than the brusque contempt he had experienced from Andros.

When Phips arrived in London in August 1688, he lost little time in establishing contact with the elder Mather. The two met to discuss New England affairs on the morning of the twenty-first, a few days after the *Good Luck and a Boy* had anchored at the Downs. They met again on the morning of 26 September, the same day on which Mather had an afternoon meeting with James II.[1] During the preceding months, Mather had worked hard and successfully to cultivate the king. In the context of the April 1688 proclamation of the second Declaration of Indulgence, which bracketed the removal of legal disabilities on Catholics with those on Protestant Dissenters, Mather had turned to advantage his prominence as a Congregational minister. By September he was confident that he was making rapid progress in his campaign against the Dominion of New England – and for the restoration of the original Massachusetts charter – both with the king and with the Lords of Trade. Thus, the landing of William of Orange at Torbay in November and the flight of James II to France some weeks later came, in this sense, at an inconvenient time.[2] However, Mather's political effectiveness did not derive only from personal access to the king. It was also based on an unusually extensive chain of relationships with Dissenting clergy and merchants in London and elsewhere. This network, drawing on both religious and kinship ties, had been developed through transatlantic correspondence links over two generations. It had been enlisted by Mather against Andros and the Dominion of New England as early as September 1687, when Mather had used 'some Gentlemen in London' as intermediaries in the transmission of a letter to James II welcoming the first Declaration of Indulgence.[3] Adjustments had to be made after the revolution, but Mather's connections proved equal to the task. Sir Henry Ashurst now emerged as the most important London supporter of the critics of the dominion. A Whig parliamentarian since the Exclusion crisis and then a London alderman, Ashurst was the leading member of London's pre-eminent Presbyterian merchant family.[4]

Adaptable as Mather's network was, from the era of the Declarations of Indulgence to the explicit Protestantism of the new regime, his chief political opponents also proved their durability. William Blathwayt only briefly lost his position as secretary for war and never loosened his grip on the Plantations Office. Sir Robert Southwell was appointed a customs commissioner in April 1689 and principal secretary of state for Ireland in 1690.[5] An even more prominent survivor of the revolution was Southwell's kinsman, the earl of Nottingham. Although sustaining his allegiance to James II until after the king's flight to France in December

1688, Nottingham soon emerged as a leading member of a group of Tory peers who facilitated the smooth transition to the new regime. In March 1689 he was appointed secretary of state.[6]

Southwell was the likely author of a letter to Nottingham in March warning that any restoration of the 'usurped Priviledges' Massachusetts had enjoyed under its old charter would 'soe Confound the Present settlement in those Parts, and their Dependance on England, that 'tis hard to say where the Mischeif will Stopp.' The letter advised that Blathwayt, 'who best knows the truth and state of things,' should be summoned directly to give advice to the new king, William of Orange.[7] In part, Southwell's concern was a result of Mather's success in taking his case directly to the king while also working through Ashurst and others to have the old charter restored through the Whig-sponsored Corporation Bill. This latter effort was to meet defeat as a result of Tory gains in the general election of 1690, but in the early months of 1689 Mather seemed to be making significant progress. He had also, by dint of two personal interviews with the king, gained a royal commitment that Andros would be recalled from his governorship.[8]

In all of this, the minor role played by Sir William Phips is established in general terms by the available evidence, but details are sparse. Beyond Cotton Mather's brief comment that, while in London, 'Sir *William* offered his best Assistances unto that Eminent Person [Increase Mather], who a little before this Revolution betook himself unto *White-Hall*,' we have no indication of Phips's activities during the later months of 1688.[9] In early 1689 he became more conspicuous. A meeting between Mather and Phips on 10 January was the first between them that Mather had recorded since September. Two days later, a circular letter was prepared for dispatch by William of Orange to all colonial governors, continuing them in office unless and until contrary orders were given. The letter to Andros was stayed at the last moment, the draft being endorsed with the words 'Memorandum[:] Upon the Application of Sir William Phipps and Mr Mather this letter was stopt: and ordered not to be sent.'[10]

More was to follow. Mather and Phips were together on the morning of 13 February, the day on which William III and Mary II formally accepted the crown, and they jointly petitioned for restoration of the old Massachusetts charter. Two separate texts exist. One (of which there is a copy in the Massachusetts Archives but no trace in English official records) invited the monarchs to declare 'by a letter under your Majesties hand and sign manual' that the former governments should be restored in all the New England colonies.[11] As Richard Johnson has noted, this use of the royal prerogative would have been unlikely to appeal to potential Whig supporters of the old charter cause, and it it is possible that the petition was never presented in this form. The one that was considered by the Privy Council on 18 February, also in the names of Phips and Mather, had the same goals but was differently framed. It argued that the proceedings by which the New England charters had been annulled were 'illegal and arbitrary,' as was the commission that had established the Dominion of New England, by which Andros had been empowered 'with four of his Councell to levie monie and make Lawes without the consent of the people by their representatives.' The abolition of the dominion therefore depended not on the royal prerogative but on a simple recognition of illegality.[12]

To establish that illegality had indeed taken place was not so simple, of course. Phips and Mather were called to a hearing before the Lords of Trade on 20 February. They went along encouraged by the fact that the order in council issued two days earlier, referring the petition to the Lords of Trade, had advised that the king was 'graciously disposed to gratifie the Petitioners.'[13] But their position was soon challenged. The only action taken on New England at the 20 February meeting was to postpone the discussion for two days and then call in Sir Robert Sawyer, who had been attorney general when the first Massachusetts charter had been abrogated in 1684. On 22 February, before an unusually large gathering of the Lords of Trade, along with interested privy councillors and again Phips and Mather, Sawyer defended the dominion and justified the annulment of the charter on the grounds of repeated abuse of power by the Massachusetts General Court. Politically divided between prominent Whigs such as Lord Mordaunt (the same who had visited the wreck in early 1688) and Tories such as Nottingham, the board drafted a report that fell far short of the blow to the dominion for which Mather and Phips had hoped. Andros should be recalled, it recommended, but he should be replaced by a provisional governor who would be constrained only by a prohibition on the raising of revenue by governor and council alone. Preparations should then be made not for restoration of the old charter but for a new 'Establishment' that would balance the rights and privileges of New Englanders with 'such a Dependance on the Crown of England as shall bee thought requisit.'[14]

Further debates of the Lords of Trade in late February and early March were inconclusive.[15] Phips's role came to an end for the time being when he sailed for Boston in mid-March, carrying copies of proclamations issued by William and Mary and thus confirmation to New England of their acceptance of the crown.[16] His departure may have been preceded by intrigues in two directions. If Cotton Mather is to be believed, Phips was contacted by 'a Messenger from the Abdicated King [who] tender'd him the Government of *New-England* if he would accept it,' but he 'thought it his Duty to refuse a *Government without an Assembly*, as a thing that was Treason in the very *Essence* of it.' Whether or not Phips behaved in such a principled manner, nothing more is heard of any such approach.[17] The other matter concerned the possibility of an insurrection in New England. Edward Randolph later maintained that Increase Mather had written to Simon Bradstreet – the last governor under the old charter government – to advocate revolt against Andros. Cotton Mather maintained, contrariwise, that any discussion of such on action by leading New Englanders centred only on the prevention of bloodshed if popular resentment against Andros threatened to provoke armed conflict. It is not altogether implausible that Phips – sailing almost immediately after Mather's productive interview with William III on 14 March – had plans to hasten the fulfilment of William's undertaking that the proclamation of the new monarchs in Massachusetts should be by 'the former magistrates.'[18] If this was so, however, his arrival on 29 May came six weeks too late to exert a significant influence on events.

On the morning of 18 April 1689, reports spread in Boston of an armed uprising. Questionable as the rumours still were, by the middle of the day a group of 'Gentlemen, Merchants, and Inhabitants of Boston, and the Country Adjacent' had proclaimed from the town-house a declaration, probably authored by Cotton Mather, that asserted the illegality of Andros's commission and detailed abuses of power under the dominion. The arrest of Andros and about fifty other officials and supporters of the dominion followed quickly.[19] Two days later a 'Council of Safety' was constituted. On 24 May the governor, deputy governor, and magistrates who had gained office in the last election under old charter rules, in 1686, resumed their duties. Political divisions persisted, however, between convinced supporters of the old charter and those whose reluctance showed them to be anxious to avoid being perceived as rebellious.[20]

This was the fluid state of affairs that greeted Phips when he arrived in Boston at the end of May. It appears to have led to an opportunity of sorts. Since Phips was not a freeman of the colony, his formal political position was considerably less than it had been during the brief period when he had seriously aspired to be provost marshal general; but, although it is unclear in what if any official capacity he acted, he was able to play a satisfying role in making the imprisonment of Andros and Randolph less comfortable. 'I am kept very inhumanely,' complained Randolph to the Lords of Trade from the common jail in Boston, 'and the Governor worse whose packett sent by expresse Order from Whitehall and letters of both publick and private Concernes of his and mine are stop'd and op'ned by Sir William Phips who says the Governor is a Rogue and shall not have his packetts nor letters and pretends an Order for so doing and keeps them from us.'[21] Yet, according to Cotton Mather, 'there were new Matters for Sir *William Phips*, in a little while, now to think upon.' As Phips settled into his new house for what was to be his longest stay in Boston since at least the early 1680s, 'he began to bethink himself, like *David*, concerning the *House* of the *God* who had surrounded him with so many favours in *his own*.'[22] The results of these meditations would not become evident for some months, but they represented the beginning of the process by which Phips would emerge in March 1690 as a member of the North Church and a freeman of the colony.

In the meantime, there were other concerns – military and political – that deserved to be pondered by Phips and other New Englanders. Of particular significance to Phips because of his origins on the Kennebec was the fall of Pemaquid to Wabanaki forces in August 1689. At the time of (or immediately after) the 18 April uprising, the Penobscot chief Madockawando had been in Boston for intended discussions with Andros, but he then left abruptly. One account a few weeks later attributed the renewed hostilities in Wabanaki territory to Madockawando's finding 'our Governor in Prisson and the Land in Confusion.'[23] The military position of the English east of the Saco River was undoubtedly weakened also by desertions and by the confusion in lines of command that stemmed from the revolution. As the siege of Pemaquid approached its end on 3 August, a Penobscot speaker was quoted as saying 'that they wanted their own country and meant to take it and the fort'; a speech after the fort's surrender predicted that now that the 'great rogue' Andros was a prisoner, the Wabanaki would have 'all their country by and by.'[24] The alarm in New England was well founded. Not only did the episode show Madockawando acting in concert with his son-in-law Jean-Vincent d'Abbadie de Saint-Castin – a former French military officer who was now living and trading on the Penobscot – but it also led to closer military cooperation between the French and Wabanaki.[25] As a by-product, it underlined the strategic significance of the Kennebec-Penobscot area from which Phips had departed so hurriedly as a result of the Wabanaki-English conflict in the previous decade.

Political developments proceeded in both England and New England. In London, Increase Mather succeeded in early July 1689 in winning the king's assurance of his 'gracious acceptance' of the efforts of the Boston revolutionaries.[26] But from then on, the balance increasingly shifted in favour of the supporters of the dominion. Letters arriving frequently from Edward Randolph portrayed New England as being in a state of political turmoil and imminent military collapse.[27] In the early spring of 1690, Randolph, Andros, and other imprisoned dominion officials arrived in England, having been released on the order of the crown. At the same time, two new Massachusetts agents – Elisha Cooke and Thomas Oakes – arrived to join Mather and Ashurst as the official representatives of the colony. The presence of the former prisoners and new agents caused the Lords of Trade to take action, demanding that the agents produce a list of complaints against Andros and the others. The agents responded with a list on 14 April, but none of them would sign the sheet: Mather and Ashurst because they had not been privy to the collection of evidence in Boston, and Cooke and Oakes apparently out of apprehension of being sued for damages. To make matters worse, when the full hearing took place on the seventeenth, Oakes and Cooke were unable to show formal credentials as agents. As a result, the Lords of Trade ruled that in the absence of proper charges, the dominion officials should be exonerated.[28] Mather's verdict on the disaster was scathing. 'Alas the Agents lately come hither,' he informed a Boston correspondent, 'are become the Ridicule of the Town, and exposed in the news letters all over the Nation; for that although they presented objections against Sir E.A. ... they declined to sign them. I have told them (and it is certayn) if they would have studyed to have gratified the enemies of New England or to have exposed themselves or the Country, they Could not have done it more effectually.'[29]

Mather's displeasure was symptomatic of the intensifying factional dispute in New England. The Council of Safety had initially tried to move cautiously and pragmatically, but it had been met with a powerful demand from the town representatives for the resumption of government according to the old charter. Elisha Cooke had argued this case from the beginning. Thomas Oakes had been chosen speaker of the representatives on 5 June 1689. In this capacity, he had presided over the drafting of their successful threat to hold up business unless the Council of Safety recanted its earlier declaration that the revolution did not imply the resumption of charter government; he had also presided over the passage of a resolution on 6 December 1689 that interpreted the royal order extending revolutionary rule as justifying 'a full exercise of Government, according to our Charter.'[30] The addition of these two to the agency in London in early 1690 testified to the power of a strain of Puritan opinion that held more unyieldingly to the old charter than either of the Mathers did.

At the other extreme was the barrage of denunciations of the revolutionary regime that had emanated from Randolph's prison cell, as well as the statements of his fellow Church of England adherents who had enjoyed high office under the dominion. Other voices were raised too, including that of Joseph Dudley, a leading member of one of the colony's principal Puritan families, who was connected by marriage to others and had been a prominent magistrate under the old charter before heading the temporary royal government of 1686 and then accepting office under Andros. That Dudley was in a category by himself was shown by his release from jail to house arrest in July 1689 until popular protest caused him to be returned to prison.[31] Church of England members who had not been dominion officials – or at least not at a high level – were also active in challenging the legitimacy of the resumption of charter forms of government. A petition of January 1690 in the name of the 'Boston members of the Church of England' had only three signatures but made up for its lack of subscribers by its forceful denunciation of the 'Seditious and Rebellious actings and proceedings' of the regime.[32]

As time passed, the revolutionary regime also gathered opponents whose dissatisfaction stemmed from a perception of ineffective government rather than from a pre-existing commitment to the dominion – though these two motivations intermingled in the thoughts and actions of some. A petition directed to the crown in January 1690 by Maine inhabitants was damaging in its praise for Andros's military conduct in his campaign against the Wabanaki and in blaming the subsequent English military disasters on 'the late insurrection and alteration of the Government att Boston.'[33] This was also a theme of the petition of twelve residents of Charlestown, who lamented 'the great disorder and confusion these parts are brought into.'[34]

The most revealing of the petitions of early 1690 was the one that carried the greatest number of signatures. Forty-five 'inhabitants of Boston and adjacent places' portrayed both New England and New York as being 'in a verry broaken and unsteady posture' following the revolution. Noting the sense of grievance that had been created by the lack of an elected assembly under the dominion, the petitioners nevertheless praised the uniting of the colonies for 'healeing the breaches amonghts us our Mutuall defence and Support and making us a Secure Bullworke against the French, and Indians.' Avoiding adverse comment on either Andros or the Council of Safety, these petitioners looked forward to the establishment of a new royal government with an assembly. First among the signatories was John Nelson, a leading member of a group of merchants who had been early members of the Council of Safety but were not freemen according to the old charter franchise and had become increasingly alienated as charter government had been resumed. Although some of the names on the petition had also appeared on more overtly antirevolutionary petitions, the signatories came from mercantile and other backgrounds that were sufficiently broad based to reinforce the document's moderate tone. Thus, between the views of, say, Elisha Cooke and Edward Randolph, there lay a body of articulate political opinion that looked towards effective government and sound military defence rather than towards either constitutional extreme.[35]

In all the documentation generated by the political debates of late 1689 and early 1690, the name of Sir William Phips is absent. Cotton Mather's biography offers two possible explanations for Phips's apparent silence on issues with which he had been closely involved in London: domestic and religious. Mather quotes Phips as reflecting on a number of occasions, 'I have no need at all to look after any further Advantages for my self in this World; I may sit still at Home if I will, and enjoy my ease for the rest of my Life.' Whether Phips's wealth was indeed sufficient to support this amount of leisure is doubtful, and in any case Mather was careful to add that Phips believed that public service was his duty despite the temptations of a quiet life. Yet when Phips was being considered in March 1690 for command of an expedition against Acadia, the diarists Samuel Sewall and Benjamin Bullivant both noted reports that Mary Spencer Phips was reluctant to give her consent and that Phips would not sail without it. Between the spring of 1689 and the late winter of 1690, Phips may well have been having a rare interlude of relatively tranquil domestic life.[36] This was also, at least in the later stages, a time of religious reflection – though whether the reflection was purely spiritual or was focused more on the benefits of an even closer identification with the Mathers is unclear from the surviving evidence. Either way, Phips made his profession of faith at the North Church on 23 March 1690.

Cotton Mather recorded the profession in full in his biography, and he took pains to point out that it was a faithful transcription 'without adding so much as one Word unto it.' Be that as it may, Mather's influence on Phips's discursive prose and biblical allusions was clearly exerted strongly at some stage. Although the statement is noticeably short of specifics on whatever sins may have given Phips cause to repent, it is revealing in a different sense. It conveyed what both Phips and Mather wished to be reported about the spiritual condition of the newly appointed major general who, the previous day, had at last accepted command of the Acadian expedition. The beginning of his religious awakening, Phips declared, had come from hearing Increase Mather preach in 1674 and from a period of spiritual direction by the elder Mather immediately afterwards; but 'the Ruins which the *Indian Wars* brought on my Affairs, and the Entanglements which my following the *Sea* laid upon me' – a tactful reference, perhaps, to the visit of the *Golden Rose* to Boston in late 1683 and early 1684 – had proved to be obstacles. Only after 'God was pleased to smile upon my *Outward Concerns*,' stated Phips, did he begin to understand the workings of Providence and understand his need for 'an Interest in the Lord Jesus Christ, and to close heartily with him.' Combined with this was his determination to serve New England:

But as soon as ever God had smiled upon me with a Turn of my Affairs, I had laid myself under the VOWS of the Lord, *That I would set my self to serve his People, and Churches here, unto the utmost of my Capacity.* I have had great Offers made to me in *England*; but the Churches of *New-England* were those which my Heart was most set upon. I knew, *That if God had a People any where, it was here*: And I *Resolved to rise and fall with them*; neglecting very great Advantages for my Worldly Interest, that I might come and enjoy the Ordinances of the Lord Jesus here.[37]

Phips's declaration was praised by Cotton Mather as showing 'Exemplary *Devotion*.' The elders and congregation evidently agreed, for Phips immediately received both baptism and admission to full membership.[38]

Other observers were as unconvinced of the blamelessness of Phips's principles of action as of his veneer of respectability. Benjamin Bullivant, albeit a hostile commentator by virtue of his pro-dominion views, described in his journal an incident that took place within a few days of Phips's baptism. The background was the arrest several weeks earlier of

Daniel Turell and John White, a joiner and younger half-brother of Phips, for debt at the behest of Joseph Smith. By 30 January 1690, Turell and White had already escaped once from prison and had then been brought before the Massachusetts council to 'Shew Cause (if any there be) why they should not be remanded to Prison.' Although they successfully requested a two-day deferral, the two were subsequently returned to jail, whence they petitioned in March for a further hearing.[39] The representatives were willing to agree, but the council refused, as Bullivant noted:

The Northend men headed by Sir William Phips. Milbourne and Way, apply to the Deputies for the discharge of Turell and White in Execution for a Just Debt the Deputies vote for theyr discharge the magistrates Opposed, as being in custody under their Commitment. Sir William Phips etc. not Contented with the opinion of the magistrates go personally to the prison, proffer the keeper 3000ll verrily to bear him harmless if he would put them at large, the Keeper refused and gives as hard Language as he receives.[40]

Bullivant's account carries a number of significant implications, especially since his journal eventually found its way into the papers of the Lords of Trade. It is hardly surprising that Phips intervened on behalf of his younger half-brother, and Turell was also known to him. Daniel Turell (or Turill) was a name shared by a father and son – the son being the one imprisoned in 1690 – who had extensive real-estate transactions in Boston in this period, particularly in the North End. In 1687, when Mary Spencer Phips had heard of her husband's success, the property she bought as the site for their house had been part-owned by the elder Daniel Turell. Presumably, the purchase meant that an amicable settlement had been reached in the dispute of 1677 in which the younger Turell had successfully sued William Phips for £13/9/–.[41]

The imprisonment of White and Turell had its origins in a venture of 1684 that corresponded closely with the treasure-seeking activities being pursued by Phips at the time. Turell and White had formed a company – with Richard Wharton, Hezekiah Usher, Joseph Smith, Thomas Mitchell, and 'several others' – for a voyage to a wreck off the Bahamas. Wharton's kinsman Goodwin Wharton was an active treasure seeker in England, described by Keith Thomas as 'continuously engaged in a treasure quest, for which he enlisted spirits, fairies and the latest resources of contemporary technology.'[42] Although Richard Wharton was not known to share Goodwin's talent for speaking to angels and disembodied spirits, his many commercial and speculative ventures showed that he was equally zealous for treasure and profit. That Richard Wharton was also an investor in Phips's Caribbean activities and that Turell witnessed the agreement of 11 January between Phips and Robert Bronson are strands of evidence that strongly suggest a relationship between the Phips and White-Turell voyages in 1684. Indeed, on 14 January 1684, Turell sold a one-eighth share of the sloop *Rosebud* to Hezekiah Usher, presumably as part of the undertaking.[43]

Some treasure had been raised by the White-Turell company by March 1684, when Thomas Mitchell received a doughboy worth £120 from an individual named John Hand. By December 1684, Mitchell had returned to Charlestown and a series of legal proceedings had begun over the doughboy and the venture as a whole. Mitchell sued Joseph Smith, who sued Turell and White. The matter was still in the courts in March 1686 when Turell and White (as defendants in the civil case against Smith) pleaded guilty to charges of making an illegitimate approach to the foreman of the jury. Apparently this faux pas had no serious consequences, and Turell and White obtained a judgment against Smith in vindication of their claim that they were the injured parties. Smith's petition for a writ of *scire facias* was then dismissed, to all appearances bringing the affair to an end. However, under what Turell later described as 'the Unjust and Arbitrary Government of Sir Edmund Andros,' Smith made another application for the writ, and eventually obtained a judgment in his favour of £200. After the fall of the dominion, with Turell and White refusing to pay, Smith had them imprisoned for debt. Thus, six years after they had begun a venture that had links with Phips, the two North End residents found themselves in jail for charges that seemed symbolic of the evils of the Andros regime. That a crowd led by Phips would descend on the jail is understandable in this context.[44]

The 'Way' referred to by Bullivant was undoubtedly Richard Way, an attorney and merchant who was a neighbour of the Phips and Turell families in the North End of Boston. A member of the North Church, Way had well-established links with the Kennebec region and with associates of Phips. He had served at one time as attorney for John Hornibrook, a Kennebec fur trader who was later an interpreter for Phips at the English-Wabanaki peace conference of August 1693. Way had also acted for Elizabeth Freake, the daughter of Phips's former employer, Thomas Clarke.[45] In 1668 Richard Way had been one of the sixty-six signatories of a petition objecting to the sentence of banishment

imposed on three Baptists.[46] That he may have retained his Baptist leanings is suggested by the fact that the other participant mentioned by
Bullivant in the Turell-White affair was William Milborne, a Baptist
preacher who had taken up residence in Boston after fleeing Bermuda in
the wake of conflicts with Governor Coney in 1684. Although 'Mr. Milborne the fifth monarchist,' as Coney described him, had left Bermuda
well before Phips visited the island in 1685, he was apparently associated with Henry Bish who sailed to England in the *Golden Rose*.[47]
Although Milborne was not a signatory of the declaration of 18 April
1689 or ever a member of the Council of Safety, he was nevertheless
described by Randolph as 'the great ringleader of the Rebellion'[48]

Phips's action on behalf of Turell and White was open to varying
interpretations. On the one hand, he could be seen as actively resisting
an injustice that was a legacy of the dominion. On the other hand, the
episode – at least as portrayed by Bullivant – could be interpreted as
raising serious questions about Phips and his behaviour. It linked him
closely with an individual, Milborne, who was held suspect by ortho-
dox Puritans for religious reasons and who – because of his role in the
rising of 18 April 1689 and, by extension, because of the even more
prominent role of his brother Jacob in the revolution in New York – was
also a target of those who had favoured the dominion. Finally, Bullivant's account, in its association of Phips with riotous behaviour and
hard language, recalled a side of his character that he had sought to
efface in his profession of faith. Clearly, respectability was not to be universally granted even on the basis of a knighthood and a well-timed
religious conversion.

Bullivant's interest in the affair of Turell and White had a further
important element. The incident had occurred virtually at the same time
as Phips's acceptance of command of the projected expedition against
Acadia, and the controversial circumstances of this appointment
ensured that all his activities would come under the close scrutiny of
those who, like Bullivant, took a cynical and pessimistic view of his
qualifications for military leadership. The impetus for the expedition
had come originally from the serious setbacks encountered by English
settlements in Wabanaki territory during the summer and fall of 1689.
The fall of Pemaquid in August had been the most conspicuous defeat,
but even the garrisons at such isolated strategic locations as Casco Bay
were small and shrinking.[49]

Many New Englanders were inclined to blame the French as much as,
or more than, the Wabanaki. Although such formulations tended to be

simplistic in attributing·to the French a control over events which they did not possess, a nascent Wabanaki-French alliance certainly existed and was becoming increasingly important in French strategic thinking. The French strategy in late 1689 and early 1690 was essentially defensive. Following the English revolution, royal instructions to the governor of New France, Jacques-René de Brisay de Denonville, had warned him to strengthen Canada's defences against possible assault from New England or New York.[50] Attack, however, could be an effective form of defence. A detailed plan for a French assault on New York, communicated in June 1689 to Denonville's successor, Louis de Buade de Frontenac et de Palluau, was shelved in the following year as a result of other demands on French forces, but Frontenac was instructed to give active encouragement to the Wabanaki in their efforts against New England.[51] A more specific reason for doing so was offered to the French crown in February 1690 by Jean-Baptiste de Lagny, the French intendant of commerce, who warned that the tumbledown fort at the Acadian headquarters of Port-Royal was indefensible and called for war to be carried into New England as a means of creating 'a diversion that may prevent them from invading Port-Royal.'[52]

In Boston, plans for the raid on Acadia had been afoot for several weeks. The possibility had been discussed in general terms since at least the fall of Pemaquid, and on 16 December – with French vessels based in Port-Royal putting increasing pressure on Massachusetts shipping – the House of Representatives resolved in favour of raising volunteers and appointing commanders 'for the Reduceing of the French on the Coast of Accada or Els where to the obedience of there Majesties of Great Britain.'[53] To all appearances, the shape and organization of the venture soon began to emerge. On 4 January 1690 the Massachusetts council heard from John Nelson, who stated that the attack on Port-Royal was necessary because 'the Origine of our mischeife is from the French' but that it was beyond the means of the overstretched public purse; he therefore proposed that it should be confided to 'Divers private Gentlemen' who would be willing to take it on as a contribution to 'the Publique Benefit.' On the same day, the representatives reaffirmed the call for volunteers and offered interested merchants the use of two sloops of war and the profits of both plunder and continuing trade on the Acadian coast. Yet the impetus soon weakened as a result of disputes over the terms on which the 'undertakers' would make their contribution to the public benefit.[54]

The project was revived only by a new series of military disasters. Late

February brought news of a devastating raid on Schenectady, New York, by French and Native forces, and just over three weeks later word was brought of a similar attack on Salmon Falls, New Hampshire. The news from Schenectady prompted Nelson to approach Samuel Sewall, and presumably others, to invest £100 in the Port-Royal expedition. But the Massachusetts General Court decided to mount a publicly organized assault.[55] Two committees were struck to coordinate the effort. A committee of five merchants took charge of logistical matters, while on 19 March an overall supervising committee was established. This group included the governor, five of the magistrates – Fitz-John Winthrop, John Richards, Elisha Hutchinson, Samuel Shrimpton, and Samuel Sewall – and Sir William Phips.[56]

The change from private to public and the composition of the supervising committee pointed to a simple political reality. Under pressure from country interests who mistrusted Boston merchants (especially those who, like Nelson, belonged to the Church of England and were not freemen) and from Cotton Mather as a political leader of clerical Puritanism, the magistrates had decided to take control. There was still doubt about who would lead the expedition. On 18 March Bartholomew Gedney was appointed, but refused. On 20 March, Penn Townsend was named as his replacement, but two days later – in Sewall's words – he 'relinquishes with Thanks' in favour of Phips. Apparently, there had been speculation that Nelson might take the command. Benjamin Bullivant disdainfully recorded: 'Mr Nelson ... was proposed for Generalissimo, and people believed it would fall so, as the fittest person for such an enterprize but the Country Deputies said he was a Merchant and not to be trusted, so it is offered to Sir William Phips.' Although both Bullivant and Sewall recorded that Mary Spencer Phips was thought likely to veto Phips's appointment, the official record affirmed that he had 'Voluntarily Offered Himself to that Service.' He was promptly made a freeman – on the eve of his religious profession, baptism, and admission to membership of the North Church.[57]

Thus Phips, on 24 March 1690, carried the title of major general as he attended the initial meeting of the 'Committee for Setting out the Forces in the expedition against the French in Nova Scotia and Lacady.' The magistrates who sat down with him included the same Governor Simon Bradstreet who had admonished him less than seven years earlier for acting above his station in life.[58] There was, however, a price. Just as his earlier association with the Navy Board and Albemarle had earned Phips the disapproval of Blathwayt and the Plantations Office, so his social and political advancement in the revolution era had depended on an increasingly close association with the Mathers and with a revolutionary regime in Boston that was far from having won universal approbation. Phips's relationship with the Mathers was a more complex one than the client-patron pattern that had character-ized his treasure-hunting years. With Increase Mather, he had collabo-rated in London, though certainly at a junior level in both age and sophistication. With Cotton Mather, who was his junior by twelve years, he stood in the role of spiritual pupil. Mather later described him as 'one whom I baptised ... one of my own Flock, and one of my dearest Friends.'[59] John Nelson, who also exercised wide influence, though in different sectors of Massachusetts society, would not have been so com-plimentary. Benjamin Bullivant wrote that when Nelson was offered the role of Phips's second-in-command in the assault on Port-Royal, he rejected it 'with Scorn and contempt.'[60] To Phips, still the parvenu in spite of his grand titles, neither scorn nor contempt was new. How much of either he would now encounter would depend largely on the outcome of the expedition.

5

The Expeditions of 1690

The preparations for the Port-Royal expedition were hasty and controversial. Not surprisingly, the recorded comments of members of the organizing committee were optimistic. Samuel Sewall noted in his diary on 24 March that eight companies were already training. 'I goe into the field,' he added with gusto, '[to] pray with the South Company, Exercise them in a few Distances, Facings, Doublings.' Governor Bradstreet wrote on the twenty-ninth to the earl of Shrewsbury, senior secretary of state, that success against Port-Royal would set the stage for an assault on Canada, provided that munitions could be supplied from England. Elisha Hutchinson, writing two days later to Elisha Cooke – a less sceptical recipient than Shrewsbury was likely to be – went so far as to assert that only a shortage of arms and ammunition was preventing the present expedition from making an attempt on Quebec. If a future expedition could be equipped with two royal frigates and the needed supplies, Hutchinson believed, the fall of Canada would easily be brought about.[1]

Critics of the regime expressed less sanguine expectations. Daniel Allin confided to Joseph Dudley on 1 April, 'I Don't find our mens spirits so hot when it comes to a Push of Reall Service as upon some occasions they have Been.' Benjamin Bullivant wrote in his journal that recruitment was initially slow and desertions went unpunished, and that when Phips mustered his men at the townhouse, 'about 80 in a Body deserted with huzza's, having been told they must find theyr own armes.' Another incident concerned a company commander named Coleman, who was appointed by Phips in preference to the commander elected by the troops. When Coleman attempted to take up his duties, he was hooted at by his company.' The soldiers won their point, for apparently Coleman was replaced by an ambitious ensign.[2] Clearly, the pro-dominion merchant Francis Foxcroft was not alone in his view when he scathingly remarked that the expedition was 'under the weighty conduct of the New England Knight.'[3]

At last, on the morning of 23 April 1690, Phips's flagship, the 42-gun, 120-man *Six Friends*, set sail for Nantasket in Boston Harbour. There it took on board the militia contingents that had been assembled on Governor's Island and Castle Island, and on 28 April it sailed northeast with four other vessels. The *Porcupine*, with 16 guns and a crew of 117, was by far the most powerful of the four, the others being the sloop *Mary* and two ketches. Due to rendezvous at Mount Desert Island were two Salem vessels, the barque *Union* and another unarmed ketch, carrying militia raised in Essex County. The total strength of the crews numbered 286, the soldiers 446. The minister Joshua Moody and three administrative officials brought the total to 736. '*He is no New Englander ...,*' Cotton Mather had preached on 20 March, '*who at such a Time as this, will not Venture his All, for this Afflicted people of God.*' What was required, he announced, was 'a brisk Salley forth upon the *French* Territories.'[4] More specifically, Phips's instructions were to sail directly to Port-Royal, reduce the fort there by articles or by storm, and then seize other French outposts in the region.[5] He did not take these orders literally. Following their successful rendezvous at Mount Desert, the New Englanders made largely unproductive visits to the *habitation* of the baron de Saint-Castin and to small French settlements at Machias and Passamaquoddy before anchoring in the basin opposite Port-Royal in the late evening of 9 May.[6]

Phips may initially have been unaware of the extreme weakness of the fort that lay at a distance across the water on the morning of 10 May. When Louis-Alexandre Des Friches de Meneval had been appointed governor of Acadia in 1687, he had expected to supervise a thorough refortification of Port-Royal and a strengthening of its garrison. The thirty soldiers sent in 1687 outnumbered those who had already been there, but the garrison was still far from formidable. Thirty more came in 1688, but with only nineteen muskets among them. As for the fortifications, the engineer Vincent Saccardy had arrived at Port-Royal in October 1689. 'Like all the engineers, he had visions that were too grandiose and disproportionate to what he had to do,' commented a critic. Saccardy had decided to raze the existing fortifications with the intention of building an elaborate new structure that more closely resembled a fortified town than a fort. He began his work of demolition despite the remonstrances of Meneval but was soon overtaken by the advancing season and was ordered by Governor Frontenac of Canada to depart. 'He left things in this state,' complained a memorandum that subsequently reached the French Ministry of Marine, 'the fort open, and thus less defensible than it had been in the first place.'[7] Plagued also by disputes with the Acadian inhabitants and by gout, Meneval pleaded for permission to return to France. If the minister would not allow it, he informed a correspondent in September, 'I assure you that at the first opportunity and regardless of the consequences I will leave here without permission, preferring a hundred times to spend three years in the Bastille than a single week here.'[8]

The Bastille might have been preferable to what Meneval was about to experience as a result of Phips's expedition. 'What I have always had reason to fear as long as I have been here has finally taken place,' he reported a few days after surrendering to Phips. In this report to France, Meneval made the New England force sound a good deal more formidable than it really was, saying that the Port-Royal basin had been invaded by 'three frigates, of 46 and 30 guns, five or six smaller ships and a landing force of eight or nine hundred troops.' His exaggeration was no doubt self-serving, for another French account of the siege gave the strength of the fleet with complete accuracy.[9] Early in the morning of 10 May, Phips had made contact with Pierre Melanson, known as Laverdure, one of two brothers who had remained at Port-Royal at the time of the English withdrawal of 1670. Laverdure's bilingualism, acquired from Huguenot origins and English connections, made him a convenient informant on the state of the garrison. Phips then weighed anchor, moved closer to Port-Royal, and sent an envoy ashore to summon Meneval to surrender. Meneval's decision was immediate. Although he went through the formality of putting the envoy under guard while the priest Louis Petit went on board the *Six Friends* for negotiations, it was understood from the beginning that capitulation would be the result.[10]

There is conflicting evidence about the events that followed, though the broad outlines are clear enough. It took Petit only half an hour to agree on the terms of capitulation with Phips, by which the garrison would be transported to France or Quebec. Although there was later dispute about the disposition of the garrison's arms and supplies, it was clear that the Acadian inhabitants were to be secure in their persons and possessions, and guaranteed freedom to exercise their Roman Catholic religion in the church at Port-Royal. Phips had refused to put the terms in writing, however, and Petit advised Meneval not to insist 'for fear of irritating him.' The following day, Phips sent his shallop for Meneval,

who came on board the *Six Friends* while the New England troops disembarked. The meeting between Phips and the governor was cordial
and, amid the complimentary exchanges, the terms of capitulation were
verbally confirmed in the presence of Petit and the French administrative official Mathieu de Goutin. The disembarkation completed, Phips
and Meneval went ashore. Then, at Phips's invitation, Meneval paraded
the French garrison in front of the church.[11]

At this point the cordiality ended and the conflicting evidence began.
The expedition journal was terse in describing what took place: 'Our
men drawn up, Possession of the Fort was given; the Governour and
Officers delivered their Swords to our General, who returned the Governour his sword and likewise to some of his Officers. The Soldiers laid
down their Arms, and were guarded to the Church, where they were
kept as Prisoners.'[12] The imprisonment of the garrison indicates that the
terms of capitulation had already broken down, and the next day's journal explained why, as well as noting the consequences for Port-Royal
and its Acadian inhabitants:

Monday 12. This Morning we went a-shoar to search for hidden goods, (for during the time of Parley they had broke open the King's Store, and Merchants
Stores, and convey'd sundry Wares into the woods) We cut down the Cross,
rifled the Church, Pu'lld down the high-Altar, breaking their Images: and
brought our Plunder, Arms and Amunition into Mr. *Nelson*'s Storehouse; *Tuesday*, 13. And so kept gathering Plunder both by land and water, and also under
ground in their Gardens, all the next day.[13]

The French accounts added more details concerning the two days of
plundering but offered a different view of how it had been precipitated.
There was no dispute about the behaviour of the French troops during
Meneval's absence on board the *Six Friends*. An account by an unidentified French officer blamed Meneval for not having left firm orders for
the garrison troops, 'who applied themselves after his departure to
drinking and pillaging.'[14] Much less clear was the extent of these mis-
deeds and their significance under the terms of capitulation. Meneval
and others maintained that the target of the troops and some Acadians
had been the personal stores of the merchant François-Marie Perrot
(who was temporarily absent from Port-Royal) and not the royal maga-
zine. Even if the royal stores had been opened, there was room for doubt
whether the agreed terms would thereby have been breached. Phips had
initially demanded the surrender of 'all the great Artillery, small Arms,

and stores of War, and whatsoever else belongs to the French King,' but it had been Petit's understanding that the garrison would march out of the fort 'in military order, with their arms and supplies.' For the anonymous French officer who described the scene after Phips's disembarkation, the first indication of treachery was when Phips ostentatiously and unexpectedly demanded Meneval's sword. Then he ordered the garrison troops disarmed, searched, relieved of their cash, and imprisoned in the church.[15]

Petit and Meneval had an explanation of Phips's conduct: 'The General seeing when he arrived at Port-Royal that, contrary to what he had thought, there was no fort at all and no defensible fortifications, and that the garrison was smaller than he had imagined, was disgusted with the honest compromise he had made. Seeking pretexts to break it, he seized upon some disorders that had taken place at Port-Royal while the governor was absent.'[16] The evidence suggests that they were mistaken. The idea that Phips had been surprised by the weak state of the fort and garrison might have been convincing had it not been for his early-morning meeting with Laverdure. Although it is not known what advice Laverdure gave, in the circumstances he would have been unlikely to misrepresent the state of the fort. Another factor was Phips's refusal to put the terms of capitulation in any written form, other than that of his letter demanding surrender, for this put him in a position to deny the existence of an 'honest compromise.'

Phips had a great deal to gain by the plundering of Port-Royal. Not only would it add to the expedition's military success by bringing personal profit to the troops and ships' crews – the importance of which for the reputation of a commander was well known to Phips from his Caribbean voyages – but it would yield military supplies and salable goods for the Massachusetts colony, to the benefit of its defensibility and financial state. With the regime under political attack for military incompetence and for raising taxes to fund the expedition at public cost, these were important considerations. There were also political dividends to be expected from the pillaging of the church. For a regime that owed much to the perception that Andros had been sympathetic to the Catholic enemy, and likewise for Phips as an acolyte of Cotton Mather, the desecration of a Roman Catholic altar was an act that could only have a solidifying effect, strengthening political and personal support.[17] The terms of capitulation, therefore, were probably intended by Phips not as a compromise but as a convenience that could be dispensed with as soon as Port-Royal had surrendered without a fight.

Phips's personal behaviour is consistent with this interpretation and also with earlier phases of his career. During Meneval's visit to the *Six Friends*, Phips apparently matched the courtly demeanour of the surrendering governor. 'When M. de Meneval had arrived on board the said commander's ship,' reported a French officer, 'he was brought to his cabin, at the back of which he was seated. On arrival, M. de Meneval made to him a deep bow, and this commander replied by inclining his head to the right and the left in the English way.' But almost immediately after reaching shore, rancour replaced courtesy. When Meneval reported to France soon afterwards, he described Phips and his lieutenants as 'very angry people, from whom I have little expectation of either mercy or good treatment.'[18] Displays of anger accompanied by hard language and threats of violence had been characteristic of Phips in many recorded instances during the previous decade. Meneval, with his aristocratic bearing but physical and military weakness, was an especially tempting target. Phips's demand for his sword, before both assembled forces, should be interpreted in this light. But there is evidence that, in this instance, Phips's displeasure took an unusual form in that he resorted to physical violence. This episode took place on 19 May after the New England troops had captured a man named La Roche, an employee of the Compagnie de la pêche sédentaire who had escaped upriver with cash and goods belonging to the company and to Perrot. Only through *la gesne* – torture – at the hands of Phips was La Roche made to reveal where he had concealed the cash box.[19]

The systematic plundering of Port-Royal, which included killing the inhabitants' livestock and sequestering Meneval's personal cash and effects, occupied some ten days. The other main effort was to induce the Acadian inhabitants to swear an oath of allegiance to William and Mary. Although in this context the documentation of the English claim to 'Port Royal, L'Accadie and Nova Scotia' was vague, Phips asserted the continuing rule of the English crown. Accordingly, Acadian inhabitants from both Port-Royal and Les Mines, in numbers that are not evident from surviving records, took an oath of allegiance to William and Mary. The journal of the expedition recorded their demonstrations of 'great Joy' and their 'great Acclamations and Rejoicings' in doing so, whereas a French account attributed the oaths to Phips's threat to burn the houses of those who refused. Both assertions may well be true, and the scenes at the oath taking must certainly have had an affinity with those on the Kennebec in 1671 – probably observed directly by the twenty-year-old William Phips – when Simon-François Daumont de

Saint-Lusson had claimed the Kennebec-Penobscot region for France amid the *joye sensible* of the English inhabitants. Where Phips in 1690 went well beyond what Saint-Lusson had accomplished in 1671 was not only in the swearing of oaths but in the selection, ostensibly by the inhabitants at large, of a president and council to govern on behalf of the English crown. The president, Charles La Tourasse, was a sergeant in the defeated garrison, and the council included prominent Acadian inhabitants. Their instructions enjoined them to make reports to the Massachusetts governor, though only 'from time to time.'[20]

With this accomplished and the plunder loaded on board ship, Phips made preparations to leave Port-Royal. Captain John Alden was dispatched in the sloop *Mary* to revisit the coastline from the St John to Penobscot rivers, to attack remaining French establishments, redeem any English captives, and try to win over Saint-Castin to the English allegiance. He was to bargain, if necessary, the freedom of a daughter of Saint-Castin captured at Port-Royal. The *Porcupine* likewise departed to harass French settlements on the Atlantic coast of Acadia and in Newfoundland.[21] Phips weighed anchor from Port-Royal on 21 May, left the basin the following day, experienced delays from calm or contrary winds, and reached Boston Harbour on the afternoon of the thirtieth. As the fleet straggled into Boston and Salem, the soldiers of the Port-Royal garrison were sent first to prison in Salem and then to find billets in Cambridge. Meneval and the priests Petit and Trouvé were placed together under house arrest. Arrangements for disposal of the plunder, meanwhile, were put in the hands of a committee, and on 6 June the goods (with the exception of the munitions) were ordered to be divided 'between the Country on one part, and the officers, Soldiers, and Seamen of the other part.' To what extent Phips profited personally is unclear, although his purchase on 13 June of a 'Brick Warehouse scituate and being near the Great Dock in Boston' for £457 is suggestive.[22]

The items brought from Port-Royal as plunder made an impressive collection. No doubt there was a ready market for the boots, shoes, and articles of clothing and certainly for the Port-Royal blacksmith's tools. The box of wafers taken from the church, along with the vestments of the priests, must have had less obvious value in the Boston of Cotton Mather, though they were certainly effective symbols of the religious significance of the expedition's success. More conventional as commodities of established trading value were the substantial quantities of furs, brandy, and cloth. There was also a total of £740 in cash, as well as guns and other military supplies, and a brigantine and two ketches.[23] The public sale of the loot, referred to by Samuel Sewall in mid-June, was an occasion to mark a significant military advance.

News of Port-Royal's fall had reached Boston on 22 May, and five days later Governor Bradstreet wrote to Jacob Leisler, leader of the revolutionary regime in New York, saying, 'Wee have received intelligence from Sir William Phipps of the Success it hath pleased God to give him.' Yet Bradstreet had to admit that 'rejoyceing therein' was 'mixt with an Alloy of sorrow.' The same week had seen two setbacks for New England. First and most serious, on 21 May, was the fall of Casco Bay's Fort Loyal to Wabanaki and French forces. Three days later the captain and numerous crew members of the warship *Rose* died in an inconclusive fight with a heavily armed French vessel off Cape Sable. Late May of 1690, in Boston or elsewhere within the rapidly shrinking confines of New England, was no time for unqualified celebration.[24]

The more sceptical observers denied any cause for celebration at all. Thomas Newton, a signatory of the Boston petition of 25 January, remarked, 'We have sufferr'd greater loss by farr at Casco than we have gained at Port Royall.' Other critics included Francis Nicholson and John Usher, both former officials of the Dominion of New England. Nicholson, who was now lieutenant-governor of Virginia, forwarded reports to London which stated that even the plunder from Port-Royal had been insufficient to prevent a deficit of £4,000 on the expedition. In similar vein, Usher relayed a correspondent's sarcastic reference to 'the greatt conquest made att port Royall' against a fort that had not a single mounted gun.[25] François-Marie Perrot, reporting to France, made the same point. Perrot, however, was inclined to put the blame on Meneval and Petit. The governor, he noted, had done nothing to make Port-Royal defensible in spite of having had adequate warning of Phips's entry into the basin: 'all of M. de Meneval's conduct was bad, and there were few who deemed it creditable.' As for Petit, said Perrot, 'In spite of his protestations, he had strong links with this nation that has always been so dear to him.'[26] Perrot was a political opponent of Meneval and the Port-Royal clergy, just as Usher was of the Boston regime, but their mutually reinforcing verdicts on the military aspects of Phips's triumph were essentially accurate. The conquest of Port-Royal had been a cheap victory over a disabled and dispirited enemy, made all the cheaper by Phips's evident determination to plunder the town in spite of the inconvenient fact that its defenders had been so anxious to capitulate.

A further criticism that was later levelled at Phips concerned the ineffectiveness of the governing council he had established at Port-Royal.

'The French at Port Royall ...,' commented a petition to the crown in early 1691, signed by sixty-one New Englanders, 'surrendered themselves upon Articles, but noe care [was] taken, to preserve the same for your Majesties service, Little annoyance given to the Enemy, by that or any other Enterprize hitherto Engaged in.' The petitioners included Nelson, Newton, and others who had signed the petitions in favour of royal government a year earlier, as well as new names such as those of Nathaniel Byfield (a merchant, formerly a resident of Rhode Island, and an early sympathizer with and publicizer of the revolution in Boston) and Cyprian Southack, who had commanded the *Porcupine* in the 1690 expedition.[27] The passage dealing with Port-Royal was on firm ground in at least two respects. First, its capture brought no lasting military advantage. Joseph Robinau de Villebon, one of Meneval's senior officers, returned from France in June 1690 and quickly moved the French headquarters to the St John Valley, where he effectively coordinated Native and French military efforts against New England. Secondly, Charles La Tourasse quickly put himself under Villebon's orders and remained as president of the council only on the basis that some collaboration with New England was unavoidable in view of Port- Royal's vulnerability to further attack.[28]

For all that, a case could be made for the Acadian council. To establish a garrison at Port-Royal would have created for New England yet another vulnerable outpost and would have detracted from available forces for the attack on Canada discussed in Boston earlier in the spring. Persuading Massachusetts militia to stay in such an isolated position would in all likelihood have proved impossible.[29] Given Acadian leanings towards pragmatism, and the influence of community members who favoured accommodation and trading contacts with the English, the council offered a way of nurturing these political tendencies until the defeat of the French could be completed by a conquest of Canada. Phips's capture of Port-Royal proved to have little lasting significance, at least by comparison with its decisive seizure in 1710 by a force led – ironically – by Francis Nicholson. Yet as elements of a strategy that included an assault on Canada, the 1690 expedition and the Acadian council were defensible enough in the short term. It was even conceivable that Phips's conduct towards Meneval and in the plundering of Port-Royal would be forgotten if he could make a successful assault on Quebec.

The momentum from the seizure of Port-Royal was more than adequate to prompt the mounting of a new expedition against the French. As Usher's informant commented, 'Here [in Boston] is greatt talk of Sending for Canada, the people generall Supposeing to have thatt upon as easy termes as [Port Royal].'[30] It took the Massachusetts General Court just four days after Phips's return to order the Canada expedition to be speedily dispatched, and on 12 June Phips was named as its general. At the council meeting that ordered his appointment, Phips was present as a member. Elected as one of the Assistants during his absence at Port-Royal, he had thus advanced further into the realms of respectability and influence.[31] The contrast with his predicament less than two years before is striking. While his political role during the era of the revolution had been slight, his association with the two Mathers had been amply rewarded. Yet his position was far from secure. With the postrevolution-ary settlement of New England still uncertain, Phips had made danger-ous enemies. The former officials and supporters of the dominion formed one conspicuous group. John Nelson, already alienated by the circum-stances of Phips's appointment to command the Port-Royal expedition, deplored the shameless plundering that had taken place and the humili-ation of Meneval. Nelson was a recognized leader of moderate merchant opinion, and the force of his displeasure was not to be underestimated.[32] For Phips, a great deal now depended on the Canada expedition: another victory, and much would be forgiven; a defeat, and the deficiencies of his conduct at Port Royal might come under closer scrutiny than his respect-able veneer could readily withstand.

The preparations for the attack on Canada were elaborate. Officials sought volunteers from all Massachusetts towns and requested assis-tance from the other New England colonies and from New York. Already, while Phips had been at sea en route to Port-Royal, New England and New York commissioners had met in New York to agree to strengthen Albany by assembling some 850 troops there. The under-standing was that this force would ultimately join with the Houdena-saunee to launch a land attack on Montreal.[33] Phips's task was to lead a seaborne assault on Quebec so that the French presence in Canada would be struck by a double blow.

As in the preparations for the Port-Royal expedition, difficulties soon arose. Joseph Dudley's assertion that there was division in the Massa-chusetts council over the merits of approving the expedition is uncon-firmed by other sources,[34] but there is clear documentation of popular unrest at Marblehead and among the interior settlements of Middlesex County, west and north of Boston. When John Alden visited Marble-head to requisition heavy guns, he was met by what the General Court described on 15 July as an 'Insurrection of the people.' This had partly been prompted by the action of local militia captains, who had ordered the beating of drums to summon the crowd. Meanwhile, in the 'frontier Townes' of Middlesex County – Concord, Sudbury, Billerica, and Stowe – Major Thomas Henchman was unable to raise his quota of volunteers for the expedition. The council curtly instructed him to make up the shortfall by levies on each town. Henchman eventually sailed for Quebec at the head of a contingent of 308, a large proportion of whom came from Sudbury. The background to both incidents lay partially in the disarray of town militias as a result of the institution, in 1689, of a nomination process for officers that amounted to popular election. But there was also the consideration of local defence. Towns vulnerable to land or sea attack were reluctant to give up their military personnel or supplies for the general good.[35]

Despite these difficulties, the colony assembled a substantial fleet under Phips's command by early August. Thirty-four vessels, again headed by Phips's *Six Friends*, carried approximately 2,300 New England troops and a native force of 50 raised in Plymouth Colony.[36] Some problems, however, remained unsolved. Governor Bradstreet and the council had formally appealed to England in late March for supplies of arms and ammunition. Although the Lords of Trade recommended compliance on 12 June, no shipment arrived until early 1691. Phips delayed his departure for Quebec in the hope of receiving these supplies, but on 10 August the advancing season dictated that he could wait no more.[37] There were also concerns about the land attack on Montreal. A New York correspondent of William Blathwayt, who reported that the force of '600 Christians and 1500 Indians' had left Albany in mid-July, was critical of the disorganized state of the New York and Connecticut forces commanded by Fitz-John Winthrop. This raised the question of whether Houdenasaunee participation would be sustained if the English effort was weak. If the Houdenasaunee pulled out, the fleet would have to attack Quebec without the strategic advantage of the double assault.[38] A further problem was that Phips lacked a pilot for the crucial passage up the St Lawrence. In late June, John Alden had been dispatched to Port-Royal in search of pilots, but his lack of success is reflected in Major Thomas Savage's later comment that the fleet 'had not one man for a pilot.'[39] A fleet that left Boston in mid-August without a pilot, with the ambition of attacking Quebec, but with limited ammunition and with no guarantee of a diversionary attack elsewhere in Canada was pinning a great deal of faith on good fortune and good weather. Phips was to enjoy neither.

The outlines of the advance and retreat of the Canada expedition between August and November 1690 are simple enough to sketch. Interpretation is more complex. The expedition spent its early weeks sailing up the coast to the mouth of the St Lawrence, its progress slowed by intermittently unfavourable weather and the need to marshal an unwieldy and straggling fleet. A storm prevented an attempt to assemble the vessels at Ile Percée, so Phips had to wait until 23 September to hold a council of war at Tadoussac.[40] The adverse weather continued, but by the morning of 6 October Phips lay opposite Quebec. Frontenac was well prepared to receive him, having returned from Montreal two days earlier. The governor had travelled to Montreal to counter the expected Houdenasaunee and English overland assault, but little defence had been required. Smallpox, divisions between Connecticut and New York officers, and the resulting disaffection of most of the Houdenasaunee force had drastically reduced the scale of the attack. What had been intended as a threat to Montreal had turned into a destructive but fleeting raid on a nearby rural area in late August, followed by a swift withdrawal. Not only was Frontenac soon free to return to Quebec but, forewarned of Phips's departure from Boston, he was able to bring with him between two and three hundred troops. Governor Louis-Hector de Callière of Montreal followed hard on his heels with more troops, while militia contingents were summoned from settlements close to Quebec. According to Silvanus Davis, who had been commander of Fort Loyal at Casco when it had fallen in the spring and was now a prisoner in Quebec, Frontenac had a force of about 2,700 at his immediate command at the time of Phips's arrival.[41]

Phips was unaware of the strength of the French position in Quebec when he dispatched Major Thomas Savage ashore with an ultimatum, in the name of William and Mary, on the morning of 6 October. This document, which was addressed to Frontenac or his deputy (indicating Phips's uncertainty over Frontenac's whereabouts), demanded total surrender within an hour, promising 'Mercy from me, as a Christian' in the case of surrender, but otherwise threatening an armed conquest that would 'when too late, make you wish you had accepted of the Favour tendered.'[42] By the time Savage came face to face with Frontenac to deliver this message, he had been led blindfold through the streets of Quebec while being jostled and ridiculed by the conveniently assembled crowds.

The theatricals continued at the fort. An account by the Boston merchant James Lloyd described the removal of Savage's blindfold in 'a

Stately Hall full of brave Martiall men.' Some confusion then arose from the translation of the ultimatum into French. According to one French account, Frontenac was dissuaded with difficulty by the bishop and intendant from having Savage summarily hanged as a pirate and as a traitor to James II. Even so, Savage retained the presence of mind ostentatiously to show Frontenac his watch and demand a reply within the hour. He did not have to wait that long. Denouncing William of Orange as a usurper, the governor characterized Phips as a rebel and as 'a man who did not honour the capitulation he had agreed upon with the governor of Port Royal.' According to the account of Frontenac's secretary Charles de Monseignat, Savage nonetheless pressed for an answer in writing and was rewarded by Frontenac's much-quoted response: 'I have no reply to make to your general except from the mouths of my cannons and by gunshots; that he will learn that this is not the way to call upon a man such as myself; let him do his best on his side, as I will on mine.' With that, Savage was bundled back on board his shallop to make his report.[43]

A council of war followed to develop a plan of attack. It was decided that John Walley, Phips's second-in-command, would land northeast of Quebec, on the opposite side of the St Charles River, with a force of some 1,200 men. A movement of ships up the St Lawrence would then create the impression that another landing was to be made south of Quebec, thus allowing Walley to cross the St Charles (which was fordable at low tide), after which he would signal to Phips. The ships of war were then to land a force of some 200 immediately below the French batteries, and Quebec would be taken by assault from the opposite directions of the lower town and the St Charles. Frontenac's strategy was to harass Walley's force with guerrilla attacks in the swampy country north of the St Charles. His aim was to induce it, when thus weakened, to cross the river at low tide and then, when the rising tide had cut off its retreat, to launch a disciplined and devastating attack by regular troops.[44]

Neither plan was carried fully into practice, because Walley did not succeed in crossing the St Charles. As the result of a series of misunderstandings between the land force and the supporting ships, the heavy guns were landed on the opposite side of the St Charles from Quebec, with no way of moving them across the river and without any boats to assist in the crossing. Also, there is no evidence that the ships ever made the diversionary movement up the St Lawrence. On the morning of 10 October, Walley went on board the *Six Friends* to propose to Phips that the troops (who were not only chilled but were dispirited by a spreading outbreak of smallpox) should be re-embarked with a view to renewing the attack elsewhere. Phips agreed. During the previous two days, without waiting for any signal from Walley, Phips had led his major warships inshore to launch a largely fruitless cannonade of the town. By now little ammunition remained and heavy return fire had damaged the *Six Friends*. A night evacuation in heavy rain on the evening of the twelfth created so much confusion that the troops inadvertently left behind five heavy guns, which were taken by the French the next morning. With these setbacks and with adverse weather preventing a further council of war, all that remained was to make an exchange of prisoners before beginning a straggling descent of the St Lawrence. As Savage concisely recorded, '[We] thought good to make the best of our way back again.'[45]

The retreat turned defeat into disaster. Many of the ships were inadequately provisioned, a reflection of the haste with which the expedition had been mounted. Smallpox continued to spread in the close quarters endured by the troops. To compound these difficulties, continuing storms delayed the passage, and low temperatures contributed to its hazards. Four of the vessels foundered. While Phips was probably accurate enough in his later claim to the Lords of Trade that he had lost only thirty men to enemy fire, the mortality rate now increased rapidly.[46] The Church of England minister Samuel Myles gave a graphic account from Boston on 12 December: 'Some of the vessells are arrived, haveing lost some halfe their men, some more some even all, many are still out there being little hopes of them, some before their Comeing out of Canada not haveing soe much as one man well on board; Great Complaints there are that there was no suitable Care, nor provision for such an Army, men being dead in holes before mist, and some haveing their Eyes and Cheeks Eaten by Ratts before found. Those men who are arrived att Boston and other places, die up and down like rotten sheep.'[47]

Myles, not a neutral observer, may have exaggerated for effect. Nevertheless, the number of deaths on the expedition probably approached four hundred, and that did not include the wounded, those who died subsequently from disease, or the new cases of smallpox that occurred when infected soldiers returned to their communities.[48] Even Bradstreet and the General Court, appealing to the crown for confirmation of charter government and for war supplies, could not disguise what they described as 'the awfull Frown of God upon us in the disappointment of this Enterprize.' Writing to Mather and the other agents in London, Bradstreet emphasized even more heavily New England's need for humility and contrition: 'Shall our ffather spit in our Face,' he asked, 'and we not be ashamed?'[49]

A more controversial question was whether Phips should be ashamed. Samuel Sewall addressed the matter directly in a letter to Increase Mather at the end of December. 'You will hear various Reports of Sir William Phips,' he informed Mather: 'I have discoursed with all sorts, and find that neither Activity nor Courage were wanting in Him; and the form of the Attack was agreed on by the Council of War.'[50] Since Sewall, like Mather, was sympathetic to Phips, his observation can be regarded more as a confirmation that criticisms were being seriously made than as any kind of reliable defence. The comments of some of Phips's critics can be similarly discounted. Myles and the anonymous correspondent of John Usher who referred scathingly to the failure before Quebec and called Phips 'our greatt Mogull' were demonstrably enemies of the Boston regime. So was the author of a letter that reached London describing the expedition's defeat as 'the most shamefull and fatall overthrow, that ever was heard of' and Phips as a 'great author of our new mischief.' James Lloyd, a long-standing business collaborator of John Nelson and a signatory of the petition of January 1690 from 'Boston and adjacent places' could also be seen as a political opponent. Lloyd yielded nothing in sarcasm to the other critics when stating his incredulity at the notion that Quebec's defenders would 'Surrender to mercy, or Conditions in Sir Williams Brest' at the behest of 'a pumpkin ffleet with the Union flag Commanded by a person [who] never did Exploit above Water.'[51]

There was more to Lloyd's letter, however, than his clever reference to Phips's underwater route to fame and fortune. As well as impugning the hasty way in which the expedition had been 'pushed into the Ocean' and criticizing its shaky financial basis on debenture loans and what he regarded as the unseemly eagerness of Walley's men to re-embark, Lloyd encapsulated the main questions that could be raised against Phips. One of them concerned the futile bombardment that Phips had begun on the evening of 8 October: 'Night and day,' commented Lloyd, 'Sir William Pelted the Hills of Quebeck [and] shott away almost all his powder.' A second criticism was that Phips had shared in the panic and confusion of the departure from Quebec to the extent that he had slipped his main anchor and cable. A more general concern, Lloyd implied, was the overall responsibility of the expedition's chief commander for a humiliating and cowardly failure. Another critic, Benjamin Davis, had just recently sold his brick warehouse to Phips, but this did not keep him from explicitly attributing 'soe much Couardize' to the defeat.[52]

Certainly, Phips did lose his sheet anchor and cable before Quebec. So did 'sundry others' of the fleet, although versions differ on whether the cause was the haste of departure or the strength of a driving wind.[53] The bombardment of the town was a more complex matter. It was undoubtedly a departure from the plan agreed at the council of war just two days before. It was also ineffective. As Louis-Armand de Lom d'Arce de Lahontan complacently reported, the walls of Quebec were 'made of an extremely hard stone' that was 'proof against bullets.'[54] Nevertheless, this episode – and the entire conduct of the Canada expedition – must be assessed not only in terms of success or failure, but also in the context of the limited options available to Phips once Frontenac and his troops reached Quebec on 4 October.

Walley's land force stood almost no chance of dislodging from Quebec a defending force that was superior in numbers and consisting of both regular troops and Canadian militia. Frontenac had just strengthened his position by erecting new palisades and redoubts, and the cold and stormy October weather added to the New Englanders' difficulties. The military historian C.P. Stacey has maintained that 'much of the explanation for the [French] victory lies in the inefficiency of the New England force.' – but Stacey's own evidence suggests that the New Englanders never even had the opportunity to prove themselves inefficient.[55] As Steven Eames has recently argued, the historiographical perception of New England militia forces as chronically amateurish and feeble underestimates the coherence of units raised from single or contiguous communities and commanded by officers whose authority stemmed from their community standing.[56] Even during the few uncomfortable days spent north of the St Charles River, Walley's force proved well able to withstand the attacks of the Canadian militia and to inflict casualties that included the leader of the Montreal contingent, Jacques Le Moyne de Sainte-Hélène, who had commanded the French forces during the Schenectady raid of the previous February.[57]

As soon as Walley interviewed a French prisoner on the evening of 8 October, however, the hopelessness of the New Englanders' task became fully evident. Walley recorded that an unconvincing effort had been made to blunt the force of the information received: 'That others might not be discouraged, wee told him [the prisoner] he was sent by the enemy to tell us a parcel of lies, but he said he had told us nothing but what we should find true.'[58] A week earlier, the situation would

have been entirely different. Silvanus Davis described severe food shortages in Quebec and the fear that had prevailed from the time of the first
reports of the New England fleet until Frontenac's arrival on 4 October.
If the ships had arrived sooner, if Frontenac had been forced by the land
attack to remain in Montreal, or even if the weather had permitted a
more prolonged siege, Davis believed that they would 'have been masters of Canada.'[59] Davis exaggerated in assuming that the capture of
Quebec would have implied in itself the fall of Canada, but he accurately identified Frontenac's return as a turning point.

The crucial element in the entire plan had been the substantial participation of the Houdenasaunee. Lacking that, success was unlikely to be
achieved. Indeed, New York's support had been so ineffective that even
a small naval force sent by Leisler in support of Phips's expedition
accomplished nothing more than a futile further pillaging of Port-Royal
(and it promptly lost its booty to three French raiders off the coast of
Long Island).[60] Just over six years later, Sir Henry Ashurst and another
Massachusetts agent attempted to persuade the English Board of Trade
that New York's neglect had been no accident; it was the result, they
said, of the merchants 'being Jealous that if Canada was conquered their
trade in furrs would diminish by the nearnesse of those of New
England, to the lakes where those furrs are cheifly taken.'[61] Their assertion was probably more accurate as a representation of ambitions nurtured by Phips in 1690 and thereafter than as an explanation of the role
of New York. But the immediate result of the failure to attack Montreal,
and of Frontenac's return to Quebec, was to make Phips's desperation in
bombarding the town – like Walley's apparent lapse into confusion and
indecision on 9 and 10 October – understandable if not justifiable in any
strict military terms.[62]

There is also another and more general explanation for the failure of
the expedition. Combined military and naval operations, while frequently attempted by English forces in this period, were notoriously
prone to failure because of uncertain communications between land and
sea and because of the likelihood of disagreements between naval commanders and those of the land forces. Also, expeditions that attempted
to carry troops over long distances were characteristically exposed to
the joint dangers of storms and disease. As Jeremy Black has pointed
out, coastal attacks on France from the 1690s onwards were remarkable
principally because they 'not only revealed the problems of amphibious
operations, but were also of singularly little diplomatic or military benefit.' J.R. Jones has similarly argued that, in general, attempts on major

centres of Spanish America were equally futile, even though isolated tri-
umphs such as that of Morgan in Panama in 1670 could be seen as the
exceptions that proved the rule.[63] Although William Blathwayt was
severely critical in early 1691 of Phips's 'shamefull and cowardly defeat
in Canada,' he subsequently gathered plenty of experience, as secretary
for war, of other damaging failures. That of Sir Francis Wheeler and
John Foulkes in Martinique during the winter of 1693 is a case in point,
while Christopher Codrington's defeat at Guadeloupe a decade later
caused Blathwayt to reflect on whether there was a pattern to the disasters that had overtaken 'all expeditions from that against Hispaniola in
Cromwell's time downwards to this last instance.' Blathwayt thought he
had found the common thread in the Admiralty's creation of problems
between land and naval commanders by insisting on the primacy of
naval strategy. A more persuasive conclusion would have been that for
combined operations against established and distant strongholds, failure was the norm unless the defences – as at Port-Royal in 1690 – were
exceptionally weak or unless the attackers had the strength, health, and
leisure to mount an extended siege.[64] Although the Canada expedition
of 1690 was ill-conceived and had disastrous results, it was no more
shameful either in design or execution than comparable attempts by
regular British forces in the same period. The paradox for Phips was
that, of his two expeditions of 1690, it was the successful one that raised
the most serious questions about the quality of his leadership, and it
was the disaster that could be more convincingly defended.

For Massachusetts, however, there was no offsetting the magnitude of
the setback represented by the defeat at Quebec. 'For the present State of
the Country in Generall I am affraid wee are allmost run on ground,'
warned James Lloyd.[65] As he made clear, the difficulty was not only military. The immediate threat to New England had in fact abated in the
short term. The postponement in the summer of 1690 of the French plan
for an attack on New York had become known to the English colonies in
the early autumn when New York vessels had captured a copy of the letter informing Frontenac and the intendant, Jean Bochart de Champigny,
that no French troops could be spared for the purpose.[66] Late autumn
brought peace overtures from the Kennebec and Androscoggin
Wabanaki, and the New England agents in London were inclined (albeit
that their chief informant was probably Phips himself) to connect the
agreement of a truce on 29 November with the capture of Port-Royal.[67]
In the longer term, however, the military position of New England
remained tenuous. Subsequent negotiations with the Wabanaki broke

down in May 1691. Meanwhile, a series of letters from French authorities to Frontenac, Champigny, and Villebon in April and May took the repulse of Phips as a victory that ought to lead to further French and Native raids on New England and New York, as well as on the Houdenasaunee, and in 1692 the French revived the plan to launch a major attack on the principal English centres.[68]

A separate though related question concerned the financial ability of the New England colonies to wage war, in the aftermath of the failure at Quebec. The New England petitioners of early 1691 – who included Lloyd – estimated that the expedition had cost Massachusetts alone 'further Arreares of at least Fifty Thousand pounds.' Even Cotton Mather, who characteristically sought to put the best possible face on the entire episode, admitted to 'Forty Thousand Pounds, more or less, now to be paid, and not a Penny in the Treasury to pay it withal.'[69] Already, two weeks before Phips's return to Boston on 19 November, the Massachusetts General Court had ordered the raising of twenty country rates, adding to what had already been a heavy burden of seventeen rates since the fall of Andros.[70] The next day, 6 November, Phips's colleagues on the council formed an unusually large ten-member committee, composed of magistrates and merchants, 'to use their Endeavours to procure the Sum of three or ffour thousand pounds in Money [i.e., cash] upon Loan for the Present Paying off the Seamen, and Soldiers at their return from Canada, and for other Emergencies upon the Publick Credit.' The lenders were to be secured not only by the proceeds of the twenty country rates but also by 'the Countries part of all such Plunder as they shall recover from the Enemy at Canada etc.'[71] Shortly afterwards, the colony's treasury was overwhelmed by the demands of those returning from Canada – and of the dependents of those who did not return – and by the need to meet them without any offsetting gains from plunder.

The decision to resort to paper currency was made on 10 December. 'Printed Bills' in denominations ranging from five shillings to five pounds, to a total not exceeding seven thousand pounds, were to be issued by a committee of the General Court created for the purpose. Although the order did not say so, the prime recipients were to be the soldiers, sailors, and other provincial creditors of the Canada expedition. In a broad sense, this development can be seen as the beginning of a process in Massachusetts that was equivalent on a smaller scale to the expansion of public credit in England, which was also influenced in its early stages by the enormous cost of warfare in the 1690s and which has

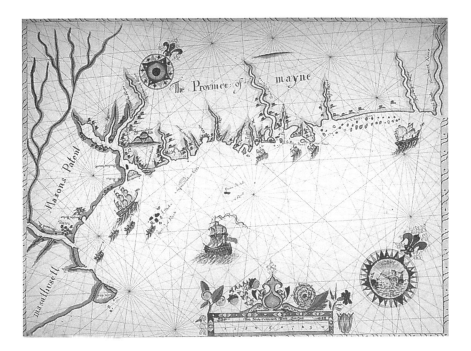

Map of the Province of Mayne, ca 1653. Courtesy of the Baxter Rare Maps Collection, Maine State Archives. Original in the British Museum

Sir William Phips, oil on canvas, attributed to Thomas Child, Boston, ca 1687–94.
Photograph by Nicholas Dean, courtesy of the Gardiner family

Coat of arms of Robert Phips of Nottingham, used by his descendants Sir
William Phips and Sir Constantine Phips

William Phips

Signature of William Phips, 3 August 1685. Great Britain, Public Record Office
(PRO), CO1/58, no. 24. Courtesy of PRO

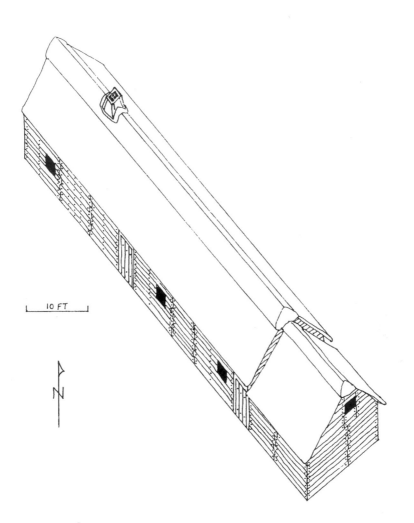

10 FT

N

Conjectural reconstruction of Structure 1 on Phips site (ME 495-14), Woolwich, Maine, by Robert L. Bradley. Courtesy of Old Fort Western, Augusta, Maine

Christopher Monck, Duke of Albemarle. Courtesy of the British Museum. A portrait of this early patron of William Phips hung in Phips's Boston house.

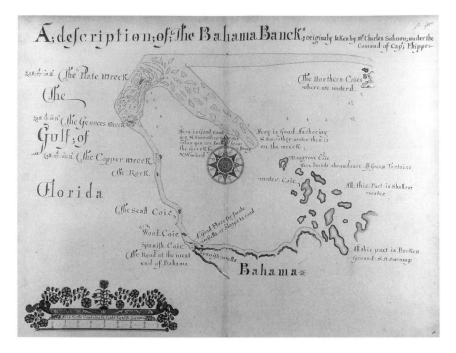

Chart of the Bahama Banks, by Charles Salmon. British Library, Sloane 45 ff. 71v–72. By permission of the British Library

Medal commemorating Phips's expedition to the Ambrosia Bank. Courtesy of Maine State Museum, Augusta, Maine

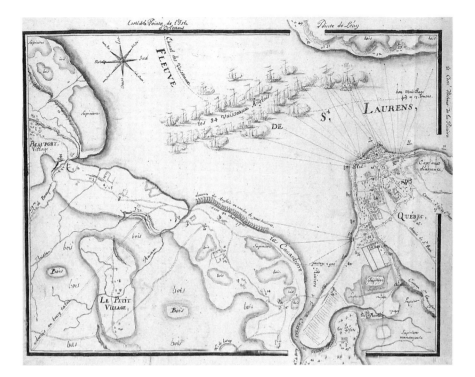

Map of the 1690 siege of Quebec. With permission of the Harvard Map
Collection

Diver excavating musket from a ship of the Phips expedition that was wrecked on its return from Quebec in 1690. The wreck is at L'Anse aux Bouleaux. Photograph by Peter Waddell, courtesy of Parks Canada

Increase Mather, by Jan Van der Spriet, 1688. Courtesy of Massachusetts
Historical Society

Sir Constantine Phips. Courtesy of the British Museum

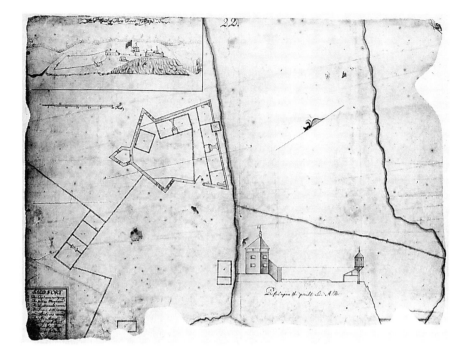

Wolfgang Romer, *The Prospect of Saco Fort*, 1699. PRO, CO700/North American Colonies, Maine/2. Photograph courtesy of Maine Historic Preservation Commission

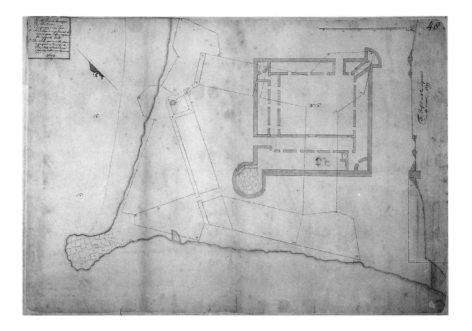

Wolfgang Romer, *The Old Fort of Pemaquid*, 1699. PRO, CO700/North American Colonies, Maine/4. Photograph courtesy of Maine Historic Preservation Commission

Wabanaki from a French mission on the St Lawrence River. Courtesy of the Bibliothèque municipale de la ville de Montréal, Collection Gagnon

The North End of Boston and the Phips mansion, in a detail from William Burgis, *A South East View of the Great Town of Boston in New England in America*, 1725. The Phips mansion is labelled no. 41. Courtesy of American Antiquarian Society

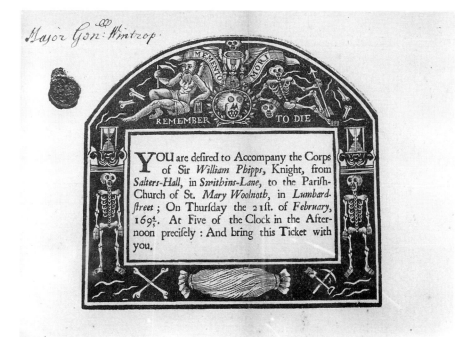

Invitation to attend the funeral of Sir William Phips, 1695. Courtesy of Massachusetts Historical Society

Josiah Eliot

C

Pietas in Patriam:

THE

LIFE

OF HIS

EXCELLENCY

Sir *William* PHIPS, Knt.

Late Captain General, and Governour
in Chief of the Province of the *Maſſachu-
ſet*-Bay,

𝔑𝔢𝔴𝔈𝔫𝔤𝔩𝔞𝔫𝔡.

Containing the Memorable *Changes* Undergone, and *Actions* Performed by Him.

By Cotton Mather

Written by one intimately acquainted with Him.

Diſcite Virtutem ex Hoc, verumque Laborem.

LONDON:

Printed by *Sam.* Bridge in *Auſtin-Friers*, for *Nath.*
Hiller at the *Princes-Arms* in *Leaden-Hall Street*,
over againſt St. *Mary-Ax*, 1697.

Title page of Cotton Mather, *Pietas in Patriam*, 1697. This was the first biography
of Sir William Phips. Courtesy of Massachusetts Historical Society

been defined by P.G.M. Dickson as the Financial Revolution. By 1712, towards the end of the wars that led up to the Treaty of Utrecht in 1713, the amount of provincial currency had risen from the initial £7,000 to some £170,000.[72] As in England, the process was controversial. In Massachusetts, the major criticism at first was that the bills represented a hasty and ultimately fraudulent expedient to disguise from the hard-pressed veterans the reality that there was no money to pay them. 'We have found a way,' wrote one critic, 'to stop the mouths and aswage the passion of the soldiers and seamen by a new mint raised here of paper money, the other good kindes being almost quite exhausted our treasury being quite empty, there are not many that take it and they that have it scarce know what to do with it.'[73]

In due course, the deeper implications of expanded public debt came to the fore, with criticism focusing on the political and patronage powers that would inevitably be wielded by major public creditors. For the time being, defenders of the scheme, such as Cotton Mather, were content to insist that it had done 'no less than save the Publick from a perfect Ruin.' Mather also had praise for the wealthy New Englanders who had supported the currency issue by buying bills in large amounts. 'Of these,' he stated, 'I think I may say, that General *Phips* was in some sort the *Leader*.' Yet Mather could not deny the quick depreciation of the bills, which he attributed to the continuing uncertainty over whether or not the old charter would be permanently restored. While there was a shortage of specie, however, there was no shortage of cynics who were willing to argue the opposite case – that it was the regime's reckless mismanagement that had both necessitated the issuing of bills and undermined any confidence that the paper currency might otherwise have commanded.[74] Along with compromising the ability of the magistrates to rule effectively, there was a legacy to any future regime that might replace them. Necessary and healthy as the generation of funds through public credit might prove to be in the longer term, it had begun in a form inseparably associated with an empty treasury, unstable finances, and a state structure that had relinquished through its virtual bankruptcy a large proportion of its capacity for effective patronage.

No other source confirms Mather's assertion of Phips's patriotically inspired purchase of public bills, though the diminished estate he left at his death may suggest such activity. In any event, both publicly and privately in late 1690, Phips faced criticisms that thwarted any attempt he might make to be seen as a public benefactor. Debate over his role in the expeditions continued well into 1691. Ultimately, John Walley bore the brunt of the blame for the failure at Quebec; he held public office in a variety of subsequent capacities, but never a military position equivalent to that he had held in 1690. Still, the close observer Thomas Savage defended Walley with the observation that 'there are some who to make themselves faultless, lay the fault upon him;' he was silent on Phips, other than describing the bombardment of Quebec as 'contrary to orders.'[75] Other critics bracketed their comments on Phips with blame for the two Mathers as instigators of the insolent disregard for royal authority that had produced both the drive towards old charter government and the issuing of commissions for the expeditions in the monarchs' names – 'the Kings honour that so presumptuously we have been shareing,' as one put it.[76] The fact that the leading opponents of the Boston regime were making an issue of the Canada failure proved to be a source of potential political strength for Phips, for it obliged the regime and its supporters to vindicate both the attempt and Phips's role in it. Secure by April 1691 in his re-election to the council with a respectable 805 votes, and sure of the active support of both Mathers, Phips had a comfortable basis from which to respond to any questions regarding Canada that might be forthcoming from the Lords of Trade.[77]

Port-Royal, however, might yet prove more difficult to explain. Frontenac was not the only observer to infer from reports of the events that Phips had acted treacherously. While the Canada expedition had been under way, John Nelson had extended personal hospitality to Meneval and had taken up the governor's cause. Shortly after Phips returned from Canada, Meneval asked for and received a hearing before the council, focusing both on the general question of the terms of capitulation of Port-Royal and on Phips's retention of his money and personal effects. 'Very fierie words between Sir William and Mr. Nelson' were noted by Sewall, who then described Phips's angry departure: 'When Sir William went out seemed to say would never come there more, had been so abus'd by said Nelson, and if Council would not right him, he would right himself.' From Meneval's point of view, the council hearing was productive in that it gave him encouragement to press his cause in London, and a few days later he obtained written permission from Bradstreet to embark.[78] Phips's response was to attempt to make good on his threat of bypassing the council. According to Meneval, Phips intervened to prevent several possible passages to England and then orchestrated a crowd action to remove Meneval physically from a vessel on which he had embarked and paid his passage. Meneval's accusation that Phips then 'brought him to Boston where, on his own authority and without the knowledge of the governor and council, he had him thrown in jail' is documented by the arrest warrant, which was signed – on no conceivable legitimate authority – by Phips on 25 December.[79]

Phips's action was transparently illegal, even though it was supported by Cotton Mather and perhaps also by the minister Joshua Moody. Samuel Sewall and the provincial secretary Isaac Addington attended a meeting with Mather and Moody at Phips's house on 29 December at which 'very sharp discourse' took place on the subject of the countermeasures taken by Meneval, which apparently included a writ obtained against Phips. As Sewall recorded, 'Mr. Mather very angrily said that they who did such things as suffering Sir William to be arrested by Meneval, were Frenchmen, or the people would say they were, &c.' The following day the council annulled the writ.[80] Thus far, the affair is revealing chiefly in its illustration of Phips's ability at this stage to manipulate the council in his own interest. Meneval was no doubt correct in describing Phips's fear that, in London, Meneval would 'make known his dishonesty and his dishonouring of his word.' The council itself can hardly have been anxious for this to happen, though it also had to consider the pressures from John Nelson and other similarly disaffected Bostonians. What made the difference, according to Meneval, was Phips's hold on *la canaille* – the mob. As Mather had hinted at the meeting on 29 December, popular anti-Catholic and anti-French sentiment was too potent a force for any leadership to be able to count on directing it. Phips, however, had demonstrated as recently as the Turell-White affair nine months earlier his ability to mobilize a crowd in support of direct action. It was this capacity, to the chagrin of Meneval and Nelson, that enabled him to act as he did with impunity in late December 1690.[81]

Nevertheless, Phips was not in as strong a position as he seemed to be. For one thing, the council's action on 30 December was not unreservedly in Phips's favour. It also led to Meneval's quiet release and included an order that Phips should return Meneval's chest and clothes. On 7 January, Bradstreet wrote in mildly insistent terms to remind Phips that he had yet to comply, and Meneval later recalled that at least some of his cash and clothes were then restored. Meneval also believed that if Phips had not given way at this point, 'there would have been a danger of sedition in the town, where the mob is the strongest.'[82] Whether or not he was exaggerating is unclear from the surviving evidence, but Phips's partial retreat is well established. It may have arisen from the same reluctance that had prevented him from crossing the line into piracy in 1684, and his ultimate preference for a chance of respectability. It may also have owed something to the intervention of Sewall and Addington, who had visited Cotton Mather on 7 January 'and expostulated with him about the discourse at Sir William's'[83]

A further significant influence was the fact that at this time Phips was under personal pressure from a different direction. On 22 December a warrant had been issued by the town of Boston to 'attach the Goods and for want thereof the body of Sir William Phips alias William Phips late Commander of the Frigott called the Golden Rose.' At issue in this and another warrant of the same date were the complaints of Robert Bronson, who was demanding the settlement of claims arising from his dealings with Phips in late 1683. Whether the timing of this suit was coincidental – warrants and summonses were served on Phips on 24 December – or whether it was arranged by supporters of Meneval is unclear. Nevertheless, as January 1691 went on, the case was being actively investigated, with depositions taken from the available participants in the treasure-hunting activities of 1684. Bronson won his case on three separate claims in county court on 27 January 1691, although the verdicts were later reversed on appeal to the Court of Assistants.[84]

Thus entangled, Phips abruptly abandoned New England for London. A letter written in Boston on 31 December 1690 had him embarking 'by this conveiance.' Although he was clearly still in Boston to receive Bradstreet's letter of 7 January, he must have left soon afterwards.[85] Cotton Mather attributed his departure, 'in the very depth of Winter, *when Sailing was now dangerous* ... in a very little Vessel,' to Phips's urgent desire to gain English support for a further attempt on Canada. 'All this while,' Mather maintained, 'CANADA was as much written upon Sir *William's* Heart, as CALLICE, they said once, was upon Queen *Mary's*.'[86] While it is true that Phips retained his interest in attacking Canada, the more urgent reality was that it had become prudent for him to leave Boston before further developments could take place on the matter of Bronson's claims. He also wanted to arrive in London before Meneval. This he accomplished, landing at Bristol in time to reach London on 4 March. In the event, Meneval sailed directly for France, arriving in April.[87]

If a report circulating in Boston is to be believed, Increase Mather had laid the groundwork for Phips to receive a friendly reception in England: 'Sir William is gon for England,' read a letter received in London by John Usher, 'of whome M. writes he may have whatt he will demand of King or Queen both for himselfe or the Country.'[88] If such a thing had ever been true, it was before the reports of the Canada failure and Meneval's complaints had crossed the Atlantic. For all of Phips's new-found church membership and military rank, he remained an outsider to those in Boston who saw in him a self-serving upstart and a rabble-rouser to boot. The ambivalence of the council on the release of Meneval suggests that even politically motivated defenders of Phips's military record might find him personally distasteful. In London, there was still the possibility that by portraying the Port-Royal expedition as a triumph, however it had been achieved, and by presenting the Canada expedition as an excusable failure and a laudable attempt, Phips's reputation could be salvaged or even enhanced. But for this to happen, the intervention of Increase Mather would be pressingly required.

6

The Charter and Beyond

The negotiations that led to the issuing of the Massachusetts charter of 1691, and the role played by Increase Mather, have been analysed frequently by historians. The role of Sir William Phips has been examined largely in the context of Phips's emergence as the first governor under the new charter, with as much attention being paid to his failings while in office as to the reasons for his appointment. 'How unsuited he was for the governorship was still to be discovered,' commented Michael G. Hall in 1988. 'For the moment he seemed a fine choice to take the sting out of the fact that Massachusetts could no longer elect its governors.'[1] While this is a defensible perspective on Phips's undoubted lack of political preparation, the months between his arrival in London in March 1691 and his departure for Boston in April 1692 were not dominated exclusively either by the charter or by the disposition of the governorship. As well as defending his conduct on the two expeditions of 1690, he was actively seeking command of a new assault on Canada as well as trying to obtain the refortification of Pemaquid and a personal share in the exploitation of natural resources on the coast of northern New England. These matters would later rank high among his preoccupations as governor, frequently overshadowing the political issues that were current in Boston and the other towns of southern New England. The appointment of Phips as governor was undoubtedly convenient for those, like the Mathers, who sought a middle position between the advocates of the old charter and those who harked back to the days of the dominion, but the irony was that Phips's attention would rarely if ever be focused on Massachusetts itself to an extent unaffected by his interests farther north and east. This division of attention was already evident during his sojourn in London in 1691 and early 1692.

After landing at Bristol, Phips made his way to London, arriving on Wednesday, 4 March 1691. Not surprisingly, he wasted no time in making contact with Increase Mather. Mather recorded in his diary that the two of them passed the afternoon and evening together. They spent the following morning in discussions at the house of Sir Henry Ashurst, and they dined together at Ashurst's at midday on the Friday after Mather had met that morning with Queen Mary's secretary, Abel Tessin d'Alonne. The interview with d'Alonne appears to have been no idle courtesy call, for on the Saturday afternoon – after Phips and Mather had spent the morning at Whitehall – d'Alonne introduced Phips 'to Kiss the Queens hand.'[2] This occasion, while no doubt brief and formal, served a purpose that was more than symbolic. Mary had proved willing in the past to exert her personal influence in favour of the interests of New England as defined by Mather, and her influence was now substantial. William III had left London in January for the Netherlands in preparation for continental military campaigning as soon as the season allowed, just as he had been absent for the entire summer of 1690. During the early days of Phips's visit to London, William was at his Netherlands country estate at Het Loo, pondering a Spanish request to attempt to raise the French siege of Mons.[3] At a time when an attack on Phips's conduct in the 1690 expeditions was likely to become the leading edge of the arguments of Mather's political opponents, it was a potentially worthwhile investment to have Phips presented to the queen as a person distinguished by loyalty and by military prowess.

During the summer of 1690 the queen had formed an increasingly close association with the earl of Nottingham. As senior secretary of state from December 1690, Nottingham had direct responsibilities for colonial and naval matters.[4] By the spring of 1691, he had emerged as a leading member of the cabinet council named to advise the queen in William's absence. The eclipse of the most committed Whigs was made all the more evident by the exclusion from the cabinet council of the earl of Monmouth, formerly Lord Mordaunt. In the most obvious sense, this political evolution was unhelpful for Mather and the other New England agents. Between February and April 1689, when the Lords of Trade had been debating the fate of the dominion, Mordaunt had been among those arguing for the recall of Andros, whereas Nottingham, the Tory, had favoured retention of Andros and of the structures binding New England tightly to the crown.

Two years later, matters were no longer so simple, for Nottingham faced serious political constraints. Within a ministry that included moderate Whigs as well as Tories, he had to coexist with colleagues who might find cause to resent the new-found ascendancy of those such as himself who had been, at best, late converts to the revolutionary cause. On the other side of the political spectrum, Nottingham had to contend with an increasingly fragile relationship with such a prominent Tory as the marquis of Carmarthen, formerly chief minister to Charles II and now lord president of the council. Thus, while Nottingham enjoyed the confidence of the monarchs, his base of political support was less secure than it seemed at first sight. He was especially vulnerable on matters connected with the naval conduct of the war. Both Nottingham and William Blathwayt, secretary for war as well as for plantations, had increasing cause for concern as 1691 failed to yield demonstrable achievements on land or at sea.[5] The junior secretary, meanwhile, was Henry Sydney. A Whig who enjoyed ready access to the court, Sydney had been successfully cultivated by Mather at least since early 1689. The fluid state of political affairs implied for Mather that, in facing old opponents, he had manoeuvring space that came not only from his own contacts with the monarchs but also from the delicate balances that high officeholders had no option but to attempt to maintain.[6]

On the other hand, Mather was working now with only intermittent collaboration from two of the four Massachusetts agents. Elisha Cooke favoured adhering to the original instructions that had enjoined the agents to press for restoration of the old charter and for further autonomy through liberty of coinage and 'such Privileges as may be of further benefit to this Colony.'[7] Mather and Ashurst, however, had begun to urge that the main effort be put into obtaining a new charter, salvaging as much as possible of the colony's earlier status. Thomas Oakes had initially appeared sympathetic to their arguments, but by early November 1690 the New England merchant Charles Lidget was reporting from London that 'Cooke and Oakes run hard for the old Charter Mather and Ashurst for a new.'[8] For a time, Mather had reason to believe that his and Ashurst's efforts might prevail, as a personal interview with William III prompted the king to refer the matter to the crown's four chief legal officers. Their draft for a new charter closely resembled the old one, but the obstacle to its implementation was the necessity for it to pass through the Lords of Trade. There it still rested, under the scrutiny of Blathwayt since early January 1691, when Phips reached London two months later.[9]

Phips's arrival presented Blathwayt with an opportunity that he seized with characteristic zest. Only two days after Phips reached London, Blathwayt had sent a copy of a French newsletter to Nottingham, who was in the Netherlands with the king. It was almost certainly the *Paris Gazette* of 26 January/5 February 1691, which had reported approvingly on Frontenac's defence of Quebec and estimated the losses of the defeated Phips at more than five hundred men.[10] For Nottingham's benefit, and presumably that of the king too, Blathwayt commented acerbically on Phips's 'shamefull and Cowardly defeat in Canada' and deftly associated this costly setback for 'the Kings credit and dominions' with the charter question. 'Under what Commission and by whose allowance,' Blathwayt wondered, 'did they presumptuously undertake this unfortunate expedition and who made this Poor Knight a Generall the same year He was publickly christ'ned at Boston?' French retaliation in the coming summer, he predicted, would do damage not just to New England but to other colonies as well. 'I foresee,' Blathwayt concluded, 'greater and irreparable mischiefs if not prevented by a higher hand for how can it be otherwise while a mean and mechanicall sort of People shall pretend to and abuse the Highest Acts of Royall Government under the colour of an imaginary Charter they have justly forfeited and which would be the most speedy means of their utter ruine if restored to them.'[11]

Nottingham's reply was inconclusive. The king, he reported, was 'troubled att the disappointment of the attempt by Sir William Phips' and expected the New England question to be 'duely considered in England.'[12] Some weeks later, on 1 April, the king left the Hague for a sojourn in England of less than a month. During that time, the separate matters of Phips's conduct at Quebec and Port-Royal were brought to a head before, respectively, the Lords of Trade and the cabinet council. The final three weeks of March were spent by Phips – guided at every step by Mather and Ashurst – in a sustained effort to gain the necessary support. Mather accompanied Phips to Whitehall on at least two mornings, and on two afternoons he 'drew up passages for Sir William' and 'wrote de Canada etc.' On the morning of 11 March, Mather and Phips visited Henry Sydney at his house, and they returned there with Ashurst on the twenty-fifth. On the twenty-first, the two visited the earl of Monmouth. The morning of the twenty-sixth they spent with Carmarthen. Phips met privately with Mather and Ashurst on frequent occasions. Meanwhile, Mather maintained infrequent contact with Cooke and Oakes and regularly visited Whitehall. On the thirtieth he met with Blathwayt in the morning and spent the afternoon in conversation with Phips. By the end of the month, Phips's role had apparently come to an end for the time being. After he and Mather had spent the morning of 31 March at Ashurst's, working together on the pamphlet that was shortly to appear under the title *Reasons for the Confirmation of the Charter Belonging to the Massachusetts Colony in New-England*, no further meetings involving Phips were noted in Mather's diary until 11 April. They dined together six days later, after which Phips disappears from the diary until late May.[13]

Mather's diary entries give no indication of the specific matters discussed at the meetings held in March. Many of his own discussions at Whitehall and elsewhere were no doubt concerned with the more general question of the charter rather than with Phips and the expeditions. Nevertheless, the importance that Phips had assumed for the time being is attested to by the obvious effort made to bring him face to face with leading Whigs, as well as with Carmarthen – who was to preside over the hearings that the Lords of Trade were to hold in April. The general lines of the approach were clear in the pamphlet being drafted on 31 March. 'His Majesties Subjects in New-England,' it reminded readers, 'have lately reduced the *French* in *Acady* unto Obedience to the Crown of England: If the like should be done in *Canada*, that would be worth Millions to the *English* Crown and Nation: not only in respect of the Bever-Trade, but in that the Fishery of those parts and of *New-found-land* also, would be entirely in the hands of the *English*.' Avoiding any direct mention of the Quebec failure, the pamphlet looked forward to the way in which the restoration of Massachusetts charter privileges would 'encourage them a second time to attempt the reducing of *Canada*' with naval support from England and good prospects of success.[14] Phips's account of the Quebec expedition – which he was instructed to prepare by order in council of 9 April but on which Mather had clearly been working in March – focused more sharply on the success at Port-Royal and the losses inflicted on the French even at Quebec, but it too hinted at the possibility of a future expedition, alluding to messages Phips claimed to have received at Quebec 'from French merchants of the best Note and Reputation, to let me know how uneasie they were under the ffrench Administration. And to assure me of their great willingness to Submit to Their Majesties Government.'[15]

By the time Phips presented his statement to the Lords of Trade on 21 April, further developments had taken place. On the ninth, Mather had had a lengthy private interview with the queen, repeatedly urging her to use her influence in favour of New England's charter privileges and also telling her, 'Sir William Phips has with many subjects in N.E.

endeavored to inlarge your Majesty's dominions, and they are ready again to Expose themselves in your Majesty's Service.'[16] Later the same day the Privy Council received at Whitehall a petition transmitted to it by Sir Purbeck Temple, uncle of John Nelson. According to Cooke (who continued to be active in matters that could be interpreted as involving defence of the old charter, as opposed to his disapproval of the pursuit of a new one), it was 'from the disappointment at Quebeck' that 'our Adversaries ... tooke courage to show themselves as they are.'[17] The petition's sixty-one signatures included those of Nelson, Charles Lidget, James Lloyd, Francis Foxcroft, and others who had signed one or more of the petitions against the Boston regime of early 1690, as well as new signatories such as Nathaniel Byfield. The petition renewed the earlier complaints of military incompetence, internal strife within New England, and absence of sound government, and used the 1690 expeditions as prime examples of the consequences. The Port-Royal venture, argued the petitioners, had caused 'Little annoyance ... to the Enemy,' while the Quebec expedition had led only to military defeat, loss of life, and financial disaster. The Privy Council referred the petition to the Lords of Trade, with the requirement that the agents be ready to respond – and Phips to give an account of the Quebec expedition – by 16 April.[18]

At this point the attack on the expeditions rapidly began to lose ground. The 16 April meeting of the Lords of Trade was postponed because Carmarthen was ill. Two days later, Mather personally presented to the king a counter-petition bearing seventy-seven signatures of English merchants trading to New England. On the twenty-first the agents presented their own response to the Lords of Trade, blaming Andros and the dominion for New England's military reverses and portraying the Port-Royal expedition as a significant victory and the attack on Canada as a discouragement to French designs on Albany. Phips also delivered his account of the Quebec expedition. The most influential appearance, however, was that of Sir Thomas Lane, brother-in-law of Sir Henry Ashurst and a signatory of the merchants' petition. As Cooke put it when reporting to Bradstreet, 'Sir Thos Lane and Several of the Merchants went up with us and appeared and spoke at the Board in the behalfe of New England. Their Answer and what was further sayd thereupon did very much damp Mr Lidgett etc. that were forward to appear against us.'[19] It is unlikely that Cooke was exaggerating. The merchants' petition submitted on 18 April was a *tour de force* by Ashurst and Mather. It represented a formidable show of strength by a number of London's foremost Whig and Dissenting merchants.

Sir Thomas Lane was in the first rank of Virginia tobacco traders; he was soon to be one of the West Jersey proprietors and was elected lord mayor of London in 1695. Among the other signatories, Sir William Ashurst (like his brother, Sir Henry) was a leading trader in Turkey and the eastern Mediterranean; he became lord mayor in 1693 and was governor of the New England Company for twenty-five years, beginning in 1695. Sir Humphrey Edwin, another prominent member of the tightly knit circle of Levant merchants, became lord mayor in 1697 and served as a director of the East India Company from 1698. Gilbert Heathcote's trading interests were concentrated in the West Indies and the Baltic but extended to the Mediterranean and North America; later a director of the East India Company and governor of the Bank of England, he was reputed to be the wealthiest London merchant of the day by the time he was elected lord mayor in 1710. In 1691 Lane, Edwin, and Sir William Ashurst were aldermen of the City; Heathcote, a member of common council, was a future alderman and member of Parliament. Sir William Ashurst had been a London MP until his defeat in the general election of 1690 (Sir Henry was more successful) but resumed his parliamentary career in 1695. While these prominent Whigs were the most conspicuous names in terms of the combination of mercantile wealth and political office, there were other signatories who were also substantial merchants trading to the Americas. These included a number of West Indies sugar merchants, such as Richard Merriweather and Stephen Mason, as well as major import traders elsewhere. The New England traders included Robert Thompson, who was governor of the New England Company from 1692 to 1695.[20]

The effect of the intervention before the Lords of Trade of these members of London's commercial elite could not fail to be substantial. Of the five members of the board who attended, the Whigs Henry Sydney and Henry Powle – a trusted supporter of Mather and now master of the rolls – were no doubt the ones who listened most sympathetically to what Lane had to say. The Tories Carmarthen, Nottingham, and Henry Compton (bishop of London) had no choice but to listen too, given the mixed character of the current ministry and the growing importance of merchant capital for a war effort that had more than doubled public expenditure since the revolution and increasingly had to be financed on a basis of public debt.[21] Nottingham's recent relations with the City, in fact, had been so strained that one reason for the appearance of so many prestigious Whig signatures on the petition may have been that it was part of their ongoing response to his efforts to intervene on behalf of

Tory candidates in two City electoral disputes in 1690. More generally, the period from late 1689 to the summer of 1690 had seen party conflicts in London in which Whig interests in the City – marshalled by the earl of Monmouth and prominently including Sir Humphrey Edwin – had used financial tactics that included not only responding slowly to requests for public loans but at other times demonstrating financial potency by making unexpected advances to the crown. While the Whigs had lost ground politically in the interim, their point had been made convincingly in fiscal terms, and this contributed to the weight carried by the petition of April 1691. Overall, the episode was a striking demonstration of the effectiveness of the network that was at the disposal, when necessary, of Mather and Ashurst.[22]

In one sense, therefore, the content of the merchants' petition was less significant than the identity of its leading signatories. Nevertheless, the text was revealing in its own way. Briefly but pointedly, it referred to the difficulties caused in New England by the withdrawal of charter rights and to the willingness of New Englanders to 'enlarge your Majesties Dominions' by taking Canada from the French. It then called for the restoration of charters and for naval support in an assault on Canada. Thus, without ever referring to the Quebec expedition of 1690, the merchants gave it their tacit sanctification as a first attempt towards a still worthy goal.[23] Although the collective response of the Lords of Trade was noncommittal, the events of the ensuing days showed that the force had gone out of the effort to associate the charter question unfavourably with the expeditions of 1690. On Blathwayt's recommendation, seven further witnesses to the state of New England were called to appear at a meeting on 27 April, the list being headed by Lidget and John Usher. According to Cooke, formal notice of the meeting was not given either to the New England agents or to certain members of the committee. However, Phips and others received word in time to attend and hear an impatient Carmarthen rebuke the new witnesses for their lack of substantive testimony.[24]

The meeting of 27 April brought an effective end to the political questions arising from the Canada expedition. In a private meeting with William III the following day, Mather abandoned the caution with which he and the others had been treating the matter by asserting outright to the king that the expedition had been 'a great and a noble undertaking.' New Englanders, he added, were 'ready to do the like again, if encouraged by your Majesty.'[25] Still to be dealt with were the complaints of Meneval regarding Phips's conduct at Port-Royal, but this proved to be

an easier and quicker matter to resolve. Arriving in France in early April
(N.S.) – late March (O.S.) – Meneval had wasted no time in setting forth
his claims of mistreatment to Louis Phélypeaux, comte de Pontchartrain, the minister of marine.[26] The detailed nature of the allegations lent
them credence, and Meneval had every incentive to present them feel-
ingly as a way of diverting attention from his defeat of the previous
year. Transmitted to England, they came before the cabinet council on
30 April. The conclusion was recorded in Nottingham's handwritten
minutes: 'Sir William Phips to be spoke with about his usage of the Governor of Port-Royal.'[27] A reprimand of sorts, it was mild enough – especially in view of the cruelty and dishonesty alleged – to close off the
issue as far as the English were concerned.

The French point of view was rather different. For Frontenac, for
instance, the Port-Royal affair and the fate of the imprisoned garrison
remained a prime example of 'the bad faith of the English.'[28] But that
was hardly Phips's concern. For him, the events of April 1691 were
important in at least two respects. First of all, successful defence of the
expeditions in England had been a personal and political necessity. Secondly, the marshalling by Mather and Ashurst of powerful Whig interests in the City of London had added a new dimension of support. It
was true that this could be seen to be more a reflection of larger political
conflicts – and possibly, too, a genuine expression of faith in the commercial benefits to be expected from a conquest of Canada – rather than
representing specific personal support for Phips. Nevertheless, it was
evidence that Phips had once again successfully integrated his own
interests with those of a network of individuals who were wealthier and
more influential than himself.

The implications for the charter question were more limited.
Exchanges between the Lords of Trade and the Massachusetts agents led
to discussion by the Privy Council on 30 April. Mather's impression was
that William III had spoken out for charter government, though with a
royal governor: 'The King ... said That he would have the *Agents* of *New-
England* Nominate a Person [as governor] that should be agreeable to the
Temper and Inclinations of the People there; only that, at this time, it
was necessary that a Military Man should be set over them; and that this
notwithstanding, he should have Charter-Priviledges Restored and
Confirmed to them.'[29] When the minute and order in council based on
this meeting appeared, however, the inclusion of the words 'as in Barbados and other Plantations' gave a very different gloss to William's
remarks. Mather recruited a number of privy councillors to attest to the

discrepancy and referred it through Sydney to the king, who was again in the Netherlands. The terms of the document, however, were never disavowed.[30] The charter question, though now free of the complications that had arisen from the brief but serious effort of Blathwayt and others to link it with the fate of the expeditions, could not readily be resolved even in the context of what were, for Mather and for Phips, the heady final days of April 1691. A much longer process of proposal and counterproposal, with the interplay of political pressures, would be required before matters began to be clarified towards the end of the summer. The central points at issue, with Blathwayt closely involved as 'an old Adversary,' concerned the powers to be exercised by the royal governor.[31]

The tide was flowing strongly in favour of a charter that would provide for a powerful royal governor, election of assembly representatives by the freeholders rather than the freemen, and in general a form of government harmonized with those that existed in other royal colonies. In part, this reflected the increasing political ascendancy of Nottingham and Carmarthen and, as Richard Johnson has pointed out, the declining attendance of the Whig members at meetings of the Lords of Trade. Yet there was probably also a strong element of truth in Nottingham's claim to the king in late July that there was 'no dispute in this matter between Partys.' The autonomy from royal influence that had characterized the old charter could be seen even by Whigs as anomalous and archaic, and arguments over such questions as the process for the appointment of judges and sheriffs were certainly not the stuff of which merchant petitions were made.[32] On some contentious issues the Lords of Trade gave ground. The committee agreed to the choosing of councillors by the assembly and to the provision of a three-year time limit on the royal power to disallow Massachusetts laws. On other points there was no concession: the choice of judges, sheriffs, and other such officers by the governor and council (the agents insisted that they should be chosen by the assembly), and the power of the governor to have a negative voice in the election of councillors by the assembly (the agents insisted that this power should reside with the assembly alone). The full Privy Council, with the queen present, instructed Nottingham on 30 July to forward the documentation to the king for a decision.[33] In doing so, Nottingham wasted neither time nor words in informing the king that the committee had 'made all the Condescensions to that people which could possibly consist with your Sovereignty over them.' On 10 August, Sydney replied from the Netherlands that the king had signified his approval of the committee's position and his refusal to 'admitt the Objections of the Agents of the said Collony.'[34]

It is at this point that it can be suggested with conviction that, for the first time, Phips began to exercise an independent role. To judge by Mather's diary, his participation in the charter debates had been limited. On 25 May he had visited Whitehall with Mather, but they had then had no further recorded meetings until they dined together with Ashurst on 10 July and again on the twenty-third. Phips and Mather spent the afternoon of the thirty-first in conversation with the other agents and the Scottish projector William Paterson.[35] Six days later, Phips, Mather, and Ashurst dined with Blathwayt and spent the afternoon in discussion with him. Mather did not record any details of this meeting except the unsurprising information that the talk was 'about N.E.' Mather had not been well, and two days later (after another afternoon meeting with Phips on 7 August) he departed to take the waters at Barnet, north of London. On 11 August he moved to nearby Totteridge to stay with an acquaintance. There, some eight miles from London, Phips found him on the twelfth. 'Upon his [Phips's] desire,' Mather recorded, 'I returned with him to London to solicit N.E. affaire.' Mather and Phips spent the morning of the thirteenth with Ashurst, following which Mather and Ashurst successively visited Nottingham and d'Alonne. Mather's diary for the fourteenth noted that he 'wrote heads for [the] charter,' in the morning. He then returned to Totteridge, where he stayed for a further twelve days.[36]

The events of 10–14 August are mysterious for a number of reasons. First of all, they were fudged by Mather in later published accounts. Both in his *Brief Account*, published later in 1691, and in a reply of 1701 to critics who charged that he had gratuitously sacrificed New England's best interests in embracing the new charter, Mather implied – though he carefully did not state it outright – that his only return to London from Totteridge had come later in August and that he had then acquiesced in the royal instructions when Nottingham showed him a copy of Sydney's letter.[37] The second oddity is that Nottingham informed Sydney in a letter dated 11 August that the Massachusetts agents were 'willing to accept their Charter upon the Termes agreed on by the Committee.' This was certainly before Sydney's letter of the previous day had reached England. It was also while Mather was out of London, and a day before Phips reached him on the twelfth.[38] Also requiring explanation is the fact that even on the nineteenth Mather's diary recorded that 'N.E. is as yet unsettled,' and he sought divine guidance on 'what to do as to that countrey [New England] submitting unto, or opposing such a settlement for the country as is insisted upon by the Lords of the Committee, etc.' Yet the following day, with Mather still out of London, Nottingham informed the Lords of Trade not only of the king's decision but of the fact that 'Sir William Phips had been with him to lett him know that the New England agents did acquiesce therein.'[39]

One possibility is that Mather, with or without some advance knowledge of the king's decision, had chosen on the thirteenth – perhaps at Phips's urging – to accept the committee's prescription for the charter, but in self-defence had felt a need to conflate the events of this visit to London with those that took place on and immediately after his subsequent return there on the twenty-sixth. One difficulty with this explanation is that Nottingham's letter was dated 11 August – though, as Johnson has suggested, it is conceivable that the letter was started on the eleventh and completed, with the addition of the New England passage, on or about the thirteenth. More crucial are the passages in Mather's diary for the nineteenth that show him to have been unaware at that time of any irrevocable developments.[40]

The other possibility is that Phips, with the collaboration of Ashurst, had made a commitment to Nottingham without Mather's knowledge. The major problem here is to find an explanation for the fact that Phips persuaded Mather to return to London on the twelfth, given that on the nineteenth Mather was still ignorant of what had taken place. However, it is consistent with two of Mather's later claims. The first was that he was taken by surprise by the news of the king's ruling, when he had been at Totteridge for an unspecified time that was less than three weeks, and that only when shown a copy of Sydney's letter by Nottingham did he set aside reports that he had been deceived.[41] The second was that his return to London to accept the terms of the charter was at the behest of 'a very great Man, and a great Friend of *New-England* [who] desired a Person of Quality to advise me to take up with what was proposed.' Neither of these descriptions was likely to be applied to Phips, but they could readily be descriptions of Ashurst and Nottingham.[42]

A more plausible explanation of the entire sequence of events is as follows. Phips and Ashurst had indeed seen Nottingham and made a commitment to accept the committee's terms – possibly in the hope of commercial advantage, though also in the belief that holding out any longer would not be in New England's interests. They brought Mather to London from the twelfth to the fourteenth to persuade him to do the same and allowed him to believe that he would be taking the lead in doing so. But Mather (who had confided to the attorney general less than three weeks earlier that the proposals of the Lords of Trade would be 'fatal to the life of New England' and that he would 'part with [his] life sooner than consent') refused to make a hasty decision. Rather, he preferred on the morning of the fourteenth to draft revised proposals on key issues which he mistakenly believed were still unresolved, and he then returned to Totteridge to wrestle with his indecision.[43] Following the meeting of the Lords of Trade on the evening of the twentieth, Phips's concession could no longer be kept secret – though its timing, indicated only in Nottingham's correspondence with Sydney, did not have to be revealed – and on the twenty-sixth Mather briefly came again to London, not fully believing what he had heard. Nottingham's display of Sydney's letter, combined with the assurances of Phips and Ashurst that the king's ruling had left them no choice by the twentieth but to submit, made up his mind. But he returned to Totteridge for another eleven days and was so uncomfortable with what he regarded as his own *volte-face* that he preferred even in later years not to reveal in published form the full sequence of events as far as he knew them.

In any event, by the second half of August, Phips had attained prominent status before the Lords of Trade, for he was summoned by name to attend the meeting of the twentieth, along with the agents.[44] From this point on, he was an active participant in the remaining discussions over the charter. By this time, too, he had re-emerged as a projector. Between late June and early September 1691 he advocated three schemes to the Lords of Trade that promised him personal benefits as well as having a purported public significance. The first and most predictable was that he should lead a new attack on Canada. As early as 7 March, just after he had reached London, a newsletter had reported that the purpose of his visit was to 'Raise More Recruites' for a renewed assault on Quebec.[45] The report would have been more nearly correct if it had specified munitions and naval support rather than recruits, but it accurately foreshadowed the persistent undercurrent of advocacy for a new expedition that characterized Phips's defence of his actions of 1690.

On 30 June he presented an explicit proposal, both to the Lords of Trade and in a petition to the king. The petition focused on the need to protect English control of 'Nova Scotia,' with its mast trees, naval stores, and expected resources of copper and other minerals. It also sought a commission for Phips to command a new expedition to Canada. The proposal to the Lords of Trade was more detailed and was directed more specifically at the conquest of Canada. Phips would need, he estimated, a third-rate or good fourth-rate warship, one hundred cannon to be sited on the Ile d'Orléans, four mortars, one thousand barrels of powder, and two thousand small arms.[46] This was a tall order given the existing expenditures on the war, and its lack of progress was indicated by Phips's presentation of a scaled-down request on 21 September. 'I have,' he claimed, 'runn a great hazard in my Voyage from New England hither, on purpose to give their Majesties an account of my whole proceedings [in the 1690 expeditions], and of the Feazableness of their being masters of Quebeck.' Two days later, Phips requested the immediate allocation of a warship for the expedition. This again was unsuccessful, but the Lords of Trade did vote on the twenty-eighth to recommend that 'a fifth Rate ffrigat may be sent to New England if a fourth Rate Cannot be spared for the Guard of that Coast and to be Employed against the ffrench as there shall be Occasion.' It was not much progress for Phips's ambitions, but it did offer a modicum of support for the notion of a new expedition under his command.[47]

Meanwhile, in August, Phips had headed a group of six petitioners for the right to mine copper and precious metals on 'the Coast of New England and of Acade, lately taken from the French.' His partners included Sir Steven Evance (or Evans) and Thomas Lake, both native New Englanders who had moved to London and become, respectively, a goldsmith and a lawyer. The other three were John Smith, a scrivener (whom it is tempting, though not possible on the basis of direct evidence, to identify with the individual who had invested in Phips's expedition of 1686–7), Thomas Porter of Shadwell, and Richard Frith Jr. Porter and Frith may have been recruited through ties Phips had established through Narbrough. Frith had ties to the Navy Board, while Shadwell was the home village of Elizabeth Hill, Narbrough's second wife. Anticipating the establishment of a mint in New England (the Massachusetts agents had been instructed to seek 'the Liberty of Coynage,' and this was unsuccessfully requested by Phips and Mather in November) they undertook to supply its needs and in the meantime to ship the minerals to England in return for a thirty-one year lease.[48] It is unclear what relationship if any this venture bore to the company headed by Sir Matthew Dudley which also sought mining rights in New England, although the presence of Sir Thomas Lane and Sir Humphrey Edwin among Dudley's partners makes it unlikely that Phips would have set up in direct competition to Dudley. The documentation on Phips's group carried the implication that its chief place of interest was the coastal areas of northern New England and Acadia, and there may well have been an informal geographical differentiation between the two. Phips's interest in developing profitable mining ventures was, however, clearly established.[49]

In September, Phips presented to the Lords of Trade a proposal concerning the timber resources of 'Piscataque, and in Nova Scotia' and their value as a source of naval stores. The committee was apparently soliciting advice on this matter; a series of questions survives among its papers focusing on the supplies that could be generated, the likely cost, and the best means of organization. Written submissions were taken from Andros and Lidget as well as Phips, but it was Phips who was summoned to appear in person. 'Sir William Phips attending,' the commitee's journal recorded, 'is Calld in and Ordered to present to the Committee some Proposalls in Writing Concerning Ship Timber, Masts and Naval Stores that may be had in New England.'[50] There were, of course, wider aspects to this discussion. One of them was the increased importance of having secure sources of naval stores as the war with France continued through its third year. Another was the fact that the purported heirs to the old proprietary grants of Maine and New Hampshire were taking advantage of the uncertainties of the charter question to press their claims.[51] Phips's statement to the Lords of Trade on timber resources was a further affirmation of the need for the boundaries of Massachusetts to be extended northeastwards, but two pieces of evidence suggest that there were also more directly commercial implications. That the committee was discussing forms of commercial organization is indicated by the presence among its papers on this question of an anonymous note that 'the best means for carrying on the trade will be by a Company.' Also, the agents' petition of 27 August carried an unusual combination of signatures. Mather signed 'by order from Sir Henry Ashurst,' while the only other signature was that of William Paterson. Although Paterson's exact role in New England affairs in August 1691 – since his meeting with Phips, Mather, and others on 31 July – is unclear, the inference that commercial schemes were involved is unavoidable given his long-standing preoccupation with a variety of enterprises.[52]

Thus, Phips the projector had established over the summer of 1691 his personal aspirations to a sphere of influence that encompassed northern New England, Acadia/Nova Scotia, and Canada. He had defined his interest in the exploitation of a variety of natural resources in the first two of these territories, and although he had not yet done so for Canada, the prominent reference to the value of the Canadian fur trade in the pamphlet published by Mather earlier in the year with Phips's likely collaboration is strongly suggestive.[53] Yet the significance of his appearance before the Lords of Trade on 2 September was not confined to territorial or commercial matters. The conclusion of his written submission, made on that day or shortly thereafter, was a request for 'sufficient order and instructions' to enable him 'to prevent the wasting of Mast Trees, by Saw Mills, or otherwise, and to improve the before mentioned, to their Majesties Advantage.'[54]

This was odd language indeed for an individual who had no formal status either within the Massachusetts agency or before the committee. It is partly explained by a statement of Elisha Cooke in a letter drafted on 10 September. Cooke had heard from a third party, he informed Bradstreet, 'that Sir William Phipps had been nominated for the Governor.'[55] Who could have made the nomination? Historians have generally considered that the crucial document was the list of proposed governor, deputy governor, and assistants that was drawn up by Mather and Ashurst, dated 18 September and received by the Lords of Trade on the twenty-second; and that in this instance, Phips was essentially a passive instrument of Mather. Indeed, Mather confided to his diary some years later, 'By my meanes [Phips] was made Governor of the Province.'[56] But this interpretation does not explain the clear emergence of Phips's candidacy before the eighteenth. Nor is it consistent with Phips's use of language to the Lords of Trade which, given the sensitivities of individuals such as Carmarthen and Nottingham, would have been recklessly presumptuous had he not enjoyed substantial support on the committee as a potential governor.[57]

The more likely inference is that while Phips's candidacy for the governorship may indeed have been influenced by Mather, the crucial involvement was that of Ashurst and Nottingham. Mather would not have forgotten the undertaking he believed the king to have made on 30 April that the agents should nominate the first governor. Nor was there any likelihood that Mather would fail to support Phips for the office, given their close association and Mather's repeated praise for Phips when defending the expeditions. Yet Phips's rapid advancement in status before the Lords of Trade occurred during a time when Mather spent all but a few days outside London and was hampered in any lobbying effort by poor health. On 3 September, Ashurst (who later commented that Phips 'had been noe more governour than Lord Lieutenant of Ireland if itt had not been for me') wrote hurriedly to Mather at Totteridge to urge him to forward that day the names of his preferred candidates for governor, deputy governor, and council. How soon Mather complied is unknown, but by the fifteenth the name of Phips appeared specifically in a submission made to the Lords of Trade by Mather in the name of the agents.

In fact, it is doubtful whether either the Lords of Trade as a body or Nottingham as secretary of state were in need of any convincing by this time.[58] The appointment had solid advantages for Nottingham in resolving what otherwise was bound to be a troublesome issue. Phips as governor would be acceptable to the queen, had at least the minimal credentials to fulfil the king's stated wish for 'a Military Man,' would be palatable to Mather, and would conciliate Ashurst and the Whig merchants. As far as the evidence shows, Phips had displayed little more than a pro forma commitment to the old charter, and indeed he had shown little apparent interest in the charter question compared with the related but distinct issues of Canada, Acadia/Nova Scotia, and Maine. In mid-August he had taken a leading role in the acceptance of the wishes of the Lords of Trade on the charter – a considerable convenience for Nottingham. Later, as governor, he persisted in writing to Nottingham in terms that implied a patron-client relationship, as when he assumed he would have Nottingham's support for a new Canada expedition and promised him personal benefit from it, or when in early 1693 he wrote: 'I am under great obligations to your Lordship, which I cannot without neglect of my duty for bear to acknowledge upon all occasions, And hope for the Continuance of your Lordships Benigne Regards.'[59] Whether or not by 1693 such a relationship existed outside Phips's hopes, the evidence supports the inference that Phips's advancement was inseparable from the meeting with Nottingham on which the secretary had reported to the Lords of Trade on 20 August 1691.

Not that his appointment as governor was a fait accompli by then or by early September. Neither the secretary of state nor the Lords of Trade appointed colonial governors. Although the senior secretary wielded a powerful influence, the power was exercised by the monarchs and the Privy Council in the context of competing demands for patronage. Once granted, office attained the status of property, and Edward Randolph for one had no doubt that Phips – or, it could be speculated, the Ashursts on his behalf – had been 'at Charge to obtain his Government.' By 4 November, however, despite the advocacy of Phips's cause, Elisha Cooke was reporting to Bradstreet, 'His Majesty has not yet declared who shall be the Governor ... there being severall that now move for it besides Sir William.' On the same day, Nottingham arranged for Mather to have an interview with the king, during which Mather recalled the king's promise of nomination by the agents, praised Phips's abilities and the success of the Port-Royal expedition, and urged that he be confirmed as governor. The appointment of a colonial-born royal governor would be unusual, but the measure gained plausibility not only from Nottingham's support but also from the City connections represented by Ashurst. Since the debacle of the dominion, moreover, the reward-to-risk equation of a New England governorship was not necessarily encouraging to more conventional candidates. The appointment of Phips did not, as it turned out, end the wielding of English political patronage (as in the case of his successor, the earl of Bellomont), but it did influence the efforts of other New Englanders – beginning with Joseph Dudley – to marshal English interests in support of their candidacy.[60]

Phips's commission was finally approved by the Privy Council on 27 November. In an effort to preserve some semblance of the military coordination that had been among the chief arguments for preserving the Dominion of New England, it included overall command of all the militias of the New England colonies.[61] By this time, too, the Massachusetts charter had passed the Great Seal. The province that Phips would govern – insofar as aboriginal possession and French claims would allow him to do so – was much larger than the original colony of Massachusetts Bay. Apparently at Mather's behest, and with little resistance, Plymouth Colony was included. Of more direct interest to Phips was the inclusion of both Maine and Nova Scotia/Acadia. Without dealing comprehensively with the older proprietary claims, the Lords of Trade began immediately after Phips's appearance on 2 September to act on the assumption that these territories would form part of the new Massachusetts colony. The proprietary claim of Samuel Allen to New Hampshire had been more vigorously pursued and was sustained, perhaps with Phips's collaboration. With this exception, and in the additional context of the continuation of the colonies of Connecticut and Rhode Island, Phips's area of government could be taken to include everything from Cape Cod to the Gulf of St Lawrence. His preoccupation as governor would be to make good on this claim and to add Canada to it.[62]

Mather was understandably elated at Phips's appointment. The new governor, he wrote in a pamphlet, was 'one that has ventured his Life to serve his Countrey,' adding that 'when *Gideon* did so, the Children of *Israel* were desirous that he should Rule over them.' It is doubtful whether Mather drew this analogy when he and Nottingham took Phips

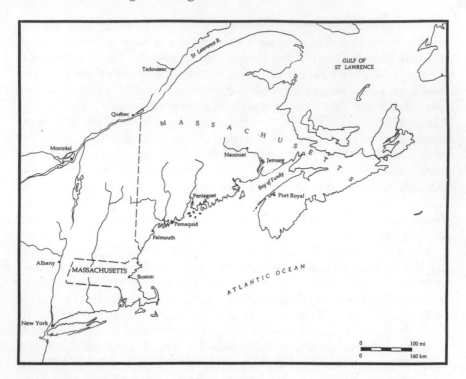

MAP 3 Northeastern North America, early 1690s, showing Massachusetts as envisaged by Sir William Phips on the basis of the 1691 charter

on 3 January 1691 to meet briefly with the king, but the interview was no doubt seen by Mather – probably misleadingly, in view of the likely role of Nottingham in Phips's nomination – as yet another instance of the ability on which he had privately congratulated himself in late November, to 'find respect and favour' in the eyes of 'the King and Queen, and the great ones at Court.' When news of the appointment reached Boston, his son Cotton Mather delightedly recorded in his diary, 'The *Governour* of the Province is not my *Enemy*, but one whom I baptised, namely *Sir William Phips*, and one of my own Flock, and one of my dearest Friends.'[63] Others were less favourably impressed. The agents Cooke and Oakes had refused to take any part in the nominations on the grounds that their instructions had been to safeguard the old charter. Cooke, reporting to Bradstreet in November, hinted that the colony should repudiate what Mather and Ashurst had done, since they had no plenipotentiary powers and had contravened their instructions. Mather's view was that Cooke and Oakes had chosen 'rather ... to save nothing than not to have the old charter just as it was.'[64] Another who disapproved, though for quite different reasons, was Blathwayt. 'Sir W. Phips,' he caustically observed to Francis Nicholson in a letter of 5 December 1691, 'is made the kings Governor of the Massachusetts and Commander in chief of the Militia in all the other colonies of New England by which means his Majesties authority is to be resetled in those parts.'[65]

Blathwayt, however, was well used to having no control over the appointment of governors, and by 28 December the Lords of Trade were ready to forward Phips's instructions to the king and council to be made final three days later. Many of the instructions were standard items that reproduced similar formulas used in other colonies, though they conspicuously did not include the duty to nurture the Church of England. Some of the provisions were more particular. Of note for Phips, and contained both in the original instructions to the Massachusetts agents and in Phips's arguments for military strength on the northeastern coastlines, was the provision for 'Ten Great Guns' to be sent to New England and for Phips 'to take care that Our Fort of Pemaquid be forthwith restored, and the said Guns placed within the Same.' Other instructions, while far from unique, have special significance in view of Phips's later actions as governor. 'You are to Encourage the Indians upon all occasions,' he was enjoined, 'so that they may apply themselves to the English Trade and Nation rather than to any other of Europe.' He was to observe the Anglo-Spanish treaty of 1670 – an ironic provision in view of Phips's earlier career in the Caribbean – and in particular to pass a law to combat the 'great disorders and depraditions dayly Committed by Pyrats and others to the prejudice of Our Allies.' This, in conjunction with the responsibilities embodied in his commission to establish and exercise vice-admiralty jurisdiction, carried the seeds of complexities to come, especially in view of concurrent allegations of illegal trade and links with pirates against such a prominent Boston merchant and supporter of the revolutionary regime as Samuel Shrimpton. But these questions, for the time being, could safely be postponed.[66]

In the meantime, Phips prepared to depart for Boston. He met occasionally with Mather, and in December he again argued the case before the Lords of Trade for naval support for New England. No longer setting his hopes on a third-rate warship, he asked for one fifth-rate and one sixth-rate warship as a minimal prerequisite for preventing the

French from taking back control of Acadia, and more ambitiously he stated that a squadron of four vessels would enable him to 'Settle all those Parts.' The result was an order in council six days later that instructed the Admiralty to provide a fourth-rate and a sixth-rate or, if these could not be spared, 'one good ship of Force.'[67] Phips and Mather were not so successful in their request that Massachusetts be granted liberty of coinage. Such a grant, they argued, would 'tend to convince and satisfie [Massachusetts inhabitants] ... that they shall be noe loosers but gainers by the new Settlement as to the Civill Government, in that Province.' Referred to the Royal Mint in January, the proposal went no further.[68] By late February, however, the new Great Seal of Massachusetts was ready for delivery to Phips, Mather receiving it from Blathwayt for transmission. Further delays then intervened before Phips and Mather embarked in late March for Boston. During the seven-week voyage, Phips travelled on the frigate *Nonsuch*, and Mather on a merchant vessel in convoy with it.[69]

Nonsuch in 1692 was an elderly fourth-rate warship of 36 guns and a complement of 150.[70] Commissioned in 1668, the vessel was now commanded by Richard Short with Abraham Hoare as lieutenant. Short, and to a lesser extent Hoare were to exert significant and unexpected influence on the course of Phips's careeer as governor – notably after Phips had accused Short of insubordination, publicly caned him on a Boston wharf in January 1693, and then bypassed Hoare in appointing a replacement for the imprisoned captain. First commissioned in April 1678 as a lieutenant, Richard Short had served only briefly before a gap in his service record that ended with his reappearance in 1689, followed by his first command two years later as captain of the fireship *Phaeton*. He took command of the *Nonsuch* in early 1692. Hoare had served as a second lieutenant, also beginning in April 1678, and had returned after a lengthy interval to serve on the *Nonsuch* from 1690 onwards. Both officers, therefore, were more senior in age than in service experience. Both had briefly begun their naval career in the context of the rapid mobilization of the Royal Navy in 1678, in anticipation of a war with France that did not take place, and had resumed it in the context of the new expansion owing to war preparations in 1689 and 1690.[71]

The voyage of the *Nonsuch* from London to Boston in the spring of 1692 generated conflicting testimony in depositions arising from the later disputes between Phips and Short. On one matter, there was no question: that en route the vessel had captured the 70-ton *Catharine*, which was on its way to La Rochelle from Martinique with a cargo of

sugar. According to George Mills, a *Nonsuch* crew member, Phips intervened on arrival in Boston and 'took her [the prize] from the said Captain Short promising the ships Company satisfaction yet never made
them any Recompense.' Benjamin Jackson, sailing as Phips's newly
acquired secretary, made the counterallegation that Short had illegally
removed and sold part of the *Catharine*'s cargo and that he had failed to
appear before the vice-admiralty court to lay any claim to the prize.[72] A
third perspective was provided by George Webster, a member of the
crew, who emphasized the cordiality of shipboard relations between the
governor and the captain. Short, Webster said, had given up his cabin to
Phips and had lodged for the duration of the voyage in the gunner's
quarters; his recollection of Phips's response to the seizure of the
Catharine was that 'Sir William said in a ffreindly Manner Captain I wish
you much Joy of your prize and many of them for I dont Expect one
Groat out of her.' However, Webster also testified that Jackson and the
purser, Matthew Cary, 'were always Contriving how to raise Animosity
and Strife between Sir William phipps and the said Captain Short and
that they continued so doing all the Time they were aboard.'[73]

When the *Nonsuch* made port in Boston on 14 May 1692, therefore, the
seeds had been sown of an animosity between captain and governor
which may or may not have already troubled the surface of their relationship. Matters became more volatile as the hard-drinking and under-
paid Short moved further into a situation of clientlike dependency on
Phips. Another factor may have been that expressed by his fellow captain Robert Fairfax, who was stationed in Boston in command of the
fifth-rate *Conception Prize* and commented, 'None that ever commands
any of their Majesties Ships in this Place was ever used with common
civility.'[74]

In the meantime, Phips's arrival in Boston fell on a spring Saturday
evening. The news of his appointment as governor had been known
since 26 January and no doubt had helped him attain on 4 May the
highest number of votes in the last election of assistants under the rules
of the old charter. His 969 votes outpolled those of both Cooke (920) and
Oakes (615), as well as those of his new deputy-governor, William
Stoughton (873), and his provincial secretary, Isaac Addington (895),
though all these men had gained election to the council, which was
superseded when Phips arrived with the new charter.[75] Samuel Sewall
described the night of Phips's disembarkation concisely: 'Sir William
arrives in the Nonsuch Frigat: Candles are lighted before He gets into
Townhouse. Eight Companies wait on Him to his house, and then on

Mr. [Increase] Mather to his. Made no volleys because 'twas Satterday night.' A more sardonic observer informed a correspondent of Francis Nicholson that Phips's instructions to desist from 'Gunns firring and Great declamations of joy' had come only after he had finished reading his commission when, seeing 'the sunne to be going of the horrizon,' he had sanctimoniously stated that he 'would not Infringe upon the lords day.' Sanctimonious or not, Phips was now installed. The same observer commented, 'Upon the wholl matter I find that North and south Boston is Greatly devided.' Like the actual or potential dissatisfaction of Richard Short, this was at present no more than a straw in the wind.[76]

That Phips had become governor of Massachusetts some sixteen months after he had hurriedly left the colony in the face of serious allegations against his conduct at Port-Royal and Quebec, not to mention his long-outstanding debts, was a remarkable feat of survival and opportunism. Although it could not have been achieved without the advocacy of Increase Mather, Phips had been far from the passive and indolent tool of Mather as depicted in some accounts. The evidence suggests that his relationship with Sir Henry Ashurst, though scantily documented, had been a launching point for his successful efforts to establish the potential economic benefits of a conquest of Canada to London merchant interests. He had also managed, probably through a politic and initially clandestine concession on the new charter, to enlist at least a necessary minimum of support for his governorship from the earl of Nottingham.

In addition, Phips had turned his attention to entrepreneurial plans that depended on the spatial extent of the new Massachusetts colony as well as on the success of his efforts to make good the extravagant territorial claims of the 1691 charter. Of the area that Phips purported to govern, there were some small corners that contained the most populous settlements of New England. Most of it, however, consisted of a great swath of aboriginal territory, with French influence felt here and there. Although Boston was the administrative and commercial centre of Massachusetts, Pemaquid was much closer to the geographic centre. Given Phips's overwhelming personal and commercial interest in the northeast and his lack of experience in provincial politics, all these dynamics – as well as his continuing military and commercial designs on Canada – carried unpredictable implications. What was clear that Phips had succeeded in harnessing his characteristically acquisitive ambitions to the demands of an empire in which fiscal imperatives had given unprecedented influence to the City merchants to whom he had presented himself with such effect. How acceptable the results would be to the Massachusetts powerbrokers who were now to be governed by this blunt and barely literate product of New England's northeastern fringe – or to the traditional arbiters of empire in the Plantations Office – was yet to be seen.

7

Statecraft and Witchcraft, 1692

When Sir William Phips arrived in Massachusetts in May 1692, he found the colony in a fragile state. Repeated military efforts, including Phips's own expeditions in 1690, had exhausted the provincial treasury without stemming the tide of Wabanaki and French advances. The revolutionary regime, still headed by the aged Simon Bradstreet, had lost all semblance of its ability to meet the military threat effectively during what the prominent minister Samuel Willard characterized soon afterwards as 'the short *Anarchy* accompanying our late Revolution.' Certainly, John Pynchon of Springfield was one influential inhabitant who welcomed Phips's governorship as offering the chance of a new beginning. At the news of Phips's arrival, Pynchon informed a correspondent, 'I greatly rejoyce, looking upon it as an answer of Prayers, and tendency to a hopeful good Settlement of this Countrey.'[1] Before such expectations could be fulfilled, however, Phips had to devise an approach to a crisis that was clearly both military and fiscal and that had its origins in the imperial conflicts that dated from 1689. The real complications, however, arose from factors that were less conspicuous.

The English reverses in the northeast were the product not only of three years of intermittent warfare but of a much longer series of military and diplomatic interactions between the English and the Wabanaki. There had been successive efforts on both sides to find a resolution to the conflicts that had arisen from English attempts to settle in Wabanaki territory, and there had also been successive breakdowns of peaceful relations. The hostilities had directly affected the English population in the areas which in earlier years had been known to the English as the Province of Maine and the Sagadahoc Territory, and were now included in Massachusetts under the charter of 1691. Migration into the region during the periods of peace had been followed by confused retreats, and this had produced serious social dislocation in the more southerly communities, where the displaced settlers had taken refuge. While the Salem witchcraft outbreak had no single or simple cause, this was an integral factor of the events there in the summer of 1692. The Salem accusations and the trials that ensued were all the more threatening to Phips and his authority because a significant number of those involved were connected with his family or that of his wife, or were known to them through their former association with the Casco Bay area and adjoining settlements. Also, as a successful treasure seeker, Phips was potentially open to accusation on the basis of traditional linkages of necromancy and other occult practices with the discovery of precious metals.

Phips's solution to these complex and volatile events was to make a display of concentrating on the simplest matter of all: a military effort to forestall any further Wabanaki gains. He avoided taking an active role in the Salem proceedings for as long as possible. This approach produced mixed results. It kept the Salem danger at arm's length while maintaining the impression of military activity. Further, it enabled Phips to make the misleading claim that his campaigning in the northeast had prevented him from acting decisively on the trials until his return. Phips's approach, however, angered Lieutenant-Governor William Stoughton, who was chief judge at the trials. Even more seriously, it threatened the integrity of the Mathers when they lent theological and intellectual justification to measures that had been taken by Phips for pragmatic reasons.

As Phips was acutely aware, the tensions between the Wabanaki and the New England settlers were far from new in the 1690s. Although dating in some senses from the beginning of English attempts at colonization, they had become acute during the 1670s and had broken into open warfare in 1676, just as King Philip's War ended in southern New England. Hostilities in Maine had continued until 1677, with the final treaty being signed in 1678. The Wabanaki prevailed in the conflict, though in the process many of their villages were destroyed, as well as those of the colonists. William Phips was only one of hundreds of people displaced by the fighting. Many never returned.[2]

The conflict also had its effects on the colony of Massachusetts, especially on Essex County. The sense of crisis originally stimulated by King Philip's War had found its expression in the jeremiads delivered by Puritan divines – led by Increase Mather – which predicted disaster for the religious experiment of New England unless worldliness was replaced by a new spiritual dedication. The conflict with the Wabanaki was seized on by Mather and others for its ability to teach spiritual lessons which might not have been adequately learned during the briefer onslaught on the tribes of southern New England. As Stephen Foster has noted, 'The Massachusetts ministry actually showed a remarkable reluctance to let the war go: they pointed to the continuing conflict in Maine as a sign that the end might still be nigh.'[3] In Essex County as elsewhere in Massachusetts, the spiritual uncertainties were accompanied by the more direct scars of the conflict.

Although relatively little fighting in King Philip's War had taken place within Essex County itself, Native forces did attack Andover, Billerica, and Rowley during the spring of 1676. Farther west, Essex militia companies took part in engagements that were costly to both sides. Among those killed defending Hadley was Freegrace Norton, a sergeant in the Essex County regiment of Samuel Appleton and the brother-in-law of Mary Spencer Phips. The most serious English defeat of the war was inflicted on Essex troops at the so-called Bloody Brook, not far from Hadley. Seventy-one were killed, almost wiping out Captain Thomas Lathrop's company. Considering that Lathrop was a prominent citizen of Beverly and that his men came from the surrounding towns, the debacle must have been painfully felt throughout Essex County.[4]

After the end of hostilities in southern New England in August 1676, the continuing English-Wabanaki struggle had a direct bearing on Essex County both militarily and in the settlement of war refugees. Essex troops were again in action and again met defeat. A company led by Newbury's Captain Benjamin Swett in support of the garrison at Black Point in the early summer of 1677 was attacked by Wabanaki forces with devastating effect, 'very few escaping,' according to the account of William Hubbard.[5] Their success against Swett's force led the Wabanaki to take the offensive by seizing English fishing and trading ships in the Gulf of Maine and raiding the island fishing settlements along the coast. In July 1677 alone, they took close to twenty fishing ketches, most of which were owned in and crewed from Salem and Marblehead. With four or five crew members on each ketch, more than eighty men may have been killed or captured in these attacks. The economic costs to the two ports also were substantial.[6]

A horrific indication of the resulting tensions occurred on 15 July 1677. Following the recapture of one of the vessels by its crew and their return to Marblehead with two captured Wabanaki sachems, an enraged crowd of women seized the two Wabanaki and stoned and beat them to death. An eyewitness reported that after the attackers had dispersed, the authorities made their way to the bodies of the sachems and 'found them with their heads off and gone, and their flesh in a manner pulled from their bones.'[7] Less dramatic though also a sign of social strain and dislocation was the gathering of refugees. Salem was a principal place of retreat for English colonists displaced from the northeast, and in January 1676 the Salem selectmen granted temporary refuge to twenty-two families. Others who went to neighbouring towns included Philip White, the half-brother of William Phips, who settled at Beverly. The immigrants included widows, orphans, and wounded soldiers. Some families were destitute, having lost all their possessions when they fled their homes. These people had to be taken in by charitable friends or be supported by public relief. As well as being a reminder of military setbacks and vulnerability, the presence of these refugees added to the already heavy burden of taxation which the hostilities had brought.[8]

Following the English-Wabanaki treaty of 1678, a gradual resettlement of English communities began in the Wabanaki territory. The returnees came from places of refuge in both Essex and Suffolk counties, and they included several members of the extended Phips family. William's older brother John Phips had died after his family had retreated to the safety of Charlestown, but his widow Elizabeth was among the Sheepscot property owners who gathered in Boston in August 1682 to organize the resettlement of their township. Elizabeth Phips petitioned officials for land in Sheepscot, citing the privations that had resulted from her husband's death after being 'driven from ... [his] very considerable quantity of land'; she also mentioned that one of her sons was determined to 'go and live where he and his brothers were born as soon as his apprenticeship is out.'[9]

Several other members of the family joined the resettlement of the Kennebec region as petitioners for the township of Newtown, at the southern end of Arrowsic Island. William's sister, Mary Phips Widger, and her fisher husband James had sought refuge at Beverly during the war. John Spencer, the brother of Mary Spencer Phips, joined the Widgers as a Newtown landowner.[10] Apparently Spencer did not remain at Newtown for very long. In 1687, confessing that he had been 'Rambling about in the wooreld and now ... [had] A desire to Get into a setled Condittion,' he had petitioned Governor Andros for confirmation of one hundred acres in Falmouth, near the mills of Silvanus Davis.[11] At the time of the petition, Spencer was living with Davis, an old acquaintance of William Phips. Sarah White Lane, Sir William's half-sister, left Boston at about the same time to move to Falmouth with her husband, Joshua Lane.[12]

Meanwhile, Anglo-Wabanaki tensions and animosities remained, heightened perhaps by the defensive precautions taken by both sides. The settlers were determined to take back their lands and rebuild their homes, while the Wabanaki once again felt the pressure of English encroachment. A new treaty in 1685 attempted to provide ways of resolving disputes, but soon afterwards, under Governor Andros, the Dominion of New England began to patent lands in the region to many potential settlers in disregard of all Native claims of ownership.[13] Problems also developed when settlers' cattle destroyed Native cornfields, when English fishermen netted the lion's share of migratory river fish, and when English fur traders aroused suspicions of unfair dealing.

In the summer and fall of 1688, these problems led to minor outbreaks of violence in several places. Efforts to negotiate the maintenance of peace came to nothing, and soon the hostilities spread.[14] Further complications soon arose from the English revolution and the formal renewal of war between England and France in May 1689. Encouraged by New York, Houdenasaunee raids plagued New France during the summer and fall.[15] The results of the English revolution in Wabanaki territory were different in that the overthrow of Andros in April 1689 led to desertions from English forts, uncertain chains of command, and, eventually, shortages of supplies, ammunition, and pay for the troops. The English defences in the Sagadahoc region were soon affected. Mary Phips Widger and James Widger were among the Newtown inhabitants who reluctantly moved to Fort Sagadahoc, at the mouth of the Kennebec, after the abandonment of two smaller forts in the area. These settlers soon petitioned Massachusetts officials for relief, 'The most of our Houses being now att This Instant in a fflame The Indians being now a burning of them, and killing our Cattle.'[16]

The skirmishing in the Sagadahoc area was a precursor of two major Wabanaki raids. On 28 June 1689 the Wabanaki attached Dover, New Hampshire, leaving twenty-three settlers dead and capturing twenty-nine. Seven weeks later, Pemaquid was taken by surprise and overrun. Successful French and Native raids on Schenectady, Salmon Falls, and Casco followed in the winter and spring of 1690, and this led to more sustained coordination between the Wabanaki and the French. The English had offered little effective resistance other than the burning of several Wabanaki villages by expeditions led by Colonel Benjamin

Church. The only remaining English settlements northeast of the Piscataqua River were Wells, York, and Kittery.[17] Even so, fighting lapsed in
late 1690 and early 1691. New Englanders speculated that it was Phips's
capture of Port-Royal earlier in the year that had prompted the
Wabanaki to agree to a ceasefire at a meeting held at Sagadahoc on
29 November 1690. At the subsequent conference at Wells on 1 May
1691, however, only an extension of the truce was agreed, and it soon
broke down.[18] Less than a year later came a further sharp reminder of
New England's vulnerability. On 24 January 1692, York experienced a
surprise winter raid in which more than a hundred people were killed or
captured. The destruction of this prosperous shire town only fifty miles
from Boston made all residents of Massachusetts acutely aware that the
French and Wabanaki could raid virtually at will.[19]

Thus, the crisis that greeted Phips on his arrival in Boston some fourteen weeks after the raid on York was undoubtedly military (and fiscal),
but it was also diplomatic. In the long term, it concerned the unresolved
question of whether a secure basis could be found that would enable the
Wabanaki to tolerate English settlement. The crisis also had social and
cultural roots, which bound the turbulent history of English-Wabanaki
relations not only to the family and friends of Sir William Phips but also
to Essex County and to the conflict that was already in its early stages in
Salem Village. There has been a long-standing scholarly and public fas-
cination with the outbreak of witchcraft in Salem. Dozens of interpretations have been advanced, ranging from genuine devil worship to ergot
poisoning. In recent years, social historians have generated a new
understanding of the episode as a phenomenon arising from local community tensions and as an expression of broader patterns in English and
New England society. Less fully explored have been the connections
between the events at Salem and the migrations back and forth between
Essex County and the northeast.[20] For Phips, these associations contributed significantly to bringing the Salem outbreak too close to be easily
managed.

One of the more prominent of the refugees of 1676 was George Burroughs. After graduating from Harvard in 1670, he had moved to Falmouth, Maine, where he served as minister until the town was
abandoned in August 1676. He then moved briefly to Salisbury, Massachusetts, and in 1680 was appointed as the new minister in Salem Village. This strife-torn community formed the western part of Salem, an
economically insecure village that had made unsuccessful efforts to gain
recognition as a separate town. It had attained a quasi-independent sta-

tus, with the power to have its own parish and minister, but it did not succeed in becoming the town of Danvers until the eighteenth century. Salem Village's semi-dependent status helped create an unsettled sense in local politics. The residents had become deeply divided over issues that included the choice of the minister, the setting of his salary, and the location of the meeting house.[21]

When Burroughs arrived, he was immediately thrust into disputes between supportive and opposing political factions within the community. Since he was the target of much of the animosity, he could do little to blunt the sharpness of divisions that had been developing for many years and had plagued the previous minister too. By early 1683, the anti-Burroughs faction had succeeded in preventing the payment of his salary. In response, he stopped meeting with the congregation and prepared to move back to the northeast. The resettlement at Falmouth was commencing, and Burroughs had been asked to return to his former community. His parishioners there included Silvanus Davis, John Spencer, and Joshua and Sarah Lane. It is not known whether Burroughs ever met Sir William Phips, but the two were certainly well known to each other through Burroughs's relationships with close family members and personal associates of the governor.[22]

Burroughs's departure did nothing to resolve the internal conflicts in Salem Village. On the contrary, as Paul Boyer and Stephen Nissenbaum have shown, the divisions continued to deepen along social, economic, and geographical lines.[23] At the same time, a further linkage was developing between Essex County and the English resettlements in the Wabanaki territory. Of the thirteen people who in 1680 had petitioned for the new township of Westcustogo (present-day Yarmouth, Maine) directly adjacent to the substantial village of Androscoggin Wabanaki at Pejebscot, at least eleven had direct ties to Essex County and eight had lived both there and at Casco Bay. Prominent among the trustees charged with initiating the new settlement was Bartholomew Gedney, a Salem merchant who already owned a large tract of Westcustogo land and had had a sawmill burned there by the Wabanaki during King Philip's War. In the 1680s, a new sawmill, a gristmill, and a house were built on the same site. Other Essex merchants also took an interest in the timber of the region. George Corwin and his son Jonathan Corwin, for example, owned sawmills on the Kennebunk river and at York. The Kennebunk operation was run by the elder Corwin's son-in-law, Eleazar Hathorne, until his death in 1680.

Thus, Essex economic interests – which had been prominent in the timber trade since the 1650s – were heavily involved in the extensive development of sawmill production that took place during the 1680s.[24] They were also heavy losers when the renewal of warfare led to the quick and decisive Wabanaki reassertions of 1689–90. Westcustogo, where no known effort had been made to legitimize the settlement by purchase or by a tribute of corn that had been specified in the 1678 treaty, was among the first areas to be contested. The English abandonment of this and other settlements in the region wiped out the investments of the Gedney, Corwin, and Hathorne families (all of which were represented among the magistrates active in the Salem trials) as well as burdening the Essex communities again with refugees. Those from whom they had fled were described by Cotton Mather, in his later reflections on the origins of the witchcraft outbreak, as 'the *Indians*, whose chief *Sagamores* are well known unto some of our Captives, to have been horrid *Sorcerers*, and hellish *Conjurers*, and such as Conversed with *Dæmons*.'[25]

Soon after the York disaster, it became obvious that something was seriously wrong in Salem Village. Earlier that winter, a group of young girls had begun to experiment with fortune-telling and other forms of magic that straddled the boundaries between witchcraft and common folkloric belief.[26] As Cotton Mather described it, they and a growing number of others were 'Arrested with many *Preternatural Vexations* upon their Bodies, and a variety of cruel Torments, which were evidently inflicted from the *Dæmons*, of the *Invisible World*.'[27] The initial symptoms appeared in the daughter of Salem Village's minister, Samuel Parris, probably in late December 1691, and several others were similarly affected in February and March. Doctors and ministers agreed that the victims were bewitched. Yet from the beginning, as Boyer and Nissenbaum have shown, there was a clear pattern to the accusations that quickly followed. The first three girls to be 'afflicted' by witchcraft included not only Betty Parris but also Ann Putnam, the daughter of a leader of the village faction that supported the minister in the disputes that had persisted from Burroughs's time and before. As the outbreak continued, most of the accusers were members of families that favoured Parris, while those accused of witchcraft, and their defenders, were drawn disproportionately from the anti-Parris group. The political division was based in part on economic differences. Parris's supporters tended to live in the western part of the village, where the poorer soil offer them a less promising future. The minister's detractors were centred in the eastern district, which was on better soil and was closer to the economic growth and opportunities (as well, perhaps, as the worldly temptations) of Salem town.[28]

The western part of the village was significant for other reasons. First, it was close to the Blind Hole, where there had been speculation about the possibility of mining copper. Several conflicting claims to this property existed by the 1680s, which may have intensified the antagonisms in Salem Village politics as well as in the witchcraft trials. Thomas Putnam Jr. who owned land adjacent to the Blind Hole, was to find that his wife, daughter, and servant girl were all among the afflicted in 1692. The appointment of Phips as governor added a further complication in view of Phips's attempt in 1691 to gain for himself and his partners a monopoly of copper and precious metal mining rights in Acadia and New England.[29]

Another significant factor was that the western part of the village was the closest to the English-Native frontier. Communities such as Andover, Billerica, and Haverhill were even closer, of course, but they were sparsely settled and obviously vulnerable to attack, as the experience of sixteen years before had shown. It was easy to see a similarity with York, which also had been a well-established community with some buffering of nearby settlement. The anxiety over the possibility of attack was not unique to the western parts of Salem Village (by midsummer, rumours of raids by small groups of French soldiers were spreading panic even in coastal Gloucester), but the village's geography explains why the fear of attack took hold there early and acutely.[30]

The linkage between the witchcraft outbreak and the raiding warfare of the early 1690s, as James Kences and others have noted, soon became explicit. Significantly, many of the afflicted were refugees from the northeast. The seeds of this association had been sown in the sermons of Samuel Parris in late 1691 and early 1692, when Parris had expounded on the coming spiritual war with the enemies of Christ, causing his parishioners to see a parallel with the alliance of French Papists and heathen Natives. Cotton Mather's later pronouncements that the Wabanaki were among the 'most devoted and resembling Children' of Satan himself, and were in the most direct sense 'Diabolical Indians,' reflected a view that had wide currency among the New Englanders who had been affected by the war. Mercy Lewis, one of the leaders of the afflicted girls, put a voice to this fear by singing 'hymns such as Psalm 149, which stressed the need 'to execute vengeance upon the heathen, and punishments upon the people.' According to Mather, the devil that afflicted Lewis and the other girls was 'of a Tawny Colour,' a description frequently applied by English observers to denote the skin colouring of native North Americans.[31]

Mercy Lewis was all too familiar with the 'heathen.' A war refugee, she was a former resident of Falmouth, and her parents may have been killed there in 1690. Of the small group of afflicted girls who were at the centre of the Salem outbreak, she was one of four who had ties to the northeast and to the conflict there. Susannah Sheldon was a refugee from Scarborough; a Godfrey Sheldon killed in the fighting of 1690 was apparently her brother. Sarah Churchill (or Churchwell) was from Saco. Mary Walcott had not lived in the Wabanaki territory, but her brother had recently been stationed there as a militia soldier.[32] In addition to these four, there was a child with refugee links who was afflicted but did not testify at the trials. Roger Toothaker, a doctor, reported two children to be 'strangely sick' and suffering from 'unwanted fits.' Their names were not recorded, but one was a child of the refugee Philip White of Beverly, who was a half-brother of Sir William Phips.[33]

Individuals with personal ties to the northeast were also prominent both as judges and as accusers during the Salem trials. Notable among them were Westcustogo proprietors and other merchants with nearby interests. Bartholomew Gedney, Jonathan Corwin, and William Hathorne – brother of Eleazar – were the presiding magistrates when most of the alleged witches were arraigned. Corwin and Gedney also sat on the court of oyer and terminer, which was created to deal with the outbreak. Jonathan Putnam, a member of one of the leading pro-Parris families who personally testified against five defendants, was a Westcustogo proprietor. So was George Ingersoll, whose slave Wonn had accused Bridget Bishop of witchcraft in 1679 and in so doing had laid the basis for Bishop's conviction and execution in 1692. Ingersoll's brother Nathaniel testified against several of the accused, and his inn was the scene of many of the examinations of purported witches. The niece by marriage of another Westcustogo proprietor, Robert Nicholson, was the afflicted girl Sarah Churchill.[34]

A significant number of the accused also had northeastern links. Two of the nineteen executed in Salem as witches – George Burroughs and Ann Pudeator – had lived for lengthy periods in the former Province of Maine. So had other accused persons, though Sarah Cloyce, Mary Bradbury, Job Tookie, Elizabeth Dicer, Nicholas Frost, and John Alden escaped with their lives. Frost and Alden were fur traders, and Alden had strong trade ties to the Wabanaki, Wuastukwiuk, and Mi'kmaq as well as to the Acadians. Alden had been one of Phips's captains in the

Port-Royal expedition of 1690, and his more recent trading voyages to that vicinity had led one of the afflicted to accuse him of treachery as well as sin: 'He sells Powder and Shot to the Indians and French, and lies with the Indian Squaes, and has Indian Papooses.'[35]

Of all the proceedings, it was the case of the former minister of Salem Village, George Burroughs, that most clearly combined the themes of local conflict and war-related tension. In 1692 Burroughs was brought back to the village under arrest to face accusations that were full of the imagery of frontier conflict. Ann Putnam, the daughter of one of the minister's strongest opponents while he had been in Salem, alleged that he had 'bewitched a grate many souldiers to death at the eastword.' Other deponents, including several militia officers, referred to Native warriors, garrison houses, and the supernatural strength that allowed Burroughs to hold a six-foot musket just by 'putting the forefinger of his right hand into the muzzle.'[36] Spectral evidence also was crucial in the cases against those accused of witchcraft. Burroughs's spectre was alleged to have appeared to a number of the afflicted to torment them and also to inform them that he had murdered both of his wives as well as other people. This type of evidence had long been introduced in witchcraft cases in both England and New England, but it had usually been given limited weight. Spectral evidence might commonly support the physical evidence in a successful prosecution, but it was rarely the prime or sole basis for conviction. Increase Mather later pointed out that the problem raised by spectral evidence lay not with belief in spectres but with the notion that the devil was sufficiently powerful to make it appear that an innocent person was responsible for an affliction. Still, George Burroughs was found guilty. On 19 August 1692 he and four other condemned witches were hanged.[37]

By this time, Sir William Phips had been in Massachusetts as governor for more than three months. His role in the witchcraft proceedings had been minimal, though he had taken two actions of serious consequence in circumstances that made decisions unavoidable. The examination of suspects had begun in Salem at the end of February, and at the time of Phips's arrival in mid-May proceedings were afoot against no fewer than forty-two persons. The first decision was forced upon him by the reality that, whatever their other dangers, the approaching witch trials were threatening to overwhelm the local court system. Phips's solution was to create a court of oyer and terminer headed by the lieutenant-governor. He acted with dispatch; the order constituting the court was passed by the Massachusetts council on 27 May, just thirteen days after his arrival. Phips also had some reason for claiming to Blathwayt in October that he had selected as judges 'people of the best prudence and figure that could then be pitched upon.' William Stoughton brought to the court not only the prestige of his office as lieutenant-governor but also two decades of almost continual public officeholding. Stoughton's associates were six of the most prominent lay leaders of New England: Samuel Sewall, Wait Winthrop, Bartholomew Gedney, Nathaniel Saltonstall, William Sargent, and John Richards.[38]

The court first met on 2 June 1692 for the trial of Bridget Bishop, the judges having decided to bypass persons who had been arraigned before her. The evidence against Bishop was considered to be the strongest of any of the cases. She had been accused of witchcraft previously, and physical evidence had been found in holes in the cellar of her house: 'several puppets made up of rags and hogs' bristles with headless pins in them.' These dolls and pins, combined with the spectral evidence of many who claimed to have been afflicted by Bishop, would probably have been enough to seal her fate whether in Salem or in a court of law in England. She was executed on 10 June.[39]

Other aspects of the witchcraft trials gave rise to disquiet in some quarters. First of all, by the time the court of oyer and terminer met, the number of the accused had risen to seventy-one. Not only had the list lengthened drastically since Phips's arrival less than three weeks earlier, but the background of the suspects and their geographical spread had taken on unusual characteristics. Witchcraft had traditionally been a localized affair, the accusations generally being made by neighbours, and the great majority of the accused being women. This pattern held in seventeenth-century New England, where some 78 per cent of those accused of witchcraft were female, and half of the men accused were relations or public supporters of women who had been denounced. Charges also tended to be class-oriented, centred among the poorer and marginalized members of the community. Leading figures served as judges in these cases but were rarely if ever accused of such a crime. Likewise, children were not commonly the targets of accusation. But in Salem, all of these boundaries were being crossed. Defendants such as Burroughs and Alden were not only males of high status, but both lived far from Salem. Alden was not even personally known to any of his accusers. They joined a list of suspects that included even five-year-old Dorcas Good. The devil appeared to be present in strength throughout the colony, among people of every age and rank.[40]

The pervasive spread of the accusations eventually brought discredit on the trials. In the short term, it was the question of spectral evidence that was the most contentious. A small group of influential men, including the Reverend Samuel Willard and the merchant Thomas Brattle, quickly rejected the proceedings as irrational and destructive. The Mathers, who were enjoying a brief period of clerical and political leadership in the wake of the new charter, took a cautious position by minimizing the value of spectral evidence without seeming to undermine the validity of the court's actions. Indeed, two days before the court's first sitting, Cotton Mather wrote to John Richards to urge that the judges should not 'lay more stress on pure specter testimony than it will bare.' It was probably at the Mathers' behest that Phips expressed his concern about spectral evidence on 13 June and called for the advice of a panel of twelve clergymen. The leading members of this body were, not surprisingly, the Mathers.[41]

The panel reported quickly. Cotton Mather drafted its findings and conveyed them to Phips on 15 June. Spectral evidence, the report declared unequivocally, was not sufficient to convict a witch or even to bring charges against a person unless supported by other evidence. In any and all circumstances, spectral evidence should be used only with 'a very critical and exquisite caution.' Moreover, if the court ignored spectral evidence altogether, this might well 'put a period unto the progress of the dreadful calamity' that was afflicting them. For all that, the report stopped well short of condemning the Salem proceedings, and it called for 'the speedy and vigorous prosecution of such as have rendered themselves obnoxious.'[42] This basic belief in the reality of witchcraft combined with the condemnation of spectral evidence must have complicated Phips's task in making a second important decision. Nathaniel Saltonstall had resigned from the court of oyer and terminer in protest at the undue use of spectral evidence. The other judges, publicly at least, held firm with Stoughton to its legitimacy as cited before the court. Phips then replaced Saltonstall with Jonathan Corwin, a leading Salem merchant and magistrate, and a known supporter of the extensive use of spectral evidence. He, Bartholomew Gedney, and William Hathorne had been the pretrial magistrates and the Salem jail was filled with people they had placed there on the sole basis of spectral evidence. With Corwin's appointment, the court was powerfully confirmed in its use of spectral evidence.[43]

In the appointment of Jonathan Corwin, Phips went far beyond the qualified expression of support for the Salem prosecutions which the Mathers and their clerical colleagues had offered, and he acted in flat contradiction to their strictures on the use of spectral evidence. Although direct indications of the reasons for the decision are lacking, the evidence strongly suggests a framework within which it can be interpreted. It is unlikely that Phips would act in petulant disregard of the Mathers' advice or that he was not sufficiently astute to realize the implications of adding Corwin to the bench. On most issues he continued to remain close to the Mathers, and Corwin's inclinations must have been plain enough even to an inexperienced governor. Possibly Phips, as the uncle of an afflicted child, identified more readily with the accusers than the accused. He no doubt shared the prevailing belief in the reality of witchcraft. Indeed, his close associate John Phillips had once linked a leg infection with 'Conjuring tricks' that had caused spectral 'Women in silk cloathing' to appear by his sickbed.[44]

However, a crucial ingredient in any reconstruction of the significance of Corwin's appointment is the fact that both Phips and his wife were clearly vulnerable to accusations of witchcraft. In the case of Mary Spencer Phips, it seems that suspicions eventually gave rise to open denunciation. While there is no surviving evidence of a formal complaint, three contemporaries linked Lady Phips directly with the Salem outbreak. The first was an anonymous letter published in pamphlet form in late 1694, its probable author Nathaniel Byfield, a political opponent of Sir William Phips. The letter made no mention of a specific accusation of witchcraft against Mary Spencer Phips, but it had her acting in Sir William's absence to issue a warrant for the release of a suspected witch. The jailer, cited as the informant for the episode, had accepted the warrant and had then been dismissed for his pains.[45] Reports that Mary Phips had been accused of more than just aiding a defendant by illegal means surfaced in print in 1700, in the Boston merchant Robert Calef's *More Wonders of the Invisible World*. When the Massachusetts council had discussed Sir William's intention to put an end to the trials, Calef recalled, praise for the governor's wisdom had been answered by sceptics who had observed sardonically that 'it was high time for him to stop it, his own Lady being accused.' Two years later the Quaker John Whiting asked rhetorically in his *Truth and Innocency Defended against Falsehood and Envy*, 'Was not the Governour's Wife [among the accused]?'[46] None of these references is individually conclusive, but taken together they identify Mary Spencer Phips as coming under suspicion at a time when it was entirely unpredictable to what level of society the denunciations would eventually reach.

There are many possible reasons why Mary Spencer Phips would have been suspected. In personal affairs she was used to acting as her husband's deputy and attorney and had been particularly active in this role in the preceding year. Some critics may already have disapproved of her independence in business dealings. This, however, was a minor matter compared to signing a warrant in the governor's absence, which would have been a flagrantly illegal act that intruded actively into the male-dominated political world of the colony. Richard Weisman has suggested that anyone who dared to protect possible witches was likely to be denounced, and Carol Karlsen has argued that her accusal fits a pattern of women without sons, or women without brothers, who 'stood in the way of orderly transmission of property from one generation of males to another.'[47] These suggestions have their merits, but the simpler and more general reality is that Mary Spencer Phips, like Sir William, was a strong candidate for accusation according to any one of a number of the prevailing criteria.

She was vulnerable, first, because of an earlier witchcraft accusation against a member of her brother-in-law's family, and this brother-in-law's widow (her sister Rebecca) was now living in Rowley, a nearby town to Salem Village. Indirect as the connection was, witchcraft was believed to pass through families, and even remote associations could be given considerable weight.[48] In this case, the episode dated from 1659, when Eleanor Bully (or Bailey) of Black Point had been accused of witchcraft by the Reverend John Thorpe. Specifically, Bully was accused of causing the death of a cow belonging to the clergyman Robert Jordan, though Jordan refused to countenance the accusation. He pointed to domestic friction as the real source of the animosity, for Thorpe boarded with the Bullys, and Eleanor had recently warned him to 'reform his life, or leave her house.' Her nephew John Bully lived in Saco with his wife Rebecca Spencer, the sister of Mary Spencer Phips. John and Rebecca had become war refugees before John's death in Boston in 1679, and Rebecca had subsequently married David Bennett of Rowley. The accusation of 1659 had been quickly dismissed when it came to court, but the case was still well known even in Essex County in the 1690s, for it was recorded in 1697 by the Reverend John Hale of Beverly in his *Modest Inquiry into the Nature of Witchcraft*.[49]

In addition to its kinship ties to an individual accused of witchcraft, the Phips household was unusual in its composition. William and Mary Phips were childless but had a number of servants, including members of groups considered heathens and outsiders in Puritan Boston. Sir William's 1696 probate inventory listed 'one negro man, boy, and negro woman,' and one of them was highly visible in a controversy during the witch trials. In late June 1692, when Phips ordered recruits to be pressed into service for an expedition against French shipping, a number of his critics described how Phips's 'Negro with a Sword by his side seized and Impressed severall free holders.'[50] The English associated Africans with the colour black, to which they attributed unpleasant connotations of evil and malignancy, and during the Salem outbreak the devil was sometimes described as a black man.[51] Another of the Phips family's servants was the granddaughter of the Penobscot Wabanaki sachem Madockawando. The Catholic daughter of his daughter Pidianske and her French husband, the baron de Saint-Castin, she had been captured by Phips at Port-Royal in 1690.[52] Taken alone, any one of these circumstances could be dismissed as harmless enough. Combined, they denoted Mary Spencer Phips as a barren woman who undermined authority, whose family included an accused witch and former parishioners of George Burroughs, and who presided over a multiracial household that included the granddaughter of one of the most prominent war leaders of Cotton Mather's *'Diabolical Indians.'* A charge against her would be all too readily believable.

A charge against Mary would also taint her husband, who had more than his own share of suspicious traits. He had grown up in close contact with Wabanaki visitors to his father's trading house and smithy, and his continued associations with the frontier and the costly war were obvious. His religious conversion had come late in life, his conversion narrative had been noticeably short on details of his repentance, and even Cotton Mather admitted that he was less than ostentatious in his devotions.[53] He was also a notoriously successful treasure seeker, a profession with ancient and well-known connections to witchcraft. In England a statute of 1542 on witchcraft, renewed in 1563, had specifically outlawed the use of occult measures to locate treasure. A more severe statute of 1604 – which remained in force until 1736 – provided the death penalty for a second offence. When these laws had been passed, barrows, mounds, and prehistoric sites had all been viewed as potential treasure troves, and their frequent excavation had led to the use of the term 'hill-digger' to denote an individual who was preoccupied with a search for instant wealth and social advancement. The equivalents in Phips's time included the quest for American silver, either in the ground or in Spanish treasure ships. Although Phips's recovery of the *Concepción* owed nothing, so far as we know, to necromancy or divination, it was open to association with the traditional magical implications of treasure. Phips's subsequent interest in mining ventures maintained this linkage. As a correspondent of the Salem merchant Bartholomew Gedney had commented in 1688, there were investors in London who 'thought copper and silver were as easily got out of the ground in N.E., as the late great treasures out of the Spanish wrecks.'[54]

·As if his ties to treasure were not enough, Phips had also associated himself with fortune-telling. Even Cotton Mather, who denounced fortune-telling as an evil akin to witchcraft, admitted that 'long before Mr. Phips came to be Sir *William*, while he sojourned in *London*, there came an old *Astrologer*, living in the Neighbourhood, who making some *Observation* of him, though he had small or no *Conversation* with him, did (howbeit by him wholly undesired) one Day send him a Paper, wherein he had, with Pretences of a Rule in *Astrology* for each Article, distinctly noted the most material Passages that were to befall this our *Phips* in the remaining part of his Life.'[55] According to Mather's account, Phips had discarded the prediction with pious scepticism and commendable speed. It had been found 'at the bottom of a Trunk' by his wife, who marvelled at its accuracy but burned it when her husband's appointment as governor confirmed yet another of the astrologer's prophecies and made her 'afraid of letting it lye any longer in the House.'

Mather took great pains to stress that both Mary and William had been troubled by the astrologer's 'undesired Paper' (he carefully avoided the word 'fortune') rather than putting any faith in it.[56] Yet the fact that it had been kept for several years could readily cast doubt on the assertion that it was unsolicited and unwanted. How widely the prediction was known about at the time is unclear, but it was evidently a matter of sufficient concern to Mather by 1697 that he went out of his way to mention it and to make a tortuous effort to impose on it a gloss favourable to Phips. The issue was eagerly seized upon by Mather's critic Robert Calef, who compared Phips to King Saul, who destroyed many witches in Israel but went to a witch to learn his fortune. Calef alleged that Phips had paid the astrologer £200 and acidly observed, 'Such predictions would have been counted at Salem, pregnant proofs of Witchcraft, and much better than what were against several that suffered there.'[57]

More generally, as the celebrated projector who had prompted a surge of speculative ventures, Phips symbolized in certain respects the unsound commercial values that could be taken as a threat to the longevity of the Puritan commonwealth. The second part of John Bunyan's *Pilgrim's Progress*, published in 1684, included an episode in which the virtuous Mr Standfast was tempted by a witch, Madam Bubble, who promised large amounts of gold if he would follow her. That the name implied an association with speculative projects is illustrated by its later application to such schemes as the South Sea Bubble of 1720. Acquisitiveness in itself was not an obstacle to godliness, as witness the economic development of seventeenth-century Massachusetts through the profits of pious and socially minded merchants, but as Stephen Innes has pointed out, the line dividing legitimate profit from the sin of greed was crossed when selfishness eclipsed social responsibility. Speculative projects that enriched individuals were notoriously corrosive of communal values, and when the riches came suddenly in the form of a vast quantity of silver and gold the further dividing line between the sinful and the diabolical could loom dangerously close.[58]

None of this ultimately led to an accusation of witchcraft against Sir William Phips, but his background does reinforce the idea that an accusation against Mary Spencer Phips was far from a freakish or random development. It also helps explain why Phips was in no position in June 1692 to antagonize the powerful Essex interests that were represented by individuals such as Bartholomew Gedney and Jonathan Corwin. Corwin's long-standing public career, notably his service as an examining magistrate, made him an obvious candidate to succeed Saltonstall on the court of oyer and terminer. His support for the wide use of spectral evidence was a price that Phips had to pay in order to avoid political disputes which, as a governor of a month's standing, he could not afford.

Corwin's appointment also gave Phips the freedom to distance himself from the Salem events by concentrating on military matters without being suspected of covert hostility to the prosecutions. Military activity, in turn, offered him an opportunity to be seen to be addressing the imminent threat that proceeded from the recent Wabanaki gains and at the same time to start to live down the failure of the expeditions of 1690. In Essex County in particular, the expeditions had produced mixed responses, ranging from the service of Gedney and George Corwin (the brother of Jonathan) as militia officers at Quebec to the unpopular reaction when John Alden attempted to remove cannon from Marblehead.[59] The charge that the expeditions had succeeded only in aggravating the currently sad state of New England's defences was more likely to be made by former supporters of the Dominion of New England than by the likes of Gedney or Corwin, but it still behoved Phips to erase the memory of the Quebec defeat as quickly and effectively as he could.

Accordingly, on 5 July 1692, Phips commissioned Benjamin Church as major-commandant of the forces. Three days later, the governor emphasized to the council the need to reinvigorate and systematize the war effort and to raise money to defend 'the Eastern Parts.' The council promptly voted to raise five hundred militia, and it established a Committee of War empowered to impress supplies for the troops. Church, meanwhile, used his fame and connections to raise a company of volunteers and a party of allied Indians.[60] In mid-August Phips and Church sailed with 450 men from Boston to Pemaquid, where – as Phips had been directed in his instructions – they planned to re-establish the abandoned fort and settlement as the northeasternmost station of Massachusetts Bay Colony.

On arrival, two companies of troops under the direction of Captains John Wing and Thomas Bancroft promptly began construction of the new fort. The work was completed subsequently under the supervision of Captain John March, the first commander of the fort, and it was named Fort William Henry in honour of the king. Although these officers oversaw the work, the fort bore Phips's clear imprint. He selected the site, choosing the high ground south of the abandoned Pemaquid village. This was the same site where in 1677 Governor Andros had constructed Fort Charles, the palisaded wooden structure that had been destroyed in the 1689 raid. Church, admittedly, was unimpressed. Asked by Phips for his opinion, the veteran of frontier warfare answered 'that his genius did not incline that way, he never had any value for them, being only nests for destructions.'[61] Nevertheless, keeping the two companies at Pemaquid, Phips gave Church command of the rest of the troops to raid the Penobscot. There they took five captives and a supply of furs and destroyed some stores of corn, though plans for an ambush failed when the Wabanaki spotted the English ships. Returning to Pemaquid, Church found the main force short of bread. The governor soon returned to Boston for supplies, ordering Church to raid the Kennebec valley. Church thereupon pursued a party of Wabanaki upriver to the falls at Taconic, burned a major village there, and destroyed many cribs of corn. The achievements of the raids were modest enough, but some semblance of English strength had been reasserted.[62]

In the meantime, the court of oyer and terminer had been rapidly discharging its backlog of cases. Between 30 June and 17 September, the judges reached guilty verdicts in every case, supporting the findings of the pretrial hearings that had focused largely on spectral evidence. By October a total of twenty-six people had been found guilty of witchcraft, and nineteen of them had been executed. Another fifty of the accused had confessed – none of whom were put to death – and the jails were full of more suspects awaiting trial. Ultimately, 142 persons would be accused.[63] Meanwhile, clerical and popular opposition to the trials had increased. Samuel Willard was prominent among the clerical critics, while the popular discontent had become very obvious when the Baptist minister William Milborne was arrested for 'very high Reflections upon their Majesties Government of this ... Province of the Massachusetts.'[64] The execution of George Burroughs had provoked disquiet, especially when Burroughs recited on the scaffold a perfect rendition of the Lord's Prayer, a task believed impossible for a witch. Even though it is unlikely that Cotton Mather, as his critic Robert Calef later alleged, had had to intervene personally to quell the discontent of the crowd assembled for the execution, both Increase and Cotton Mather remarked that Burroughs's conviction was just, thereby further contributing to their dilemma over the trials.[65]

When Phips arrived back in Boston from Pemaquid on 29 September, it seemed to him that there was 'a strange ferment of dissatisfaction, which was increased by some hott spirritts that blew up the flame, but on enquiry into the matter,' he said, 'I found that the devill had taken upon him the name and shape of severall persons who were doubtlesse innocent.' Among the latter, he no doubt counted his wife. Accordingly, Phips suspended the proceedings. By late October he was ready for the next step and sent a bill to the Massachusetts General Court for the dissolution of the court of oyer and terminer. It passed in the assembly by thirty-three votes to twenty-nine. Despite the wish of Stoughton and at least some of the judges that the court should not be discontinued as a result of this narrow vote, Samuel Sewall recorded tersely on 29 October that when the matter had been raised to Phips, the 'Governour said it must fall.'[66] A few weeks later, the Superior Court of Judicature was established with Stoughton as chief justice. Its tasks included hearing the remaining witchcraft cases. Meeting in four sessions in the winter and spring of 1693, this new court did not allow the use of spectral evidence. It accepted few indictments and convicted only three suspects, all of whom had confessed. Some months later, Phips ordered a general pardon and the release from prison of the remaining convicted persons.[67]

Stoughton's resentment became acute when Phips issued these pardons. The lieutenant-governor, described by Phips as 'inraged, and filled with passionate anger,' promptly quit the bench.[68] This incident undoubtedly added to the friction between the two, although Stoughton already had close ties with Joseph Dudley and had shown little enthusiasm for serving a governor whom he had so contemptuously cross-questioned less than a decade before when Phips had been captain of the *Golden Rose*. From Phips's standpoint, the position of the Mathers was a more serious concern. Increase Mather had made a direct attack on spectral evidence in his *Cases of Conscience Concerning Evil Spirits Impersonating Men*, which was published with a date of 1693 but was already in circulation in Boston in the fall of 1692.[69] This work gave an added justification to Phips's action in stopping the trials, but it did not resolve a fundamental dilemma. If spectral evidence was illegitimate as used by the court of oyer and terminer, then accused persons had been wrongly charged, imprisoned, and even executed. If, on the other hand, spectral evidence was legitimate as used, then what was the justification for Phips's intervention? Phips, furthermore, had created the court and had appointed Jonathan Corwin to it at a crucial time. The Mathers had supported the convictions, yet at the same time they had expressed doubt about spectral evidence.

The most thorough attempt at an answer came in Cotton Mather's *Wonders of the Invisible World*, dated 1693, though also in circulation before the end of 1692. In his effort to justify both the ending of the trials and the actions of the judges, the younger Mather minimized the difference of opinion over spectral evidence and discussed in detail only five of the witchcraft cases – all of which depended on physical as well as spectral evidence. The transparently self-serving intention of his argument, along with rumours of disagreement between him and his father, did lasting damage to Cotton Mather's reputation.[70] The reality, however, was that Phips, with the acquiescence and frequent advice (not always heeded) of both Mathers, had handled the Salem outbreak in a pragmatic and political way. He could not afford to be drawn into the intense and claustrophobic drama of the Salem struggles because of his close personal involvement and that of his wife. Only by allowing and even encouraging the trials to proceed could the new governor keep his distance. By late September and early October, the situation had changed because of the powerful opposition that had developed against the proceedings. In view of the suspicions about Mary Spencer Phips, the best way of avoiding personal damage was now by intervening to end the trials. The fact that one of the others accused at this point was Margaret Thatcher, mother-in-law of Jonathan Corwin, may have done something to blunt any resentment which Essex merchant interests might have felt about Phips's action. At the same time as discontinuing the trials, he imposed a ban on the publication of any material bearing on the Salem outbreak. While this measure risked the criticism that the governor was improperly constraining the confession of sin, if sin there had been in the proceedings, it effectively ensured that for the time being the Mathers had the last word.[71]

Phips justified his actions in a letter to Blathwayt on 12 October 1692, when he claimed that he had been 'almost the whole time of the proceeding abroad in the Service of their Majesties in the easterne part of the Countrey and depended upon the Judgment of the Court as to a right method of proceeding in cases of witchcrafte.'[72] This statement was misleading and self-serving. Even though Phips was no doubt busy with preparations for his expedition to Pemaquid, there is no evidence to suggest that he left Boston before mid-August. The scattered records of this period do not allow a complete piecing together of his activities from day to day, but a general pattern can be discerned. He was present in Boston on 25 June, when he ordered the arrest of William Milborne. The General Court met from 27 June to 2 July and Phips was present, for on 30 June he called for a council meeting on 8 July. At that meeting, he announced his intention of going to Pemaquid to begin work on Fort William Henry. The council had further meetings on 18, 21, and 25, primarily on military matters, and on 1 August Phips began direct preparations for his departure. On that day, he authorized Stoughton to act as governor in his absence. Within a few days, the expedition departed, reaching Pemaquid on 11 August. In early September, Phips was back in Boston to gather supplies for his troops. His subsequent return to Pemaquid was brief, for he arrived back in Boston on 29 September. By this time the court of oyer and terminer had existed for four months, during which period Phips had been absent from Boston only between five and six weeks. Had he so chosen, he could have attended all the sittings of the court of oyer and terminer except those of 9 and 17 September. It is even possible that he was in Boston on those days too. Phips was undoubtedly distant from the Salem proceedings, but it was a distance of choice rather than necessity.[73]

For all Phips's dissimulation, avoiding political division was impossible. Any reconciliation with Stoughton that was achieved by Cotton Mather's *Wonders of the Invisible World* came at the expense of damaging Mather's reputation and his ability to mediate between Phips and the politically active of the colony.[74] Nevertheless, Phips had begun to reestablish an English military presence in the Wabanaki lands. Sustaining this effort would depend on further military and diplomatic exchanges with the non-English inhabitants of the entire northeastern territories claimed under the Massachusetts charter of 1691.

8

Frontier Governor and Projector, 1692–1694

The military conjuncture that greeted Sir William Phips in May 1692 was difficult and complex, and not only in the Wabanaki territory. The charter of 1691 defined Massachusetts as including the entire area from the Piscataqua River up to and including 'the Country or Territory Commonly Called Accadia or Nova Scotia.' This broad swathe of northeastern North America was seen by Phips as having enormous economic potential for both the empire and himself.[1] The difficulty was that beyond Wells the territories were firmly controlled by the Wabanaki, Wuastukwiuk, and Mi'kmaq, as well as being subject to French influence that radiated outwards from the headquarters of Commandant Joseph Robinau de Villebon on the St John River. Phips, throughout his governorship, expended much of his energy in efforts to consolidate and extend what influence the English did enjoy in the region and in seeking possible economic opportunities. The thrust of this activity was necessarily diplomatic as well as military, and Phips claimed success not only in concluding a treaty with the Wabanaki in August 1693 but in inducing some Acadians to renew the oath of allegiance they had taken in 1690. In reality, however, no firm English grip was established on the northeastern areas. Rather, paradoxes arose that stemmed from the inherent difficulties of cross-cultural interaction and from the constraints imposed on Phips by the English need to conduct negotiations using terminologies of allegiance and subjection that preserved the fiction of imperial control. Ultimately, Phips was unable significantly to advance either his own economic interests or those of the London-based merchants who had supported his plans to extend the rule of Massachusetts not only northeastwards but into Canada itself.

Since Phips's departure from New England in early 1691, the English ability to influence events among the Acadians and throughout the Mi'kmaq and Wuastukwiuk territories had significantly deteriorated. Because of Joseph Robinau de Villebon's arrival in Port-Royal in June 1690, his assumption of military command from a base at Jemseg later that summer, and the subsequent failure of Phips's Quebec expedition, the Acadian council set up by Phips at Port-Royal had soon lost any semblance of representing an English governing authority. Villebon was willing for it to continue as a front to insulate the Port-Royal inhabitants from reprisals exacted by visiting English naval vessels, but he maintained close contact with the nominal president of the council, his former sergeant, Charles La Tourasse. 'I must say,' Villebon commented of La Tourasse in 1693, 'that, since my coming into this country, he has carried out all my orders with the greatest exactitude.'[2] John Alden, throughout late 1690 and early 1691, had continued his long-standing practice of trading on the Acadian coast, but the testimony of a New England soldier held captive for a time on the St John River indicates that Alden was immune from attack only because he supplied food and ammunition (just as his Salem accusers later asserted) to the French at Jemseg.[3]

Two events in 1691 further eroded the already tenuous basis for an English reassertion in the Wuastukwiuk-Mi'kmaq region. By the end of the year, Villebon had begun construction of a new fort at Naxouat, some thirty miles upriver from Jemseg. Although small, the fort was readily defensible against hostile forces advancing up the St John valley and was conveniently close to portage routes connecting to the Penobscot. Following its completion in the winter of 1692, Villebon used it with great effect as a headquarters for the coordination of French and Native raids on New England.[4] The most disastrous episode of 1691 for the English, however, had taken place earlier in the year. On 4 June the Massachusetts council had agreed to authorize an effort by a group of merchants headed by John Nelson to establish a fort and garrison at Port-Royal, in the interests of the English crown and for the security of New England, and also – buttressed by a trade monopoly in the region – in the interests of the merchants themselves. The venture began a few weeks later, Nelson and others setting out in a vessel commanded by Alden. An attempt to win over Saint-Castin failed. Trade at Port-Royal was more successful, but the settling of a garrison there proved beyond the power of the small expedition. Turning towards the mouth of the St John in pursuit of further trade, the ship was overtaken in late September by a French frigate, newly arrived after returning Villebon from a visit to France. As the acerbic Samuel Ravenscroft informed Francis Nicholson, the *Soleil d'Afrique* promptly 'tooke all the Pillgarlicks prisoners.'[5]

As Villebon was fully aware, this setback was commercially damaging to the English as well as being a military humiliation. Writing to Governor Bradstreet in October, and contrasting his own courteous behaviour with Phips's treachery at Port-Royal in 1690, Villebon demanded that Alden, who had been sent to Boston on parole, return with the remaining members of the Port-Royal garrison and other French prisoners. Nelson was to be sent to Quebec to await the results of Alden's voyage and a possible prisoner exchange. In the meantime, Villebon visited Port-Royal to reassert French authority. Although he did not formally abolish Phips's council, the news of his action reached England as representing his 'having lately retaken Port Royall.'[6] A bungled attempt by Massachusetts the following May to restore only a few of the Port-Royal garrison members was followed by the abrupt departure of Alden from the mouth of the St John with two captured Acadians and the personal effects of the restored prisoners. Villebon's denunciation of English bad faith must have reached Boston within days of Phips's arrival as governor. Not only did the affair guarantee the continuing imprisonment of Nelson, but it caused Villebon to promise retaliation. 'I have equipped a ship to cruise outside Boston to take prizes,' he wrote. 'One will be sent back to you with this letter. I know no surer means of bringing it to your hand.'[7]

The threat was a serious one. The ship was that of Pierre Maisonnat, known as Baptiste, who enjoyed extraordinary success as a privateer until his capture and imprisonment in Boston in 1697.[8] Baptiste's presence put immediate pressure on Phips to respond. Although competing demands arose from the military successes of the Wabanaki and the growing crisis in Salem, Phips dispatched the *Nonsuch* to Port-Royal in June. If Villebon's account is to be believed, Captain Short – who had apparently been reluctant to undertake the voyage in the first place – enjoyed limited success in his discussions with the inhabitants. When Short tried to convince the settlers to take up arms against other Frenchmen, the furthest they would go was to promise neutrality.[9]

It is not clear how many return visits were made by the *Nonsuch* or the *Conception Prize*, the other naval vessel stationed in Boston. Villebon implied that one of them was at Port-Royal in the late autumn, and this is corroborated by the fact that in early October – at which time Pierre Le Moyne d'Iberville was at Pentagoet with a naval squadron – Phips told Blathwayt, 'I have caused the inhabitants of Port-Royal to renew their oath of aleigance to their Majesties, and because a French man of warr was Expected there, I have ordered their Majesties Ship Conception thither, to secure them.'[10] What is less clear about Phips's report is the basis on which he claimed that the Acadians had renewed their oath. That Villebon made no mention of an English visit to Port-Royal between June and the late fall suggests that Phips was referring to Short's inconclusive conversations there. Phips no doubt understood the Acadian response better than he was willing to report to London, and would privately have agreed with Villebon's comment on the ambivalent role of La Tourasse that 'without these compromises it would be impossible to exist in this country.'[11]

Phips made no report at all to England on his other major initiative regarding the French in Acadia during the autumn of 1692, and for good reason. It arose when Phips received a letter smuggled out of Quebec by John Nelson, using two French deserters as couriers, to warn of a planned French assault on Wells, the Isles of Shoals, and Piscataqua by d'Iberville and land forces.[12] Despite Nelson's plea that the letter be used discreetly, Phips saw an opportunity for an unorthodox stroke. Sending the two deserters to Pentagoet, where the attack was expected to be launched, Phips apparently hoped that they would kidnap or even kill Saint-Castin. The unlikely plan went irretrievably awry when two Acadians pressed into service as guides promptly turned the deserters over to Saint-Castin and d'Iberville, who court-martialled and executed the would-be spies. The effort cost Nelson the latitude he had previously enjoyed as a prisoner in Quebec, and soon afterwards he was sent into extended captivity in France. The planned French attack, meanwhile, involved only ineffective raids before d'Iberville departed for France in November. Nelson believed that Phips had deliberately betrayed him, and the claim was made more plausible by Cotton Mather's clumsy efforts in later years to dissociate himself from the scheme. At best, the plan was reckless and ill-judged. The evidence suggests that Phips saw it as a way to repay Nelson for his role in the Meneval affair and at the same time remove from the scene an individual whose aspirations in the northeastern territories were too close to Phips's own to be readily tolerated.[13]

In general, Phips's approach to Acadia remained indirect. Despite intermittent discussion of an assault on Naxouat, none materialized. Criticizing the slow pace with which 'these gentlemen of Boston and their generals' thought and acted, as well as noting the exhaustion of

Massachusetts by a long and expensive war, Villebon informed the French minister of marine in 1694, 'I do not believe ... that they will come and see us very soon.'[14] He was right. Phips preferred to maintain the fiction – and, to a limited extent, the substance – of English influence at Port-Royal by encouraging Acadian trading contacts with New England and by sending shipments of provisions to Port-Royal from time to time. As early as May 1691, Abraham Boudrot and Jean Martel, as Acadian inhabitants 'Included and under the present Subjection of those parts to the Crowne of England,' had petitioned the Massachusetts council for the freedom of trade promised by Phips in 1690 and owed to them (they believed) by 'this place [Massachusetts], who ought to be their protectors.'[15] Martel and Boudrot traded with Boston in later years, and Boudrot in particular appears to have formed a relationship with Phips. As governor, Phips defended Boudrot vigorously against allegations by customs collectors that his trade with Boston was illegal.[16] Phips was also fond of claiming that he received notice of French shipping movements from his contacts at Port-Royal. Certainly, in the period immediately following Phips's governorship, Charles Melanson regularly provided such information. He was no doubt helped by the fact that his brother, Pierre Melanson, was Villebon's 'captain of the coast' at the time.[17]

There was another side to Phips's relationship with the Acadians, however, and one that was influenced by his characteristic indiscretion. Jean Martel, who was related by marriage to Villebon, was a business partner of the privateer Baptiste.[18] Worse yet, Abraham Boudrot was systematically passing information to Villebon. Not only was Boudrot presumably the individual described by Villebon in 1694 as having 'made a pretence of attaching himself to William Phips so that he might more easily become acquainted with his views,' but he was also explicitly identified by the French commandant as having twice been inside Fort William Henry at Pemaquid and thus being able to provide a detailed description of its defences. Fort William Henry had also been reconnoitred in Wabanaki disguise by a French officer, Claude-Sébastien de Villieu, but there is no doubt of the value attributed by Villebon to Boudrot's reports from there and from Boston.[19] Nor could Phips forestall the occasional outbreak of violence during English-Acadian trade, as in the incident at Beaubassin in the spring of 1693 when, according to French reports, two New England supply vessels had gratuitously attacked the inhabitants; or, according to the New Englanders, they themselves had been ambushed by 'a party of French and Indians.'

Boudrot reported to Villebon that Phips had declared, perhaps with more bravado than conviction, 'that he would make inquiries and see who was wrong.'[20]

However imperfectly Phips coped with the complex details of dealing with the Acadian population, he was well aware that the English did not wield enough military force to intimidate and that consequently there had to be some form of accommodation. He reported differently to England: assertions that the Acadians' oaths of allegiance had been renewed were good enough for Blathwayt and Nottingham. In reality, Phips proceeded more cautiously and politically, perhaps even appreciating – despite his misplaced confidence in Boudrot – the virtue of nurturing a pro-English faction among the Acadians.

Building a faction was a technique that could also be applied to the Wabanaki, although when Phips first arrived as governor in May 1692 military confrontation was unavoidable for the time being. Massachusetts had been losing ground in a difficult war for more than three years. Phips's immediate priority was to try and wrest the initiative from the Wabanaki, as was shown by Church's raids during the summer of 1692 and by Phips's own efforts at Pemaquid. Yet the summer's campaigning ended on a tentative note, for supply shortages intervened and Phips returned to Pemaquid in September with only a small amount of bread. With all foodstuffs running low, even though the fort had largely been built, Phips, Church, and the expedition returned to Boston, leaving March in command. Phips had intended to use the *Nonsuch* and *Conception Prize* to protect and supply Fort William Henry while it was under construction, but Richard Short and the *Conception*'s commander, Robert Fairfax, were strongly against the idea. The uncertainty of their supply lines and the difficulty of winter navigation in Pemaquid harbour were the reasons they gave for their reluctance to stay – and on one occasion for their departure, in defiance of Phips's orders. The consequences for both Short and Phips would be far-reaching.[21]

The construction and protection of Fort William Henry increasingly preoccupied Phips. It was the centrepiece of his effort, both for imperial reasons and for his own political and commercial benefit, to make good on the northeastern territorial claims that had been advanced in the Massachusetts charter of 1691. So concerned was Phips with the progress of construction that he returned in October 1692 to take personal charge for a period of time. Between August 1692 and July 1694, he made seven known trips to Pemaquid, and he may well have made more. The first three involved the construction of the fort.[22] His other visits were in order to make and keep the peace with the Wabanaki and pursue commercial ventures.

In all of this, the purported strength of Fort William Henry was crucial. A very different structure from the wooden forts built in the region earlier in the seventeenth century, the new stronghold was an imposing stone fortification built from more than two thousand cartloads of fieldstones. The compound measured more than one hundred feet on each side, and the walls ranged from ten to twenty-two feet in height. The huge western bastion, twenty-nine feet high, dominated the surrounding landscape. William Henry was strongly armed, though there were conflicting reports about the details. Cotton Mather wrote that it had 'fourteen (if not eighteen) guns mounted, whereof six were eighteen-pounders,' while Boudrot's report to Villebon identified a battery of sixteen twelve- and sixteen-pound guns, as well as several four- and six-pounders.[23] Its usual garrison of sixty soldiers was adequate to defend the fort but not enough to give it the capability to take the offensive against the Wabanaki.

There is every likelihood that Phips himself was responsible for the design of the Pemaquid fort. With evident pride, he informed the earl of Nottingham in September 1693, 'I have Caused a Large Stone Fort to bee built att Pemaquid ... and have kept an army in readynesse wherewith I have attaqued the Indians when ever they appeared upon our Frontiers, and often drove them from their Quarters, The Fort is Sufficient to resist all the Indians in america.'[24] Phips was too boastful, as the events of 1696 proved. The fort's quick surrender to a French and Wabanaki force in August of that year exposed serious flaws in its design. As early as January 1693, one John Dottin, who had recently met with John Nelson in France, had condemned its weakness: 'Its built in such a place that ships can come and storm it so its in great danger and the fort of no great force, had the fort been built further up the bay that no ships could come to batter it it would be of great safeguard against the Indians.'[25]

More damaging still, was the fort's orientation to face assault from the sea, and its virtual lack of firepower on the two landward sides. Villebon's conclusion after studying this layout was that an attacking force could readily land at nearby New Harbour and then travel the short distance to the fort's more vulnerable eastern side. Other elements of the design proved equally short-sighted. The buildings were not bomb-proof, so a mortar attack could potentially be lethal; the fort's well was outside the compound, severely limiting the capacity to withstand a siege; and the masonry of the fort was poorly mortared, causing cannon platforms to crack when the fort's ordnance was fired at attacking forces. With a single round stone tower and an opposed flanker, the fort had more of a medieval appearance than the star-shaped fortifications that were in vogue in Europe at that time. Reportedly, William Henry cost £20,000 to build, an enormous sum equal to two-thirds of the budget for the government of Massachusetts Bay for 1692. Despite the cost, the project bore the marks of an effort by a dedicated but amateurish group, led by the governor.[26]

Strategically too, the location of the fort proved to be risky. Pemaquid was more than seventy-five miles from the nearest surviving English settlement at Wells, and it was a hundred miles from Portsmouth, the nearest military centre of any significance. This was a point repeatedly made in later years in efforts by the Massachusetts House of Representatives to resist royal orders to rebuild at Pemaquid. In 1703, for example, the Representatives informed Governor Joseph Dudley that the crown had been misled on such questions as 'the little Advantage it was formerly to us although not lesse than Twenty Thousand Pounds expended' and 'the Scituation being out of the ordinary Way of the Indians, and more than One Hundred Miles distance from any English Plantation.'[27]

For all that, the building of Fort William Henry in 1692 had its own logic. Although Pemaquid had been abandoned during King Philip's War and was again destroyed in 1689, in Phips's day these losses could be attributed to inadequate defences and poor preparation. Colonists had only been gone for three years, and Massachusetts had for many years officially encouraged – even instructed – settlers to remain on the frontier and defend themselves. In the context of the early 1690s, a fort at Pemaquid could be seen as a key contribution to making this approach work. Phips clearly did not envisage that Fort William Henry would be an isolated outpost for long. The faithful Cotton Mather praised the location of the fort 'in the very Heart of the Country now possessed by the Enemy' and credited it as a reason for the Wabanaki's willingness to sign a treaty with Phips in 1693. Villebon, while noting the fort's vulnerabilities, was inclined to agree.[28]

Phips also had personal reasons for building William Henry at Pemaquid. He still owned the family homestead at Nequasset, and many of his relatives and friends had been forced out of their homes a second time. Some may even have been living with Phips, or at his expense, in Boston. A major fort at Pemaquid would eventually allow these people to return home and would increase the value of Phips's property to boot. Suspicion over such motives may have contributed to the way in which the costs of the fort's construction and garrison caused it to be 'continually complained of as one of the "countrie's grievances,"' as Increase Mather admitted.[29]

The most explicit criticism of Phips's actions in the region, however, focused on a different form of self-interest. John Usher alleged in 1694 that Phips's intentions in his dealings with the Wabanaki had been directed at self-enrichment, aiming 'only to Carry on an Indian Trade.'[30] Usher oversimplified, for Phips's personal ambitions were inseparable from imperial assertions as he conceived them, but the allegation was not without merit. The speculator who had found riches in the Caribbean also saw a potential treasure in Wabanaki furs and lands and in those that lay farther afield in the territories known to the French as Acadia and Canada. The building of Fort William Henry might well be a grievance to those colonists whose frame of reference was the long-settled area of southeastern New England; but Phips's conception of Massachusetts – its geographical shape and its economic future – was bound more closely to the charter of 1691 and to the interests of imperially minded projectors such as himself.

Pemaquid and the Kennebec region had long been central to the English fur trade, in which Phips's father and many others had been involved. The trade had also long been important to the Wabanaki, who by the 1670s had come to rely on guns, flints, powder, and shot for their hunting, on iron spear points and hooks for their fishing, and on steel knives and copper kettles for preparing and cooking their food. Their clothing came principally from European textiles. They regularly traded for English and French foodstuffs, especially in the early spring, which the Wabanaki referred to as the starving time.[31] The importance of guns and ammunition for their hunting was underlined by an observation which Thomas Gardner, the leading Pemaquid fur trader at the time, made to Governor John Leverett of Massachusetts in September 1675. Appealing to Leverett to repeal the trade ban which Massachusetts had recently placed on the Wabanaki in view of the spreading hostilities of King Philip's War, Gardner had noted 'These Indianes in these parts did never Apeare dissatisfied untill their Armes weare Taken Away.' He feared that they would be driven to the French for these supplies or forced to go to war, for they 'live most by Hunting' and have 'nothing for their suport Almost in these parts but their guns.'

Less than two years later, Gardner's view was corroborated in the statement of a number of Kennebec sachems, who stated that in winter conditions 'for want of our gons there was severall starved.' Skills with traditional weapons, including such an essential technology as flint-knapping, which had once been passed on from one generation to the next, had apparently declined as the Wabanaki came to rely on guns. Firearms help them harvest pelts and food; the pelts in turn were used to buy powder, shot, and other goods. The cycle carried the potential of giving European traders considerable power of leverage over the Wabanaki, although this was offset by the accessibility of competing English and French suppliers, especially after the emergence in the early 1690s of direct Wabanaki-French military cooperation. Even so, as late as 1691, the captive Mark Emerson described his native captors as going hungry for want of powder and shot to hunt fowl.[32]

Trade therefore had considerable attractions both for the Wabanaki and for Phips. But trade required accommodation rather than hostility. During the summer of 1693, accommodation prevailed in circumstances that gave scope for Phips to claim a military and political triumph, to which he was only partly entitled at best. On 7 July Phips reported to the Massachusetts council that Wabanaki representatives had come to Pemaquid and wished to discuss peace. A ceasefire was agreed two weeks later, being signed on behalf of the Wabanaki by the Penobscot leader Madockawando, leading Kennebec sachems Egeremet and Moxus, and nine others. The written text of the truce bound the parties to meet again at Pemaquid within twenty days 'to make and conclude a firm and lasting peace.' The news of this agreement reached Boston in time to be reported to the Massachusetts council on 25 July. The next day, Phips informed the council that he would be going to Pemaquid to take personal charge of the negotiations, which duly began on 10 August.[33]

The situation seemed promising, for the preceding year had been a difficult one for the French-Wabanaki alliance. In the summer of 1692, a substantial combined force led by Madockawando, Egeremet, Moxus, and others had been unable to take Wells, even though the town had been protected only by a small number of garrison troops and local militia. As Villebon later recorded, the Native forces had taken this as 'a bad augury,' and even the persuasions of Saint-Castin had been insufficient to prevent a retreat.[34] At the same time, as in any long- drawn-out conflict, the Wabanaki economy was suffering from distractions that prevented normal hunting and planting. The effects were compounded when Phips and Church took the offensive. One of Church's raids burned several villages on the Penobscot and Kennebec, and although few Wabanaki lives were lost, many crucial supplies were destroyed.

French resources were inadequate at the time to meet the need created. Then, early in the summer of 1693, forces under Major James Converse constructed another stone fortress, this one on the Saco River.

The English seemed to be growing stronger, and the French were not proving to be effective allies. In the fall of 1692, Saint-Castin and a Wabanaki war party had rendezvoused with two French ships for an attack on Fort William Henry; but much to the disgust of the Wabanaki, the French captains had refused to participate in the attack when bad weather loomed. By April 1693, Phips was proudly reporting to London on the success of the fort: 'I understand by some Captives, that have been lately redeemed, that it is a great Check to the Indians, and that my destroying their Corne the last yeare, put them into a Miserable Condittion all the winter ... The Indians begin to appear in small partyes upon our Frontiers, but I have ordered two or three hundred men to drive them away.'[35]

Despite his bravado, Phips was urgently in need of peace. The events of the summer and fall of 1692 had given the first effective demonstration since 1689 that New England was not entirely defenceless in its conflict with the Wabanaki. Even so, the English retrenchments of those three years had not been significantly reversed, nor had there been any substantial resettlement. Politically, Phips was under severe pressure from a variety of directions. Within Massachusetts, the expense of building Fort William Henry was already a matter of controversy and was becoming subsumed into Phips's quarrels on a wider front with the House of Representatives and its speaker Nathaniel Byfield. The matter was in the process of moving from the relative gentility of the council's request in February 1693 that the crown take responsibility for expenditures on the fort, to the bluntness of the House resolution in December that 'the imployment [at Pemaquid] of any money out of the publick treasury' was a breach of assembly privilege.[36]

Like all the political tensions involving Phips at this time, these were intensified by the disputes over his relations with Richard Short and the customs collector Jahleel Brenton. Meanwhile, outside Massachusetts, Phips was in ill repute in several quarters for his parsimony with military assistance. John Usher had complained to the Lords of Trade that in April 1693 Phips had withdrawn Massachusetts soldiers from vulnerable areas of New Hampshire 'and left the poor out Towns, to stand upon their own defence.'[37] During the weeks immediately before the Pemaquid meeting in August, Phips had refused aid to New York in an angry confrontation with a messenger from Governor Benjamin Fletcher. In a frosty exchange of correspondence with Admiral Sir Francis Wheeler, he had also declined to send troops to support Wheeler against either Quebec or Plaisance.[38] In the sure knowledge that news of these altercations would soon find its way to the Plantations Office, Phips was desperate for a success that would help justify his actions as well as furthering his economic ventures in the northeast.

Among Phips's reasons for refusing Wheeler was his assertion that 'an Expedition [is] now forming against the Indian Enemy in the Eastern parts which will require a considerable number of men.' In early August, Villebon received a report from two Frenchmen, former prisoners who had left Boston around 18 July, that an eight-hundred-man force was being assembled to sail from Boston to Acadia with Naxouat as its target. How accurate the information was is difficult to gauge; Villebon noted dismissively the following year that the New Englanders' failure to persuade 'their Indian followers to oppose ours' had made the effort ineffective. Certainly, the expedition was not mentioned in other standard contemporary accounts, such as that of Cotton Mather. Yet Isaac Addington wrote to Blathwayt some months later that the negotiations at Pemaquid 'hapned just at the time when fresh Forces raysed for an Expedition to visit their head Quarters were advanced on that design as far as the mouth of the Kennebeck River, being purposely so contrived.' Thus, Phips arrived for the meeting with as impressive a show of military force as he could muster. The two hundred Wabanaki who attended were also, according to Addington, well arrayed: 'having been lately supplied with ammunition and what else they wanted, from the French ... [they] appeared in a very good habit and plight of body.'[39]

The meeting extended over two days and resulted on 11 August 1693 in a written peace treaty. It consisted of two instruments, one signed by Phips and the other by thirteen Wabanaki, including Egeremet and Madockawando. The terms set down were unprecedented in Wabanaki-English relations. Attributing years of 'bloody war' to Wabanaki adherence to the 'ill Counsells' of the French, the paper signed by the Wabanaki promised 'hearty subjection and obedience unto the Crown of England' on behalf of 'all the Indians belonging unto the several Rivers aforesaid [Penobscot, Kennebec, Androscoggin, Saco], and of all other Indians ... from Merrimack River unto the most Easterly bounds of ... [Massachusetts].' Peace was to be established and captives returned; the Wabanaki were to abandon the French alliance; the English fur trade was to be regulated by the Massachusetts government, and future disputes were to be settled in English courts. As regards land, the English were to enjoy 'all and singular their Rights of Land and former Settlements and Possessions.' The instrument signed by Phips, on the other hand, merely promised peace, and this was conditional on the Wabanaki's adherence to their undertakings.[40] The treaty has been labelled by some historians as one that 'only formalized misunderstandings' between the Wabanaki and the English. Phips's own assessment, as presented a month later to the earl of Nottingham, allowed for no ambiguities. His successful military tactics and the building of Fort William Henry, wrote Phips, had so discouraged the Wabanaki 'that in despair ... they have laid downe their armes, and their Sagamores or Princes have desired an everlasting peace, and Cast themselves upon their Majesties Grace.'[41]

The treaty of 1693 was far removed in both tone and content from that of 1678, which had recognized English settlement only on Wabanaki sufferance. Similarly, the 1693 provision for dispute resolution in English courts contrasted with the 1685 agreement's statement that traditional forms of resolution would be maintained by both sides. Even so, Addington's account included no corroboration of the Wabanaki 'despair' mentioned by Phips, though it did note the nearby presence of the English expeditionary force. Important interpretive questions arise from the nature of the discussions that preceded the signing. In Sir William Phips, Wabanaki negotiators faced an adversary quite different from any they had met before, for they had known him since childhood. Phips himself claimed in a petition to the crown later in 1693 that his 'personall acquaintance with the Chiefe Sagamores of those Indians' had been 'a Principall reason why they have soe freely subjected Themselves unto your Majestie without standing upon Termes Haveing left the articles of peace unto your Petitioners Discretion Submitting to every Demand without any objection.'[42] To attribute such credulity to experienced negotiators such as Madockawando and Egeremet is unconvincing. Nevertheless, Phips was an unprecedentedly intimate adversary, and the proceedings were indeed short. It is likely that he used as a negotiating tool whatever personal credibility he had.

A further question is raised by Isaac Addington's later report to Blathwayt that Phips, on 10 August, would accept nothing less than submission to the English crown and that the Wabanaki representatives conferred overnight and 'readily agreed' the next day. The interpretive problem lies in the related realities that the Wabanaki, by Addington's own account, were well supplied and armed at the time, and that – as the missionary Thury later observed – the Native leaders who were most committed to peace with the English were 'among ... the most prominent' and yet had to contend with a more sceptical faction that might later gain sufficient influence to predominate in the consensual counsels of the tribes.[43] A humiliating submission was not a plausible result of either of these considerations.

As in later negotiations between the Wabanaki and the English in which the verbal exchanges were recorded in detail, cross-cultural agreement was fraught with complexities. Matters such as peace, trade, landholding, and dispute resolution had immediate practical consequences, which ensured that any misunderstandings could be identified and corrected through later experience; but abstract matters such as sovereignty and submission were much more liable to be understood differently by the two sides, producing a gap in perception that even the most honest efforts at linguistic translation were incapable of bridging. Indeed, translation – insofar, for example, as it might equate the English concept of the authority of a king with the nonauthoritarian Wabanaki familial analogy of a father – might be actively misleading to both sides. It is in this context, along with that of Phips's pressing need for a peace that he could portray as a submission, that the treaty of 1693 must be interpreted.[44] Like Phips's claims that he had caused the Acadians to renew their oaths, his claims to have subjected the Wabanaki deserve the sceptical scrutiny of historians. They may even have caused some wry amusement to those with whom Phips had sat down to negotiate over the years, such as Robert Bronson or Louis-Alexandre Des Friches de Meneval.

Be that as it may, the English-Wabanaki treaty did bring peace for a time and thus gave Phips the opportunity to pursue other goals. One of these was the launching of another assault on Quebec, which Phips urged in a letter to Nottingham in January 1694. Smallpox had hit Quebec, Phips argued, and it might be ready to fall to him in an expedition in the spring.[45] As well as having its own military and economic importance, the fall of Canada would weaken the ability of the Wabanaki, Wuastukwiuk, and Mi'kmaq to maintain control of their territories. Thus, Phips may have envisaged a circular and self-fulfilling process by which the 1693 treaty, by providing peace in the short term, would make it possible to substantiate in some way its more extravagant claims, such as the subjection of the Wabanaki and the notion that its terms extended to 'all other Indians ... unto the most Easterly bounds' of Massachusetts, as defined in the 1691 charter.[46] The reaction of the French to the treaty confirmed that they saw it as a serious threat. Villebon gave strong encouragement to the pro-French Wabanaki led by the Penobscot sachem Taxous, who less than a month after the treaty indicated that he hoped to prepare a large war party for the spring. In late May 1694, Taxous visited Villebon to confirm these plans, and he resolved to recruit Madockawando to join the attack.[47]

The most immediately significant aspect of the treaty for both Phips and the Wabanaki, however, was that it reinstated trade and regulated English traders in order to avoid the abuses and disorders that had so often endangered Wabanaki-English relations in the past.[48] While he undoubtedly appreciated the value of stable trade on favourable terms as a means of nurturing a harmonious relationship with the Wabanaki, he also had more personal ambitions.[49] Exactly a month after the Wabanaki treaty, he addressed himself in obsequious terms to Blathwayt. 'This peace,' he suggested, 'hath put into our hands an opperturnity of doeing something that may be of considerable advantage to both of us if you are pleased to accept it ... It is concerning the Beaver and Peltry Trade with those Indians which I know will bee worth two thousand pounds per annum if not much more all Charges Deducted.' Suggesting that they each make an initial investment of £500, Phips requested Blathwayt to 'procure for mee their Majesties Letters Pattents for that Trade.' While Blathwayt was not always averse to involvement in profitable colonial schemes, there is no evidence that he replied to this approach. As well as being hindered by Blathwayt's long-standing disapproval of him, along with scepticism about his exploits, Phips may not have advanced his cause by making some disparaging remarks about Joseph Dudley – whom Blathwayt found more congenial but whom Phips referred to in this letter as 'mine and this Countreyes Enemye.'[50]

Just over three weeks later, Phips again wrote to Blathwayt, this time enclosing a petition for presentation to the crown at Blathwayt's discretion. Whether the petition was ever presented is not known, but it certainly offered a clear statement of Phips's commercial ambitions. Requesting a monopoly of the fur trade 'from Saco Eastward to the utmost Bounds of [Massachusetts],' Phips cited his 'personall acquaintance with the Chiefe Sagamores of those Indians,' his loss of personal property in the region because of the Wabanaki-English hostilities, and his 'very considerable Charge for the Management of the Cannada and Port Royall Expeditions.'[51] Not noticeably discouraged by the silence that greeted this proposal, Phips soon took a more direct approach to the matter of landed property in the region. In late December he undertook a dangerous winter voyage to Pemaquid to meet again with

Wabanaki representatives, and he reported to Nottingham that the peace was holding despite French efforts to disrupt it. Following Phips's further sojourn there in May 1694, Addington for one was much less sanguine, citing the 'unwearied sollicitations of the French Emissarys' among the Wabanaki.[52] The key to the fulfilment of Addington's fears, however, lay in Phips's own acquisitiveness.

During his stay at Pemaquid in May, Phips purchased a large tract of land from Madockawando, the leading sachem of the Penobscot Wabanaki. It consisted principally of the St George River Valley, a tract of thousands of acres, and the deed was witnessed on 5 May by Egeremet and by Madockawando's cousin, Wenemoet. The following day, in a virtually identical deed, Silvanus Davis bought a nearby tract from both Madockawando and Egeremet.[53] The two deeds together represent an anomaly in the overall pattern of seventeenth-century land transactions between the Wabanaki and the English in that the overwhelming majority of the transactions occurred from the late 1640s to the outbreak of King Philip's War. Only a very small number of deeds were recorded in the 1680s and 1690s, a time of increasing conflict between the two groups. The Phips and Davis transactions clearly formed part of a meeting that reaffirmed the treaty of 1693. The Wabanaki leaders had been entertained by Phips on board the *Conception Prize*, anchored in the harbour at Pemaquid, in circumstances that were recorded by the French officer Villieu after a conversation with a Wabanaki eyewitness. As Villieu reported it:

The Governor had invited the chiefs into his cabin with his officers and his interpreter, and two hours later the two Indians had come out, and going to the side of the vessel, had thrown their hatchets into the sea, in order, they said, to make it impossible for them or their descendants to recover them again. Afterwards, the Governor gave them his hand in token of friendship, and they drank one another's health, and went into the saloon where they had supper. This led M. de Villieu to think that peace had been concluded, and he informed M. de Thury, who was quite prepared to believe it.[54]

Both Phips and Davis may well have viewed the signing of these deeds as an important ceremonial confirmation of the successful outcome of negotiations for continuing the peace. The deeds do not specify exactly what Phips gave in exchange for the land, though a deposition of 1736 indicates that Phips gave Madockawando a large number of silver coins.[55] Why would Madockawando, with the cooperation of Egeremet, sell this land? Traditionally it has been argued that aboriginal inhabitants, not understanding the English perception of a property transaction, were easily cheated out of land. While this may have been true in the earliest years of the English presence, the practical implications of both trade and land sales appear to have been well understood by the Wabanaki by the mid-seventeenth century. Clearly, the sachems knew in 1694 that the land had been sold to Phips, for it was one of their compatriots who relayed this information to Villieu a few days later.[56] Translation difficulties are also an unlikely explanation of the results of a meeting involving a land transaction, for this was not an abstract matter like sovereignty and allegiance. The episode may be explained in part by declining Wabanaki use of the land. The reduced Native population now tended to inhabit the more northerly area surrounding the Penobscot River and Bay, with its rich natural resources. At the same time, an English presence on the coast east of Pemaquid would be an advantage for Madockawando, saving him the need to journey to Pemaquid to trade. In the eighteenth century, a trading house was established on the St George River and was used extensively by the Penobscot.

For the faction led by Taxous the deeds came to represent a formidable political weapon. Until this time, Taxous, Villieu, and the Abbé Thury had been making little headway in their efforts to induce the Wabanaki to break the peace, but the news of the land transactions had what Villieu described as 'a wonderful effect.' Within three weeks, enough Penobscot warriors had joined Taxous to induce Madockawando to agree to create consensus by participating in raids on English settlements in the Piscataqua region. Kennebec forces also took part, indicating (though direct evidence is lacking) that Egeremet had been no more successful than Madockawando in advocating the legitimacy of the land sales.[57] Madockawando and Egeremet had allowed their actions to be tainted by the appearance of self-interest, in contrast to the traditionally collective process for authorization of land sales by the sachems. Madockawando may also have been damaged in this instance by the fact that he was not a native-born member of the Penobscot; he was a Maliseet speaker from the St John Valley who had risen to leadership among the Penobscot by 1675, presumably through marriage. Madockawando's participation in the raids of the summer of 1694 did not avert his decline in power and influence between then and his death in an epidemic in 1698.[58] The hostilities, in which more than 150 colonists died or were captured between July and October 1694, brought an end for the time being to any prospect of stable Wabanaki-English accommodation.[59]

Sir William Phips's influence in the northeastern region declined as steeply as that of Madockawando. Phips, too, was confronted with damaging allegations of greed and self-interest. John Usher had condemned the 1693 treaty from the first for what he interpreted as Phips's unscrupulous neglect of the interests of the New Hampshire settlements. Now, in the context of the first raid in July on Oyster River, Usher's verdict was scathing. His theme was soon taken up more widely among Phips's political opponents. An anonymous report reaching London in September 1694 had Phips making a personal gain of £2,000 by 'Tradeing to Eastward by Monopolizing the Trade in his own hands.' A 'Letter from New England,' printed and distributed as a pamphlet later in the year, defined the results of the 1693 treaty in similar terms: 'Sir *William* being to have the trade of Beaver to himself and Company, by his Sloop from time to time for about ten months, supplies them with all things to pursue their depredations upon us.'[60] Even Thury, reporting to Frontenac on a visit that Phips made to Pemaquid in late July, had heard rumours that a major reason for Phips's expedition was to 'appease the New Englanders who had blamed him for all the damage they [the Wabanaki] had done to them, because the result of his assurances, that the peace he had made with the natives was genuine, was that they had all let down their guard.' Phips, on his return to Boston, reported to the Massachusetts council that he had found some of the Wabanaki to be 'very friendly.' But mid-September, in a letter to Secretary of State Sir John Trenchard, he was admitting the extent of the hostilities, though giving them a self-serving gloss connected with his recent recall to face his critics in London: 'Our Eastern Sagamores upon the newes of my going home seem to abandon that good Regard for the English, whereunto by God's blessing I had brought and kept them.'[61]

The land transactions of the summer of 1694 thus proved to have serious consequences for Phips's personal and political goals in the region. Yet had the peace held, the results could have been different. Phips's dealings with Madockawando and Egeremet, while ultimately unsuccessful, were revealing in terms of his aims and aspirations. The shipboard meeting in Pemaquid harbour had reaffirmed the peace, a point of strength for a governor who was already facing the possibility of recall. Moreover maintaining the Wabanaki as allies isolated the French and strengthened Phips's chances for leading another expedition to attack Quebec. No doubt, Phips planned to press his case for another expedition if he proved able to clear his name in England. The St George River was the next major drainage east of Pemaquid and a logical place for the next series of towns to be planted once the war was over. Phips had long been considering this area for new settlement. While in England in 1691 he had drawn up a list of twelve harbours and other places in New England and Acadia that would be suitable sites for new settlements. The first name on the list was 'Puttdumquoar' – Phips's clumsy attempt to write 'Matonquoog,' the mouth of the St George River. A healthy return awaited the astute proprietor of such a parcel once the French were defeated and settlement could begin.[62]

There was a complication, though, in the fact that the land had another claimant to ownership aside from the Wabanaki. A patent of 1630 was still held by the Leverett family, one of the most influential in Massachusetts. Many years later, Phips's adopted son Spencer reached an agreement with the Leverett heirs to exchange the Madockawando deed for a 10 per cent share of the original patent.[63] In the meantime, since the 1693 treaty had opened up to Phips direct profits from the fur trade (which he vainly hoped to secure further through an official monopoly), the 1694 land deed offered the prospect of lucrative land speculation. It also promised landholding that was more in keeping with his status as New England's first knight than his previously modest holdings in Boston and the neck of land that comprised most of the family farm at Nequasset.[64] Although the farm was sizable, Phips probably did not consider it a worthy rural estate for a knight, for it was a sign of his poor childhood and humble origins. Now, by signing a single deed, Phips had purchased thousands of acres of land that made him a great landowner – at least on paper, and assuming that the authority of Madockawando and Egeremet could be sustained.

Phips had a further venture in mind for the region, as witness his petition of August 1691 for the mining rights to New England and Acadia. Phips and his fellow petitioners – Thomas Lake Jr, Sir Steven Evance (or Evans), John Smith, Thomas Porter of Shadwell, and Richard Frith Jr – claimed to know the region well and believed that it contained silver and copper mines. Phips almost certainly had direct knowledge of at least one silver mine in the Saco River Valley, for its development had been attempted unsucccessfully in the early 1660s by the prominent Saco landholder William Phillips. In partnership with his son-in-law John Alden, Phillips had sold shares to members of his family and to leading Boston merchants, including Thomas Clarke. No serious efforts appear to have been made at that time to work the mine, but Phips was in a good position to be aware of its existence; his brother-in-law John Spencer had lived on the Saco and had witnessed Phillips's purchase of the land from a Wabanaki vendor as well as his sale of a share of the mine.[65]

At least one of Phips's fellow petitioners, Thomas Lake, probably knew of this mine as well. Lake's father and namesake was the Thomas Lake who had been a long-time partner of Thomas Clarke in many of his ventures, and through Clarke it is possible that the senior Lake may have had a small interest in the mine. Born in New England, Thomas Lake Jr had moved to England to become a lawyer at the Middle Temple and was the heir of a well-connected uncle, Sir Edward Lake. Lake's career had similarities with that of Sir Stephen Evance, another of the petitioners. Evance had been born in New Haven into one of the wealthiest merchant families in Connecticut. In the early 1670s he had moved to England with his widowed mother and his siblings. Becoming a banker and goldsmith of wealth and standing, he was knighted in 1690, thereby becoming the second native-born New Englander to be so honoured. He was also a prominent public creditor and, during the summer of 1691, an active speculator in stocks. Evance may have been drawn into the partnership by Lake, for the two families were old friends. Thomas Lake Jr's mother was Lydia Goodyear, the daughter of Stephen Goodyear, merchant and lieutenant-governor of New Haven. When the Evances sold their property in New Haven to return to England, Thomas Lake Sr was the buyer. With family ties and a common background, Thomas Lake Jr and Sir Stephen Evance had presumably remained in touch with each other.

The petitioners were thus a powerful and well-organized group, a reflection of Phips's circle of contacts and the faith he appeared to have instilled in the investors. The group included three notably wealthy men of New England origin, two of them knights and the third a nephew of a knight. Phips provided the experience as a successful projector, Lake had the legal connections, and no mining operation could be complete without a goldsmith, such as Evance. The other investors also brought their money and talents.[66]

Nothing ever came of Phips's petition, but he was not the only one interested in the mining operation on the Saco. George Turfrey, a merchant with ties in both Boston and Saco, had written in 1687 to Blathwayt – who referred to him in one document as Cousin Treffrey – in pursuit of the rights to the Saco River mine, promising 50 per cent of the profit to Blathwayt. Despite all this interest, there is no evidence that the silver mine was worked before the nineteenth century. Meanwhile, in addition to the efforts of the Phips group and Turfrey, a group led by Sir Matthew Dudley continued to seek a charter for a major copper-mining operation and a copper mint. In January 1694 Dudley noted that just as soon as they had their charter they proposed to send between £5,000 and £10,000 to New England to hire workers and materials for the copper works. The group was also ready to invest £40,000 to buy land for timber and naval stores.[67]

Phips was strangely silent about the Dudley enterprise, considering his own efforts to develop enterprises in both mining and timber. His interest in timber had first been broached to the Lords of Trade in September 1691, and in April 1693 he renewed his request for directions to enable him to 'make some proposals as to providing naval stores and other things of the kind.' He added, 'If such produce be encouraged there may well be supplied for the Royal Navy, and I shall study that it may be done at cheaper than ordinary rates.'[68] By the spring of 1694, Sir Henry Ashurst and Sir Stephen Evance appear to have been working against the Dudley proposal. Dire consequences would follow for Massachusetts, they warned, if a patent were granted to an English group seeking to engross the mines and timber of New England. They proposed instead that within a year they should bring over a supply of naval stores, which could be examined for quality, along with an official estimate from the Massachusetts government of the quantities that could be supplied regularly. Ashurst's strained relations with Phips at the time make it unlikely that the governor was an intended beneficiary of this intervention. In any event, the matter remained unsettled well beyond Phips's lifetime.[69]

Phips's efforts to use his governorship to advance his aspirations as a projector on the frontier of New England thus ended in failure. So did his related attempt to reach a firm accommodation with the Wabanaki, since the peace was threatened by Wabanaki factional disputes and the activities of the French, as well as being undermined by Phips's own acquisitiveness. Phips paid a political as well as a personal price for these setbacks, having committed so much of his energy, resources, and prestige to the northeastern region. His efforts to maintain a semblance of English influence in the Acadian communities also had limited success. Nevertheless, his actions did have a certain consistency. First, they reflected a geographical perception of Massachusetts that conformed with the charter of 1691, with its wider boundaries than Massachusetts had traditionally enjoyed. This implied that there was correspondingly less attention given by Phips to southern New England. Secondly, Phips's commercial view of the northeastern expansion of New England, in which exploitation of natural resources would precede settlement, implied a need to reach an accommodation with the non-English population. However much the written terms of the treaty of 1693 may have differed from what the Wabanaki understood them to be, Phips was well aware that peace was a necessary prerequisite for trade and then for English settlement. Another model of accommodation was evident in his support of Acadian merchants. Thirdly, Phips was aware of the strategic advantages that could be gained for the English interest in this entire region by a successful assault on Canada. In all of these ways, events in the northeast were connected not only with the potential development of imperial trade but also with the socio-economic functioning of New England as a whole. This in turn was intimately linked with the ebb and flow of Phips's more purely political fortunes as governor.

9

Factional Currents, 1692–1694

During the spring of 1692, soon after the arrival of Sir William Phips as governor, Cotton Mather had circulated a paper of 'political fables' among his friends and political acquaintances in Boston. The first fable, 'The New Settlement of the Birds in New England,' took as its premise the loss of an old charter by which the birds had formerly 'maintained good order among themselves.' After the efforts of a few dedicated agents of the flocks had led to a 'comfortable settlement' by – of all deities – Jupiter, in the form of a new charter, the birds were divided and uncertain. Some believed that if Jupiter would not restore them to 'all their ancient circumstances' they should refuse the charter even if the result was an even less palatable regime. Other more reasonable birds wanted 'to accept the offers of Jupiter; and if anything were yet grievous, they might shortly see a fitter season to ask further favors.' The charter Jupiter offered, it seemed, contained many provisions which 'all the other American birds would part with more than half the feathers on their backs to purchase.'[1]

Another fable, 'The Elephant's Case a Little Stated,' began with the plight of a popular elephant who had been chosen by Jupiter to be 'governour over the wilderness.' Murmurings soon began among the other beasts. It was true that 'they had nothing to say against the elephant; he was as good as he was great; he loved his king and country better than himself, and was as universally beloved.' But 'they feared he was but a shoeing-horn'; in a year or two, he might be replaced by a cruel and oppressive regime. The genial elephant, however, pointed out that guarantees now existed to guard against arbitrary rule. 'And if, after all that I have done for you,' he continued in a vein that soon brought joyful assent from the assembled beasts, 'not only employing of my purse, but also venturing my life to serve you, you have no better name for me than a shoeing-horn, yet I have at least obtained this for you, that you have time to shape your foot, so as, whatever shoe comes, it shall sit easy upon you.'[2]

The fables were as elephantine in style and conception as they were in metaphor, yet they represented a significant appeal to those who had cherished the hope that the old charter would be restored. Not only was the good elephant (the large and increasingly overweight Sir William Phips) a governor deserving of support, but the birds and beasts now had a priceless opportunity to secure their liberty by cheerfully accepting the 1691 charter and working diligently through the institutions it prescribed. The charter was better than none at all, and if the colony acted in a wise and timely fashion, it could protect itself from future excesses, even if a governor like Andros ever again found office. In the fables, Cotton Mather was echoing themes already developed in a more conventional form by his father. Increase Mather had argued similarly in favour of the new charter in a tract published in London in late 1691, in which he had described Phips as 'one that has ventured his Life' in the service of New England. 'When *Gideon* did so,' he continued, 'the Children of *Israel* were desirous that he should Rule over them.' Phips was, by this logic, the choice of New Englanders for governor in all moral reality if not actually by the electoral mechanisms of the old charter.[3]

The Mathers directed their efforts at securing support from at least two kinds of readers. The first group consisted of those who had become disillusioned both with the perceived excesses of the Dominion of New England and with the political and military torpor of the revolutionary regime that had succeeded it. They included merchants who looked for a return to as much economic stability as could be expected in time of war, as well as the inhabitants of outlying parts of New England whose concerns were directly military. Both religious and political sensibilities defined the second group: those who feared that the charter of 1691 represented a betrayal of New England's distinctive institutions and ultimately of its Puritan mission. The Mathers, who a short time before might have been expected to share these misgivings, now sought to demonstrate that the new charter was in effect a moral continuation of the old. Clearly, they did not design their arguments to make converts in the thin but not uninfluential ranks of those who had supported the dominion and had suffered through the revolution to prove it. Not only did these individuals have sympathizers at the Plantations Office in Whitehall, but they also had in Joseph Dudley a credible alternative to the upstart Sir William Phips.

As Richard Johnson has pointed out, there has been considerable confusion among historians about just who were the real political enemies of Phips and the Mathers. Many scholars have long assumed that the advocates of the old charter presented the greatest danger, as witness the attention given to them by the public statements of the Mathers and the references in Phips's early official letters to, for example, the 'Secrett discontent' of those who yearned for the former charter.[4] The reality was more complex. From the beginning, Phips faced opposition from two directions: from the supporters of the old charter and from the royalist faction led (largely *in absentia*) by Dudley. The first group could mobilize powerful support and had a prestigious advocate in the person of Elisha Cooke but might reasonably be expected to become accessible over time to the argument that the 1691 charter worked well in practice to sustain essential liberties. The second group was the more hardened in its opposition. The common experience of personal privations beginning in April 1689 provided emotional force, while the role of Dudley as a prospective governor not only sharpened the focus of attempts to undermine Phips but offered the possibility of growing support drawn from those who had family or commercial ties with Dudley himself. There was little point, for Phips, in trying to appeal to the royalist group, and it is significant that the Mathers did not try to do so either. But from the beginning, they tried to isolate this form of opposition by co-opting both political moderates and those whose commitment to the Puritan mission – like that of the Mathers themselves – did not preclude their conversion away from the old charter.

At first, there seemed a realistic chance that all might go well. Politically, Phips's governorship can be divided broadly into three phases. The early months represented a period of apparently successful though flawed consolidation. The year 1693 brought a series of conflicts, to which Phips contributed through his inexperience and his ill-considered actions. The final months, prior to Phips's recall in late 1694, saw a reconciliation with Cooke and the old charter group that held out the possibility of real political gains for Phips at the expense of Dudley and his supporters. All of this, however, lay far in the future as Cotton Mather cheerfully wrote in his diary on 29 April 1692, 'Instead, of my being made a Sacrifice to wicked *Rulers*, all the *Councellors* of the Province, are of my own Father's Nomination.'[5]

The new charter called for twenty-eight councillors, eighteen of

whom were to be landholders or residents from within the old boundaries of Massachusetts, while four were to be from Plymouth, three from
the former Province of Maine, and one from the lands east of the Kennebec River. Increase Mather's nominees were to sit until May 1693;
thenceforward, all councillors were to be elected by the representatives,
subject to a veto by the governor. Mather had selected largely from
among those he judged to be loyal to him and favourable to Phips,
drawing heavily on magistrates who were currently in office. Eleven of
the new councillors were already sitting as Massachusetts magistrates,
and all four of Plymouth's councillors held office in that colony. Gone
were six of the sitting assistants, including Cooke, Oakes, and Deputy-
Governor Danforth. These steadfast supporters of the 1629 charter had
traditionally been political allies of Increase Mather, but he now gave
preference to more pragmatic individuals such as the new deputy-
governor, William Stoughton, and the councillor Bartholomew Gedney,
who had served under both the 1629 charter and the dominion. In all,
ten new councillors would sit for Massachusetts, seven of whom had
served on the Council of Safety. Four of them were members of the
Mathers' church. (Clearly personal friends as well as political moderates
were to help build the ruling coalition.)[6]

The early indications were promising enough. Samuel Sewall
recorded on 4 May 1692, ten days before Phips's arrival in Boston, that
the new governor had attained the highest number of votes in the last
election of assistants to be held under the old charter rules. In truth, this
was hardly surprising, for it was already well known that Phips would
soon arrive as governor, and obviously it would not be prudent to vote
against him. Yet the fact that he had outpolled such men as Stoughton
and Cooke lent support to the contention that he was a morally justifiable choice as governor.[7] Phips had barely disembarked from the *Nonsuch* when he made a speech assuring his listeners 'that he would not
Abridge them of theire Ancient lawes and Customes but all the privil-
lages and lawes and liberties as was prackticall in the days of ould
should be as they were before and that he, would uphould and main-
taine them.' By 18 June the Massachusetts General Court had approved
a resolution appointing a day of public thanksgiving for the safe arrival
of Phips and Mather and for the new charter, and five days later Mather
felt confident enough to send a note to the earl of Nottingham describing the favourable reception the charter had received.[8] One sceptical
observer, Joshua Broadbent, saw elements of farce in the celebrations
that greeted the new governor's landing in Boston, but the favourable

reaction of John Pynchon – who in early 1691 had been one of the signers of the 'Humble Address' that had attacked the revolutionary regime in Boston – was indicative that hopes for a moderate coalition were not altogether misplaced.[9]

Much depended on the ability of Phips and the General Court to work effectively to re-establish the institutional framework of government and justice that had fallen into disrepair following the demise both of the 1629 charter and the dominion, and at the same time to provide some solid evidence for claim that old liberties would be safeguarded under the new charter. With so much to be accomplished, it is not surprising that one of the first acts passed during the initial legislative session, which began on 8 June 1692, provided for the continuation of all existing laws of Massachusetts and Plymouth until November. When the end of the fall session approached, with many issues still outstanding, the General Court made the continuation indefinite. In the meantime, what Johnson has called 'a torrent of legislation' had begun.[10] On the afternoon of 8 June, in a ceremony that symbolized the new relationship between royal governor and assembly, leading members of the House of Representatives visited Phips to present to him their speaker, William Bond. Bond then requested that a list of 'accustomed priviledges of an English assembly' be recognized, to which the governor 'readily consented.'[11]

With this important formality completed, over the ensuing weeks and months a series of measures followed that were aimed at safeguarding more widely defined liberties. In implied recollection of the loss of land titles under the dominion and the efforts of Andros and others to profit from it, an act was passed that granted uncontested ownership of a tract that was possessed unmolested for three years.[12] An 'Act Setting Forth General Privilidges' held the colony exempt from all taxes except those raised by the General Court, and two measures affirmed the freedom of colonists from arbitrary imprisonment.[13] Illegal imprisonment was not the only matter of judicial process that had been controversial under Andros. Once arrested, the dominion's critics maintained, a defendant had been likely to face a packed jury selected by the governor's appointee, the county sheriff. Therefore, a new law called for jurors to be picked by the towns, not the sheriffs. In another effort to curb the powers of the sheriff, an elected county treasurer was to administered county taxes.[14] These measures, in combination with the need for council approval of a sheriff's appointment, severely limited the power of this office, which had attracted so much criticism under the dominion and had been the focus of Phips's brief and humiliating attempt in the summer of 1688 to assert his powers as provost marshal general.

The evidence suggests that Phips, as governor, gave active support to this legislative effort to distinguish the new regime sharply from the dominion. He was forthcoming with his assent, and further measures contributed to the prospects of his gaining broadly based support. The creation of naval offices for the entry and clearance of vessels from major ports appealed to merchants who feared the intrusion of the royal customs service into their business. The chartering of Harvard College was especially significant to its president, Increase Mather, but it also pleased other members of the Puritan elite and probably even political opponents such as Cooke.[15] In addition, Phips allowed the council alone to make appointments to judgeships and other offices. This deviated from the charter, which had established the governor's right to make appointments to the bench, albeit with the advice and consent of the council.[16] A more substantive reorganization of the courts followed during the legislative session of November 1692. While the new and anglicized judicial structures resembled those that had briefly prevailed under the dominion the context was the charter provision which provided the Massachusetts General Court with 'full Power and Authority to Erect and Constitute Judicatories and Courts of Record or other Courts' and which also provided a right to regular elections and meetings of the assembly. A convincing case could therefore be made that anglicization implied no more than a superficial resemblance to the controversial practices of the dominion.[17]

Whatever the merits of all of this legislation, Phips can hardly be credited with personal involvement in the details of its creation. By his own statement to Blathwayt, he depended on Stoughton in the framing of the bills, and the lieutenant-governor no doubt drew in turn from whatever legal expertise was available.[18] For all that, there was a provisional quality to all the legislation in that the charter reserved to the crown the power of disallowance within three years. When the time came, a number of the most important measures were disallowed, though some of them were then altered by the General Court and resubmitted. The resulting transatlantic tug-of-war threatened to result in a long-term state of confusion.[19] Isaac Addington, the provincial secretary, admitted to Blathwayt when he forwarded the legislation of 1692–3 for transmission to the crown that the laws were only 'so far agreeable to the Laws and Statutes of England as the circumstances of the place and people may well admit of.' A long-standing supporter of the old charter and a kinsman of Elisha Cooke, Addington then added some comments which serve as the nearest approach to an impartial report on the political aspects of Phips's initial months in office. 'If any thing be offered by way of complaint against the administration of the Government here, in which some restless Spirits may not be wanting, We pray to be notified thereof, that so We may make our defense ... The distresses of the War and Taxes necessarily required for defreying the Charges thereof has rendred our circumstances more difficult, tho his Excellency has meditated to manage the Government with what possible Ease may be.'[20]

Addington's remarkably favourable assessment of Phips's role provides a valuable counterweight to the views of historians who have portrayed Phips as 'a bad ruler' who was 'weak, ineffective, and crude' or as one who was 'hopelessly incompetent.'[21] Still, less promising indications also emerged in the politics of his first year in office. These problems partly concerned elements of the relationship between governor and assembly over which Phips could exercise limited control. Questions relating to the relative powers of governor and assembly were to persist in Massachusetts throughout much of the eighteenth century. In fact, some of the issues facing Phips in the aftermath of the revolution settlement were paralleled by those encountered by the last royal governor, Thomas Hutchinson, during the period preceding another revolution some eighty years later.

The important question of Phips's salary, for example, quickly became contentious. Only in early 1693 did the assembly, exercising its power of the purse, decide to compensate the governor. Even then, it carefully avoided the award of a regular salary, choosing instead to vote Phips a sum of £500 for his 'service and expense since his arrival.' Phips assented to the grant but lost little time in protesting to the Lords of Trade and unsuccessfully petitioning the crown to mandate to the assembly the settling of an adequate salary.[22] Twice more in the remaining years of Phips's governorship, the assembly provided him only with special allocations of £500, referring both in June and October 1694 to his 'great service' in the office but making no gesture in the direction of settled remuneration.[23] Even though the issue was one that would plague Massachusetts politics for decades to come, there is good reason to conclude that Phips took the General Court's refusal of a salary as a personal affront and that, regardless of whether this interpretation was accurate, he had genuine cause for complaint.

On 27 February 1693 Phips wrote to Blathwayt to underline the inadequacy of the 'gratuity' recently voted by the assembly. Making it clear that he was referring to Cooke and the old charter advocates, he blamed 'some persons, whose Envy prompts them to oppose every thing that is for my creditt or advantage.' He lacked the wherewithal, he informed Blathwayt 'to bear up the Grandure' of his office.[24] Limited available evidence on Phips's personal finances suggests that this was not an idle plea. When he died in 1695, his probate inventory totalled £3,379. Real estate and loans would have raised the estate's value to about £5,000. Unless he had sizable unrecorded assets, Phips's estate was greatly diminished from the £11,000 he had received from the treasure of the *Concepción*.[25] Although a small portion of the profits may have gone to unofficial investors such as Richard Wharton, Robert Bronson, and John Hull, a decline of perhaps as much as £6,000 in eight years indicates serious mismanagement – or possible losses from speculation in the paper currency of 1690. Lack of cash could be a major hindrance to a royal governor, who was expected to look and act the part. His household needed to be suitably furnished, and hospitality was closely related to patronage.

Phips's probate inventory, taken in 1696, does indicate a high material standard of living to an extent that must have contributed to his reduced estate. His clothing and furnishings alone were appraised at £400, which was more than twice the value of the entire estate of the average contemporary Bostonian.[26] The brick house on Charter Street – one of the finest in Boston at the time, with a commanding view of the harbour from its location at the extreme North End – contained silk quilts and curtains, clocks, books, 237 pounds of pewterware, a case of crystal bottles, six chairs worked with oriental carpeting, more than £400 of silver plate, and other valuable items. Yet there is little indication that the house was used for entertaining. Even Increase Mather recorded only four visits to Sir William's mansion in 1693. The only mention in Sewall's diary of any hospitality extended by Phips was when he and Increase Mather 'treated' visiting English naval officers in June 1693, but even that took place in Cambridge, presumably at Harvard College. Sewall himself, a wealthy and sociable councillor whose family was well known to Phips, was apparently never invited socially to the governor's house, even after Phips had accepted an invitation in late 1692 to take a glass of brandy at Sewall's home.[27] While social unease may partly explain such a lapse in etiquette, it is also likely that the accumulation of unreimbursed expenses during the legislative session, as well as the expense of maintaining the appropriate 'Grandure,' severely strained Phips's cash reserves. Awaiting the pleasure of the assembly thus exacted a personal as well as political price and was an affront that Phips was unlikely to have taken well.

Beyond the immediate friction, there was an unpredictability about the future composition of the assembly that proceeded from the act passed in November 1692 'for ascertaining the number and regulating the house of representatives.' Under the old charter, every town had been entitled to send three representatives. In practice, none except Boston – and, recently, Charlestown – did so. A smaller town commonly sent one member if any, or recruited a Bostonian to represent it. Between 1674 and 1686 the House of Representatives had an average of thirty-six members representing twenty-nine towns, attendance being greater when major questions had to be decided.[28] By contrast, an enormous and unwieldy General Court resulted in May 1692 from the last elections held under the rules of the old charter. Most towns sent two representatives to what was obviously, given the new charter and governor, a momentous gathering. Add to these the thirty-nine members from the former Plymouth Colony and four from Martha's Vineyard and Nantucket, and the result was that Phips was greeted by no fewer than one hundred and fifty-four representatives.[29] The new regulations of November 1692 ensured that this would not happen again by reducing the size of the assembly and altering the distribution of membership. While allowing proportionally greater representation than before to Boston and the larger port towns, the legislation addressed the complaints of towns that saw a significant amount of their local taxes going to pay the expenses of their representatives. Now smaller towns could send fewer representatives or, in the case of the smallest towns, no representative at all.[30]

The result was that the composition of the assembly in the next session, in May 1693, was altogether different from that of the previous year. Most towns returned to their earlier practice of sending one representative, and some smaller communities sent none. The seventy-two members in attendance constituted a house that was much larger than those of the 1670s and 1680s but was less than half the size of the first meeting of the representatives who had worked in fair harmony with Phips during 1692–3. There were other significant differences too. Of the seventy-two representatives, the majority had not sat in the previous house: only thirty-three incumbents were returned. As well, there was a notable geographical shift in the membership, for the decrease in membership was unevenly distributed.

Boston had sent its full allowance of four representatives, but this was not a universal trend. Of the counties, the representation of Suffolk was the least diminished, going from twenty-five to sixteen members. The areas of the long-established Massachusetts Bay Colony settlement were, in general, the most fully represented, while Plymouth, the islands, and the northeast had only a fraction of the attendees of the previous year. York County, the former Province of Maine, had sent eight representatives in 1692 but sent only one in 1693. Bristol, Plymouth, and Barnstable counties (the old Plymouth Colony) dropped from thirty-nine to twelve, and the islands from four to one. Together, these areas outside the old Massachusetts Bay Colony had held one-third of the representation in 1692 (51 out of 154). In 1693 their interest had slipped to fourteen, or 19.4 per cent, and was less numerous even than the sixteen-member group from Suffolk County.

Moreover, the disparity was more striking than it appeared at first sight, for some of the representatives of the more distant towns were actually Bostonians. Electing such a representative was cost-effective, for these individuals incurred no costs for travel or accommodation, and if they were prominent merchants, they might have significant political and economic influence to wield on behalf of their constituents. In sum, therefore, the apportionment act had created the potential for Boston and the other major towns – and notably their merchants – to wield disproportionate power in the new assembly. This presaged serious problems for Phips, who drew significant support from such outlying towns as those in the northeast and, led by John Pynchon, in the Connecticut Valley.[31]

A further difficulty for Phips, and one which also arose from the events during his early months as governor, was connected with the political legacy of the Salem witchcraft proceedings. Phips's efforts to distance himself from the trials, followed by his intervention to bring them to an end, served the immediate purpose of avoiding the consequences that could have flowed from his being drawn into disputes that would have been complicated by family involvement. The price, however, was heavy, and not only because the trials threatened to draw attention to Phips's unorthodox past and the suspicious connections of his wife. It concerned the Mathers, especially Cotton, whose intellectual contortions in justifying Phips's actions in relation to the trials were seen by critics as amounting to a loss of integrity. For Phips, the greatest loss was the ability of the Mathers to act effectively as mediators between himself and a political elite of which he knew little from his own experience.

One side of the problem was the alienation of certain individuals who had been potential political supporters of Phips and the Mathers but who also had close personal ties with Joseph Dudley. Samuel Willard, Dudley's brother-in-law, who in the early days of the Salem trials had collaborated closely with the Mathers in their opposition to spectral evidence, had been mortally offended by their subsequent waverings, which he considered compromising to his own probity. By the spring of 1694, Willard was devoting his election sermon to a denunciation of Phips's governorship.[32] Then there was Lieutenant-Governor William Stoughton, who had been a long-standing political ally of Dudley, despite their differences in 1689. Although Stoughton's scepticism of Phips can be traced farther back than the Salem outbreak, his anger at the suspension of the trials dealt one more blow to the prospects of the brokering by Increase Mather of a stable and moderate coalition. Ever so cautiously, Stoughton began privately to write about the shortcomings of Phips and to urge, as he did to Blathwayt in October 1693, that the 'great abilities' of Dudley demanded his return to public office in Massachusetts.[33]

Stoughton was also receiving private encouragement from a seemingly unlikely quarter – Sir Henry Ashurst in London. In October 1692 Ashurst wrote two letters to Massachusetts, one to Increase Mather and one to Stoughton, which reveal the beginning of a breach between himself and Phips. The letter to Mather, on 18 October, began with pleasantries but soon turned to criticism of the provincial government. 'I thought itt very Extraordinary,' he confided, 'that they should not send me their Address to the King nor acquaint me with the Laws they had agreed of for Confirmation which I onnely heard of by accident att Mr. Blaithwait's office which looked like a Contempt or att Least I tooke itt soe.' Ashurst was especially disappointed by the governor, who 'hath forgott Sir William Phipps freinds.' He complained that Phips had not even thanked him for his efforts, though Phips would not have 'been Governor ... If itt had not been for me.' Ashurst stressed, not entirely convincingly, that he had worked to get Phips the office because he believed it to be in the public interest, and he added, 'It did not sway me a farthing his promisses of £100000 advantage.' The complaints were vaguely worded, and they were not altogether clarified by a cryptic reference to the possible influence on Phips of 'the lies of Sir. S. E.' (presumably Sir Stephen Evance, the London merchant and banker who had been a co-petitioner with Phips in 1691 for the right to mine for precious metals in Acadia and New England). The chief importance of the letter, however, is its revelation of Ashurst's hostility to Phips.[34]

Ashurst's letter to Stoughton four days later was more blunt, to the point that he implored Stoughton 'by all our freindshipp [that] you will Lett none see this Letter.' He expressed pleasure at Stoughton's approval of the new charter; stating 'This hath reconsiled me much to Mr. Dudley who was allwayes of that Opinion.' As for Phips, Ashurst sounded a distinctly bitter and sarcastic note in declaring, 'I doe not meane he should performe the 100 part he promised me but I expected a Civill Letter he had been noe more governour then Lord Lieutenant of Ireland if itt had not been for me ... As little as he thinks I am I may pos- sybley have Interest Enough to unhorse him.' Promising his good offices to the colony and to Stoughton himself, Ashurst went on to suggest, 'When Nova Scotia is Settled it would please me to have Some tract of land by the Country given to me as a gratuity for my Service.'[35]

The contents of this letter, including the explicit withdrawal of sup- port for Phips in favour of his opponents, are less surprising when con- sidered in a long-term context. Ashurst had trade ties with Dudley and his partner Daniel Allin, as well as with Stoughton, which were already well-established in 1684, the date of the earliest extant letters between them. These men were therefore among Ashurst's oldest contacts in New England.[36] Ashurst's mention of Phips's attempt to influence him with money, and of intrigues with Sir Stephen Evance, may even have been intended specifically to discredit Phips with the Mathers. The ref- erence to 'Sir S. E.' is missing from the Stoughton letter, and only two months later Ashurst wrote to Evance's brother John at Aleppo in the hope of initiating trade ties.[37] Be that as it may, Ashurst could not have given a clearer signal of support to Stoughton in the event that the dep- uty-governor were to break with Phips.

Nor, to complicate matters further, were Phips's relations with the old charter group in good repair. Apart from the damage done by the Salem episode, animosities had lingered from the conflicts in London between Increase Mather and Elisha Cooke over the merits of the 1691 charter. Cooke had returned to Boston from London on 23 October 1692, and some weeks later he observed a day of thanksgiving for his safe arrival. The guests at his house included a large gathering not only of old charter supporters but also of more pragmatic individuals such as Samuel Shrimpton. Conspicuously absent were the Mathers, so much so that Samuel Sewall noted it in his diary: 'Mr. Mather not there, nor Mr. Cotton Mather. The good Lord unite us in his Fear, and remove our Animosities.'[38]

Relations between the Mathers and Cooke remained frosty, and on the morning of 31 May 1693 it was a hostile and defensive Increase Mather who preached the election-day sermon before the representatives. The text for *The Great Blessing of Primitive Counsellours* came from Isaiah 1:28, 'I will Restore thy Counsellours as at the Beginning.' While Mather enumerated yet again the advantages of the 1691 charter, gave general warnings against dissent, and defended his efforts in London, he also delivered a blunt and specific message regarding the election of council members by the representatives. 'No governor,' Mather declared, 'will take those into his council, who are *Malecontents*, and do what in them is, to make others to be Disaffected to the Government. No Governour can take such men into his Bosome.' Even though, during the charter negotiations, Mather had argued strongly against the governor's having a 'negative voice' (or veto) over council appointments, he was now openly urging Phips to use this power if necessary.[39]

The irony of Mather's reversal can hardly have been lost on the representatives, and his threats probably did more harm than good to the cause he sought to advance. As Mather was no doubt aware, this General Court was already guaranteed to be more troublesome to Phips than the last. The assembly members elected under the new regulations included not only a solid representation of those still committed to the merits of the old charter over the new, but also a smaller but well-focused group of those who opposed Phips from the royalist side. Daniel Allin, elected to represent Oxford, was a business partner of Joseph Dudley, whose son Thomas Dudley was also a house member. Allin, along with the members Benjamin Davis, Francis Foxcroft, and Richard Sprague, had been signatories of the major petitions of 1690 and 1691 in favour of royal intervention against the revolutionary regime. They were joined by three members from Bristol County who had not been active opponents of the previous regime but had been alienated by Phips as governor.

The central figure of the trio was Jahleel Brenton, the royal collector of customs for New England. Brenton had been in conflict with Phips over the operation of the naval offices, which were in competition with his own interests and authority, and just two days before the opening of the General Court he had come off the worst in a personal confrontation with the governor on a Boston wharf. Brenton represented Freetown in the assembly, while his brother Ebenezer sat for Swansea, and Ebenezer's brother-in-law Nathaniel Byfield for Bristol. Byfield, who was also related by marriage to William Stoughton, had recently clashed with Phips when he had supported the naval captain Richard Short, whom Phips had publicly disgraced and dismissed from command of the *Nonsuch*. In a political culture where family and business connections were crucial to the solidifying of alliances, these members gave every appearance of having the ability to create a solid faction, and the connections with Dudley and Stoughton added a further dimension that was potentially dangerous to Phips. Collectively, they exemplified the large turnover in house membership: of all of them, only Sprague had previously served in the General Court.[40]

Also a sign of approaching difficulty for Phips in the new General Court was the unavailability of a number of the existing councillors to be candidates for re-election. Two councillors, John Joyliffe and the aged Simon Bradstreet, withdrew because of ill health. Stephen Mason, a London merchant who had been made a councillor by Increase Mather in thanks for his work for the charter, also had to be replaced. Samuel Appleton, who was near the end of a long public career and in declining health, may have withdrawn as well. Captain John Alcock, commander of one of the few garrisons in York to survive the 1692 Candlemas raid, was probably too busy to stand for office again in 1693.[41] When the voting took place on 31 May, the numerical strength of the old charter cause among the representatives was demonstrated, even though factional lines on the council were not altogether clearly drawn.

Samuel Sewall recorded the votes for council, and they provide a rare chance to examine political divisions during Phips's regime. Eleven members of the council received anywhere from fifty-five to seventy-seven votes, indicating widespread support for them regardless of their politics. They included Sewall, Thomas Danforth, John Richards, and Wait Winthrop, all of whom had strong leanings towards the old charter cause. Danforth, the former deputy-governor, had been ostentatiously omitted by Mather from the former council. John Phillips and John Pynchon, meanwhile, were known supporters of Phips. This voting pattern suggests the continuing importance of deference and personal ties, even amid the growing factionalism. In addition, Stoughton and Addington were formally voted onto the council while continuing to hold office as deputy-governor and provincial secretary, respectively. The most conspicuous candidate to be elected, however – albeit with only thirty-one votes – was Elisha Cooke.[42]

Cooke's election flew directly in the face of Mather's admonitions, and Phips reacted quickly. 'His Excellency,' read the terse language of the council minutes of June, 'signified and declared in writing his acceptance and approbation of all the persons newly chosen Councillors or

Assistants for the yeare ensueing. Except Mr. Elisha Cooke.' The general impression, according to Sewall, was that the governor had exercised his veto specifically on Mather's advice.[43] While the contents of Mather's election sermon indicate that there was some obvious reason for this supposition, in fact Phips himself had observed to Blathwayt some three months earlier, 'I am Glad their Majesties have given a Negative Voyce, although I did use some arguments against it when in England.' Phips had complained repeatedly to London that Cooke and like-minded persons had attempted 'to clogg me in the management of their Majesties affaires here And in secrett designes against mee otherwayes.' He included Addington, 'who as hee is nerely related to Dr Cooke is alsoe firmly ingaged in the Same interest.' Although Cooke was undoubtedly a political opponent of the governor at this point, the role of Addington is far less clear. But it is significant that Phips was attempting to have Addington replaced as provincial secretary by his own personal secretary, Benjamin Jackson, and was arguing this case in the same letters in which he was surreptitiously accusing Addington of disloyal conduct.[44] Be that as it may, it is clear that Phips needed no prompting from Mather to mistrust Elisha Cooke.

Nevertheless, it soon became evident that the rejection of Cooke had been a political blunder. The consequences were swift and severe. As Sewall recorded, there was 'great wrath about Mr. Cook's being refused,' and the anger was not confined to Cooke's immediate political circle. Phips's action had raised the spectre of arbitrary rule, and for a time it brought a veneer of unity to the opposition in the assembly. When new voting took place on 2 June for the council position that would have been filled by Cooke, the successful candidate was the innocuous Daniel Pierce. More important than the result, however, was the fact that Joseph Dudley, who had briefly returned from New York to his Roxbury home and was soon to proceed to London, had allowed his name to stand and had been defeated by only a single vote. Pierce's nineteen votes and Dudley's eighteen had been closely followed by the seventeen votes gathered by the third candidate, Samuel Shrimpton.[45]

Hard on the heels of this election came another in which Phips suffered a further rebuke. John Phillips, the provincial treasurer, was a close adviser and associate of the governor. In the council election of 31 May, he had received a solid endorsement of fifty-five votes; but when the time came to elect a treasurer three days later, Phillips could muster only twenty-two votes to the twenty-eight of his principal opponent, James Taylor. This may have been partly a reflection of doubts about Phillips's performance as treasurer, but it is difficult to avoid the conclusion that the climate of the election had been dramatically altered by the immediately preceding events.[46] Not only that, but the pro-Dudley opposition was able to seize the initiative even further by successfully prompting the assembly to pass a resolution demanding that Phillips give a full accounting for the expenditure of public moneys 'since his Excellencies Arrivall' and that a committee be struck to conduct the investigation. The eight members named to this body included Byfield, Foxcroft, Sprague, Jahleel Brenton, and Thomas Dudley.[47]

Not for several months would the matter of Phillips's accounts come back before the General Court, but in the meantime the governor's political standing had been gravely weakened. Dudley, privately arguing his own cause and receiving encouragement from Blathwayt, had not only expressed the hope that 'Sir William's time will be but short' but had attacked the 1692–3 laws as amounting to a return to the old charter.[48] It was ironic that the discomfiture of Cooke had been so clearly beneficial for the old nemesis of the original charter. The irony seems to have been clear at least to Thomas Danforth, who along with the governor was engaged in urgent but fruitless attempts to reconcile Dudley's opponents. 'Mr. Danforth,' noted Sewall on 8 June, 'labours to bring Mr. Mather and Cook together, but I think in vain.'[49] On June 30 Phips invited Increase Mather, Cooke, and Oakes to his mansion, but the meeting failed to end the quarrel. Danforth made another effort to reduce the tensions just over a month later, when he and Sewall attended the assembly to try to end the impasse on a bill that would allow Phillips to collect rate arrears from his period as treasurer. A revised bill was passed on 14 July, but by this time Phips was about to take a different approach. Angered by the representatives' treatment of Phillips and by the failure of a measure that would have further reformed the rules governing the assembly, Phips abruptly dissolved the house on 15 July.[50]

The new assembly, which first met in November 1693, proved to be even more conflict-filled than the old, although it sowed the seeds for a modest political recovery by Phips. On 16 November a majority of the representatives were induced to vote to join with the council in making an address to the crown that focused mainly on the continuing need for naval defence of the New England coast but opened with an expression of thanks for the appointment of Phips, Stoughton, and Addington – 'persons from amongst Ourselves, naturally disposed to promote your

Majesties interest, and very acceptable to your Majesties Loyal Subjects.'[51] Any illusion that this might be the signal for a period of political quiescence was rudely disrupted five days later. On the eighteenth, a Saturday, Phips called in the house speaker, who was now Nathaniel Byfield, and demanded an explanation of why the representatives were not sitting that day. Informed that an adjournment had been voted until the following Tuesday, Phips expressed 'resentment' that this had been done without his permission but eventually acquiesced. When the house resumed on the twenty-first, Phips used the pretext of the adjournment to declare to a joint session of assembly and council that 'whereas the Speaker had bin the occasion of sundry disorders Committed by [the representatives] ... the least that he could do was to dismiss the speaker from his place.' Refusing to allow Byfield to respond, Phips ordered the representatives to choose a successor.[52]

Mediation resolved the affair by the following morning, after the representatives had demanded to know by what power the governor had acted, 'no president of Like nature being known to this house.' Eventually, the assembly apologized for adjourning without permission, and Byfield remained as speaker.[53] Phips immediately returned to the attack, focusing on reform of the assembly's regulations. With his support, a bill dealing primarily with the obligation of elected representatives to attend whenever the assembly was summoned was drafted to include a clause specifying that all representatives must be freeholders and residents of the town they represented. This would end the practice by which Boston residents such as Byfield could represent outlying towns, and it would also greatly curb the influence in the General Court of the Boston interests who opposed Phips.

Not surprisingly, the measure was vigorously opposed by many representatives and councillors, especially those who lived in Boston – and not only by opponents of the governor. After a fiery debate, it barely passed in the house, and it was forwarded to the council with a protest signed by twenty-one opponents. Among them were Allin, both Brentons, Byfield, Davis, and Sprague. After both the clause and the protest had been repeatedly read to the council on 28 November, Phips having absented himself, a positive vote of nine to eight was recorded.[54] Phips had prevailed, but the margins had been so thin that it remained to be seen whether the residency requirement for representatives would be enforced during the coming spring. Voting lines and allegiances had remained fluid, with no clear 'court' and 'country' groupings formed as might have taken place under the rule of a governor such as Dudley.

Under Phips, the group that bore the closest resemblance to a 'court' faction was irrevocably opposed to the governor. It remained to be seen whether enough of Cooke's rural supporters could be won over to rehabilitate the working relationship between governor and assembly that had been so jeopardized in the spring of 1693.

In the meantime, other issues smouldered on. The assembly made an explicit assertion of its financial privileges in early December: 'that before any money bee raised in the Province ... [the representatives] bee advised for what uses it is to bee improved and that to imploy any money from time to time raised by the Generall Assembly of the said Province for any other Uses than what it is directed to in the Act is a grievance.' Although this resolution was directed generally at the use of the money raised in recent years for war it specifically targeted the building and maintaining of Fort William Henry at Pemaquid.[55] Then there was the matter of the former provincial treasurer. On 22 November, Byfield, Sprague, Allin, and Davis, sitting as the committee on John Phillips's accounts, produced a list of 'exceptions,' to which Phillips replied after the report had been sent to the council. The matters raised were diverse, though one that struck close to Phips was the allegation that a sum of £95/10/9 had been expended from public funds for the hire and wages of the sloop *Mary*, ostensibly on public duty but in fact sent out on 'Private Service.' The voyage was not specified, but the *Mary* had been used for supply and trade voyages to Port-Royal and other Acadian centres, including the visit to Beaubassin that had led to a short pitched battle with French and Native forces in the spring of 1693. Phillips, in reply, maintained that a distinction had to be made between hire of the vessel and wages for the ship's company, and that public funds had been used legitimately for the latter.

Adjournment of the General Court intervened on 16 December to forestall further inquiries for the time being (as Joseph Dudley sourly noted in a letter to Blathwayt).[56] Immediately before the adjournment, however, Phips gave assent to the striking of a new committee that would examine Phillips's accounts in the context of a wider mandate to inquire into the expending of the approximately £40,000 on provincial bills of credit. Although Byfield and Allin were members, they were balanced by the addition of six others, including – interestingly – Elisha Cooke. This group eventually reported in February that Phillips was owed more than £833. The report was read by the council as the last act in its capacity as upper house before the dissolution of the General Court on 3 March 1694.[57]

The two General Courts of 1693–4 had been costly for Phips in political terms. The consequences of Cooke's exclusion from the council had not been confined to the disaffection of Cooke and his immediate political entourage; and Phips's conflicts with Byfield and his associates in the assembly remained unresolved by either the dissolution of July 1693 or that of March 1694. For most of 1693, Phips had been fighting a battle on two fronts, although the involvement of Cooke in the lessening of tensions over Phillips's accounts in early 1694 was a sign that this phase might be coming to an end. It was clear that the meeting of the new General Court would see a further and possibly decisive jockeying for position among competing political interests. Few, however, could have anticipated how dramatic the events would be. The formal minutes of 30 May tersely record that on that day Phips raised an objection to six assembly members who were, according to him, non-residents of the towns they had come to represent.[58] The most detailed account, however, was contained in a letter written to Joseph Dudley and promptly conveyed by him to the Plantations Office. Although it was unsigned, internal evidence identifies the author as Nathaniel Byfield. After the representatives had convened early in the morning, Byfield recounted, they had waited in vain for about two hours to be sworn in, and were then summoned to the council chamber. There, they were addressed by Phips:

The Governour said that he observed there was many more of the Gentlemen of Boston then could serve for that towne and for some reasons which he should give hereafter he did Declare that Byfield Capt. Davis Capt. Dudley Capt. Clarke and Capt. ffoxcroft if he were present should not have their oaths and the rest should be sworne all at once, which was done not without some confusion, Byfield replyed to his Excellency that the house of representatives were proper judges of their own members, to which his Excellency commanded Silence saying he would allow of no taulke there.[59]

Phips also intervened to prevent the swearing of Samuel Legge as the representative for Marblehead. Legge, who was a veteran of the Canada expedition of 1690 and had served with Phips on the organizing committee for that venture, was no political opponent of the governor. This relationship was a central factor in the episode that began soon afterwards in the assembly chamber in the Boston townhouse:

When Capt. Legg was come into the house of representatives he said he would

Stay there for all the Governor and would not go out till rejected by the house which was presently tould his Excellency ... upon which his Excellency with great fury without his hatt came in to the house of representatives and said that he was informed that some of the said persons he had just now excepted against, where still there and had since said they would not go out of the house till the house putt them out he added he wish he knew who it was said so upon which Capt. Legg hasted to him being on the other side the roome, and said he was the man that said it, and was still of the same mind to which the Governour Replyed he had nothing against him and could wish he had bin returned for Boston and he could freely have imbraced him, but for the other Gentlemen he had something else to say to them and if the house would not turne them out he would turne them all oute presently.[60]

All of the controverted members eventually left the house, and business was resumed under a new speaker, Nehemiah Jewett, who was decribed by a critic of the affair as 'a practising Sow-Gelder.'[61] The exchange with Legge, however, is revealing for it indicates the partisan dimensions of Phips's actions. Although the incident can hardly have been stage-managed, it was turned to good effect by a governor whose display of rage was found – not for the first time in his career – to be surprisingly mutable in the right circumstances. Two important messages had been communicated. One was that, since Phips was determined to apply the residency rule even to an individual to whom he might reasonably have looked for political support, his intention was not to use it selectively as part of a generalized attack on the privileges of the assembly. Given that the action would inevitably stir memories of conflicts between Stuart monarchs and the House of Commons, and notably the personal arrival of Charles I in the Commons chamber in his attempt of January 1642 to have five members arrested, this was a crucial point to be made if there was to be a chance of avoiding the widespread anger that had greeted the rejection of Cooke a year earlier.[62] Secondly, by distinguishing so clearly between Legge and the others, Phips had bluntly stated his objection to the politics of the royalist faction and, by implication, of its support for Dudley. In this sense, the episode marked his overt entry into partisan politics and the end of an era during which he had too often given careless offence to potential allies. Finally, Phips was starting to act politically, if not to raise a 'court' party as such, then at least to draw clear and consistent support from rural areas and from those whose affection for the old charter might be turned to good account by raising the spectre of Dudley and the dominion.

Forceful criticism was to be expected, of course. Its first conspicuous expression was from a quarter that could easily be damaging to Phips – the election sermon delivered later on 30 May by Dudley's brother-in-law, Samuel Willard. Willard's sermon was entitled *The Character of a Good Ruler*, and as well as offering a reply to Mather's sermon of the previous year, it took issue in guarded but unmistakable terms both with the residency rule and with Phips's method of enforcing it.[63] Byfield, writing to Dudley, commended Willard but was not optimistic that the sermon would make any difference to the direction of events. He was far more outspoken a few weeks later in a letter to John Usher: 'Our Governor's Treatment of the Assembly in the yeare Past hath bin such as I doe thinke noe place belonging to the English Nation can paralell.'[64] The problem with these Whiggish sentiments, however, was that they carried little conviction when expressed by an individual whose closest political associates had been supporters and beneficiaries of the dominion. The notion that the likes of Byfield, Foxcroft, or Allin could put themselves at the head of a movement to preserve the privileges of the assembly was bound to be met with scepticism from most members. This was an irony that tended to reflect even on the weight carried by the opinion of a respected cleric such as Willard, and it was one that Phips now set out to exploit to the full.

Late in the day on 30 May 1694, the representatives presented the council with their twenty-eight nominees for the new council. Elisha Cooke was one of them, and this time there was no veto. The following day, Phips gave his written approbation to all the candidates. Three days later, Cooke took his oath and was seated at the council table.[65] Soon the council was discussing a measure described as an 'additional Bill for setting forth general priviledges,' which received Phips's assent on 8 June. The act affirmed the right of the House of Representatives under the charter to 'all the liberties and priviledges of an English assembly.' The choice and appointment of all civil officers, unless otherwise provided in the charter, was to belong 'of right ... to the great and general court or assembly.' The power of the purse was explicitly affirmed, as was the right of the house to know for 'what uses and improvement' moneys were being raised. All warrants issued by the governor and council for expenditures were to specify the authorizing vote of the assembly and justify the expense in terms of the purpose of which the assembly had originally been advised. Although the crown eventually disallowed this legislation, its immediate effect was to address financial issues that had been raised by the assembly over the preceding year, to reaffirm privileges, and in so doing to isolate further the complaints of Byfield and the other rejected members.[66] Another gesture of conciliation, symbolic but revealing, came on 19 June when Phips consented to the paying of £100 each to Cooke and Thomas Oakes, as well as the settlement of some outstanding expenses, 'as a Reward for their services in their Late agency in England.'[67]

Other measures may also have contributed to the rapprochement between governor and assembly, including an act to regulate the English side of the northeastern fur trade, which might offset any lingering associations of Phips's diplomacy of 1693 and 1694 with his desire for a personal monopoly of the trade.[68] At no time did Phips's efforts to gain support from the old charter advocates become more clear than when on 14 September 1694 – already recalled to face his critics in London – he was invited to take a glass of wine with the representatives and made what was probably an impromptu speech: 'His Excellency declared to them he satt uneasie in his place, for that he was not Chosen by the Country, and although the King had Sent for him home, Yett the love he had for his Countrie, made him doe two things for them, and now was the time, the one was to procure the Choise of Governor Deputie Governor, and Secretarie by the people, and the procureing the Antient Charter and the priviledges thereof.' He also promised to try to get the crown to pay the construction and garrisoning costs of Fort William Henry.[69] The latter ambition was more attainable than the first, but as Phips undoubtedly knew, neither was likely. Even so, the speech was well suited to its audience.

In general, although Phips's relations with the assembly were not always as harmonious as Cotton Mather later attempted to show, the governor's anonymous critic was not seriously mistaken in asserting that by the autumn of 1694 'in that House his Address, and what else he pleases runs smooth.'[70] The address referred to was directed to the crown by the council and assembly, and dated 31 October. Dealing mainly with the military state to which Massachusetts had been reduced by the hostility of the Wabanaki, it concluded by imploring 'that Complaints of a personal Concern may not be improved to deprive us of your Majesties Captain General and Governour Sir William Phips, at this time especially of whose integrity for your Majesties service we are well assured.'[71]

Although the political distance that Phips had travelled *en route* between the setbacks of 1693 and this declaration should not be underestimated, a full assessment of the purely political aspects of his governorship is hindered by lack of evidence on certain important questions. Prime among them is whose advice he was receiving and heeding. According to Stoughton, Phips did not pay attention to the council; instead, he listened to 'prejudiced persons' who held the council in disrespect. The impression of the New York envoy Chidley Brooke was that Phips 'selects his company out of the Mobb, for the most part, amongst whom Noys and Strutt, pass for witt, and prowis.'[72] Yet some of the individuals who can be identified as companions and likely advisers fit neither description. For instance, there is no reason to doubt Cotton Mather's assertion that John Phillips was close to Phips personally as well as politically. Other councillors who had business as well as political ties with Phips were John Foster and Silvanus Davis.[73] The influence of the Mathers themselves is more questionable, especially after the fiasco of Increase Mather's election sermon of May 1693. While Phips presumably met both father and son regularly at church, the diary of Increase Mather shows no evidence of more private meetings on a regular basis. Increase, after hearing about Phips's recall, lost little time in writing to Blathwayt in July 1694 on the governor's behalf, yet Phips's speech to the representatives two months later went much further towards an unfavourable contrast of the new charter with the old than either Mather could comfortably have done.[74] On balance, the evidence suggests that the time spent with Phips by Phillips, Davis, and Foster – in such contexts as in business discussions and on voyages to Pemaquid – provided better access to the governor than did a compromised relationship with the Mathers.

There were others who might more readily qualify for the contempt of such observers as Stoughton and Brooke, for instance, Phips's secretary, Benjamin Jackson, and the New York political exile, Abraham Gouverneur. Jackson clearly had frequent access to the governor, while Gouverneur travelled with him at times and witnessed legal documents on his behalf. Yet the extent of any influence they may have exerted on political matters is unclear. So are the implications of the popularity that Phips enjoyed among the working class of Boston's North End. That he retained a following there is suggested not only by the intelligence information of Villebon but by the observation of Samuel Sewall that at the arrival in Boston in May 1695 of the news of Phips's death, 'people ... [were] generally sad.' There is no evidence, however, that he headed crowd actions while he was governor as he had done at least twice in 1690.[75] Phips's social role in the North End had shifted over the years. That he maintained contact with individuals of dubious reputation is exemplified in his holding a £100 mortgage for Edward and Deborah Creek. The Creeks kept the Half Moon tavern, a haunt of Maine refugees, and they had been warned out of Boston some years earlier on charges of attempting to burn down the city.

The mortgage also illustrates Phips's emergence, primarily through the business dealings conducted by his wife, as a landlord and mortgage holder on a substantial scale. The Phipses' landholdings steadily increased with the acquisition of properties near their house and also, in October 1692, of the wharfside land on which stood the Salutation tavern.[76] Sir William Phips frequented the waterfront, and his demonstrated ability to mobilize support there remained a source of disdainfully expressed unease for his opponents. His social class identity in the North End was now ambiguous, however, and it was not a crucial element in his approach to factional politicking in which the push and pull of religious sensibilities and economic interests were central; class conflict took on the aspect of rural rather than urban disaffection.

However Phips's political strategies were generated, he had made considerable progress by the autumn of 1694 towards reproducing the fabled achievement of Cotton Mather's elephant in reconciling the other beasts to his rule. Ironically, he had achieved this by moving steadily towards an admission (for the benefit of the representatives who still yearned for the old charter) of imperfections in the charter of 1691. Deprived in the aftermath of the Salem trials of the full benefit of the Mathers' help in smoothing his political path, and thrown into a dangerous isolation by his ill-advised rejection of Elisha Cooke in May 1693, Phips had recovered by going on the attack against the old royalist faction, which now favoured the ambitions of Joseph Dudley, and by reaching a reconciliation with the advocates of the old charter. Success to this extent in the internal political affairs of the colony did not, however, guarantee Phips the opportunity to pursue his ambitions regarding the northeastern parts of greater Massachusetts and a renewed assault on Canada. That luxury would come, if at all, when certain other conflicts had been resolved in an imperial context.

10

Imperial Governorship: Conflicts and Clientage, 1692–1693

'Sir W.P. having been at Charge to obtain his Government not knowing how long it will last, drives on furiously.'[1] Edward Randolph's evaluation, written in a letter to William Blathwayt just over four months after Sir William Phips had arrived in Boston as governor, was directed specifically at Phips's outfitting of a speculative cruise against French shipping at the mouth of the St Lawrence and at the building of Fort William Henry at Pemaquid. It also drew attention by implication to the difficulty of Phips's position as a governor who neither enjoyed solid support from Blathwayt's Plantations Office nor had the means of distributing patronage effectively within Massachusetts. Although colonial governors were not easily unseated, repeated complaints could and did make a cumulative impression in London. Arbitrary rule in any form or indiscreet use of the office for personal gain, or a demonstrable failure to concert defence forces effectively, were allegations that were apt to be taken seriously.[2]

In this context, the security of Phips's tenure deteriorated noticeably during his first year in office. The reasons were connected in part with the strife between political factions in Massachusetts, which led to the governor's alienation by the spring of 1693 of both the royalist and the old charter groups. The antagonism of Sir Henry Ashurst and the conspicuous availability of Joseph Dudley as an alternative governor (the precedent for a New England–born appointee having been set, ironically, by Phips's own governorship) ensured that evidence of internal dissent would be transmitted efficiently to Whitehall. In addition, there was a range of issues that had a more directly imperial significance: the exercise of admiralty jurisdiction, relations with other governors, and relations with naval commanders stationed in Massachusetts and with other directly appointed crown officials.

In all these areas, Phips aroused serious complaint. His blustering aggressiveness was partly to blame, and his frequent quarrels undoubtedly drew further attention to the 'lowness of his Education and parts' which had so impressed itself on the older Puritan rulers of Massachusetts.[3] Yet Phips's disputes were not entirely the result of his personal shortcomings. They stemmed also from his pressing need to pursue aggressive and profitable exploits, notably in the northeast and against Canada, as a basis for what little patronage power he could wield. From this resulted conflicts of strategy or interest with others who also held royal office and who considered their own sources of redress in London to be equal or superior to those of the governor. In the imperial arena as in the internal politics of Massachusetts, the spring and summer of 1693 marked for Phips a nadir of sorts, to be followed by a brittle but definable recovery.

Phips's preoccupation with a renewed assault on Canada had been evident long before his departure for Massachusetts as governor, in his repeated proposals to the Lords of Trade in June and September 1691.[4] However, his instructions made no reference to the matter. In October 1692 he returned to his habitual theme. To both Nottingham and Blathwayt he urged the royal outfitting of an expedition under his command, promising that it would have widespread support in New England.[5] To Blathwayt, he also stressed the personal advantages of the plan:

The Conquest [of Canada] ... will not onely be worth Millions to the Englishe Nation But from thence may arise unto your Selfe a Considerable yearly income And my Endeavours and forwardnesse to Serve you herein shall be according to the greatnesse of the Kindnesses received from you I would desire his Majesties particular instructions in that affaire for the people throughout this Goverment doe declare that if his Majestie orders mee to Command in that Expedition there shall be noe need of presseing men.

This approach proved fruitless. Since the tone of the letter indicated some confusion over who would be the patron and who the client, it may even have played a role in the subsequent decision to attack Canada with a squadron that was already in the Caribbean under the command of Sir Francis Wheeler, with Phips playing a relatively minor part. Certainly, Blathwayt issued a thinly veiled warning to Phips, reminding him, 'Your honor as well as duty is concerned to mannage the [Wheeler] Expedition and the preparations towards it with chearfulness vigor and dispatch.' For good measure, he also enlisted Increase Mather's influence to ensure that Phips would 'Easily acquiesce ... in leaving the cheif command as his Majesty has determined it.'[6]

Others took Phips's aspirations more seriously. A memorandum sent to France from Canada by members of the Jesuit order in the spring of 1692 anticipated an attack on Canada that summer on grounds that were explicitly associated with Phips's ambitions. 'This is chiefly proved,' the Jesuits wrote, 'by the return of Phips to Boston, whom the Prince of Orange has made governor and has given him two or three warships, with soldiers to strengthen his fleet. He [Phips] has declared that he wishes to restore the honour of the English and to recover at whatever peril to his life the anchor and five cannons he lost when he lifted his siege of Quebec.' The English designs concerning Quebec, they added, had as their goal 'through the capture of this post, to make themselves masters of all North America, its fish and furs, and the territories of the interior.' Although no attack materialized during the summer of 1692, Frontenac for one was not reassured, citing in September an intelligence report that 'Phips still intends to turn his efforts to come and visit us again next year, which obliges me to take all the precautions I can to give him a good reception.'[7] In fact, not quite three weeks earlier, Phips's intentions had been signalled in a raid on French shipping traffic to Canada.

The voyage of the *Swan* and *Elizabeth and Sarah* gave an early indication of the complexities of the attitude towards Canada taken by Phips as governor and of its implications for the effectiveness of his rule. Superficially, the raid was a great success. Phips boasted to London that the two vessels sent to the lower St Lawrence had 'landed men in severall places, and burnt many of their howses, and have taken a french flyboate, in the mouth of the River, laden with Wine, brandy, and other french goods.' The French supply vessel *St Jacob* had indeed been captured near Anticosti Island on 18 August 1692, and it had been declared a lawful prize by Phips, sitting as vice-admiral, in early October.[8] The fuller reality, however, was that the expedition had begun with controversy and ended in recrimination, and had lasting results in creating animosities that damaged Phips in an imperial context over the ensuing months and years.

The controversy began soon after Phips issued a warrant for the impressment of boats, guns, and men on 21 June. Apparently, he delegated the impressment of men to Captain Richard Short, whose violent late-night efforts to find seamen – whether to impress them or to locate missing members of his own crew – led two members of the General Court to swear out complaints that they had been turned out of their beds and assaulted.[9] Some months later, Nathaniel Byfield headed a group of Phips's political opponents who wrote to Blathwayt contemptuously dismissing what they interpreted as Phips's efforts to put the blame for the impressments solely on Short. They also made charges relating to the commercial organization of the voyage, which they portrayed as 'a private designe' to use the power of impressment for Phips's own benefit, with none of the proceeds from the *St Jacob* even being reserved for the royal tenth. Phips's version, naturally, was different. The impressments, he maintained, were part of an early attempt to mount the expedition as a public venture. Only when he found the public treasury unequal to the expense did he 'admitt severall merchants, that would advance mony to be concerned; when they were ready to saile the men were put to their choice, whither to go or stay, upon which some went on shoare, and all the rest went as Volunteers.'[10]

Later depositions by those most closely involved did not confirm Phips's assertion of a change from public to private organization. The *Swan* was owned by Andrew Belcher, the brigantine *Elizabeth and Sarah* by Timothy Clarke and Nathaniel Oliver. All three owners were prominent merchants. Clarke, Oliver, and Belcher recalled that after having initial misgivings, they had agreed that Phips could use their vessels provided he supplied the men and remitted the king's tenth. Clarke stated that Phips had admitted that the treasury was empty and had floated the possibility of impressment, even though he 'doubted not of Volunteers enough by reason of his giving the King's Tenths.' The merchants maintained that impressments had indeed taken place. Oliver recalled that although all but a few had subsequently been signed on for shares, he was 'very well satisfied that halfe the men on board would have left the Vessell if they could, but being forced to go, chose rather to signe than to take Kings pay.' One of the impressed men who eventually signed on as a volunteer was William Snowton, who confirmed that the 'one or two' who had refused had not been released from service. As for Phips's personal interest in the voyage, the shipowners' testimony indicated that he had a three-eighths share of the *Elizabeth and Sarah* and a one-eighth share of the *Swan*. The net proceeds were estimated with some variations but approached £9,000.[11] The most likely inference is that the fiction of voluntary service was introduced primarily as an expedient to offset the well-founded charges (which were promptly relayed to London by Edward Randolph) that Phips was using impressment for his personal gain.[12]

As well as generating damaging allegations that could be used in the future by political opponents, the affair illustrated the weakness of Phips's powers of patronage as governor. Regardless of how his political support might ebb and flow, Phips inevitably had to deal with strong commercial interests within the colony; and not only was the provincial treasury exhausted, but prominent Boston and Salem merchants – Andrew Belcher among them – were beginning to press for repayment of the advances they had earlier made for war expenses. Some of these merchants had not yet been reimbursed for ships lost on the Quebec expedition, and their petitions thus had the added potential of bringing political embarrassment to Phips.[13] A governor in this situation could easily assume a role that was more like that of a suppliant in relation to public creditors. Furthermore, Phips's personal resources were small. His fortune from the voyage of the *James and Mary* had been sufficient to buy respectability but not, for a colonial governor, affluence.

Moreover, although he was able to benefit from some long-standing Phips-White and Spencer family contacts, his social origins limited the strength of his personal connections in merchant circles. Thus, no matter how much Phips might seek the company of merchants in Samuel Shrimpton's Exchange tavern in Boston, he operated within real limitations. Certainly, expedients such as the impressments for the August 1692 voyage were clumsy and dishonest, even taking into account the flexibility of the boundary between personal and public activity for governors of the era; but when Richard Short observed that 'Sir William hates all ... Those that dus not condesend to his Privite Intrest for him and all his Counsell are Marchants,' or when Governor Benjamin Fletcher of New York referred to Phips as 'a machin[e] moved by every Phanatical finger, The Contempt of wise men and sport of the fooles,' there was a context that went beyond personal failings, however real those might be.[14]

Fletcher's withering comment was also a result of his quarrels with Phips, an experience he shared with the other colonial neighbours of Massachusetts. Phips's disputes with adjoining jurisdictions fell into three broad categories: those that stemmed from boundary issues predating his governorship; those that were connected with his command of New England militias; and those directly related to his military and political priorities. Fletcher and the colony of New York were concerned with disagreements in all three categories.

A long-standing boundary dispute concerned Martha's Vineyard and Nantucket. Although the two islands were specifically included in the Massachusetts charter of 1691, the Martha's Vineyard resident and missionary John Mayhew appealed to New York during the summer of 1692 and received an assurance that the New York council would continue to regard the islands as included within its territory. Expressions of concern from opponents of Mayhew on both islands led Phips to take the matter up with Fletcher and caused the Massachusetts council to issue a new commission of the peace for Martha's Vineyard.[15] In February 1693 the New York council responded by reasserting its right to the island, but by that time the substance of the dispute had been overtaken in significance by the embitterment of relations between Phips and Fletcher, which it had helped create. Both complained to London, Fletcher citing sarcastically 'the principles and sentiments of that Knight' and protestesting, 'He has seized upon Martins [Martha's] Vineyard which has ever been part of this Government ... I must nott Levy warr Against him tho provoked by his unmannerly Letter to meet him there.' Phips, meanwhile, portrayed himself as the injured party, describing Fletcher's sending of a messenger 'to tell mee, hee designed to be early in the spring at Martha's Vinyard, to take upon him the Government thereof, and expects me to meet him there, which messenger, I may Justly terme a herauld, for he delivered his message, as a challenge.'[16]

Phips's commission to command all the New England militias also had implications for New York, though some of the tensions it caused were internal to New England. Phips's unsuccessful efforts to assert control of the Rhode Island militia ran afoul of factional conflicts in that colony.[17] The situation was further complicated by an existing border dispute between Massachusetts and Rhode Island, which led briefly to violence in Bristol County in late 1692. A group of insurgents (whom Phips dismissed as 'giddy and brain sick fellows') had claimed that the town of Little Compton, on the eastern shore of Narragansett Bay, lay within the bounds of Rhode Island. They were dissuaded only after being besieged and arrested by a local militia force, which was defending the Massachusetts claim to the territory.[18] Phips had enjoyed the active support of such prominent Bristol County military leaders as Benjamin Church and John Walley, the same officer who had led the unsuccessful land force at Quebec in 1690. On the other hand, several of his most tenacious political opponents, including Nathaniel Byfield and Jahleel Brenton, were among those wealthy members of the House of

Representatives who had close ties with the Bristol County towns and with residents who felt an affinity with Rhode Island.[19]

Phips's list of enemies also included Lieutenant-Governor John Usher of New Hampshire. The two were old adversaries from the era of the Revolution of 1688–9. Usher was now acting permanently for the absentee governor of New Hampshire, Samuel Allen, whose commission specifically recognized the supremacy of Phips in military matters.[20] Usher wrote to Phips in that context in October 1692, in a short-lived and probably disingenuous attempt at neighbourly fence mending. Criticizing the appointment of Allen, he proposed that he should take charge of the actual disposition of the troops and officers appointed for New Hampshire by Phips. Usher concluded the letter by asking Phips not to be swayed against him by 'whatt ever ill minded prejudiced persons may buz in your Ears, whereby to create differences between your Excellency and my selfe.' Phips's response was to turn the approach aside with a crude play on words: 'Their Majesties affaires shall not suffer ... by my being bussed in the ears (as you terme itt) by evill minded and prejudiced persons.' He then packaged up Usher's letter, with its embarrassing contents, and sent it to Blathwayt as proof of New Hampshire's instability, which he had recently used as an argument for that colony's absorption by Massachusetts.[21] Subsequent sources of friction included control of the Piscataqua River for customs purposes and the more personal matter of the Massachusetts council's refusal to repay approximately £1,000 which Usher claimed to have disbursed from his own funds while serving as treasurer under the Dominion of New England.[22] Even though Usher was exaggerating when he told the Lords of Trade in April 1693, 'I judge by the Nextt Ships you will hear the province Massachusetts and province of Hampshire are in a Civill warr,' the hostility was palpable in the official exchanges between the two colonies, and Usher remained Phips's dogged and at times effective foe.[23]

In Connecticut, as in Rhode Island and New Hampshire, the question of Phips's control over the militia was complicated by other issues. In this case, the outcome of a confused series of demands for Connecticut support of Phips's eastern campaigns, and of the defence of Deerfield, Massachusetts, became entangled with a territorial dispute between the towns of Enfield, Massachusetts, and Windsor, Connecticut. By February 1693, the uncompromising nature of Phips's demands had been replaced by a conciliatory appeal to Connecticut as a neighbour. In March, John Pynchon travelled to Hartford to assert Phips's commission but eventually settled for a promise of soldiers for Deerfield and of cash for Phips's efforts against the Wabanaki.[24] However, the Lords of Trade, recognizing the strategic affinities of Connecticut and New York, had already decided to revoke Phips's commission in this case in favour of New York. Fletcher's commission was dated 1 May 1693, though he too had difficulty in asserting authority in Connecticut.[25]

Underlying this change was the wider issue of disagreement between Fletcher and Phips on the entire question of strategy vis-à-vis Canada and on the relative importance of the territories northeast of New England compared with those between and above the Connecticut and Hudson valleys. Fletcher and the New York council were not averse to a new attack on Canada, but since they had no confidence in Phips's ability to lead a seaborne attack on Quebec and since there was always the possibility of a French-Houdenasaunee reconciliation, they favoured awaiting direct English naval assistance. In the meantime, New York's priorities were defensive, aimed at safeguarding settlements and trade against enemy raids. This policy called for assistance from New England for the protection of New York and the vigorous defence of the Connecticut Valley by the New England colonies, and it included requests to London for the absorption of Connecticut by New York. But Phips, too, was mistrustful, mindful of New York's failure to carry through with its planned attack on Montreal in 1690. In any case, he had commercial and political reasons for concentrating New England's limited military resources on aggressive campaigning against the Wabanaki. This he intended to follow with accommodation and then with a renewed assault on Canada.[26]

Thus, the disputes between New York and Phips on this question went deeper than control of militias and were symptomatic of different aims and priorities. Phips did write to Fletcher in a more conciliatory vein in July 1693, praising Fletcher's success in his recent negotiations with the Houdenasaunee, but this was an isolated exception in a troubled relationship, and it may simply have been laying the groundwork for some reciprocal praise of Phips in the event that he succeeded in making peace with the Wabanaki. A few weeks later Phips wrote to Fletcher portraying the Wabanaki treaty of August 1693 as a triumph of his personal diplomacy.[27] Fletcher's guarded reply expressed pleasure at Phips's news and at the prospect (which he must have known to be unlikely) that the treaty would free up the two hundred New England troops he had repeatedly requested for the defence of New York.[28] Privately, his view of Phips's achievement was undoubtedly more sceptical.

Most of Phips's quarrels with neighbouring jurisdictions had originated in 1692 as disputes that had some foundation in differences over boundaries, powers, or matters of strategy. In many cases, these continued into 1693. During the first half of 1693, Phips also became entangled in a series of conflicts that were more personal in nature and more threatening to his imperial reputation. The first of these, which had begun in 1692, further émbittered Phips's relations with New York and was carefully relayed to London by Usher. It concerned Abraham Gouverneur, who had been a prominent member of the Leislerian regime in revolutionary New York but had then been imprisoned and had left the colony in 1692 claiming to have been released. Fletcher, who as governor had quickly identified himself with the anti-Leislerian faction, maintained that Gouverneur had escaped while on parole. By October 1692, Gouverneur had reached Boston and had a private interview with Phips. Describing this meeting in a letter to his parents, Gouverneur wrote that Phips had accused the New York council of Jacobitism, had called Fletcher 'a poor beggar ... [who] sees but money and not the good of the country,' and had mused, 'If what Governor Leisler and ye have don be ill how [come] their Majesties to sit upon the throne.'

None of this was substantially different from the conclusions that were reached later in the 1690s by Fletcher's successor as governor, the earl of Bellomont. Nor was Phips alone in identifying Fletcher's peculations.[29] Expressed privately, the comments were not in themselves inflammatory. On 5 January 1693, however, Fletcher announced to the New York council that Gouverneur's letter had come into his hands and that 'words tending to Sedition' had been uttered at the meeting between Gouverneur and Phips. Fletcher wrote to Phips the next day, saying that if the letter was accurate, 'you have forgott your Duty to their Majesties and your manners to gentlemen,' and demanding Gouverneur's arrest and return to New York. To Joseph Dudley, meanwhile, Fletcher described Phips as 'the incendiary or rather the Bellows that Blows up the Dyeing embers of former Discontents.'[30] The charge was an overelaborate effort to build on Phips's brief conversation with Gouverneur, but Phips promptly repeated his remarks to the messenger carrying Fletcher's letter. Indeed, he went even further. In the presence of Usher and others, Phips reportedly 'reflected extraordinarily' on Fletcher and the anti-Leislerians, and then, after fulminating about New York's designs on Martha's Vineyard, 'went on vindicateing of Leisliur.' Two days later, on 19 January, the performance was repeated in part before the Massachusetts council, on which occasion Phips publicly described the messenger as 'an Impudent Sawcy pitiful Jackanapes.'[31]

Phips's written reply to Fletcher the following week took a somewhat different approach. Phips claimed that Fletcher had deliberately misread Gouverneur's letter in order to credit Phips with opinions that only Gouverneur had expressed – a point already made by Gouverneur in a letter written to Fletcher the day after the confrontation before the council. Phips refused to surrender Gouverneur, who thereafter became a regular member of his entourage. He vigorously repeated the Massachusetts claim to Martha's Vineyard, and he responded to Fletcher's insults by stating, 'Your absurd abusive letter plainly demonstrates that if (as you say) I have forgott my manners to Gentlemen I have forgott what you never had.'[32] Angry letters also reached London from both Phips and his New York critics, and although the affair then subsided quickly enough, it had most certainly added to the number and vehemence of Phips's detractors.[33]

Even more damaging in an imperial context was Phips's quarrel with Captain Richard Short. Their scuffle on a public wharf in Boston, at 9.00 AM on 4 January 1693, was brief and inglorious. Accounts differed about which of them was the aggressor. The affair had been precipitated by a verbal exchange in which Phips had demanded that Short supply men for a voyage to Pemaquid, and Short had responded angrily to the governor's charges that he had too often hired out his seamen for private voyages. According to Short's son Joseph, who witnessed the dispute, Phips called Short 'a Lay or whore' and then assaulted him with his cane. Phips maintained that he was being threatened by Short and that he gave him only 'a small blow,' which, said Phips 'I designed should bee all and was to make him know his distance.'[34] On the violence that followed and on who got the better of it, there was no dispute. According to two other eyewitnesses – John March, the Pemaquid commander, and Nathaniel Hatch, commander of the vessel bound for Pemaquid – Phips called Short a liar, whereupon Short stepped forward and 'shook his Cane ... not regarding his respect to the Governor his Insolent carriage and ill Language provok'd the Governor to strike him, and the said Captain Short after the first blow with all imaginable violence return'd the 2d and continued to strike many blows at the Governor's head and other parts of his Body untill the Governor threw him on the grownd he rising again persisted in striking the Governor untill his Excellency with his Cane disabled him from striking any more.' An anonymous letter writer who corroborated the accounts of Short and his son as well as that of the other naval captain, Robert Fairfax, added an important detail – that Short had a disabled right hand – and he

summed up the episode very differently: 'Sir William gives him the lye
the Rascal the Lubber and strikes him Short I suppose with his left hand
gives him one Rap and falls by accedent backwards over a Gunn and
then the poor Sole is beaten lustily back and sides and head broken.'
Soon afterwards, Short was arrested by a warrant from Phips and was
thrown into the common jail.[35]

Historians have frequently viewed this episode as a defining moment
in Phips's career, seeing it as an unmistakable demonstration of the
violence of his character and the rude incompetence of his governorship. When the antecedents of the incident are closely examined, however, the evidence – while not supporting Phips's version of events –
suggests inferences that are more finely nuanced. It is true that
Pemaquid had been a point of friction between the two, and this was
the element that Phips chose to emphasize in his self-justifications to
London, along with Short's alleged drunkenness, cruelty, and incompetence. Benjamin Jackson attested that as early as mid-September 1692,
Short had disobeyed an order to sail for Pemaquid in favour of stopping
at Piscataqua. The desertion of Pemaquid by both Short and Fairfax in
the autumn was another point of contention. Finally, as Phips would
have it, Short had declined to make a winter voyage to Pemaquid but
had agreed to 'Supply a Sloop with men, Provisions, and Ammunition,
to goe between Boston, and Pemaquid, as their Majesties Service Should
require.' It was Short's reneging on this promise, Phips asserted, that
had led to the incident on 4 January.[36]

Short and Fairfax told the story differently, stressing the dangers of
anchorage in Pemaquid harbour and the uncertainties of their provi-
sioning. As well, Fairfax relayed to the Admiralty the reports he had
heard of Phips's previous threats of violence to Short. Short confirmed
these and recalled that on one trip to Pemaquid he had lost his anchor
and cable through 'the Governor then being on board and by his advise-
ing the Pilote.' Fairfax also put a different complexion on the immediate
issue: 'Some friends of the Governor, having occasion to man a Merchantman for a short voyage, desired Captain Shortt to spare them some
men during his lying by the Wharfe, which he refused to do until they
influenced the Governor to desire and consent to it, who told Capt.
Shortt, that it was a safe voyage and short, and would be a kindness to
his men, as well as his friends ... The ship being saild, the Governor
sends an Order to him to send 4 men more into the Mary sloop for
Pemaquid, and to get 36 more ready for other service, which Captain
Shortt refused.'[37]

Here they were touching on the heart of the quarrel, though the issue was treated circumspectly by both Phips and the captains. From the time of the *Nonsuch*'s voyage to New England in the spring of 1692, the names of Phips and Short can be linked with commercial arrangements that promised profit to both but delivered it more regularly to Phips than to Short. Suggestive though not conclusive are the events surrounding the capture of the *Catharine* during the voyage. The vessel had been condemned as a lawful prize in July 1692 and had subsequently been sold. At the time, the episode passed without any public controversy, but Benjamin Jackson later testified that Short had clandestinely removed from the *Catharine* 'severall large packs or Baggs of Cotton Wooll with severall Casks of other Goods' and had sold them to the merchants Andrew Belcher and Francis Foxcroft for £200. According to other evidence, which came to light later still, Phips himself had 'sent for' at least one cask of sugar for which no receipt was given. Phips's critics later alleged that he had profited from the prize to the amount of some £1,000.[38] Jackson mentioned that Short had complained, in private conversations that Phips had taken the prize from him, but Jackson also pointed out that Short had not appeared at the Court of Admiralty proceedings to press any claim. Another observer noted that from this time forward Short became 'a perfect bigot to Sir William.' The most persuasive inference, therefore, from the murky dealings that followed the seizure of the *Catharine* is that a relationship of mutual convenience had been initiated between Phips and Short. Given the likelihood that Phips was using Fort William Henry as a base for personal trading activities, his demands for seamen from the *Nonsuch* to crew 'Country Sloops' carrying supplies for Pemaquid can be interpreted in the same light.[39]

More explicitly documented were the arrangements made during the autumn of 1692 for the service of *Nonsuch* seamen on commercial voyages to Virginia and the Caribbean. Thomas Dobbins, who was appointed by Phips to be Short's successor in command of the *Nonsuch*, later attested:

Sometime in the month of November 1692 or thereabouts Capt. Short spared sixteen men belonging to Nonsuch Friggat unto Capt. Benjamin Emes for manning of his ship on a voyage to Saltatudos, two of them did not return (being said to be kil'd) but the rest did, and that when Capt. Emes paid the said men their Wages, he stopt Twenty shillings per month of each man, as he said for Capt. Short from the time they were shipt with Capt. Emes, until Capt. Short was suspended, and that said Capt. Short spared two men unto Mr. Lynde Master of another Vessell, and one to John Halsey another Master.[40]

Dobbins was not an unbiased observer, and he made no mention either of his own financial interest in the wages of the men shipped with Emes or of the role of Phips. Other sources confirm Short's participation and add details on that of Phips. The seaman who went with John Halsey to Virginia had indeed agreed to pay Short twenty shillings per month. Halsey was probably connected by marriage to the governor, demonstrating another link in the Phips family web.[41]

More elaborate were the preparations for the voyage of Emes in the prize vessel St Jacob to the salt pans of Tortuga Salada. Emes recalled in a later deposition that the crew of sixteen men and a boy had agreed to pay Short twenty shillings per man per month. According to Nathaniel Byfield and others, Short had declared widely at the time that he had agreed only 'at Sir William's request and direction.' But Emes gave an account of a meeting at Phips's house which suggests that Short had a more active role than he admitted, and which also sheds light on the role of Phips. 'Capt. Short and the Deponent did go to the Governours house,' Emes recalled, 'and there Capt Short asked the Governour if he might let the men go with the Deponent, and also desired an order of the Governor then the Governor answered and said, he knew what he had to do, for he was there Captain.' Phips had then added the significant observation that 'it might do well.'[42]

Significant elements of the winter voyage of the St Jacob remain unclear, including the nature of Phips's interest. Whether he had a direct stake in the voyage, whether he was being paid for encouraging or manoeuvring Short into supplying seamen, or whether he was simply doing so as a way of dispensing favours to merchants whose political support he sought is not established by the evidence. Nor is the purpose of the voyage. Although the normal goal of a voyage to Tortuga Salada was to take on a cargo of salt, the St Jacob was absent from Boston for almost five months before returning in late April 1693 with salt and brazilletta wood, which was promptly unloaded with the permission of Benjamin Jackson. Since the route to Tortuga Salada passed close to the Ambrosia Bank, and bearing in mind Cotton Mather's observation that Phips had learned at some time before his death in 1695 about the location of another wreck, which he hoped eventually to salvage, it is tempting to speculate on a return to the vicinity of the wreck of the Concepción. On this there is no direct evidence. It is noteworthy that a contemporary

later recorded that Phips had offered to contribute £1,000 to the fortification of New Providence Island in exchange for a grant of Hog Island,
just offshore from the town of Nassau, but unfortunately he did not
state when Phips made this offer.[43] Short did eventually receive a share
of the wages of the fifteen surviving crew members, although Dobbins
received twice as much. Long before then, and before his confrontation
with Phips, Short had apparently repented of his decision to become
involved. Byfield, Foxcroft, and other critics of Phips reported to Blathwayt that they had considered the arrangements 'amisse and more than
the Capt. could well answer,' and that on the basis of their advice Short
had resolved to refuse any similar approaches in future.[44]

Considered in this context, the caning of Richard Short was not an act
of random cruelty and undisciplined violence. Rather, it represented the
public chastisement of a disloyal client by a governor whose patronage
powers were so weak that he could not afford to overlook Short's
change of heart, which had been at least partly ispired by the advice of
an opposing political faction. As noted earlier, personal violence was as
rare in Phips as verbal abuse was common. On the few convincingly
documented occasions when it took place, it was calculated – as during
the 1684 mutiny on the *Golden Rose* or at Port-Royal in 1690. Phips had
been warned that Short was going to refuse to hire him any of his men.
Benjamin Jackson, attempting to portray Short as the aggressor,
reported that he had heard that Short had told associates the previous
evening 'that he would goe and huff the Governor next morning.' More
reliable was the account given by John March of a conversation he himself had had with Short. He had asked Short 'whether his men were
ready which he had promised should go with us in their Majesties sloop
the Mary to Pemaquid.' To this, said March, Short had replied 'No, but
he would wait on the Governour in the morning.' March had suggested
that Short need not do so 'unless he would let the Governour have the
men desired, which said Short said he scorned to do, or words to that
purpose.' Since March was with Phips early the next morning, before
Phips met Short on the wharf, he had plenty of time to tell Phips of
Short's response. Thus, any premeditation of violence was more likely
to have been on Phips's side than on Short's.[45]

The hiring out of naval seamen was not an unusual practice, but in this
case it was on such a large scale that, in the words of one observer, it
would have 'dismantled' Short's ship. For a tarpaulin officer who had
only recently resumed his naval career in middle age, the temptations
had been real but the returns disappointing. As Fairfax put it in an

oblique but revealing reference to Short's clientage, 'I am well assurd that Captain Shortt hath behaved himself with great civility to Sir William Phipps and his friends, as well in their passage aboard him, as since he came into the Country, and am as sure that he never met with any other return than ... hard usage, tho' he wanted not for large promises.'[46]

For Short, the hard usage continued long after 4 January 1693, in circumstances that led ultimately to farce rather than high drama. From what his supporters described as 'the Common Stinking Prison,' Short was transferred on Phips's order to Castle Island.[47] On 1 March Phips orded him to be moved to the merchant vessel *Walter and Thomas* for transportation to England, where he was to be delivered either to Nottingham personally or to the Admiralty. The choice of vessel was a poor one. The *Walter and Thomas* was owned by Nathaniel Byfield and John Mico, and Byfield's sympathy with Short was no secret. Mico was a less conspicuous figure, though he reportedly nursed a grievance over having been assessed in 1692, on Phips's orders, with an unusually high fine for nonperformance of militia duties.[48] When the *Walter and Thomas* left Boston, it made for the Piscataqua River with the intention of picking up three pro-Short deserters from the *Nonsuch*, who had been sheltered in Byfield's Boston warehouse. Word of this having leaked out, the vessel was pursued by a sloop from the *Nonsuch* with Dobbins aboard as well as the purser, Matthew Cary. The master of the *Walter and Thomas*, Jeremiah Tay (or Toy) put into Cape Ann in an attempt to hide, but he was seized there by Dobbins and Cary and brought back to Boston, to be held under close arrest on the *Nonsuch*. Short and the deserters, in the meantime, had escaped at Cape Ann to make their way to Portsmouth and a hospitable welcome from Usher.[49]

After refusing to accept offers of bail from Byfield and Mico, Phips ordered Tay's release on 13 March, by which time the captain had spent a week in captivity. Understandably, Tay was anxious to leave Boston as quickly as possible. He proceeded to Portsmouth, where the *Walter and Thomas* had been brought in the meantime by the authority of its owners. Byfield also made for the Piscataqua, and was followed some days later by Phips. At a meeting at a house on Great Island on 29 March, Phips demanded in Byfield's presence that Tay surrender Short and the deserters. When this was refused, Phips vented his anger by tearing the seal off the warrant he had originally given for Short's transportation. He later boarded the *Walter and Thomas*, to which Tay had not yet returned, and broke into the main cabin to seize those of Short's possessions that were aboard.[50] Among those most offended by this incident was Usher, who complained that Phips had invaded his jurisdiction. Phips complained in turn that his attempt on 31 March to assert his command of the New Hampshire militia at the Portsmouth fort, immediately before leaving the Piscataqua for Boston, had been thwarted by a 'Corporall, with a file of Musqueteers,' who had barred his entry to the fort. Richard Short, preparing to make his way overland to New York, carried with him the image of Phips entering an alehouse to have his militia commission read, and of how, when 'about 5 or 6 Carpenters came to him no Gentleman would go near him he carryed himself so dirty.'[51] Thus, the entire episode ended with Phips portraying himself, through gratuitous displays of aggression, as petty, vindictive, and undignified.

The Short affair had significant consequences for certain individuals. Short himself returned to Boston in the summer of 1693, having been advised by Fairfax to arrange a meeting with Admiral Sir Francis Wheeler, who was in Boston harbour with the remains of his West Indian fleet. According to one report, Wheeler refused to support Short, whose service record does not show him receiving another command.[52] Dobbins failed to have the Admiralty confirm his new rank as captain, despite Phips's recommendation of him (apocryphally or not) as the boatman who had taken William of Orange ashore at Torbay in 1688. Short may have been nearer the truth of Dobbins's qualifications when he asserted that the governor 'hath put in a Commander which will condesend to his private interest and tends upon Phips as a Boy.' By September 1694, Dobbins had relinquished the *Nonsuch* to a new captain and was commanding the Massachusetts *Province Galley*. Abraham Hoare, the *Nonsuch*'s lieutenant (who had protested Dobbins's appointment as captain on the grounds that the normal practice would have been to promote the lieutenant) retained that position.[53]

The evidence suggests that Phips now sought alternative ways of combining private and public affairs. In April 1693 he announced to the Admiralty the building of a 'yacht' of eighteen guns and asked 'that this Vessell may bee in their Majesties pay, as a sixth rate, onely Six months in the year, which will bee in the Summer time, and that I may imploy her in the winter otherwise.' The results of this initiative are unclear; Phips's request was put to the consideration of the Admiralty commissioners in June, and the yacht (having been sold for £1,800) duly appeared in the inventory of his estate some years later, but there is no evidence of its being used for public purposes.[54] For Phips, the chief immediate consequence of the Short affair was that it entrenched the enmity of Byfield and his merchant associates and bound them more closely to old political opponents such as Usher and Dudley. Matters were not improved for the governor by the difficulties of the Wheeler expedition during the summer of 1693 and a related incident, which again inflamed his relations with New York.

The Wheeler expedition had been conceived by Blathwayt in the spring of 1692 with the encouragement of Nottingham. Nottingham had nominated Sir Francis Wheeler to command, and Colonel John Foulkes was later added as the land commander. The purpose of the venture was to take French islands in the West Indies. It was one of the long-standing series of English naval efforts against the French and Spanish Caribbean that had almost uniformly been disastrous.[55] The Wheeler expedition was no exception. Even though the characteristic problems of weather and epidemic disease were well known, the fleet sailed in late December, was delayed in Barbados for several weeks, lost many of the troops to disease, and was then decisively repulsed in a spring assault on Martinique. By 12 June 1693, the ships were beginning to straggle into Boston harbour. 'Severall of the Frigotts come up above Long-Island,' noted Samuel Sewall on the thirteenth. 'Sir Francis [Wheeler] came to Noddle's-Island yesterday.' Ten days later, Sewall noted that Wheeler and his commanders were 'Treated' at Cambridge by Phips and Increase Mather. However convivial the occasion may have been, the conversation would have been bound to dwell on the failure of the expedition to date, and to touch also on Phips's professed surprise that its next target was to be Canada.[56]

An attack on Canada had not been part of the original plan, though Blathwayt had observed in late July 1692 that the expedition 'may proceed to New England if it be towards the Spring and serve the Purposes in those parts.' Phips had received orders to assist in victualling the fleet if called upon by Wheeler, and he had responded fulsomely in March with a promise of 'all imaginable dilligence.'[57] At that time, the royal order to Phips to prepare supplies and reinforcements for Wheeler's attack on Canada had been signed but not yet sent. Dated 2 February 1693, it was still awaiting dispatch with the Virginia fleet two months later. An alternative plan hastily devised by Nottingham to send another copy of the order to Ireland, and thence by a quick passage to New England, was approved by Blathwayt but failed when the transatlantic vessel was captured by the French. Not until 24 September, long after Wheeler had departed, did the original order reach Boston. Even Blathwayt's letter of 20 February, summoning Phips to undertake cheerfully his limited role as commander of New England volunteers, arrived only in late July.[58] Thus, technically at least, Phips had every right to express surprise when Wheeler arrived in June. Nevertheless, a reference in a letter that had left Boston in March 1693 raises the possibility that the expedition's plan to attack Canada had already been rumoured. The writer of this letter had observed that the year's tax assessments would provide 'a summe very fit to be managed by an able Generall for the reduction of Kebeck who I am well assured if their Majesties please may be here before half that money be gathered.' In some quarters, the imminence of the attack on Canada was assumed simply from Wheeler's arrival. By the beginning of July – mid-July in the English calendar – a report had been received in Quebec, derived from a prisoner taken by the Wabanaki at Pemaquid, that Wheeler's fleet had set sail for Quebec.

The response of the New York council when it learned on 17 July of the expedition's arrival was to send one of its members immediately to Boston to welcome Wheeler and offer assistance.[59] The reaction in Massachusetts was very different. When Wheeler communicated with Phips on 8 July, specifically requesting a written response, his letter was strictly formal and clearly followed an earlier verbal exchange. Referring to the attack on Canada, Wheeler wrote: 'Your Excellency was pleased to tell me that you had received no orders nor notice from his Majesty of the Expedition, and that it was necessary that the Forces for that service should be at least 4000 strong That we ought to have sailed hence on that Service by the First of July at the farthest, and that it was most absolutely necessary, That to have raised your Forces and to have carried on your Correspondence with New Yorke the Neighbouring Colonies and the Indians in Amity with the English you should have had at least four monthes time.' Starting that an epidemic which had ravaged the expedtion had subsided among the 650 remaining troops as well as among the seamen, Wheeler asked Phips what should be done next.

Phips's response four days later, after consulting the council, was equally formal and again stated his opinion that the forces were insufficient and the year too far advanced for Quebec to be attempted. Taking up an alternative suggestion advanced by Wheeler, Phips praised the idea of a raid on the French Newfoundland ports of Plaisance and St Pierre. However, when Wheeler asked later in the month for a Massachusetts contingent of four hundred to assist in carrying out this plan, Phips replied that he had to refuse, and he was ready with a number of reasons: his lack of authority to require out-of-province service without the approval of the recently dismissed assembly; the need for troops for his eastern expedition, and the reluctance of many to venture on board ships that had so recently harboured an epidemic of yellow fever.[60] Wheeler left soon afterwards and apparently did make a brief raid on Plaisance. He finally reached Spithead in October.[61]

Phips took a defensive tone in a series of letters to London explaining why he had been unable to assist Wheeler. On 11 September he told Nottingham that he had not had 'the least intimation of such a designe' and was 'much grieved for the misfortune of looseing at this time so good an oppertunity of subdueing Cannada.' He wrote in similar vein to Blathwayt on the twenty-sixth, noting the arrival of the royal order just two days earlier and the lack of any chance to prepare 'for that designe which I soe much thirst after.' However, Phips's distress did not prevent him from continuing to thirst after new orders to 'give *mee* opertunity to accomplishe that Necessary and much desired Service, which I should Cheerfully attempt although with the greatest Hazzard.'[62] The evidence suggests that the lost orders were not so much a source of regret to Phips as a fortunate excuse for avoiding an expedition that he could not have commanded. In fact, his arguments against proceeding to Quebec were not without merit. Despite the more genuine regret expressed in New York for a lost opportunity, even Fletcher was inclined to agree that the depleted expedition would have been inadequate for the task.[63] Yet it was the way in which Phips's arguments were deployed and the effect they produced on Wheeler that were more striking than their substance.

As with so many of Phips's travails of 1693, it was not only the main incident that was significant. The most dramatic scene connected with the Wheeler expedition was a meeting between Phips and the New York emissary, Chidley Brooke. Brooke had arrived in Boston on the evening of 27 July and had found Phips and Wheeler together at the governor's house. According to Brooke's report to Fletcher, this encounter consisted of a 'flatt Harrangue' by Phips on the costs of the war for Massachusetts. Brooke was invited to return the next day but did not find Phips at home until the morning of 1 August. Then, in the presence of an unidentified member of the Massachusetts council and some others who had arrived with Brooke, he gave Phips an account of New York's military weakness and it need for help. This apparently put Phips 'into a ferment.' Fletcher's demand for two hundred soldiers produced 'a Rude passion,' while a request for New England commissioners to attend a meeting to agree on quotas for New York's financial and military assistance 'Aggravated his former heat.'

Brooke finally decided to leave. The council member, he later said, 'seemd asham'd of his [Phips's] behavior, and desir'd me to blame his education for what I saw. I told him his governor was very hott. he Returnd; Sir you must pardon him his dogg-days, he cannot help it.' For good measure, Brooke added some further conclusions: 'I do observe the people here are highly Tax'd and no less displeas'd at the ill peni-worthe they have for their money their Governor is little fear'd and less Lov'd. he selects his company out of the Mobb, for the most part, amongst whom Noys and Strutt, pass for witt, and prowis; som few of the better sort pay him respect and complement, for their own sake, rather than any esteem they have for him; the rest ridicule him.'[64] Brooke's verdict should not necessarily be taken at face value. Villebon, for one, had deduced from the reports he received from Boston that the fact that Phips 'had not forgotten his origin' was a source of political and military strength rather than a weakness. Nevertheless, there was a real question of how many enemies Phips could afford to make through his displays of anger, especially when complaints began to focus in a more coordinated way on the Plantations Office. Following Brooke's verbal report to the New York council on 24 August, his written assessment was promptly forwarded to London by Fletcher.[65]

Phips seems to have believed that he enjoyed firm support from both Blathwayt and Nottingham. Joseph Dudley observed to Blathwayt in February 1693, 'The present Masters of this Country ... say here that My Lord Nottingham and your Honnor will get passed by his Majesty whatever they shall offer. I perfectly hope the Contrary.'[66] Phips's seven letters to Nottingham between 15 and 28 September (six of them dealing with distinct elements of his governorship and one being a note acknowledging 'great obligations to your Lordship') were matched in number though not exactly in content by his letters to Blathwayt from 20 to 27 September. Taken together, they represent a major attempt at favourable self-portrayal by a governor who was fond of boasting that 'he knew how things went at Whitehall.'[67] At times Phips could make this claim believable even to his critics. Nathaniel Byfield recalled in 1694 a conversation on the principle of whether taxpayers from the old Plymouth Colony should be liable retrospectively for the expenses of Massachusetts agents prior to the charter of 1691, 'to which his Excel-lency with great earnestness of Speritt gott up said yt was a white hall stroake; to which I could make no Answer supposeing he Knew white hall better than my selfe.'[68] The reality was, however, that although Phips's personal history with Nottingham may have given some slender basis for a continuing relationship, his credit with the Plantations Office was not only low but sank even lower each time he cast aspersions on Blathwayt's established clients.

Dudley and Usher, and to a lesser degree Addington and Stoughton, were frequent New England correspondents of Blathwayt. So, from New York, were Fletcher and Brooke. For Phips to imagine that he could persuade Blathwayt that Dudley was 'this Countreyes Enemye' or that he could readily have Addington replaced as provincial secretary by Benjamin Jackson because of Addington's 'Perverse humour' showed remarkable naivety. Addington, in fact, wrote letters that were more supportive of Phips than most of those Blathwayt received.[69] Not that Blathwayt's disapproval was in itself a lethal threat. Colonial governors could be dismissed only by the crown, which had appointed them. If the Plantations Office had been in control of appointments, Phips would never have been a candidate in the first place. Yet for a governor whose patronage resources were slim and had to be eked out by dubious actions, the danger of having the opposition distilled into a coherent faction was not one to be ignored. Joseph Dudley, for one, took a long step in this direction in the wake of the Short affair when he gave a personal endorsement of the letter supporting Short, which Byfield, Foxcroft, and others had written to Blathwayt, and followed it five days later with a direct attack of his own. 'It is hoped,' he informed Blathwayt, 'that Sir William's time will be but short and I am Confident if his Managements were well represented it would soon Issue, he is very Unhappy [i.e., unsuited, unfit] in himself and in such as he is pleased to make choice of for advisers.'[70] Sir Henry Ashurst, meanwhile, continued to regard Phips at best as an ingrate. Phips, in his first year as governor, had run dangerously low on both imperial patrons and colonial clients.

11

Imperial Governorship:
Recall, 1693–1694

On 4 July 1694, Sir William Phips received official notice of his recall to England to face the charges of his critics in a hearing before the Privy Council. As well as the grievances of Richard Short, there were two other areas of complaint. One concerned abuses of admiralty jurisdiction, especially in connection with Phips's condemnation of the prize vessels *Catharine* and *St Jacob* in 1692. The other, which proved to be crucial in the process leading to Phips's recall, consisted of accusations by the customs collector Jahleel Brenton regarding Phips's personal conduct and his alleged violations of the Navigation Acts. The thread that bound together all the complaints was their relation to Phips's involvement in illegal and self-serving commercial activities, whether through his use of Short for impressments and as a source of seamen to be hired out for commercial voyages, through embezzlement of the royal share of prize revenues, or through outright illicit trade. Yet, as the charges were set out and the evidence assembled, another issue began to overshadow these commercial questions: the linkage between the violent assaults allegedly committed by Phips against both Short and Brenton. This was, at least potentially, a much easier matter for Phips to answer. The nature of the evidence put Phips in a stronger position than his opponents had expected, and at the same time he was solidifying his political position within the colony. By the time he departed for London in November 1694, his description of the summons as a demonstration of 'Royall ffavor [in] granting mee the oportunity to make my defense' was not altogether inapt in view of the events of the preceding four months.[1]

Jahleel Brenton's petition was considered by the customs commissioners in November 1693. Brenton attacked the regulation of trade in

Massachusetts on a wide front, citing the denial of his right to control the entry and clearance of vessels, the condoning of illegal trade by Phips and the courts, and Phips's own 'private Trades.' In illustration, the collector described two apparently flagrant cases of abuse. In one, he recounted how he had repeatedly prosecuted Samuel Shrimpton's brigantine *Mary* for trading directly with continental Europe, only to be rebuffed by the courts and see Shrimpton break into the royal warehouse to recover a seized cargo. The other case, as Brenton described it, was even more dramatic:

That there lately arrived a sloop called the Good Luck Thomas Wake Master who pretended to come from the Island of providence being loaden with Indico ffustick and other goods of the growth of Jamaica and no certificate being produced for the said goods Your Petitioner made seizure thereof and got part of the said Goods (to the value of about One thousand pounds new England money) unto their Majesties Storehouse Whereupon the Governor Sir William phips with those that belonged to the said Sloop and others to the number of about fifty persons attending him came to the said Storehouse and there Laying violent hands upon your petitioner, pulling and dragging him about the wharfe at the said Storehouse and striking him severall blows upon the brest and other parts of his body and striking him on the face with his fist abusing him with all manner of Barbarous Language threatning to beat him untill he broake all of his bones and then Commit him to prison if he did not immediatly deliver all the said Goods seized and put in the said Storehouse: Your petitioner Considering the station that the said Sir William phips stands in there by their Majesties appointment thought it better to submitt to this Arbitrary act of force and suffer him to have the goods rather than to duel with him or to suffer from him what he so Arbitrarily threatned and therefore submitted to him having the said goods, declaring at the same time that the said goods still remained under seizure for their Majesties.[2]

This intriguing story may have been added to the petition as an afterthought. It occupied considerably less space than the allegations regarding the *Mary*, and since the incident had taken place on 29 May 1693, almost two months before the petition was dispatched, it seems unlikely that immediate outrage was the principal force moving Brenton to act. Alternatively and more probably, the account of Phips's allegedly violent intervention, with its similarity to the fracas between Phips and Short in January, was adopted by Brenton as an especially forceful ending to his broader attack, at a time when extensive accounts of the Short affair were still reaching London. Either way, it was clearly this part of the petition that most caught the attention of the customs commissioners, Sir Robert Southwell among them, as they forwarded it to the Treasury with an almost word-for-word repetition of Brenton's version of the confrontation and a plea for redress of 'a Violence of this high nature.' The customs commissioners added the detail, which had not appeared in the petition, that Brenton had later been informed that 'the said Sir William Phips and John ffoster one of their Majesties Councill [of Massachusetts] had bought all the said Goods at a low rate.'³ The imputed parallel between the Short and Brenton affairs, and the implication that the two reinforced each other as illustrations of Phips's characteristically violent behaviour, proved to be attractive to the Lords of Trade, who linked the complaints of Short with those of Brenton in a joint hearing in mid-January 1694.⁴

The quarrel between Brenton and Phips on 29 May 1693 had arisen from a long-standing series of disputes. As early as 8 September 1692, Brenton had formally requested Phips to cease obstructing him in the discharge of his duties, thereby contesting Phips's assertions of the primacy of the governor's powers over those of the collector. When Edward Randolph had arrived in Boston six days earlier, he had found Brenton 'full of Complaints.' Randolph was no great admirer of Brenton, who had displaced him as collector after the Revolution of 1688–9, possibly at the behest of Increase Mather. Declaring himself troubled by Brenton's record of being 'irreguler and arbitrary in his proceedings,' Randolph associated the collector with Byfield in the questionable sale of an illegal Scottish cargo in late 1691. Nevertheless, he broached the collector's grievances to Phips, who responded with the threat, said Randolph, that 'he would drubb me if I had not been under his Roofe.'⁵ By mid-October 1692, Phips was informing Blathwayt that he had complained about Brenton to the customs commissioners, accusing him of 'neglect of his duty and injustice to their Majesties, and abuse of their Subjects.' Brenton in turn petitioned the Privy Council against abuses of trade in New England, and this prompted an inconclusive hearing in December 1692.⁶

Animosity and conflicting self-interest were not the only causes of conflict between Phips and Brenton. Their quarrel was also an extension of the dispute over trade regulation that was connected with the origins of the Navigation Acts, a dispute that had been waged intermittently in New England since the passage through the English parliament of the Plantation Duty Act of 1673. This act had supplemented the Navigation

Acts of 1651, 1660, and 1663, which had established the principle that colonial trade should be confined to English or English colonial vessels, that continental European goods could be carried to the colonies only by way of England, and that there were certain 'enumerated' colonial products that could be exported only to England or to an English colony. The enumerated goods were largely produced in the West Indies and in the southern colonies of North America, and did not include New England's principal exports – fish, timber, and agricultural products.

The act of 1673 attempted to close a loophole that had become evident in intercolonial trade, notably the shipment of enumerated goods to New England without payment of duties. In many cases, the enumerated commodities were being transshipped in New England and then carried directly to continental Europe. The act imposed duties, payable at the time of loading, on enumerated goods that were sent to another colony without a bond being given that they would be carried to England. It also provided for enforcement of these impositions by customs officers, who were to be established in the colonies. Left unclear was the relationship between the customs officials and the colonial governors, whose overall authority had been recognized in the earlier Navigation Acts. In Massachusetts, the General Court attempted without success to resolve the question in 1682, following a series of seizures of vessels and cargoes by Randolph, which had disrupted the business of Samuel Shrimpton and a number of other merchants. The proposed Naval Office Act upheld the colonial authority as opposed to that of the customs collector in all areas except collection of the duties imposed in 1673 – a minor role in a colony where no enumerated commodities were produced. The colony's own 'naval officers' were to be responsible for entry and clearance of vessels at the major Massachusetts ports. Governor Bradstreet, however, withheld approval, and the matter lapsed with the end of the old charter regime in 1684.[7]

One of the earliest legislative enactments of Phips's regime, to which he speedily gave his assent in July 1692, was an act to establish naval offices at Boston, Salem, and five other ports. The naval officer appointed for Boston was Phips's private secretary, Benjamin Jackson. As for Brenton, Phips and the council made their position clear in a formal declaration. The collector's claim to enter and clear vessels, and the 'unnecessary and unreasonable Fees' that went with this, was rejected in favour of the naval offices; and although it was stated that the collector would receive 'all encouragement and assistance ... in the due Execution of his Commission,' the absence of enumerated goods produced in New

England meant, in effect, that he had little or nothing to do.[8] As an interpretation of the act of 1673, this was later rejected both by the Privy Council's disallowance of the Naval Office Act in 1695 and by the passage of a further Navigation Act the following year, among whose many provisions was the subordination of naval officers to customs collectors. But for the time being, the action of the General Court was decisive. Justifying it to the customs commissioners in January 1693, Phips promised that the Navigation Acts would be 'carefully observed' and that the collector would be supported in his remaining duties: 'to make discovery of false Certificates and to prevent ffrauds.'[9] Brenton, meanwhile, had been fighting court battles along the same lines as his predecessor, Randolph. As in the early 1680s, a salient target was Shrimpton's trade with continental Europe. The case of the *Mary*, about which Brenton complained in his petition of July 1693, went eventually to the Privy Council, which in 1697 gave a judgment against the collector. In the meantime, Brenton's petition linked this matter with the establishment of the naval offices, 'which hath proved a great Incouragement to persons in Committing frauds and practising unlawfull trades,' and with the personal actions of Phips.[10]

The rivalry between Brenton and the Boston naval office is well documented, as is the confusion it created. The experience in August 1692 of Henry Graven, master of the New York sloop *Elizabeth*, was typical. Graven entered the naval office and received permission to land his cargo, but while the unloading was in progress, one of Brenton's 'waiters' confiscated the naval office permit. Graven's subsequent visit to the customs house led to a threat of seizure by Brenton, whereupon the master – who had presumably paid the two-shilling fee for entry through the naval office, and more for any certificates required – was relieved of another seven shillings as the fee for completing further entry formalities through the customs office. Another bewildered master was Jeremiah Tay. The eventful voyage that briefly had Richard Short as a passenger on his ship had begun with conflicting demands by Brenton and Jackson for documentation on the bonding of the *Walter and Thomas*.[11]

Equally clear is the close personal involvement of Phips in support of Jackson. Jackson was twenty-four years old when he gave evidence at the admiralty trial of the *Catharine* in July 1692. He remains an obscure figure, and we get only a glimpse of him from Phips's description when vainly attempting to persuade Blathwayt that Jackson should replace Addington as provincial secretary: 'Hee is of Cheshire in England, and came over with mee, hee hath to my great Satisfaction Served mee, as my Secretary, in all my buisinis since my comeing overlast and now understands the manner and Circumstances of this Countrey, and who are my friends, and who my Enemyes.' Jackson had probably accompanied Phips from England as early as 1689. That he lodged at Phips's house is suggested by the testimony of Henry Francklyn and William Hill, as Brenton's waiters, that they had repeatedly made approaches to him there with demands for certificates. On one such occasion, the meeting was delayed while Jackson finished his dinner. Edward Randolph, in 1692, had taken a characteristically acerbic view of the relationship between Phips and Jackson. 'I have nothing to say to Sir William's naval officer,' Randolph observed to John Usher: 'he keeps him chained up as your Bitch is at home.' The analogy notwithstanding, one of Jackson's roles as private secretary appears to have been to disguise Phips's lack of full literacy, and he was one of the few who can be identified as genuine intimates of the governor.[12]

Phips's interventions ranged from counselling shipmasters to do their business with Jackson, rather than Brenton, to using more forceful methods. When Thomas Cobbitt arrived from London in October 1693 commanding the ship *Elizabeth*, he took the precaution of immediately meeting with Phips. But taking the governor's advice to see Jackson did not insulate Cobbitt from all difficulties. For several days he was enmeshed in the conflicting demands of the naval officer and the collector, though he later testified that meeting Jackson had saved him the inconvenience of having his cargo inspected; Jackson had kept the coquet carrying details of the cargo, and he never made use of it to verify the contents.[13]

More direct was Phips's involvement on the autumn day in 1693 when, during one of his walks on the waterfront, he was stopped by Abraham Boudrot and Benjamin Faneuil, who told him that Brenton had ordered the seizure of their latest cargo of furs from Acadia and that this was being attended to right then by Francklyn and Hill. Phips took the opportunity to declare that Boudrot and Faneuil were 'as good or better English men than the Collector is, and let him seize them if he dare. If he doth, I will break his head.' The retreat of Francklyn and Hill was followed by the rapid unloading of the cargo, so no seizure took place. Nor did it on a later occasion, when Francklyn and Hill encountered Boudrot with a load of furs, feathers, and wheat, even though the two officials were able to establish that 'the said Boudrot's mariners owned themselves to be Frenchmen.' Phips, of course, would have maintained that

Acadians such as Boudrot, or such as Charles de La Tour, who also was trading regularly from Port-Royal, were indeed legitimate visitors on the basis of the oaths he claimed to have obtained from the Acadians.[14] According to the testimony of a shipowner towards whom he had been less forthcoming, however, the governor was often willing to accommodate even those whose traffic was more clearly illicit. James Leblond testified that he and Timothy Clarke had gone to Phips's house to seek release for their brigantine *Sarah*, which apparently had been seized by the naval office for carrying contraband, and Phips had informed them that 'through his clemency he had released above twelve or fourteen Vessells that had transgressed but he was resolved to do so no more.'[15]

Whether Phips kept the resolve is far from clear. But the protection he had afforded some shipowners can hardly have been given free. To be sure, the most thoroughgoing allegations regarding breaches of the Navigation Acts in Massachusetts came from those who were not disinterested. Charles Lidget, who in 1693 identified the practice of fraudulent clearing for Bermuda by merchants trading to the Wabanaki and French even in times of hostility, had been a close associate of Shrimpton before the revolution but had not negotiated the revolutionary era with the same suppleness, and he had left Boston for London under pressure from his creditors.[16] John Usher, whose business affairs in Boston had suffered for the same reason, and who had shared with Lidget both imprisonment and then unsuccessful lobbying in London against Phips and Mather, was especially vehement on the establishment of a naval office at Kittery. Just across the Piscataqua River from Portsmouth, this office represented for Usher 'onely a Cloak to Robb the King, as to violateing the Acts of Navigation.' More specifically, he reported that ships were being allowed to dock at the secluded Isles of Shoals and were directly exchanging enumerated goods for French, Spanish, and Dutch products. Brenton, Usher maintained, 'is dilligent and faithfull in his place and thatts enough to be mallign'd by the Government.' Benjamin Fletcher, meanwhile, was less specific but equally firm in declaring to Blathwayt from New York, 'The Neighbouring Collonys ... Robb us of all trade, by imposeing noe duties, the Acct for navigation nott observed or vallued.'[17]

This was not quite true. The evidence suggests that there was no lack of appreciation in Massachusetts for the Navigation Acts as long as they were interpreted and enforced in a way that restrained non-English competition without unduly restricting New England merchant activity. Still, Fletcher and the other critics were not fundamentally mistaken either about Phips or about the doubtful legality of much of the trading. In this area, Phips's self-interest and political imperatives coincided. In the most general terms, his entire career had been built on profit and the hope of profit, in the Caribbean and northeastern areas, towards which significant portions of New England's extralegal trade was directed. As well as his own interests in northeastern trade and privateering (and perhaps in the Caribbean too, as suggested by his attempt to obtain a grant of Hog Island), he stood to gain by fostering similar trade by others, receiving gifts in exchange for favours or profiting from the cheap purchase of illegal goods. The same possibilities, of course, were open to Brenton and Byfield, or would be if they could wrest control from Phips and the naval office. Politically too, it was expedient for Phips to adopt an accommodating view of trade regulation, for councillors such as John Foster and Samuel Shrimpton were well worth cultivating. Indeed, as Brenton pointed out in late 1694, some council members had even admitted in the context of the allegations against Phips that 'the Collector had complained to the King against them all, and therefore they were all concerned.'[18]

In all of this, the case of the *Good Luck* was not exceptional until Brenton's complaint of physical violence by Phips gave it additional significance. A fifteen-ton sloop of Providence Island, the *Good Luck* had arrived in Boston on 25 May 1693 with a cargo of enumerated goods: cotton wool, fustic, indigo, and logwood. The owners were Samuel Freith of Providence Island, who had accompanied the vessel to Boston, and his brother Daniel. Their Boston correspondent David Edwards later testified that Phips had personally authorized the *Good Luck*'s entry and that the certificate of entry had been signed by Jackson. Jackson recalled that he had initially had doubts about the legitimacy of the vessel's documentation but was satisfied after Phips had interrogated its master, Thomas Wake. Edwards also stated, confirming in part the assertion made to the customs commissioners, that the bulk of the cargo had been bought by John Foster. Phips had bought the balance of eight small iron cannons, though not until several weeks later, in July. Edwards gave no indication that the price had been unusually low, though Foster recalled hearing Freith observe that the sale would depend on 'reasonable' terms being offered.[19]

The smooth progress towards landing the cargo was interrupted by suspicions raised by Brenton's deputy. It emerged, too, that the *Good Luck*'s certificate of clearance from the Bahamas had specified only in general terms the commodities carried, leaving blank spaces for the quantities. Wake's explanation that the Jamaican-produced goods had been salvaged from a wreck en route and that this plan had been approved by the governor of the Bahamas did not convince the collector. Accordingly the *Good Luck* and its cargo were seized.[20] Brenton personally led the seizure immediately after meeting with Captain Robert Fairfax aboard the *Conception Prize*. Seamen from the frigate secured the *Good Luck*, which was then removed to the customs dock. To what extent this represented an established pattern of collaboration is unclear, though some four months earlier Captain Fairfax – no friend to Phips, in the wake of the Short affair – had reported to the Admiralty that his ability to buy provisions in Boston had depended on Brenton's extending to him more than £700 of credit.[21]

The seizure of the *Good Luck* involved harsh exchanges from the beginning. Thomas Wake claimed that Brenton had threatened to 'stob' him (stab him), though Brenton maintained that he had said only that he would 'stop' Wake from landing an illegal cargo. Foster stated that when he arrived at the customs dock, he had remonstrated with Brenton, whereupon the collector had declared, 'What! you thought to have a bargain, but you shall not.' By the time Foster had broached the legal niceties of the case with Judge Samuel Sewall, Wake and Samuel Freith had sought out Phips and brought him to the wharf, where the *Good Luck* was in the process of being unloaded.

Brenton's version of what followed included the punching and caning by Phips which he described in his petition. John Foster's account, which can be taken as equally partisan, had Brenton refusing the governor's order to reload the cargo and Phips declaring 'that he would make him do it or else lay him fast, or words to that purpose.' Foster admitted to having seen Phips use his cane to restrain Brenton from leaving the wharf as well as giving the collector 'some Chucks under the Chin,' but he maintained, 'No strikeing or beating of him did I see.' The real pattern of events would not be established with any reliability until the evidence of other witnesses was collated more than a year after the incident. In the meantime, the day belonged to Phips in the sense that Brenton conceded the vessel and its cargo and that both Foster and Phips went on to complete their purchases. Brenton's petition two months later represented an effort to make the episode a telling one in the context of the more general dispute over the regulation of trade and who in Boston controlled it.[22]

Also prominent among the complaints against Phips as they emerged from the initial hearings of the Lords of Trade were those related to admiralty jurisdiction. One grievance concerned the disposition of the

Catharine and Phips's ignoring the claims of both Richard Short and the crown. Added to it was the case of the *St Jacob*, in which the royal share had again been neglected. In this case, it was alleged that Phips had caused the terms of the condemnation of the vessel to be changed as a result of protests that private profit was being made from a voyage supposedly mounted in the interests of the crown. A critic of Phips summarized the accusation concisely:

Sir *William* himself sat Judge upon one *French* Prize, sold for Ten Thousand Pounds, which he divided to the last penny, between himself the Captors, and Undertakers, and finding presently that it was publickly observed that the Privateer that took her, was called the Kings Ship and Men, Guns, Provisions and Stores, Impressed for her in the Kings name, and their Commission was for their Majesties Service for that expedition, which would come out some time or other, he orders his Court again, takes in and Razes the first Judgment, wherein all regard was seemingly had to their Majesties, and gives out another Decree with all it's teeth beaten out, lest it should Bite him. And now the Judgment upon File hath not so much as his Majesties name in it, *Presto*! Be gone Sir, and then all is well.[23]

Like so many of the allegations made against Phips, this one lacks comprehensive documentation, though certain key elements of it can be corroborated. Phips's personal profit from the cruise of the *Swan* and the *Elizabeth and Sarah* was confirmed by Andrew Belcher and Timothy Clarke as owners of the vessels involved, and Brenton's deputy later attested that the same Belcher and Clarke had borrowed the copy of the condemnation deposited at the office of the customs collector and had later replaced it with one that differed from the original.[24] Taken together with the controversy surrounding Phips's efforts to conceal the role of impressment in the mounting of the expedition, the charge was clearly one that would require answering.

There were also some matters that were absent from the formal complaints against Phips but swirled around the more explicitly defined issues. One of these concerned appointments. The letter about the *St. Jacob* alleged that Phips had made appointments of admiralty court officers that were beyond his powers. Certainly, his clerk of admiralty was his personal secretary Benjamin Jackson; and the two assistants at the vice-admiralty court that deliberated on the *Catharine* were political friends of both Phips and Increase Mather: John Richards and John Foster.

Edward Randolph later made a similar suggestion regarding the position of attorney general, observing that Phips's first appointment had been Thomas Newton, whom the governor had dismissed in favour of Anthony Checkley, 'upon his vigorous prosecuting Offenders, against the Acts of Trade.' Randolph described Checkley as 'a man ignorant in the Laws of England, and one that has bin (if not still) an illegall Trader.' Phips had not mentioned Newton when he wrote to Blathwayt in October 1692 saying that Checkley was 'the most fitt person I could pitch upon here.' Newton had been a practising lawyer in New England since 1688, and the position he had undoubtedly held was that of crown attorney before the court of oyer and terminer during the early phases of the Salem trials; he later claimed that he had for a time 'executed the office of Attorney-General.' In 1692 he was displaced from his Salem role on the appointment of Checkley, who had first been appointed attorney general in June 1689 under the revolutionary regime. It was Checkley, as attorney general, who presented the case for the condemnation of the *Catharine* on 27 July 1692. Randolph was therefore not entirely accurate in presenting his accusation. Nevertheless, considering that Newton had been a signatory of the major petitions against the revolutionary regime, the choice of Checkley undoubtedly represented someone who was politically acceptable over one whose direct qualifications were much stronger.[25]

Another repeated allegation of Phips's critics was that he had received cash generated by piracy. This suggestion did not reach the Lords of Trade in specific terms until September 1694, and even then it was contained only in an anonymous set of 'Sir William Phips Accounts,' but there had long been general allegations regarding Massachusetts connections with piracy which were often linked with the name of Samuel Shrimpton.[26] Earlier in 1694, Joseph Dudley had passed on to the Lords of Trade a letter from Nathaniel Byfield that went to the brink of accusation in noting the presence in Boston of a crew headed by a Captain Tew, 'who have brott in vast quantitys of Gold and Silver which they have gott in all Likelyehood very wickedly.' Since Phips was absent at Pemaquid, Stoughton issued a warrant against them, only to see his action reversed when Phips returned. 'Much might be added,' Byfield concluded, 'about the power of Gold which I leave to a better penn then mine to enlarge upon.' Phips did take depositions from members of the crew of Tew's sloop *Amity*, who supplied narratives of a privateering commission from Bermuda and a cruise off the African coast that yielded a treasure-carrying prize which might – or might not – have been

French.[27] Phips's subsequent actions are not clear from the surviving evidence, but the 'Accounts' attributed to him included both £500 in 'Arabian Gold' received from pirates in 1692–3 and £1,000 in 'Arabian Gold in the year 1694 received of pirates he giving them liberty to come to Boston from Roade Island.' For good measure, they also listed an amount of £900 in connection with the *Trempeuse*, a French privateer taken by the *Nonsuch* in July 1693, and £1,000 in the general category of 'setting as judge in Admiralty withoutt Commission and putting mony into his pockett.'[28]

During the autumn and winter of 1693–4, these accusations took no systematic or coherent form. It was the complaints of Short and Brenton that were the focus of the early hearings in London on Phips's discharge of his duties. Brenton's petition, which the customs commissioners had referred to the Treasury, was then passed on to the Lords of Trade. On 6 December 1693 they agreed that Phips appeared to have discouraged ship masters from clearing with Brenton, and they recommended an investigation by commissioners yet to be named. On the following day the Privy Council approved the recommendation while also formally referring Short's complaint to the Lords of Trade. In Short's petition he had not only summarized his suffering at Phips's hands between January and March 1693; he had also complained of Phips's taking the *Catharine* from him, and he claimed a rightful share of the proceeds of the prize for himself and the crew of the *Nonsuch*. There matters stood at the end of 1693, with no explicit linkage between the two complaints beyond the obvious fact that Phips was the target and potential respondent in each case.[29]

While the minuet of references, investigations, and recommendations proceeded, the more robust dance of lobbying and jostling for position was beginning to take its more private course. Phips had taken the precaution of sending Benjamin Jackson to London as his personal agent, and Sir Henry Ashurst continued to act as agent of the colony. Ashurst was joined now and for some years to come by Constantine Phips. A London attorney of growing reputation and a prominent Tory, Constantine was Sir William Phips's second cousin and had apparently been appointed colonial agent at the governor's behest.[30] For William Stoughton, however, the role of the colonial agents was secondary to the influence that should be exerted by the Plantations Office. When writing to Blathwayt in late October 1693, the lieutenant-governor's cautious entry into the issues raised by Phips's difficulties took the form of an observation on the general conduct of government in Massachusetts. 'I fear,' Stoughton commented, 'that in too many particulars, we have fallen short of so great a duty.' Praising the Wheeler expedition, in intent if not in achievement, he went on to express the hope that royal favour to New England would be shown in the appointment of Joseph Dudley and his son to 'publick stations amongst us.' The elder Dudley's 'great abilities,' Stoughton informed Blathwayt, 'are much wanted [i.e., missed] here.'[31]

Joseph Dudley himself was more direct. When writing to Blathwayt in early December, he focused on recent upheavals in the House of Representatives over such matters as John Phillips's accounts and the legislation disqualifying members who were not residents of the towns that had elected them.[32] A contributory issue had been the composition of the address to the crown that had made an elaborate expression of thanks for the appointment of Phips, Stoughton, and Addington. The document had been adopted by the council and, ironically, had been endorsed by Byfield as speaker. The irony lay in the fact that Byfield had joined almost half of the other representatives in opposing the dispatch of the address. As later summarized in an anonymous account that was either written or heavily influenced by Byfield, the draft address 'was brought into our House of Commons, and was Read, and Considered, Sliced and Season'd, and disposed of like a Cucumber; but it was soon discovered, that it was obstructed but by Twenty Three of Fifty (whereof the Speaker was one) ... and that they were Gentlemen principally of *Boston*, who were too near Sir *William* to think well of him, but served in the House, for several Towns and Villages at some distance.'[33] Dudley's comment to Blathwayt emphasized the narrow majorities attained in both houses by the bill on non-residents and warned, 'Continuall Indulgences ... will gratifye and Confirme our loose and alien principles and may at length under malign Influences dissolve our Strict dependance upon the Crown.'[34]

This was an argument well calculated to appeal to Blathwayt and other long-standing critics who had opposed not only the old charter but also the efforts of Increase Mather during and after the revolution, and who regarded Phips as a stalking-horse for both. When the formal processes continued in London early in 1694, a number of these critics found themselves promised an influential role. The ten names recommended by the customs commissioners on 4 January 1694 to act as commissioners investigating Brenton's complaints were certainly not selected with impartiality in mind. They included Byfield, Dudley, and other political foes of Phips, such as Daniel Allin, Francis Foxcroft, Francis Nicholson, Richard Sprague, and John Usher. Four of the ten – Allin, Byfield, Foxcroft, and Sprague – had recently signed their names along-side that of Brenton as representatives protesting against the exclusion of non-residents.[35]

Another setback for Phips came four days later. Despite a petition from Jackson asking for a delay so that he could prepare an answer to the complaints against the governor and if need be send to Boston for Phips's own answer, the Lords of Trade announced on 8 January their intention to proceed to a hearing at their next meeting on the twelfth and to invite representation from the Treasury and Admiralty. An unusually large attendance was recorded at the meeting; but as John Povey wrote to the Admiralty without explanation, the hearing was postponed for another three days.[36] On the fifteenth, verbal arguments were heard, and evidence was ordered to be submitted in writing on the Short case within four days. On the nineteenth, when another unusually large attendance included not only the core of regular participants but also Lord Falkland, who had been one of Phips's sponsors in the voyage of the *James and Mary*, the Lords of Trade considered a variety of depositions and other written evidence. They then formulated an account of the facts of the case, which largely conformed with the complaints of Short and the depositions in his favour, rather than agreeing with the arguments made by Jackson and others.[37]

Since this report was intended for the crown, the focus now shifted to the Privy Council. Jackson again attempted to temporize, arguing that the inclusion of the allegation that Phips had embezzled the royal tenths while sitting in admiralty court was new and had found him unprepared, and that this matter should be considered with Brenton's complaints rather than Short's. The Privy Council, however, elected on 1 February to sustain the linkage between the two cases which had been made when both were combined in the hearing of the Lords of Trade just over two weeks before. 'The Lords of the Committee,' read an endorsement to the report of the Lords of Trade on the Short affair, 'were asked by his Majesty to Consider of the Bringing Sir William Phips to answer before his Majesty in Councill the full Complaints of Mr Brenton and Captain Short.'[38]

From this point, matters progressed swiftly and predictably. Meeting the following day, the Lords of Trade formally recommended Phips's recall to England 'by the first shipping.' Evidence was to be collected on all the complaints, and Phips was instructed 'not to Intermeddle in any other manner, than by the offering to the Lieutenant Governor and

Councill such proofs as he shall desire may be made before them on his own behalf.' Stoughton was to supervise the collection of evidence and to govern in Phips's absence. This recommendation was closely followed in the royal order that was issued later in the month, in which the complaints of both Short and Brenton were specified for investigation along with the events surrounding the affair of the *St Jacob*. Committed to a courier in early April, the order reached Boston for delivery to Phips on 4 July 1694.[39]

Insofar as any conclusions had been drawn by the Lords of Trade, and by implication endorsed by the Privy Council, they were unfavourable to Phips. Nevertheless, the results of the deliberations were by no means disastrous from his point of view. First, as his initial response pointed out, he now had the opportunity to answer the charges directly. He also had time to gather support. Side-stepping the instruction to embark immediately, he promised only to depart when the evidence was collected, and he further excused himself by saying that he had to go to Pemaquid. Secondly, entrusting the investigation to Stoughton and the council meant that those recommended by the customs commissioners had no role to play other than as possible witnesses. Furthermore, since Phips was entitled, as governor, to attend council meetings, the direction that he not 'intermeddle' with the process could be interpreted as being no barrier to his presence alongside the other councillors while evidence was being given. Thirdly, rumours were circulating in Boston by the spring of 1694 that Dudley had seriously overstated the case against Phips. 'It is suggested ... to our good honest Councillors and Country men' Byfield informed Dudley in June, 'that you lost yourself very much by saying before the Lords [of Trade] by a publick hearing that Sir W: had not done any good thing since he was Governour and that you were taken up severely and asked if the makeing the peace with the Indians at the eastward were not a good thing and that you had nothing to say in answer.' Clearly, much still depended on the evidence that was collected and on the expected hearing before the Privy Council.[40]

In the meantime, the opinions of others were varied. Increase Mather waited barely twenty-four hours before writing to Blathwayt in what was inevitably a futile effort to enlist the secretary's support for Phips's continuation in office. 'I am sure,' wrote Mather, 'that hee is Zelous in promoting their Majesties Interest, and that hee is beloved by the generality of people throughout the province: And that hee has a great Veneration for your selfe in particular; and you will find him ready to comply with your Directions on all occasions.' The opinion of William Stoughton was different, though he did not dispute Phips's zeal. Stoughton's formal response to the royal letter was brief, promising only to proceed without delay. His more personal view was later expressed to Blathwayt with the significant rider that 'considerable persons' hoped that Dudley would be appointed governor if Phips was dismissed. Stoughton's evaluation of Phips's tenure was severe in the characteristically cautious way of one whose capacity for survival in both the imperial and the New England political contexts was second only to that of Dudley himself. 'His fidelity to their Majesties, and good intentions in the main, cannot by any one bee questioned,' Stoughton commented, 'it hath been his misfortune to doe too many things upon his own single opinion, or with adherence to the advises of others, more than to those of their Majesties Councill, often much dissatisfyed thereby. His personall prejudices also, and compliances with prejudiced persons, have run him upon putting too great disrespects, upon some worthy men, that might have been otherwise very serviceable.'[41]

Joseph Robinau de Villebon offered yet another perspective on Phips's recall when writing to France of the class-based antagonism towards Phips as a social upstart and noting that it was balanced politically by the governor's equally class-based enjoyment of popular confidence. He added that Stoughton was 'only a simple inexperienced citizen' compared with the military rank and experience of Phips. 'This leads me to believe,' the French commandant continued, 'that during his absence there will be other changes in their plans, and it would be easy, at this time, to profit by the dissension which is certain to arise among them.'[42] The relish with which Villebon identified a military opportunity was not misplaced. His assessment was an illustration of the serious military problems that continued to be encountered by all of the northern English colonies even as evidence was being collected in Boston on the complaints against Phips, which in turn involved Phips in further disputes and recriminations with neighbouring colonies.

Prime among these were his continuing exchanges with Usher. The Wabanaki raids on Oyster River and neighbouring New Hampshire settlements during the second half of July 1694 had ignited the always smouldering bitterness between the two men. When Usher's urgent request for the support of one hundred Massachusetts troops was denied by Phips on the grounds that the charter forbade him to order the militia outside the province without the consent of the assembly, Usher responded with scorn and incredulity. After Phips had left for

Pemaquid, Stoughton apparently reversed the decision, but no Massachusetts forces reached New Hampshire, and Stoughton was forced to apologize in early August for the deficiencies of military organization, which he attributed to 'the refractorynesse of the people and ... [the] want of brisk Commanders.' Usher's complaint was duly dispatched to the Lords of Trade in September.[43] During Phips's absence, Stoughton was also left with the task of trying to persuade the governor and council of Connecticut to supply military support for New York. Massachusetts, Stoughton argued, was fully stretched by its warfare with the Wabanaki, and he hoped that Connecticut, 'lying so much neerer to the place,' would respond to Fletcher's appeals. Fletcher had enjoyed no more success than Phips in asserting control over the Connecticut militia, and Stoughton's efforts also proved fruitless.[44]

Phips's relations with New York, meanwhile, took a more constructive turn after he wrote to Fletcher in late June 1694 to propose that they collaborate in their efforts to preserve the English-Houdenasaunee friendship. Fletcher brought the letter to the New York council, with some observations which the council minutes discreetly recorded as a reference to Phips's 'Long Silence and ... neglect of all his Excellency's [Fletcher's] proposalls for the defence of the frontiers.' Nevertheless, the result was a sharing of information as well as a contribution by Massachusetts to the gifts presented to the Houdenasaunee.[45] Even so, it is unlikely that Phips's reputation with Fletcher and his political circle had significantly progressed from the point in October 1693 when New York's attorney general, James Graham, had informed Edward Randolph about Fitz-John Winthrop's role in the Connecticut militia dispute and had gone on to say that both Phips and Winthrop deserved a 'woodden sword rather than to be honoured beyond their meritt.'[46]

Despite the pressing demands on Phips, Stoughton, and the Massachusetts council during the summer and autumn of 1694, the gathering of evidence proceeded. Stoughton presented the royal order to the council on 5 July, and 17 July was set as the first day for evidence to be heard. Brenton appeared in person to submit affidavits in support of his complaints, and Phips also was there. Both were given the power to summon any witnesses they wished to have heard. There was a break in the hearings when Phips went to Pemaquid following the raid on Oyster River, but they were resumed on 14 August and continued, approximately at weekly intervals, until 17 September. There was then a month-long hiatus. The next session was held on 17 October, attended by Byfield as 'attourney to Mr. Brenton,' and there was another one three days later, at which the process was 'shut up.'[47] Benjamin Jackson apparently caused some consternation on 15 November when he announced his intention to submit additional statements. Sewall described a hasty council meeting at Phips's house, a delay in order to allow Byfield to comment, and a decision after 'much debate at the Townhouse' to allow Jackson to proceed. His additional material was packaged separately from the other evidence, with a note from Stoughton indicating that it had been accepted by the council at Phips's request so that he should not regard himself as 'neglected or injured.'[48] With that, the 109 pages of evidence were ready for transmission to London by the first available ship.

Phips's opinion of what had taken place is nowhere recorded, though in a letter of 18 September to Secretary of State Sir John Trenchard he did refer to 'the Depositions referring to matters between me and my Calumnious Adversaries' and to 'the Accusations of my Enemies, whose notorious malice is already become the Discourse and Wonder of the Countrey where I have had the Honour to be usefull unto their Majesties Interests.' This much was predictable enough. More disinterested was Isaac Addington's, opinion. He informed Blathwayt that Stoughton had been 'very studious to observe his Majesties Commands in directing that affair with an equal hand, and allowed free liberty to all persons to offer what they had to say in those matters.'[49] Jahleel Brenton would not have agreed with this assessment, as was clear from his later restatement of his charges, which included a thorough indictment of the hearings:

All the before mentioned Articles are Proved upon Oath, before the the Lieutenant Governor and Councill, the said Sir William Phips endeavored all he could to hindere the Proof thereof, sometimes threatning the Wittnesses that their Eares ought to be Cutt of, and sometimes barring (as he Called it) others from Swearing. Some of the Councill also Publicly declared themselves Partys in the Cause, Saying the Collector had complained to the King against them all, and therefore they were all concerned, the Councill allso refused to let Severall Wittnesses be sworne which the Collector brought before them, and endeavored as much as in them lay, to Baffle and Trappan those that did swear. There are diverse other matters of a high nature relating to Sir William Phips, which if a Commission may be Granted to Persons unbiassed, the Collector will give Securety to Prove.[50]

Brenton's complaints may have had some substance. Undoubtedly, the presence of Phips in the council chamber would have exerted an influence on some of the deponents. Nevertheless, Addington's description of Stoughton's steady control of the process deserves to be given considerable weight, especially when one remembers that Stoughton was no political friend of Phips. A more likely explanation of Brenton's displeasure is that he was aware of the weakness of the evidence supporting the charge that he had been assaulted by Phips.

In the case of Richard Short, the evidence gathered by Stoughton and the council added no more than a few details to what was already widely known. Francis Foxcroft had testified on Phips's refusal to accept bail for the imprisoned Short, thereby reinforcing Short's complaint of harsh treatment. Depositions about Phips's boarding of the *Walter and Thomas* at Piscataqua confirmed the known sequence of events. However, the accounts emphasizing Phips's anger and his calling Jeremiah Tay 'a Rogue and a Rascal' were counterbalanced by others that were more favourable to him; among these was the complaint of the purser of the *Nonsuch*, Matthew Cary, that he had been arbitrarily imprisoned in Portsmouth at the behest of Tay and Byfield.[51] The main revelations, however, concerned Short's involvement in lending out seamen for commercial voyages and the payments he had received. One deponent, Walter Willett, said that Benjamin Emes had maintained that the monthly payment of twenty shillings to Short had been a voluntary tribute rather than one that was made on the captain's demand, but the overall force of the testimony offered no corroboration for this.[52]

In general, the new evidence was little different from what had emerged from the hearings of the Lords of Trade in January, except that Short's probity had been more effectively challenged. To that extent, the outcome was favourable to Phips. On the admiralty questions, Phips's defences had always been thin, and they remained so. Depositions established clearly that he had profited from the capture of the *St Jacob*, that the waiver of the royal share had been promised by him in advance, that men and munitions had been impressed, and that there had been irregularities in the admiralty court. A possible mitigating argument might still have been made on the basis of Phips's indisputable ignorance of the subtleties of admiralty jurisprudence, but the presumption that he had overstepped the bounds of legitimate self-interest arose unmistakably from the evidence. As a vignette, several of the depositions submitted by Benjamin Jackson on 15 November 1694 concerned actions taken by Jackson in the capacity of clerk of the admiralty. That Jackson was designated admiralty clerk and a naval officer as well as being Phips's private secretary, agent, and candidate for provincial secretary was a comment in itself on Phips's conduct as vice-admiral.[53]

As for the complaints made by Brenton, the thrust of the evidence was quite different. The evidence of competition and conflict between Brenton and the naval office was clear and unsurprising. Brenton's 'waiters,' Hill and Francklyn, testified at length on suspicious shipments and on the obstacles put in the way of their investigations, though they admitted under questioning that they had never been refused access to 'Cocquets, Bonds, or Entrys' of the naval office – which was one of Brenton's specific allegations – and that 'not till of late' had they ever asked to see those documents.[54] By far the greatest proportion of the evidence on customs matters concerned the case of the *Good Luck*. Some of the testimony concerned the entry formalities undergone by Thomas Wake and his vessel, and the shifting fortunes of the cargo. Most of it dealt with the altercation between Phips and Brenton, to which fourteen eyewitnesses addressed themselves. All agreed that a loud argument had taken place after Phips had hurried onto the customs wharf. Hill and Francklyn had Phips calling Brenton 'Rogue, Rascall and Villaine.' They and Timothy Clarke (who had become a political critic of Phips since opposing the bill on non-resident representatives and had been in conversation with Brenton when the incident began) described threats from Phips to the effect that 'he would break his head and bones and send him to Gaol.' Other witnesses said that Phips, in more reasoned vein, had informed the collector, 'You shall not break open hatches and rob men of their Goods if you can seize it in a lawful way you may, and shall have a fair Tryal for it.'[55]

On the key contentions that Phips had arrived with a crowd of some fifty persons and had assaulted Brenton with his fist and cane, the evidence offered Brenton scant support. Hill and Francklyn at first loyally maintained that Phips had struck Brenton and dragged him around the wharf, but they later qualified their testimony: 'Upon the Question put to the Evidences about the word dragging they explained themselves to intend pulling and shoving the Collector standing upon his Feet, and by strikeing they do not intend downright blows but say the Governour struck the Collector several blows downwards with his Cane upon the shoulder and thighs.' Every other witness of this episode denied seeing Phips strike a blow. Several recalled that he had gesticulated with his cane and had used both it and his hands to stop Brenton from leaving the wharf and some confirmed Foster's description of Phips giving Brenton 'Chucks under the Chin.' For example, the house carpenter John Barnard, who had been repairing a nearby warehouse, declared that 'he saw the Governour hold up his Cane at the Collector, and might touch him with it, but fetched no stroke at him, pusht him with his hand towards the Warehouse, and chuckt him under the Chin.' Other witnesses recalled seeing Brenton put a hand on his sword, though he had not drawn it.[56]

As for the crowd, not even Hill and Francklyn confirmed Brenton's version. Byfield made an attempt to do so, but when questioned he had to admit that he had arrived after the 'noyse and tumult' had begun and that he had observed only 'that the persons present did generally abet and countenance Sir William Phips in his Proceedings against the Collector, and brought him drink But this Deponent did not see any to take notice of the Collector, or any way to countenance him.' Other witnesses contradicted Brenton directly. John Barnard, for instance, stated that Phips had arrived with 'no attendance,' while others said he had been followed only by Wake and the goldsmith William Rous. There was no doubt that a crowd had soon gathered, and it is likely that most were more favourably disposed towards Phips than to Brenton. On the other hand, the crowd included the seamen from the *Conception Prize* who had been assisting Brenton. Hill and Francklyn noted that one of them, thinking that Phips was slighting Fairfax and the ship, had exclaimed, 'Damn his Blood, do's he say a little Kings ship, if I had him in place where, I'de burst the belly of him '[57] It was not only Phips who was capable of threats and abusive language. Nor, despite Phips's ability to orchestrate crowd actions, did this spontaneous gathering of onlookers constitute the threatening mob invoked by Brenton in his petition.

Although Brenton's allegation of the manipulation of witnesses and unfair questioning cannot entirely be set aside, the balance of the evidence against his version of the events on 29 May 1693 was clear and conspicuous. For Phips to launch a physical attack against Brenton would have been a remarkable anomaly in a person who rarely resorted to violence, and then only when there was a well-defined immediate goal. No such purpose suggests itself in the case of Brenton, and a number of the witnesses quoted Phips – with minor variations – as saying repeatedly in the course of the exchange that 'he did not, nor would he ever hinder him [Brenton] in the Execution of his Office, but assist him all he could, but yet would not suffer such illegal actions.'[58] This comment indicates that anger had not caused the governor to overlook the need to assert that while the collector had legitimate duties, granting or seizing entry certificates and was not among them.

The evidence contained a further clue about the undercurrents of the *Good Luck* affair. One of the witnesses on the wharf, Joshua Winsor, described a conversation he had had just afterwards with the merchant David Waterhouse, who had been on his way to Marblehead to buy the *Good Luck*'s cargo but had been forestalled when the vessel had put in at Boston. For this he blamed Phips and Foster. Waterhouse, along with John Nelson, Byfield, Richard Sprague, and others, had been among the merchants who had sat for a time on the Council of Safety but had then parted company with the revolutionary regime and signed the New England petition of early 1691. More recently, he had joined Byfield and others in writing to Blathwayt in support of Richard Short.[59] The *Good Luck* affair can be understood on various levels. Personal conflict between Phips and Brenton was one, disputed jurisdiction over entering cargoes another, but a third was the commercial rivalry and the competition for patronage opportunities that underlay all the tensions over port regulation.

Be that as it may, the evidence collected by Stoughton and the council from July to November 1694 left Brenton, and also Byfield, in an isolated position. It is unlikely that Brenton and Byfield had expected the tale of Phips's assault to assume such significance – they had probably seen it simply as a vignette that would lend credence to the more substantive charges – but the customs commissioners had seized on it from the start. The subsequent linkage of the Short and Brenton complaints had focused attention even more on Phips's personal behaviour, and the collection of evidence but reinforced this focus. As a result, Brenton and his supporters were left with the unwelcome task of justifying in detail a story which, at best, they had greatly exaggerated for effect. One result of this situation was a feeling of frustration, which can be seen so clearly in Brenton's restatement of November 1694. But there were also deeper implications.

Neither Brenton nor Byfield enjoyed a secure basis of political support. Brenton's personal origins were in Rhode Island, as the son of a wealthy Newport merchant. Byfield, English-born, had come to Massachusetts in 1674 and had resided for a time in Boston. His political base, however, was where he had been living between then and 1692, in rural Bristol County at the southwestern extreme of the old Plymouth colony, close to the disputed boundary with Rhode Island.[60] Like the brothers Jahleel and Ebenezer Brenton, Byfield had been damaged politically by the disqualification of non-resident representatives. The rebuttal of a key accusation against Phips would represent a further setback.

At a deeper level, Brenton and Byfield also lacked secure status within the political faction to which they belonged. Byfield had held minor office under the Dominion of New England, though he had adjusted easily to the revolution. Jahleel Brenton reputedly owed his appointment as collector to Increase Mather but had made enemies of a significant number of Boston merchants through his customs activities. Never close to the old charter group and now alienated from the pragmatic supporters of the new charter regime, Brenton and Byfield had not shared the experience of deprivation during the revolution that was common to such committed opponents of Phips as Dudley, Foxcroft, and Usher. Nor did they, in themselves, have worthwhile connections in London. Byfield had admitted as much when he said that Phips 'Knew white hall better than my selfe,' and according to Brenton's deputies Hill and Francklyn, Phips had used much the same words to Brenton during the altercation of 29 May 1693 when Brenton's had threatened to appeal to London: 'I think I know Whitehall a little better than you do.'[61] In time, Byfield's growing association with Dudley would bring handsome political returns, but on 13 November 1694 it seemed to Isaac Addington that 'the particular fflames which have been blown up and possibly shone abroad ... [are] pretty well extinguished and uncomfortable heats occasioned by those Fires allaied.'[62]

Addington's assessment was borne out by the perceptible solidification of political support that Phips was enjoying within the colony. To merchant members of the council whose interests ran contrary to those of Brenton, Phips's quarrel with the collector was a recommendation in itself. His rapprochement with the assembly, especially with the old charter advocates, had become particularly clear in his cordial visit to the House of Representatives on 14 September, when he had promised to make efforts in London to have the ancient charter privileges restored. Thus, the events that preceded Phips's departure gave him some reason to regard his summons to England as an opportunity rather than a threat. It is true that he still had to face the resentment of Sir Henry Ashurst, but this would be offset by the presence of another colonial agent, his cousin Constantine Phips. If he could face down his critics before the Privy Council, he would return strengthened in both imperial and colonial contexts. He might even be able to extricate himself from the political thickets of southern New England sufficiently to get on with the real business of making good commercial use of the northeastern boundaries in the 1691 charter and then to extend English influence through the defeat of the French in Canada.

Before Phips left, his political opponents presented him with yet another challenge. On 1 November his client Thomas Dobbins was arrested on a suit brought by Captain Jeremiah Tay for unlawful confinement and ill-treatment during Tay's week-long captivity aboard the *Nonsuch* in March 1693. When Dobbins was committed to prison he refused to supply bail, but as Samuel Sewall recorded, 'Sir William Phips rescued him, and told the Sheriff He would send him, the Sheriff, to prison, if he touch'd him, which occasioned very warm discourse between Him and the Lieutenant Governour.' More was to come the following week when Dobbins was summoned to court, again refused to give bail, and 'Between Sheriff and Keeper is [was] carried to Goal, which makes great Wrath.' This time there was no rescue. The hearing was inconclusive, but Phips's name was prominent in the proceedings, since Dobbins defended himself by citing the governor's warrant for Tay to be detained.

Phips made his feelings plain two days later by boycotting a farewell dinner given in his honour by Stoughton and the council. Both of the Mathers and John Foster also stayed away, but the most conspicuously empty chair was that 'at the upper end of the Table.'[63] Cotton Mather's subsequent excuse to Sewall that he was 'sick of a grievous pain in his face' rang hollow enough to give the impression of peevishness and pique. Yet both the timing of the suit and the court appearance of Joseph Dudley's son Thomas as attorney for Tay suggest that Phips had some reason for his resentment, at least as far as Stoughton was concerned. Coming more than eighteen months after the event, the suit not only reflected on Phips but also gave a none-too-subtle warning to clients and allies of the departing governor as to what they might face in his absence.[64]

Nevertheless, on the Saturday evening of the following week, 17 November, there was no evident trace of these conflicts or even of the arguments that had preceded the last-minute presentation of Jackson's depositions two days earlier. Phips was accompanied to the wharf by Stoughton and all the council members who were in town, as well as by a group which Sewall described as including 'Mr. Cotton Mather, Captains of Frigatts, Justices and many other Gentlemen.' According to Mather, the governor graciously told his critics 'that he *freely forgave them all*.' If he did indeed say this, Sewall made no mention of it, preferring to note that a departure after dark on the eve of the Sabbath created some awkwardness and that he had turned for home as soon as Phips's vessel made sail. 'Guns at the Castle were fired about seven,' recorded Sewall as the last of Phips's numerous transatlantic voyages began. 'Governour had his Flagg in main Top.'[65]

12

Endings

On 7 December 1694 a vessel arrived at Cowes carrying news that Sir William Phips was preparing to sail from Boston. Phips reached London on 1 January 1695, whereupon he was immediately arrested in connection with a £20,000 legal action brought against him by Joseph Dudley and another individual. Although details of the affair have not survived, Sir Henry Ashurst attributed it to Dudley's efforts to be named as Phips's successor. 'Mr. D– thought himself as sure of being governor,' Ashurst later wrote to Increase Mather, 'as you are of my friendship.' Ashurst bailed Phips out, his sense of responsibility as an accredited agent of Massachusetts perhaps outweighing his personal disillusionment with the governor, or perhaps he was swayed by Phips's complaints that he was the victim of a powerful group of enemies. 'I could not believe what Sir William Phips told me of Mr. Stoughton and Mr. Addington,' wrote Ashurst to Mather. 'I perceive I had wrong notions of things.'[1] Matters now appeared to improve for Phips. He quickly petitioned the crown for an early hearing at which he could answer 'the Imputation of such great Crimes as are falsely Laid to his ... Charge.' The petition was referred from the Privy Council to the Lords of Trade, who in late January had formally received the evidence collected in Boston and now agreed, on 13 February, to set a date 'as soon as Mr Brent [sic] and Captain Short the Complainants are ready.'[2]

There is little reliable evidence regarding Phips's activities during his weeks of waiting. Cotton Mather, plausibly enough, had him pursuing his long-standing interests in the trade in timber and naval stores and in a further expedition against Canada, as well as seeking royal permission for a new treasure-seeking venture in the Caribbean after his eventual and honourable 'Dismission from his Government.' Phips certainly paid

close attention to the proceedings of the Lords of Trade. Fitz-John Winthrop, who was in London as agent for Connecticut, wrote of attending
with him 'the Councill Chamber at White Hall' on 12 February. By then
Phips had a heavy cold. According to Winthrop, it was 'the usual dis-
temper to strangers, which hung about him very much, but kept him not
within.' Returning to his lodgings on the evening of the twelfth, Phips
took a turn for the worse. Although he was bled, this failed to produce
any lasting relief from what was probably a severe attack of influenza,
and his fever increased on the sixteenth. On the next day, a Sunday
afternoon, Winthrop went to see him and 'found him extreme ill, scarce
able to breath; and soe continued all night, and about nine of the clock in
the morning departed very easely.'[3]

Phips was buried on the afternoon of 21 February 1695 at the church
of St Mary Woolnoth, in Lombard Street in the City of London. Winthrop believed that had he lived, 'all would have been well.' Cotton
Mather recorded that during Phips's last illness he had received 'the
Honour of a Visit from a very Eminent Person at *Whitehall*, who upon
sufficient Assurance, bad him *Get well as fast as he could, for in one Months
time he should again be dispatched away to his Government of* New-
England.'[4] Certainly, the evidence that Brenton would have brought
against him was weak. Ashurst appears to have been leaning once again
in favour of Phips, and the efforts of Constantine Phips might in any
case have offset any lingering animosity on Ashurst's part.

Samuel Sewall recorded in his diary that the news of Phips's death
reached Boston on 5 May, 'at which people are generally sad.' Guns
were fired in mourning the next day, and on the eighth Sewall visited
Mary Spencer Phips. '[She] takes on heavily for the death of Sir William,' Sewall noted. Reproachful that Stoughton and the council 'were
not so kind to him as they should have been,' she later found solace in
placing a white marble monument in the church where her husband
was interred. Intricately adorned in bas-relief, it depicted such images
as the scene of Phips's treasure hunt and his family coat of arms.[5] At a
memorial service in Boston, Phips was eulogized by Increase Mather,
who declared, '*New-England* knows not yet what they have lost!' Others
were more concerned with the succession. The early talk was of Dudley,
but by the summer Fitz-John Winthrop was reporting that the new governor would be Richard Coote, earl of Bellomont, an Irish peer and a
prominent Whig. Dudley finally had his turn in 1701, following Bellomont's death.[6]

Phips's immediate legacy was mixed, in both personal and provincial affairs. His will was simple enough, leaving all his property to Mary Spencer Phips save for five shillings left to his brother James, whom he had supported over the years but who had apparently predeceased him. The other provisions related only to the eventuality of the intestate deaths of his widow and their adopted son Spencer Phips. The inventory included household goods, silver plate valued at not quite £415, the yacht he had had built in 1693 (which was now sold for £1,800), a one-sixteenth share of the merchant vessel *Friendship*, and 'one negro man, boy, and negro woman.' With miscellaneous items but not including either real estate holdings or loans and mortgages, the value was set at £3,377/19/–. Phips's major real estate holdings, which included several waterfront properties and even the Salutation tavern, had originally been purchased for almost £1,500. Outstanding mortgages probably took the real total of his estate to some £5,000. This indicates considerable shrinkage of his wealth since the voyage of 1686-7. Yet even with his fortune eroded, the value of Phips's estate was exceptional in Boston at the time. Of the 304 decedents there between 1685 and 1699 who left probate inventories, only seven had estates worth more than £2,000. The wealthiest 10 per cent had estates ranging in value from £1,155 to £3,417 – an upper extreme only slightly higher than Phips's total.[7]

Following Sir William's death, Mary Spencer Phips stepped out of her husband's shadow and openly began to direct the business ventures of the family. She purchased shares in ships, granted mortgages, and continued to own wharves, warehouses, and the tavern. Well prepared by her years as Sir William's deputy and attorney as well as by her background as a merchant's daughter, she seems to have relished her role and the independence it offered. She outlived Sir William by eleven years, but only in 1701 did she remarry. Her third husband, Peter Sargeant, was a prominent Boston merchant and a kinsman of Sir Henry Ashurst.

Mary died on 20 January 1706.[8] Her will included a number of small bequests and annuities to family and friends. Sir William Phips's long-lived mother received an annuity of ten pounds, while Andrew Belcher, John Foster, and Increase Mather, all of whom were associates of Sir William as well as of Mary, collected bequests of ten pounds each. The bulk of the estate passed to Spencer Phips. A 1703 Harvard graduate who was listed first in his class because of the status of his family, Spencer was politically active over a long period. He served on the Massachusetts council almost continuously from 1721 to 1732, and was then deputy governor from 1733 until his death in 1757. He undertook a variety of public tasks and seemed to maintain his adoptive father's interest in relations with Native inhabitants. He was a trustee of the Natick Indians, he treated with the Houdenasaunee and Wabanaki, and he served as commissioner for the New England Company.[9]

Spencer Phips married Elizabeth Hutchinson, daughter of the prominent merchant Eliakim Hutchinson. They sold Sir William's house and raised a family of ten children on a large farm that consisted of much of present-day East Cambridge. Seven of their children survived to adulthood, though not all lived long lives. Spencer Jr died as a young lieutenant at Annapolis Royal, the Nova Scotia outpost that had borne the name Port-Royal when briefly captured by Sir William in 1690. The oldest son, William, graduated from Harvard after a scandalous career there, served on the 1745 expedition to Louisbourg, and in 1750 was stationed at Fort Frederick at Pemaquid. There he died in 1751, commander of the fort that had been built on the ruins of his grandfather's Fort William Henry. Another son, David, also went to Louisbourg and later served as a naval officer on the Great Lakes during the Seven Years' War. A Loyalist, he and his family moved to Halifax, Nova Scotia, in 1776, at the cost of the confiscation of his entire estate, which included portraits of Sir William Phips and the duke of Albemarle. David Phips eventually moved to England, where he died aged 87 in Bath in 1811. The family thus returned to the West Country which James Phips had left close to two hundred years before.[10]

Politically and militarily, Sir William Phips bequeathed continuing difficulties to his acting successor, Stoughton. Hostilities continued in the Wabanaki territory, and Pemaquid fell to the Wabanaki in the summer of 1696. Meanwhile, in June 1695 the Lords of Trade in London concluded their scrutiny of the first batch of statutes enacted in Massachusetts after Phips's arrival as governor. Some were confirmed, others disallowed or referred to the legal officers of the crown. Among those disallowed was the act establishing the naval offices, and in 1696 a further Navigation Act provided new and effective machinery for enforcing the authority of royal customs collectors in the colonies. Jahleel Brenton continued in office in New England until 1707. Even so, the rights and wrongs of his behaviour during Phips's governorship were still being controverted before the newly established Board of Trade (the successor to the Privy Council committee usually known as the Lords of Trade) at the end of July 1696, even as the siege of Fort William Henry was about to begin.[11]

Shortly afterwards, John Nelson – newly released from imprisonment

in France – put much of the responsibility for the devastating effectiveness of the Wabanaki-French alliance on 'that Late foolish and unhapie
Expedition from New England [to Quebec] by Sir William Phips, as All-
soe, for want of due care of settlement in the Countries of Nova Scotia
affter the takeing of Port Royall.' Others blamed Phips for more personal losses. John Usher attempted in 1697 to persuade the Board of
Trade that the non-payment of his accounts dating from the era of the
Dominion of New England had been the result of 'some groundless
prejudice conceived against your petitioner by ... Sir William Phipps.'
With more obvious justification, though little chance of success, Des
Friches de Meneval claimed satisfaction in 1700 from Phips's widow
and heirs for the retention by Phips of his money and personal effects.[12]

Meneval would no doubt have been interested to know that the epi-
taphs suggested for Phips in an anonymous commemorative broadside
poem, published in Boston in 1695, were 'A PUBLICK SPIRIT'S GONE. *Or
but name* PHIPS; *more needs not be exprest*; *Both* Englands, *and next* Ages,
tell the Rest.'[13] In the years immediately following Phips's death, there
was no shortage of detractors who must have found the sentiment as
naive as the poem's breathless grandiloquence. Historical perspective,
however, allows for a more nuanced judgment. Obviously, Phips was
not as righteous and merciful as Increase Mather's eulogy proclaimed.
His behaviour, though sometimes crudely straightforward, had more
than its share of ambiguities which had as much to do with his social
mobility as they did with morality. Nor was he a successful governor,
in his own terms or anyone else's, except perhaps the Mathers'. To be
sure, his career in office was left untidy and unfinished at the time of
his death, and none can say what might have followed a successful
defence of his record before the Lords of Trade. Yet his historical
importance rests more on the circumstances which he confronted and
the processes in which he took part than on any simple estimate of success or failure.

Phips should be understood in part as a projector, a promoter of
schemes that promised enrichment for himself and for any patrons or
investors he was able to attract. His tenacious pursuit of treasure in the
Caribbean provides the clearest example. His hopes for development of
the fur trade in northern New England and Acadia/Nova Scotia, along
with trade in timber and naval stores, and mines for precious metals
had similar aims. The conquest of Canada, for which Phips never ceased
to hope – except when it threatened to be carried out under a command
other than his own – would have implied at least the potential of a lucra-

tive fur trade and the exploitation of a range of other resources. Mather recorded that towards the close of Phips's life his thoughts turned back to the Caribbean. That he intended to resume 'his old *Fishing-Trade*,' conditional no doubt on the continuing elusiveness of a new Canada expedition, is also suggested by his effort to obtain a grant of Hog Island, opposite Nassau. Certainly, if Defoe is to be believed, Phips's 'strange Performance' in salvaging the *Concepción* had 'set a great many Heads on work to contrive something for themselves,' a phenomenon that was no doubt reflected in the conversation at Phips's only known meeting with William Paterson in July 1691.[14] As a projector, Phips had only one great success. But it was enough to sustain an acquisitiveness that pervaded all of his later activities.

Phips was also a political figure. To this he came late, though with some preparation derived from earlier experience. Finding the right patronage was as much a part of the political culture of late-seventeenth-century England and Anglo-America as it was essential to successful treasure seeking. Commanding a vessel in which the shares of the crew were essentially equal was, among other things, a political task. It was one in which Phips made successful use of the tools of hard language and the calculated provocation of his social superiors. These techniques had their uses for a colonial governor, as was seen in Phips's ability to derive support from Boston's North End, but they also had their drawbacks. Patronage, moreover, was a more complex matter in the labyrinthine networks of postrevolutionary Whitehall than it had been in the more socially fluid context of the Navy Board.

Thus, Phips relied heavily on Increase Mather's political and commercial contacts, and he put them to good use. It was no minor feat to progress in the space of a few months from being the butt of William Blathwayt's scorn – as in March 1691 when he was belittled for his 'shamefull and cowardly defeat in Canada' – to dining with Blathwayt, Mather, and Ashurst in August, and then shortly afterwards emerging as the leading candidate for the governorship.[15] The evidence suggested that Phips participated actively in this process, with the crucial assistance of Sir Henry Ashurst. Once he was appointed, however, Phips's lack of solid political experience soon became clear, as did the limitations of his patronage in London. If he thought, as some of his letters indicate, that he could count on Blathwayt and the earl of Nottingham for support, he was mistaken. His alienation of Ashurst by the fall of 1692 further undermined his repeated claims that he had influence in Whitehall, although his rapprochement with Ashurst in early 1695 and the increasing role of Constantine Phips suggest that the damage was not beyond repair.

As governor, Phips also had the disadvantage that his personal patronage engine was dangerously small. He had neither sufficient personal wealth (beyond the diminishing proceeds from the *Concepción*) nor high enough social status to give him leverage with the politically active strata of Massachusetts society. He also lacked the social graces that might otherwise have smoothed his path. There is no evidence that Phips entertained in the way that his successors did, and there is every indication that he was at his most comfortable when on his walks on the Boston waterfront, when providing a dinner for ship's carpenters, or when undertaking one of his frequent sojourns at Pemaquid.[16] Patronage opportunities, for him, stemmed largely from the encouragement of quasi-military expeditions against the French, from which merchants could be promised private profit (and sometimes attain it), and from his control of trade through the naval offices. Thus, if there is a connection between Phips's quarrels with Short and Brenton, it lies not in his supposedly violent and impulsive character but in the reality that each of these opponents in his own way threatened the governor's already meagre ability to extend patronage. In this context, Phips had difficulty in meeting problems that were to become familiar to later governors: the matter of his salary, the extent of his powers, and his response to political factionalism in the colony and across the Atlantic. Although it has been suggested that in the late 1690s the earl of Bellomont was the first colonial governor to be deliberately targeted by 'London-American interests,' the activities of Dudley, Ashurst, Byfield, and Stoughton indicate that Phips had been so honoured some years before.[17]

Phips's political difficulties, as well as stemming, at least initially, from his personal lack of relevant experience and resources, thus reflected the characteristic structures and dynamics of the empire. In an imperial context, his significance lay also in his handling of problems that were to become increasingly acute for British imperialism during the eighteenth century. The harnessing together of commercial and strategic objectives which became so evident following the Revolution of 1688–9 (and of which the support of Phips and Mather by leading City merchants in 1691 was an early indication) implied that English and then British hegemony would be asserted over large areas of North America, and eventually over large areas of the world, where there was little if any British settlement. The financial revolution that created both the 'military-fiscal state' defined by John Brewer and the connections between landed and monied interests embodied in the 'gentlemanly capitalism' of P.J. Cain and A.G. Hopkins was in its early days during Phips's lifetime.[18] Even so, the expanding roles of the state and of the monied interests that were the sources of public credit were already perceptible.

Crucially lacking, however, were the tools to resolve the paradoxes that could arise where imperial expansion confronted the well-entrenched position of non-English peoples, whether aboriginal or colonial. Massachusetts, under the charter of 1691, was a colony of greater complexity than historians have normally recognized. While it retained certain characteristics of a colony of settlement, notably in the areas that immediately surrounded Massachusetts Bay itself, it was geographically dominated by territories in which English hegemony had yet to be convincingly asserted. Although Phips's diplomatic efforts to resolve this paradox were ultimately unsuccessful, he was not mistaken in his recognition that – at least for the time being – negotiated relationships with non-English peoples were essential to the establishment of a widespread English sphere of influence in greater Massachusetts.

Yet within the more limited confines of Puritan New England, antagonism and mistrust were easily aroused by the same characteristics that gave weight to the imperial Phips. Aggressive, acquisitive, and pragmatic in his alliances, Phips was an unorthodox figure both socially and politically. His origins were obscure and peripheral, his language and manners left much to be desired, and he was rumoured to lack any but the most basic literacy. His religious awakening came late in life, at a time convenient for his political advancement, and was based on a conversion narrative characterized by less than the usual quotient of heartfelt repentance. His successful pursuit of riches through treasure seeking could be taken as an affront to the communal values that alone could justify accumulated wealth. Even politically, he had never attained or sought the opportunity to serve the common good as a town selectman or representative to the General Court.

There was, to be sure, another side to the equation. Phips was clearly able to forge relationships with at least some of the Boston merchants who enjoyed the kind of respectability that had been recognizable in his wife's father and in her first husband – the kind of modest but solid respectability to which Phips himself could have aspired had he continued his steady progress from shipwright to sea captain to merchant. His alliance with the Mathers was not an unmixed political blessing, and its usefulness was perceptibly reduced after the Salem outbreak, but it did open some important doors – to church membership, for example. Phips's own political efforts were not always effective, but they did enable him by 1694 to combat the pro-Dudley faction successfully by establishing an understanding with the advocates of the old charter.

How this alliance would have evolved if his position as governor had been confirmed in 1695 is a matter for speculation, but at the time of his death it offered him his most promising route towards political security. Implying as it did the support of rural members of the House of Representatives, it also held out the prospect of a reconciliation of sorts: of an assured place for the unconventional governor in the political and cultural milieu of the Puritan commonwealth while he continued to advance his own interests within the commercial and military framework of the empire. All would have depended, of course, on the outcome of the hearing that was forestalled by his death. Yet it is in paradoxes such as this that Sir William Phips's historical significance chiefly lies. Wholly successful in none of his pursuits – except briefly as a treasure seeker – and at times a conspicuous failure, he nevertheless was neither a simple nor a ridiculous figure. Helped and hindered by his obscure origins, Phips struggled for advancement and illustrated the fluid nature of the late-seventeenth-century empire as much by his limitations as by his ultimately modest attainments.

Notes

In this study, we have used the shortened form of endnote citation. Full details of sources cited are provided only in the bibliography. In all references to dates, the appropriate calendar style has been retained – the Julian calendar where the citation is from an English source, the Gregorian calendar where it is French – except that the years have been modernized in all cases to begin on 1 January. Quotations have been rendered exactly as written, with the following exceptions for clarity: standard abbreviations have been expanded; the thorn has been changed to 'th' and the ampersand to 'and' or 'et' as appropriate; where they are interchangeable, the letters 'v' and 'j' have been changed to 'u' and 'i'; superscript letters have been lowered.

Abbreviations

AAS	American Antiquarian Society
AC	Archives nationales, Archives des colonies, France
AGI	Archivo General de Indias, Spain
BL	British Library
BodL	Bodleian Library, Oxford University
CKS	Kent Archives Office, Centre for Kentish Studies
CWBK	Colonial Williamsburg, Blathwayt Papers
DAB	*Dictionary of American Biography*
DCB	*Dictionary of Canadian Biography*
DNB	*Dictionary of National Biography*
HLBP	Huntington Library, Blathwayt Papers
HMC	Historical Manuscripts Commission, Great Britain
MA	Massachusetts State Archives
MHS	Massachusetts Historical Society

NMM   National Maritime Museum, Great Britain
OED   *Oxford English Dictionary*, 2nd edition
PRO   Public Record Office, Great Britain
UNP   University of Nottingham, Portland Mss

Preface

1 Cotton Mather, *Diary*, 1: 148; Cotton Mather, 'Pietas in Patriam: The Life of His Excellency Sir William Phips, Knt.,' in Mather, *Magnalia Christi Americana* (hereafter Mather, 'Pietas in Patriam'), 280.
2 Ibid., 281, 288, 341–7.
3 Willard, *The Character of a Good Ruler*; Calef, *More Wonders of the Invisible World*. See also Gura, 'Cotton Mather's *Life of Phips*,' 440–57.
4 Goold, 'Sir William Phips,'; Bowen, 'Life of Sir William Phips,' 99.
5 Lounsberry, *Sir William Phips*, xi–xii.
6 Thayer, *Sir William Phips, Adventurer and Statesman*, esp. 67–8.
7 See Johnson, 'Charles McLean Andrews and the Invention of American Colonial History,' esp. 532; Goggin, 'Challenging Sexual Discrimination in the Historical Profession,' 778–9, 794–5; *Directory of American Scholars*, 6th ed., 1 (1974), 29.
8 Barnes, 'The Rise of William Phips,' 271–94, and 'Phippius Maximus,' 532–53.
9 C.P. Stacey, 'Phips, Sir William,' DCB, 1: 544–6; Richard R. Johnson, 'Sir William Phips,' in Gallay, *Colonial Wars of North America*, 563–5.
10 Karraker, 'The Treasure Expedition of Captain William Phips to the Bahama Banks,' 731–52; Karraker, 'Spanish Treasure, Casual Revenue of the Crown,' 301–18; George, 'The Treasure Trove of William Phips,' 294–318; Karraker, *The Hispaniola Treasure*.
11 Earle, *Treasure of the* Concepción.
12 For early examples, see Stacey, 'Sir William Phips' Attack on Quebec, 1690,' in his *Introduction to the Study of Military History for Canadian Students*, 56; Miller, *The New England Mind: From Colony to Province*, 167, 177, 209.
13 Hall, *The Last American Puritan*, 265; Levin, *Cotton Mather*, 178.
14 Miller, *The New England Mind: From Colony to Province*, 209; Sosin, *English America and the Revolution of 1688*, 204, 224, 227.
15 Mather, 'Pietas in Patriam,' 343; see also Puck's speech in Shakespeare's *Midsummer Night's Dream*, act 3, scene 2.
16 Lethbridge, *Here Lies Gold*, 149, 153.
17 Baker, 'Trouble to the Eastward,' and 'A Scratch with a Bear's Paw,'; Reid, *Acadia, Maine, and New Scotland*; Daigle, 'Nos amis les ennemis; Morrison, *The Embattled Northeast*.

18 Johnson, *John Nelson* and *Adjustment to Empire;* Godfrey, *Pursuit of Profit and Preferment in Colonial North America.*

19 Rediker, *Between the Devil and the Deep Blue Sea;* Davies, *Gentlemen and Tarpaulins;* Hornstein, *The Restoration Navy and English Foreign Trade.*

20 Dickson, *The Financial Revolution in England;* Jones, *War and Economy in the Age of William III and Marlborough;* De Krey, *A Fractured Society;* Olson, *Making the Empire Work.*

21 Brewer, *The Sinews of Power;* Cain and Hopkins, *British Imperialism: Innovation and Expansion, 1688–1914.* See also the essays in Stone, ed., *An Imperial State at War,* and for a useful historiographical discussion, Bowen, *Elites, Enterprise and the Making of the British Overseas Empire,* 3–21.

22 Defoe, *Essay upon Projects.*

23 Lockridge, *A New England Town;* Demos, *A Little Commonwealth;* Greven, *Four Generations.* Earlier works that also influenced this flowering of community study included Powell, *Puritan Village,* and Rutman, *Winthrop's Boston.*

24 Boyer and Nissenbaum, *Salem Possessed;* Demos, *Entertaining Satan;* Hall, *Worlds of Wonder, Days of Judgment.*

25 Innes, *Creating the Commonwealth.* For differentiation of Innes's interpretation of Puritan commercial values from the portrayals in the earlier community studies, see ibid., 41–5.

26 Clark, *The Eastern Frontier;* Camp, *Archaeological Investigations at Pemaquid;* Bradley, 'Was the Plantation Despicable?'; See also Emerson W. Baker, 'A Guide to Sources on Maine in the Age of Discovery,' in Howell and Baker, *Maine in the Age of Discovery.*

27 For further discussion and a review of the ambiguities of conventional delineations, see Bourque, 'Ethnicity on the Maritime Peninsula.' The separation of the Wuastukwiuk from the Penobscot Wabanaki is problematic in this period, and there remains considerable debate about the stage which the separation of these groups by language and ethnicity had reached by Phips's lifetime.

1: Early Life, 1651–1682

1 Cotton Mather, 'Pietas in Patriam: The Life of His Excellency Sir William Phips, Knt.,' in Mather, *Magnalia Christi Americana* (hereafter Mather, 'Pietas in Patriam'), 278.

2 See Gura, 'Cotton Mather's *Life of Phips,*' 447–53; Canup, *Out of the Wilderness,* 218.

3 Noyes, Libby, and Davis, eds., *Genealogical Dictionary of Maine and New Hampshire,* 115, 550. In this study, we will not normally make use of geographical terms that are anachronistic in the relevant period. Thus, we will

make limited use of the term 'Maine,' except insofar as we refer to the English perception of that portion of the Wabanaki territory – between the Piscataqua and Kennebec rivers – that was intermittently designated by the English as 'the Province of Maine' between 1622 and 1691. Between 1622 and 1629, this term was applied to a larger area, from the Merrimack to the Kennebec rivers. See Reid, *Maine, Charles II, and Massachusetts*, passim.

4 Pedigree of Francis Phips, 11 March 1664, BODL, Rawlinson MSS, D 865, 86.

5 Sir Henry Ashurst to William Stoughton, 14 November 1693, BODL, Ashurst Papers, Letterbook of Sir Henry Ashurst, 90.

6 The monument does not survive, but it was first described in the 'New View of London' in 1708. See 'Monument of Sir William Phipps in London,' *New England Historical and Genealogical Register* 4 (1850), 290. The coat of arms consisted of sable, a trefoil slipt, with an orl of eight mullets argent. See also Pedigree of Francis Phipps, 11 March 1664, BODL, Rawlinson MSS, D 865, 86.

7 Examination of William Phips, 30 July 1631, in 'Edward Ashley, Trader at Penobscot,' *Massachusetts Historical Society Proceedings* 45 (1911–12), 63; Spencer, *Pioneers on Maine Rivers*, 388. James Phips is the only one of the children not to be recorded in the Mangotsfield parish records. Possibly he was born during a gap in the records from December 1602 to February 1604, although this would have made him at least twenty-two when he began his apprenticeship. There can be little doubt he is of this family, as there appears to have been only one William Phips in Mangotsfield, and James's apprentice record indicates that his father was William (St James's Church, Mangotsfield Parish, Gloucestershire, Baptism Registers, 1591–1602, 1603–20).

8 Edwin A. Churchill, 'Introduction: Colonial Pemaquid,' in Camp, *Archaeological Investigations at Pemaquid*, ix–x; Sacks, *The Widening Gate*, 50, 66–8, 226–7.

9 Bristol Record Office, Bristol Apprentice Registers, 1532–1658; Sacks, *The Widening Gate*, 122, 320–1; Noyes, Libby, and Davis, eds., *Genealogical Dictionary of Maine and New Hampshire*, 115.

10 Lincoln County Deeds, 18: 115; *York Deeds*, 17: 190; Harald Prins, 'Chief Rawandagon, Alias Robinhood: Native "Lord of Misrule" in the Maine Wilderness' in Grumet, *Northeastern Indian Lives, 1632–1816*, 93–115; Bristol Record Office, Bristol Apprentice Registers, 1532–1658; Frank White, personal communication, 1995. On these matters, we are much indebted to Frank White, who generously shared the results of his research on the Bristol connections of the Phips and White families. The John White apprenticed to Aldworth cannot be identified conclusively with the White who was associated with James Phips, but the likelihood is strong. On Aldworth and other aspects of Pemaquid's earliest years, see DePaoli, 'Beaver, Blankets, Liquor, and Politics,' 170–7.

11 Bradley, 'Was the Plantation Despicable?' 11–17. For a discussion of English settlement patterns in the area, see Baker, 'English Settlement Patterns and Site Characteristics in Seventeenth-Century Maine.'

12 *Suffolk Deeds*, 3: 100–1; Libby, Noyes, and Davis, eds., *Genealogical Dictionary of Maine and New Hampshire*, 304, 403–4; Alexander Brown to John Winslow, May 10, 1667, Kennebec Proprietors' Papers, MaineHistorical Society.

13 Proclamation, 1 November 1622, in Brigham, ed., *British Royal Proclamations*, 33–4; Pory to Sir Francis Wyatt, 1622, in James, ed., *Three Visitors to Early Plymouth*, 16, 32; Vaughan, *New England Frontier*, 227–8.

14 Christopher Levett, 'A Voyage into New England,' in Howell and Baker, *Maine in the Age of Discovery*, 54; Thwaites, ed., *Jesuit Relations* 37, (1899), 249.

15 Shurtleff, ed., *Records of the Governor and Company of Massachusetts Bay*, vol. 4, pt 2, 364–6; Josselyn, *Colonial Traveler*, 103–4.

16 Examination of William Phips, 30 July 1631, in 'Edward Ashley, Trader at Penobscot,' *Massachusetts Historical Society Proceedings* 45 (1911–12), 63.

17 Mather 'Pietas in Patriam,' 337. For an interpretation of early Native weapons use that differs from ours in the importance attached to firearms, albeit in a military context, see Given, *A Most Pernicious Thing*, 87–92. On William Phips, brother of James and uncle of Sir William, see Shurtleff, ed., *Records of the Colony of New Plymouth*, 1: 92; Spencer, *Pioneers on Maine Rivers*, 383, 388. For William's return to Bristol, we are indebted to the unpublished research of Frank White in the Bristol Record Office.

18 Mather, 'Pietas in Patriam,' 278.

19 Bradley, 'Was the Plantation Despicable?' 11–17; Baker et al., 'Earthfast Architecture in Early Maine.'

20 Bradley, 'Was the Plantation Despicable?', 11–17.

21 Baker et al., 'Earthfast Architecture in Early Maine.'

22 Mather, 'Pietas in Patriam,' 278.

23 Noyes, Libby, and Davis, eds., *Genealogical Dictionary of Maine and New Hampshire*, 550–1, 746–7; personal communication, Frank White to Emerson Baker, July 1996.

24 For family size in early New England, see Greven, *Four Generations*, 30–1, 111–12.

25 Noyes, Libby, and Davis, eds., *Genealogical Dictionary of Maine and New Hampshire*, 550–1, 746–7. On the importance of kinship connections, see Cressy, *Coming Over*, 263–91; Demos, *A Little Commonwealth*, 118–25.

26 See Reid, *Acadia, Maine, and New Scotland*, 135–6.

27 Grant of Council for New England, 22 April 1635, PRO, CO1/8, no. 56; Reid, *Acadia, Maine, and New Scotland*, 83.

28 Cranmer, *Cushnoc*, 24–30.
29 Baker, *The Clarke & Lake Company*, 9–10, and 'Trouble to the Eastward,' 120.
30 Reid, *Acadia, Maine, and New Scotland*, 149–53; Lovejoy, *The Glorious Revolution in America*, 122–9; *Province and Court Records of Maine*, 1: 243–5.
31 Petition, 18 May 1672, MA, Suffolk County Court Files, no. 1117; proceedings of the Massachusetts commissioners, 22 July 1674, MA, vol. 3, 306–8; Baker, *Maritime History of Bath, Maine and the Kennebec Region*, 29–30.
32 For a discussion of order and disorder in the fishing settlements of Essex County, Massachusetts, see Vickers, *Farmers and Fishermen*, 138–40.
33 Talon to Colbert, 11 November 1671, AC, C11A, vol. 3, 187–8.
34 Josselyn, *Colonial Traveler*, 140; 'Memorial of the Subscribers, Who Usually Follow the Fishing Business, on the Eastern Coasts of the Province,' 28 February 1759, *Documentary History of the State of Maine*, 13: 156–7; Baker, *Maritime History of Bath, Maine, and the Kennebec Region*, 36.
35 Carroll, *Timber Economy of Puritan New England*, 102–9; William Hubbard, 'A Narrative of the Troubles with the Indians in New England from Piscataqua to Pemaquid,' in Drake, ed., *The Indian Wars in New England*, 223–4
36 Report of royal commissioners, in Cartwright to [Arlington], 14 December 1665, PRO, CO1/19, no. 143.
37 Baker, *Maritime History of Bath, Maine, and the Kennebec Region*, 31–8.
38 Hubbard, 'A Narrative of the Troubles with the Indians in New England from Piscataqua to Pemaquid,' in Drake, ed., *The Indian Wars in New England*, 73, 223.
39 Mather, 'Pietas in Patriam,' 278. The biblical allusions, as pointed out in Murdock's edition of Mather's *Magnalia Christi Americana*, 461, are to 2 Samuel 7:8, and Psalms 78:70–1.
40 Morison, ed., *Records of Suffolk County Court*, 30: 857–8; Suffolk County Court File, no. 1682. Although the date of the case was 30 October 1677, the evidence makes it clear that the incident occurred prior to Phips's departure from the family home in 1676.
41 Mather, 'Pietas in Patriam,' 279; Noyes, Libby, and Davis, eds., *Genealogical Dictionary of Maine and New Hampshire*, 293–4, 746, 767. On farm childhood, see Vickers, *Farmers and Fishermen*, 64–7.
42 Noyes, Libby, and Davis, *Genealogical Dictionary of Maine and New Hampshire*, 766–7; Owen, *History of Bath*, 37–8. Wiswell later moved to Duxbury in Plymouth Colony. He was in London, serving as Plymouth's agent, at the time of Phips's appointment as governor of Massachusetts (Lovejoy, *Glorious Revolution in America*, 348–50).
43 Mather, 'Pietas in Patriam,' 296; Baker, *The Clarke & Lake Company*, 7–9, 16; Hall, *The Last American Puritan*, 41, 49–50, 338–43. See also Baker, *Maritime History of Bath, Maine, and the Kennebec Region*, 37.

44 Inventory of the estate of John Hull, 2 May 1673, Suffolk County Probate File, 661; Noyes, Libby, and Davis, *Genealogical Dictionary of Maine and New Hampshire*, 357, 651.

45 *Suffolk Deeds*, 3: 100–1; DePaoli, 'Beaver, Blankets, Liquor, and Politics,' 179–81.

46 Noyes, Libby, and Davis, eds., *Genealogical Dictionary of Maine and New Hampshire*, 651; Baker, *The Clarke & Lake Company*, 7–9.

47 Biddeford Town Records (Typescript in Dyer Library, Saco, Maine), 1: 6, 8.

48 Mather, 'Pietas in Patriam,' 279; 'Administration of the Estate of Roger Spencer, 14 May 1675,' Suffolk County Probate File, 736; Biddeford Town Records (Dyer Library, Saco), 1: 6–9, 116; *York Deeds*, 1: 76, 113.

49 Sewall, *Diary*, 5 May 1695, 1: 331.

50 Ulrich, *Goodwives*, 35–50; *Suffolk Deeds*, 15:1, 4, 16, 51, 131, 149, 210; 16:111, 242, 390; and 17:188, 221–4; Mather, 'Pietas in Patriam,' 340.

51 Knepp Journal, 3 January 1684, BL, Egerton MSS, 2526, 19; Sewall, *Diary*, 21 October 1687, 1:152; ibid., 22 March 1690, 1:254–5; Journal of Benjamin Bullivant, 18 March 1690 [*sic* for 22 March], PRO, CO5/855, no. 94. For details of Lady Phips's widowhood, see chapter 12.

52 Baxter, ed., Trelawny Papers, *Documentary History of the State of Maine*, 3:165; Morison, ed., *Records of Suffolk County Court*, 30:874–5, 887; Baker, *Colonial Vessels*; personal communication, Nicholas Dean to Emerson Baker, February 1994.

53 Baker, 'Trouble to the Eastward,' 188–99.

54 Baker, *The Clarke & Lake Company*, 14–15.

55 Mather, 'Pietas in Patriam,' 279; see also 461 for the biblical reference to Noah in Hebrews 11:7.

56 Konig, *Law and Society in Puritan Massachusetts*, 74–82.

57 Morison, ed., *Records of Suffolk County Court*, 30:791, 807, 857–8, 874–5, 887; Suffolk County Court File, no. 1682.

58 Mather, 'Pietas in Patriam,' 341.

59 Ibid., 279; 'A Letter from New England,' 1 November 1694, PRO, CO5/858, no. 41A.

60 On 'trick' signatures, see Lockridge, *Literacy in Colonial New England*, 16. See Cressy, *Literacy and the Social Order*, 53–61, for an argument that such signatures were rare in England because marks remained socially acceptable. For Phips, however, as an ambitious individual moving from the Kennebec – an area of low literacy – to the relatively high literacy of Boston and nearby towns, reliance on a mark would have seemed an unwelcome distinction.

61 Extract of a letter from Boston [24 March 1693], PRO, CO5/857, no. 41; messenger's narrative, January 1693, PRO, CO5/751, no. 18 (i).

62 Lockridge, *Literacy in Colonial New England*, 22, 27, 37, 43–7; Cressy, *Literacy*

and the Social Order, 74–5, 141. See also Monaghan, 'Family Literacy in Early Eighteenth-century Boston,' 342–70; Steele, *The English Atlantic*, 265.

63 John Higginson to John How, 1 August 1694, in Moody, ed., *The Saltonstall Papers, Volume 1:*, 214.

64 Testimony of Thomas Baker, 14 November 1683, Knepp Journal, 14 November 1683, BL, Egerton MSS, 2526, 11; Sewall, *Diary*, 1 November 1694, 1:322; Usher to Phips, 15 October 1692, PRO, CO5/857, no. 8; Phips to Usher, 18 October 1692, PRO, CO5/924, no. 18 (i); Mather, 'Pietas in Patriam,' 280.

65 'Relation de la prise du Port-Royal par des habitans de Baston et de Selan commandez par Vuillam Phips le 21e May 1690' (hereafter 'Relation de la prise'), in Doughty, *Report of the Work of the Archives Branch for the Year 1912*, app. F, 68–9. For fuller discussion of this element of Phips's behaviour, see Baker and Reid, 'Sir William Phips, Violence, and the Historians'

66 Chidley Brooke to Benjamin Fletcher, 2 August 1693, PRO, CO5/1038, no. 23.

67 Sewall, *Diary*, 19 November 1692, 1:300–1; Diary of Increase Mather, AAS.

68 Fletcher to Phips, 6 January 1693, PRO, CO5/751, no. 18 (i); Phips to Fletcher, 27 January 1693, ibid., no. 18 (iii). On harsh language and its implied refusal of deference, see also Rediker, *Between the Devil and the Deep Blue Sea*, 164–9; Vickers, *Farmers and Fishermen*, 139–40.

2: The Making of a Projector

1 Cotton Mather, 'Pietas in Patriam,' 280; On the economic linkages characteristic of the maritime economy of seventeenth-century New England, see also Innes, *Creating the Commonwealth*, 271–305.

2 See Bailyn, *New England Merchants*, 134–6, 194–7.

3 Defoe, *Essay upon Projects*, 11, 15–18, 24, 27, 33–5. See also J.D. Alsop, 'The Age of the Projectors: British Imperial Strategy in the North Atlantic in the War of the Spanish Succession,' *Acadiensis* 21, no. 1 (Autumn 1991), 30–53.

4 Mather, 'Pietas in Patriam,' 280.

5 'Att a Court of Assistants or Court of Admiralty Held at Boston 15th June 1682,' in Noble, *Records of the Court of Assistants*, 1:211–12.

6 Edward Randolph to Sir Robert Southwell, 19 August 1683, in Toppan and Goodrick, eds., *Randolph Letters*, 3: 262; 'Relation of the Arrival of the Ship James and Mary,' in Dispatch of Don Pedro Ronquillo, AGI, IN2699, 248.

7 Dispatch of Don Pedro Ronquillo, 23 June 1687, AGI, IN2699, 232–3; Earle, *Treasure of the* Concepción, 120; Dyer, *Life of Sir John Narbrough*, 11; DNB, 14:89–91.

8 Report of James Farmer, n.d., BL, Sloane MSS, vol. 3984, 191.

9 Sir Thomas Lynch to Robert Clarke [1682], PRO, CO1/49, no. 35 (i).

10 See Dunn, *Sugar and Slaves*, 156–60; Thornton, *West-India Policy*, 202–3, 219–20, 222–3.

11 William Blathwayt to Sir Robert Southwell, 28 May 1682, UNP, PWV 52/53 (a); Blathwayt to Southwell, 19 August 1682, UNP, PWV 52/59. The buccaneers to whom Blathwayt specifically referred had recently returned from a cruise on the west coast of South America, led by Bartholomew Sharpe (Esquemeling, *Buccaneers of America*, 257–83). See also Murison, 'William Blathwayt's Empire,' 68; Thornton, *West-India Policy*, 233–4.

12 DNB, 7:870–1.

13 See Dyer, *Life of Sir John Narbrough*, 57–91; see also journal of *Sweepstakes*, May 1669 – July 1671, CKS, Naval Papers, U515/03.

14 Expedition Journal, April 1680 – January 1682, CKS, U515/09. See also Esquemeling, *Buccaneers of America*, 257–83, 289–475.

15 List of lieutenants and captains, 1660–88, PRO, ADM10/10, entry for Bartholomew Sharp, n.p.; Esquemeling, *Buccaneers of America*, 282–3.

16 Order, 2 April 1683, PRO, ADM2/1750, 309; journal of *Bonetta*, 8 April 1683 – 19 July 1686, BODL, Rawlinson MSS, A300. According to one account, Sharpe's passage to the Caribbean had been forbidden by 'either ... the Privy Council or the Court of Admiralty' out of concern for further conflicts with the Spanish (Esquemeling, *Buccaneers of America*, 283). For further discussion of the origins and events of the *Bonetta* expedition, see Earle, *Treasure of the Concepción*, 118–23, 129–43.

17 Admiralty commissioners to Navy Board, 19 June 1683, PRO, ADM106/55, n.p.; Edward Randolph to Sir Robert Southwell, 19 August 1683, in Toppan and Goodrick, eds., *Randolph Letters*, 3:262; 'Golden Rose Prize: A Survey-Book,' 20 August 1683, PRO, ADM1/3554, 451–65.

18 Navy Board to Samuel Pepys, 25 February 1685, PRO, ADM1/3554, 449. Both Narbrough and Haddock were among the commissioners who signed this letter.

19 Crokat, *A Consolatory Letter*, preface; Dyer, *Life of Sir John Narbrough*, 164; on Nottingham, see DNB, 7:1–5. Precedents for the lending of a royal vessel for commercial purposes included the loan of the *Eaglet* to the Hudson's Bay Company in 1668. See Gough, 'The Adventurers of England Trading into Hudson's Bay,' 37–8.

20 Articles between William Phips and the ship's company of the *Rose*, 13 July 1683, BL, Egerton MSS, vol. 2526, 32.

21 Naval listings, 1546–1714, BL, Add. MSS, vol. 9336, 120; W.B. Rowbotham, 'Pepys List of Ships and Officers, 1660–1688,' manuscript in PRO, 47; *London Gazette*, nos. 1617, 1618, May 1681; Dyer, *Life of Sir John Narbrough*, 211.

22 Baker, *Piracy and Diplomacy in Seventeenth-Century North Africa*, 84–5. On the

size and composition of the Algerian fleet, see Hornstein, *Restoration Navy and English Foreign Trade*, 110–11.

23 'Golden Rose Prize: A Survey-Book,' 20 August 1683, PRO, ADM1/3554, 465.

24 Charles II to William Stoughton and Joseph Dudley, 27 February 1684, PRO, CO389/4, 172–3.

25 Naval listings, 1686–87, BL, Add. MSS, vol. 9313, 29; Knepp Journal, BL, Egerton MSS, 2526, 1–22; 'A description of the Bahama Banck, originaly taken by Mr. Charles Salmon, under the Comand of Capt Phipps,' BL, Sloane MSS, vol. 45, 72.

26 Charles II to William Stoughton and Joseph Dudley, 27 February 1684, PRO, CO389/4, 172–3.

27 Articles, 13 July 1683, BL, Egerton MSS, vol. 2526, 32. See also Edward Randolph to William Blathwayt, 3 September 1683, in Toppan and Goodrick, eds., *Randolph Letters*, 6:147.

28 Knepp Journal, 6, 8 October 1683, BL, Egerton MSS, 2526, 5.

29 Ibid., 31 December 1683, 19.

30 Ibid., 5 September 1683, 1; petition of Charles Salmon [11 December 1686], PRO, T4/3, 425.

31 Knepp Journal, 14 January 1684, BL, Egerton MSS, 2526, 20.

32 Henry Guy to navy commissioners, 10 July 1683, PRO, T27/7, 183; Guy to Sir Robert Howard et al., 14 July 1683, PRO, T61/2, 245.

33 Knepp Journal, 13–20 September 1683, BL, Egerton MSS, 2526, 16; ibid., 21 January 1684, 2–3, 20–1.

34 Receipt, William Phips to Robert Bronson, 4 December 1683, MA, vol. 36, 343; receipt, Phips to Bronson, 7 December 1683, ibid., 343a; account of Bronson, 13 December 1683, ibid., 343b; declaration of Phips, ibid., 350.

35 Articles of agreement, Phips-Bronson, 11 January 1684, Ibid., 352; declaration of Phips, 14 January 1684, ibid., 351; warrants, 22 December 1690, ibid., 344–5; Simon Bradstreet to Phips, 7 January 1691, ibid., 263a.

36 Mather, 'Pietas in Patriam,' 281–2; deposition of Henry Dickeson, 24 January 1691, MA, vol. 36, 348a; deposition of William Bryant, 29 January 1691, ibid., 349; Hender Molesworth to William Blathwayt, 30 September 1684, CWBP, vol. 25, folder 1.

37 Rediker, *Between the Devil and the Deep Blue Sea*, 264. See also ibid., 118–19; Bromley, *Corsairs and Navies*, 11–12; Zahedieh, 'A Frugal, Prudential and Hopeful Trade,' 150, 157–8.

38 Knepp Journal, 8, 9 January 1684, BL, Egerton MSS, 2526, 19–20; articles of agreement, William Phips – Francis Rogers, 5 January 1684, MA, vol. 36, 346–7; Daniel Defoe, *History of the Pyrates*, quoted in Rediker, *Between the Devil and the Deep Blue Sea*, 262.

39 Rediker, *Between the Devil and the Deep Blue Sea*, 166, 278; Knepp Journal, 6
    October 1683, BL, Egerton MSS, 2526, 5.
40 Ibid., 3 January 1684, 19.
41 Ibid., 21 January 1684, 21.
42 Ibid., 21 December 1683, 17.
43 Ibid., 1–12 November 1683, 8–10, 12.
44 Ibid., 14 November 1683, 11–13.
45 Ibid., 14, 19, 27 November, 13 December 1683, 13–15.
46 Petition of Thomas Jenner, 4 July 1656, PRO, CO1/13, no. 3; Middlesex County
    Court Files, *Tead v. Collicott*, 1657; Baker, 'Trouble to the Eastward,' 133–9,
    226–7; Reid, *Acadia, Maine, and New Scotland*, 135–41; Knepp Journal, 16
    December 1683, BL, Egerton MSS, 2526, 15.
47 Ibid., 20–3 December 1683, 15–18.
48 Ibid., 22 March 1684, 21.
49 Molesworth to Blathwayt, 18 November 1684, PRO, CO1/56, no. 82.
50 Ibid.
51 The importance of salutes and of naval patronage is discussed in Davies,
    Gentlemen and Tarpaulins, 62–6. Also on patronage, as well as the views of
    Blathwayt on Anglo-Spanish commercial relations in the Caribbean, see
    Murison, 'William Blathwayt's Empire,' 13, 64.
52 Knepp Journal, 31 October, BL, Egerton MSS, 2526, 16; ibid., 26 November
    1683, 8, 13–14.
53 Ibid., 19 January, 12 March, 15 April, 2 May 1684, 21–2.
54 Depositions of John Carlile and Edward Pell [26 January 1691], MA, vol. 36,
    353; Henry Guy to Sir Richard Haddock, 12 April 1686, PRO, T27/9, 319;
    Henry Guy to the Royal Mint, 24 November 1686, PRO, T27/10, 32; Henry
    Guy to the Royal Mint, 14 March 1687, PRO, T61/6.
55 Deposition of William Bryant, 29 January 1691, MA, vol. 36, 349. See also dep-
    osition of Henry Dickeson, 24 January 1691, ibid., 348a.
56 Mather, 'Pietas in Patriam,' 281.
57 Ibid., 281–2. On mutinies, and on the articles governing pirate voyages, see
    Rediker, *Between the Devil and the Deep Blue Sea*, 228–35, 261–6.
58 Hender Molesworth to William Blathwayt, 30 September 1684, CWBP, vol. 25,
    folder 1; Mather, 'Pietas in Patriam,' 282; deposition of Henry Dickeson, 24
    January 1691, MA, vol. 36, 348a; deposition of William Bryant, 29 January
    1691, ibid., 349.
59 Earle, *Treasure of the* Concepción, 154–5, 197–8; journal of *Bonetta*, BODL, Raw-
    linson MSS, A300, 64.
60 Mather, 'Pietas in Patriam,' 282–3.
61 Deposition of William Bryant, 29 January 1691, MA, vol. 36, 349.

62 Richard Coney to the Lords of Trade, 4 June 1685, PRO, CO1/57, no. 136. On the series of disputes that complicated colonial affairs in Bermuda in the wake of the dissolution of the Bermuda Company in 1684, see Kennedy, *Isle of Devils*, 245–56; Wilkinson, *The Adventurers of Bermuda*, 374–84.

63 Deposition of William Phips [1685?], PRO, CO1/57, no. 170; Richard Coney to William Phips, 5 June 1685, PRO, CO1/57, no. 140. The date of Phips's deposition is problematic. The contents suggest that it was given soon after his two-month stay in Bermuda, and it is filed with papers from 1685. However, Phips defined his age at the time as 'about 40 years.' Since he was only thirty-four when he visited Bermuda, the discrepancy raises the possibility that the deposition was given some years later and then filed with the earlier material; or, more likely, that Phips for some reason gave his age incorrectly. The source for Phips's actual age is a firm and precise statement in Mather, 'Pietas in Patriam,' 278.

64 Phips to Sunderland, 3 August 1685, PRO, CO1/58, no. 24; Blathwayt to 'Mr. Graham,' 4 August 1685, ibid., no. 28.

65 Journal of the Lords of Trade, 23 February 1685, PRO, CO391/5, 96–7.

66 Henry Guy to Sir Richard Haddock and Sir John Narbrough, 26 January 1686, PRO, T27/9, 257; Guy to Phips, 30 March 1686, ibid., 314; Guy to Samuel Pepys, 19 April 1686, ibid., 324; Guy to Haddock and Narbrough, 15 May 1686, ibid., 348; George, 'The Treasure Trove of William Phips,' 295. The *Golden Rose* was sold by the crown in 1687 (PRO, Rowbotham, 'Pepys List of Ships and Officers,' 47).

67 'Some brief remarks ...' [1687], BODL, Rawlinson MSS, A171, 205; Earle, *The Treasure of the* Concepción, 160–1.

68 Mather, 'Pietas in Patriam,' 283; Brewer, *The Sinews of Power*, 58.

69 Duke of Beaufort to the duchess of Beaufort, 16 June 1687, Great Britain, HMC, *Twelfth Report, Appendix*, Part 9, 90.

70 'Testimony of Christopher Monck, Duke of Albemarle,' [1687], PRO, C10/227/63. Some secondary accounts assert that Albemarle had also been involved with the voyage of the *Golden Rose*. See, for example, Ward, *Christopher Monck, Duke of Albemarle*, 243–4, and Thayer, *Sir William Phips, Adventurer and Statesman*, 14–16. This suggestion finds no support in primary sources and appears to be conclusively rebutted by Albemarle's own testimony regarding the date of his first knowledge of the wreck.

71 Blathwayt to Southwell, 4 August 1685, UNP, PWV53/2; Ward, *Christopher Monck, Duke of Albemarle*, 195–220.

72 Earle, *Treasure of the* Concepción, 162–3.

73 Blathwayt to Southwell, 17 April 1686, UNP, PWV53/30; Ward, *Christopher Monck, Duke of Albemarle*, 233–62.

74 'Testimony of Sir William Phips' [1687], PRO, C10/227/63; 'Testimony of Sir John Narbrough' [1687], ibid.

75 Earle, *Treasure of the* Concepción, 164.

76 Complaint of Smith [1687], PRO, CO10/227/63; testimony of Phips [1687], ibid.; testimony of Albemarle [1687], ibid.

77 Albemarle to Lord Dartmouth, 18 August 1686, Great Britain, HMC, *Eleventh Report, Appendix*, part 5, 131; Earle, *Treasure of the* Concepción, 164.

78 List of disbursements [1687], PRO, C10/227/63; further account of John Smith [1687], ibid.

79 Richard Wharton to Hezekiah Usher, 29 September 1687, MA, vol. 37, 160; deposition of Samuel Newman, 7 July 1691, ibid., 159a. Newman also referred to a payment of £80 to Wharton by Francis Rogers, but linked it specifically to the purchase of a share of the *Rosebud*. The matter, also noted by Wharton in his letter to Usher of 29 September 1687 may therefore have related to transactions connected with the 1683–5 voyage rather than that of 1686–7.

80 Duke of Beaufort to the duchess of Beaufort, 16 June 1687, Great Britain, HMC, *Twelfth Report, Appendix*, part 9, 90

81 Complaint of John Smith [1687], PRO, C10/227/63.

82 Order, 18 July 1686, PRO, ADM2/1741, 263.

83 Sir John Narbrough and Isaac Foxcroft to Albemarle [1686], Northampton-shire Record Office, Albemarle Papers, no. 118.

84 Order, 20 February 1687, PRO, ADM2/1741, 378–9; letters patent, 4 March 1687, PRO, C66/3291, no. 6.

85 Scott, *Constitution and Finance*, 2:484–5.

86 Mather, 'Pietas in Patriam,' 283; Earle, *Treasure of the Concepción*, 174.

87 Deposition of Thomas Smith, 20 January 1685, PRO, CO1/56, no. 9 (i); Hender Molesworth to William Blathwayt, 25 November 1685, PRO, CO138/5, 119–21.

88 Journal of *Henry*, 24 September 1686 – 16 March 1687, CKS, U515/010, 2–3, 6–8.

89 Ibid., 10.

90 Ibid., 9–10; journal of *James and Mary*, 11 December 1686 – 4 June 1687, BL, Sloane MSS, vol. 50, 34–5.

91 Ibid., 99–7; journal of *Henry*, 10–11. The journal of the *James and Mary*, written on the reverse of another ship's journal, is foliated in reverse order.

92 Journal of *Henry*, 11. The point regarding diversion of attention from the real purpose of the expedition is made in Earle, *Treasure of the* Concepción, 172.

93 Journal of *James and Mary*, 96; journal of *Henry*, 12–13.

94 Ibid., 14. Other accounts of the discovery of the wreck can be found in Mather, 'Pietas in Patriam,' 283–4, and in Sir Hans Sloane to Sir Arthur Raw-

don, 21 May 1687, in Berwick, ed., *Rawdon Papers*, 388–91. Both of these are second–hand descriptions, however, and as Peter Earle has pointed out, they appear to have fanciful elements and add nothing reliable to the first-hand account in the journal of the *Henry* (Earle, *Treasure of the* Concepción, 174–5).
95 Journal of *Henry*, 15–18.
96 Journal of *James and Mary*, 93; Mather, 'Pietas in Patriam,' 284. The term 'sow,' or 'pig,' was frequently used to denote an ingot of precious metal. See OED, 11: 806 and 16: 81. 'Bar' is self-explanatory, while neither 'Champene' nor 'dow boy' (or 'doughboy') appears in any of the standard dictionaries. 'Doughboy,' however, was a term frequently used and presumably referred to a piece of silver resembling in shape and size the dumpling of boiled flour that bore this name. See oed, 4: 986.
97 Defoe, *Essay upon Projects*, 16.

3: Treasure Gained and Patrons Lost

1 Journal of *James and Mary*, 92–3; journal of *Henry*, 18.
2 Ibid., 18–19; journal of *James and Mary*, 40–2, 91–2.
3 Ibid., 86–90; journal of *Henry*, 19–20.
4 Earle, *Treasure of the* Concepción, 182–8. See also Bowden, 'Gleaning Treasure from the Silver Bank,' 90–105.
5 Journal of *James and Mary*, 80, 81.
6 Ibid., 81, 84; journal of *Henry*, 21–2; Earle, *Treasure of the* Concepción, 185–8. For Atherley's claim, see Henry Hordesnell to Lords of the Treasury, 28 January 1688, PRO, T64/88, 306. On seventeenth-century diving technology, see (despite inaccuracies on the specific activities of Phips) Beebe, *Half Mile Down*, 42–59.
7 Journal of *James and Mary*, 75–82.
8 Ibid., 71–4; Mather, 'Pietas in Patriam,' 285.
9 Ibid.; warrant of James II, 24 January 1688, PRO, T2/12, 345.
10 Journal of *James and Mary*, 58–71; John Verney to Sir Ralph Verney, 15 June 1687, Great Britain, HMC, *Seventh Report of the Royal Commission on Historical Manuscripts*, part 1, *Report and Appendix*, 482.
11 Warrant to Sir Roger Strickland, 8 June 1687, PRO, ADM2/1727, 139; warrant to Sir Cloudesley Shovell, 8 June 1687, ibid., 192–3; Treasury order, 9 June 1687, PRO, T11/11, 45; dispatch of Don Pedro Ronquillo, 7 July 1687, AGI, IN2699, 243–5; King to William Joyner, 12 June 1687, PRO, ADM2/1741, 418. See also Hans Sloane to Sir Arthur Rawdon, 21 May [sic for June] 1687, in Berwick, ed. *Rawdon Papers*, 388–91.
12 Henry Guy to officers of Royal Mint, 28 June 1687, PRO, T27/11, 133; royal

warrant, 24 January 1688, PRO, T52/12, 345; Earle, *Treasure of the* Concepción, 191–3; George, 'The Treasure Trove of William Phips,' 311–12.

13 *An Exact and Perfect Relation of the Arrival of the Ship the James and Mary Captain Phipps Commander; London Gazette,* 30 June – 4 July 1687.

14 Charles Bertie to the countess of Rutland, 9 June 1687, Great Britain, HMC, *Twelfth Report, Appendix,* part 5, 114; duke of Beaufort to duchess of Beaufort, 16 June 1687, Great Britain, HMC, *Twelfth Report, Appendix,* part 9, 90; letter to John Ellis, 14 May 1687 [*sic* for 14 June], Ellis, ed., *The Ellis Correspondence,* 1:296–7; Evelyn, *Diary,* 4: 552; Luttrell, *Brief Historical Relation,* 1:407.

15 Scott, *Constitution and Finance,* 1:326–7. See also Clapham, *Bank of England,* 1:13–14, and Keynes, *Treatise on Money,* 2:151.

16 Keynes, *Treatise on Money,* 2:156–7; Earle, *Treasure of the* Concepción, 193. As a contribution to public finance, the royal share of some £21,000 was small compared with overall revenues, but it did represent rather more than one-third of the annual value of proceeds from the post office in the late 1680s. See Mitchell and Deane, *Abstract of British Historical Statistics,* 386, and Karraker, 'Spanish Treasure, Casual Revenue of the Crown,' 301–18. On the bullion outflow from England that was developing during the later 1680s, and the clipping of silver coins, see Jones, *War and Economy in the Age of William III and Marlborough,* 18–19, 141, 229–34.

17 Mather, 'Pietas in Patriam,' 286. For the calculation of Phips's share of the treasure, see Earle, *Treasure of the* Concepción, 194, 201.

18 Edmond Sawbell to Messrs. Goodwin and Martin, 28 July 1687, Great Britain, HMC, *Report on the Manuscripts of the Marquess of Downshire,* 1:256.

19 Newsletter to Sir William Trumbull, 30 June 1687, ibid., 1:252; *London Gazette,* 30 June – 4 July 1687; Luttrell, *Brief Historical Relation,* 408.

20 Knepp Journal, 14 November 1683, BL, Egerton MSS, 2526, 13.

21 William Blathwayt to the earl of Nottingham, 6 March 1691, PRO, SP63d/353, no. 55; abstract of letter of Francis Foxcroft, 2 April 1690, PRO, CO5/855, no. 79.

22 See Davies, *Gentlemen and Tarpaulins,* 229–30.

23 Sewall, *Diary,* 21 October 1687, 1:152.

24 Defoe, *Essay upon Projects,* 27. On Albemarle's melting his silver, see newsletter to Sir William Trumbull, 30 June 1687, Great Britain, HMC, *Report on the Manuscripts of the Marquess of Downshire,* 1:252.

25 John Povey to Sir Robert Southwell, 11 June 1687, UNP, PWV61.

26 Dispatch of Francesco Terriesi, 20 June 1687, BL, Add. MSS, vol. 25,374, 143–6; Letter of Don Pedro Ronquillo, 10 December 1687, PRO, SP94/72, 201–2; Povey to Southwell, 24 December 1687, UNP, PWV61; newsletter, 7 January 1688, Great Britain, HMC, *Report on the Manuscripts of the Marquess of Down-*

shire, 1:285; Hans Sloane to Sir Arthur Rawdon, 21 May [*sic* for June] 1687, in Berwick, ed., *Rawdon Papers*, 388–91. For fuller discussion of the Spanish protests, see Earle, *Treasure of the* Concepción, 194–8. On Anglo-Spanish relations more generally, see Thornton, *West-India Policy*, 97–8, 114–15, 229–30, and Hornstein, *Restoration Navy and English Foreign Trade*, 228–41.

27   Statement of John Smith [1687], PRO, C10/227/63.
28   Testimony of Sir William Phips [1687], ibid.
29   Affidavit of John Smith, 21 July 1687, PRO, C41/27, no. 1229, Trinity Term; complaint of Lord Falkland et al., 8 December 1693, PRO, C8/540/85.
30   Earle, *Treasure of the* Concepción, 197–8; James II to the Treasury, 9 September 1687, PRO, T52/12, 266.
31   Treasury warrant, 3 September 1688, PRO, T54/12, 351; Henry Guy to the Royal Mint, 5 September 1688, PRO, T27/11, 434; Treasury warrant, 17 September 1688, PRO, T54/12, 351–2; Privy Council order, 9 September 1688, in Grant and Munro, eds., *Acts of the Privy Council of England: Colonial Series*, 2:101.
32   Deposition of Samuel Newman, 7 July 1691, MA, vol. 37, 159a.
33   Richard Wharton to Hezekiah Usher, 29 September 1687, ibid., 160.
34   Patent, 13 August 1687, PRO, C66/3298, no. 16; Mather, 'Pietas in Patriam,' 287–8.
35   Minutes, 14 June 1687, BODL, Sloane MSS, A189, 370; James II to navy commissioners, 14 June 1687, PRO, ADM106/68.
36   Minutes, 14 June 1687, BODL, Sloane MSS, A189, 370; notes on agreement of 14 June 1687, ibid., 371; warrant, 28 June 1687, PRO, T52/12, 199–203; patent, 12 August 1687, PRO, C66/3297, no. 1.
37   Letter to John Ellis, 30 July 1687, Ellis, ed., *Ellis Correspondence*, 1:325.
38   Sir John Narbrough to Sir James Hayes, 29 November 1687, NMM, LBK1, 3.
39   On 'good voyages' and the profits that naval captains could make from carrying cargoes of silver plate until the practice was banned in 1686, see Davies, *Gentlemen and Tarpaulins*, 179–84.
40   Captain's journal of *Foresight*, 15 December 1687, PRO, ADM/35/2; lieutenant's journal of *Foresight*, 15 December 1687, NMM, L/F/198; William Croft to Lord Dartmouth, 7 January 1688, HMC, *Eleventh Report, Appendix*, part 5, 135–6.
41   Complaint of Lord Falkland et al., 8 December 1693, PRO, C8/540/85.
42   Captain's journal of *Foresight*, 5 February 1688, PRO, ADM/35/2; Narbrough to Albemarle, 17 February 1688, NMM, LBK1, 5–6. On Mordaunt, see DNB, 13:840–1.
43   Journal of *Assistance*, 29 February 1688, PRO, ADM51/68; journal of *Swan*, PRO, ADM51/3987, 35–6; journal of *Falcon*, 21 February – 10 May 1688, PRO, ADM51/345.

44 Complaint of Lord Falkland et al., 8 December 1693, PRO, c8/540/85; Narbrough to Hayes, 29 November 1687, NMM, LBK1, 3. Neale, in his capacity as master, had supervised the weighing of the treasure brought to Deptford by Phips in June 1687 (warrant, 24 January 1688, PRO, T52/12, 345).

45 Newsletter to Sir William Trumbull, 9 July 1687, Great Britain, HMC, *Report on the Manuscripts of the Marquess of Downshire*, 1:254; captain's journal of *Foresight*, 15–18 July 1687, PRO, ADM/35/2; letter to John Ellis, 30 July 1687, Ellis, ed., *Ellis Correspondence*, 1:325; lieutenant's Journal of *Foresight*, 13 August 1687, NMM, L/F/198; Narbrough to [Albemarle], [January 1688], NMM, LBK1, 4; Earle, *Treasure of the* Concepción, 203–4.

46 Lieutenant's journal of *Foresight*, 15 September 1687, NMM, L/F/198; *Autobiography of Sir John Bramston*, 299–300; Narbrough to Hayes, 29 November 1687, NMM, LBK1, 3.

47 Captain's journal of *Foresight*, 28 September, 16 November 1687, PRO, ADM/35/2; Narbrough to Hayes, 15 October 1687, NMM, LBK1, 2; Narbrough to Hayes, 29 November 1687, ibid., 3.

48 See Mather, 'Pietas in Patriam,' 288–9.

49 Captain's journal of *Foresight*, 7 December 1687, PRO, ADM/35/2.

50 Letter of Narbrough, 14 April 1688, NMM, LBK1, 14; captain's journal of *Foresight*, 5–15 December 1687, PRO, ADM/35/2; lieutenant's journal of *Foresight*, 5–15 December 1687, NMM, L/F/198.

51 Narbrough to Falkland, 4 May 1688, NMM, LBK1, 19–20. For full consideration of the cargo of the *Concepción* and its value, and the amounts already salvaged, see Earle, *Treasure of the* Concepción, 209–12.

52 Narbrough to [Albemarle], [January 1688], NMM, LBK1, 4; captain's journal of *Foresight*, 10 December 1687, PRO, ADM/35/2; Narbrough to the investors, 14 April 1688, NMM, LBK1, 16; Narbrough to Falkland, 4 May 1688, ibid., 19–20; Narbrough to Albemarle, 26 May 1688, ibid., 23; lieutenant's journal of *Foresight*, 18 March, 1, 15, 29 April 1688, NMM, L/F/198.

53 Captain's journal of *Foresight*, 8 May 1688, PRO, ADM/35/2; lieutenant's journal of *Foresight*, 8 May 1688, NMM, L/F/198; Narbrough to Phips, 26 May 1688, NMM, LBK1, 35. The captain of the *Falcon* was also in some doubt, recording that 'Sir Wm Phipps sayled, I beleive for New England' (journal of *Falcon*, 8 May 1688, PRO, ADM51/345).

54 Captain's journal of *Foresight*, 1 February, 7 March 1688, PRO, ADM/35/2; lieutenant's journal of *Foresight*, 1 February, 7 March 1688, NMM/L/F/198.

55 Captain's journal of *Foresight*, 22–9 February 1688, PRO, ADM/35/2; Narbrough to Albemarle, 8 March 1688, NMM, LBK1, 8; Sir Nathaniel Johnson to Lords of Trade, 20 February, PRO, co1/64, no. 25. DNB suggests that Mordaunt's real purpose may have been to recruit Narbrough for William of

Orange. There is no record, however, of any meeting between the two, and Narbrough specifically observed to Albemarle that he had not seen Mordaunt (DNB, 13:840–1; Narbrough to Albemarle, 8 March 1688, NMM, LBK1, 8).

56 Captain's journal of *Foresight*, 9, 14 April 1688, PRO, ADM/35/2; Earle, *Treasure of the* Concepción, 214.

57 Captain's journal of *Foresight*, 21, 22 April, 27 May 1688, PRO, ADM/35/2; lieutenant's journal of *Foresight*, 27 May 1688, NMM, L/F/198; Samuel Jackson to Samuel Pepys, 20 July 1688, BODL, Sloane MSS, A179, 70.

58 Samuel Jackson to Samuel Pepys, ibid.; lieutenant's journal of *Foresight*, 2 August 1688, NMM, L/F/198.

59 Blathwayt to Southwell, 5 May 1688, UNP, PWV53/68; Povey to Southwell, 21 February, 1 March 1688, UNP, PWV61.

60 Blathwayt to Southwell, 19 June 1688, UNP, PWV53/69.

61 Letter to John Ellis, 8 July 1688, Ellis, ed., *Ellis Correspondence*, 2:30.

62 James II to Albemarle, 22 January 1688, PRO, CO138/6, 63–7; Albemarle to Lords of Trade, 11 February 1688, PRO, CO1/64, no. 19; Hender Molesworth to Lords of the Treasury, 28 February 1688, ibid., no. 26; Albemarle to Lords of Trade, 6 March 1688, ibid., no. 30; Albemarle to Lords of Trade, 16 April 1688, ibid., no. 51; Albemarle to Lords of Trade, 6 June 1688, PRO, CO1/65, no. 2; Dunn, *Sugar and Slaves*, 160–1; Ollard, *Man of War*, 199; Ward, *Christopher Monck, Duke of Albemarle*, 291–315.

63 Henry Hordesnell to Lords of Trade, 28 January 1688, PRO, CO1/64, no. 12.

64 Blathwayt to Southwell, 17 April 1686, UNP, PWV53/30.

65 Povey to Southwell, 20 May 1686, UNP, PWV60; Blathwayt to Southwell, 22 May 1686, UNP, PWV53/34; Povey to Southwell, 26 May 1686, UNP, PWV60; Commission of Sir Edmund Andros, 3 June 1686, PRO, CO5/904, 270–81.

66 Johnson, *Adjustment to Empire*, 53–7, 63–5.

67 Mather, 'Pietas in Patriam,' 289–91; Johnson, *Adjustment to Empire*, 71–83.

68 Hall, *Edward Randolph and the American Colonies*, 95–7.

69 Blathwayt to Southwell, 5 May 1688, UNP, PWV53/68. For the context of Blathwayt's comments on the wives of Randolph and Andros, see also Randolph to Blathwayt, 5 August 1687, 16 January 1688, Toppan and Goodrick, eds., *Randolph Letters*, 6:225, 238; Sewall, *Diary*, 22 January, 10 February 1688, 1:158–60.

70 Mather, 'Pietas in Patriam,' 288–9.

71 Barnes, 'The Rise of William Phips,' 283–4.

72 See Johnson, *Adjustment to Empire*, 81–3.

73 Andros to Lords of Trade, 7 July 1688, PRO, CO1/65, no. 19.

74 Sewall, *Diary*, 1 June, 4 July 1688, 1:169, 172.

75 Phips to Andros [30 June 1688], MA, vol. 129, 14. Although this document is

undated, the date assigned to it in the volume index is consistent with the hearing of the issue by the council of the Dominion during the first week of July.

76 Andros to Fitz-John Winthrop, 5 July 1688, Massachusetts Historical Society *Collections*, 6th ser. 3:488; minute, 6 July 1688, MA, vol. 129, 30; testimony of Edward Randolph, 7 July 1688, ibid., 29a. Phips also blamed Robert Mason, proprietary claimant to New Hampshire, as another councillor who had opposed the dismissal of the sheriffs.

77 Clearance, 7 July 1688, MA, vol. 7, p. 51; Sewall, *Diary*, 16 July 1688, 1:173; journal of *Falcon*, 17 August 1688, PRO, ADM51/345.

78 Letter to John Ellis, 24 July 1688, Ellis, ed., *Ellis Correspondence*, 2:67; Hans Sloane, 'Account of the Illness and Death of the Duke of Albemarle,' BL, Sloane MSS, vol. 3984, 282–4; Ward, *Christopher Monck, Duke of Albemarle*, 316–22.

79 Complaint of Lord Falkland et al., 8 December 1693, PRO, C8/540/85; warrant, 20 August 1688, PRO, T52/13, 83–6; Earle, *Treasure of the* Concepción, 217.

80 Thomas Monck to Sir William Phips, 1 November 1688, Suffolk Deeds, 15:16.

81 Sewall, *Diary*, 3 June 1688, 1:169.

82 Blathwayt to Southwell, 19 June 1688, UNP, PWV53/69.

83 Diary of Increase Mather (typescript), 30 May, 1 June, 2 July, 26 September, 16 October 1688, AAS; Hall, *The Last American Puritan*, 214–17, 221–3.

4: Respectability and Revolution

1 Diary of Increase Mather, 21 August, 26 September 1688, AAS.

2 Hall, *The Last American Puritan*, 212–17; Jones, *The Revolution of 1688 in England*, 98–127; J.R. Jones, 'James II's Revolution: Royal Policies, 1686–92,' in Israel, *The Anglo-Dutch Moment*, 56–66. On the role of the Lords of Trade as an influential committee of the Privy Council advising the crown on both colonial and trade matters, see Steele, *Politics of Colonial Policy*, 8–10.

3 Hall, *The Last American Puritan*, 207–10, 214; Bremer, *Congregational Communion*, 181–5, 247–8; Cressy, *Coming Over*, 272–4; Olson, *Making the Empire Work*, 45, 49.

4 Bremer, *Congregational Communion*, 248–9; De Krey, *A Fractured Society*, 76–7, 88–90; Hall, *The Last American Puritan*, 220–1; Olson, *Making the Empire Work*, 49.

5 Webb, 'William Blathwayt, Imperial Fixer: From Popish Plot to Glorious Revolution,' 20–1; Webb, 'William Blathwayt, Imperial Fixer: Muddling Through to Empire, 1689–1717,' 373–4; DNB, 18:709.

6 Horwitz, *Revolution Politicks*, 64–85.

7 [Sir Robert Southwell?] to Earl of Nottingham, 23 March 1689, HLBP, BL 418.
8 Hall, *The Last American Puritan*, 222–3, 229; Johnson, *Adjustment to Empire*, 145.
9 Mather, 'Pietas in Patriam,' 292.
10 Diary of Increase Mather, 10 January 1689, AAS; William of Orange to Sir Edmund Andros (draft), 12 January 1689, PRO, CO5/905, 41–2.
11 Diary of Increase Mather, 13 February 1689, AAS; petition of Sir William Phips and Increase Mather, n.d., MA, vol. 129, 317.
12 Petition of Sir William Phips and Increase Mather [18 February 1689], PRO, CO/751, no. 2; Johnson, *Adjustment to Empire*, 147–8.
13 Order in council, 18 February 1689, PRO, CO5/751, no. 2. The order is entered in the margin of the petition of Phips and Mather.
14 Journal of Lords of Trade, 20, 22 February 1689, PRO, CO391/6, 199–203; entry book of Roger Morrice [c. 22 February 1689], in Moody and Simmons, eds., *Glorious Revolution in Massachusetts*, 430. For political analysis, see Johnson, *Adjustment to Empire*, 146–50. Johnson suggests that Phips may have played an active role in lobbying Mordaunt on Mather's behalf because of their shared Caribbean experience; this is possible, although direct evidence is lacking (*Adjustment to Empire*, 148).
15 See Simmons, 'Historical Introduction,' in Moody and Simmons, eds., *Glorious Revolution in Massachusetts*, 20–3; Johnson, *Adjustment to Empire*, 152–5, 160–3.
16 Sewall, *Diary*, 18 March 1689, 1:204; Captain John George to the Admiralty, 12 June 1689, PRO, CO5/855, no. 15. News of the accession of William and Mary had already reached New England through less formal channels by late March (Steele, *The English Atlantic*, 104).
17 Mather, 'Pietas in Patriam,' 292.
18 Edward Randolph to Lords of Trade, 5 September 1689, PRO, CO5/855, no. 34; Mather, 'Pietas in Patriam,' 293–4; Increase Mather, *Autobiography*, 332. Among secondary analyses, Barnes (*The Dominion of New England*, 237–8) is inclined to take Randolph's accusation seriously, while Johnson (*Adjustment to Empire*, 88–90) and Lovejoy (*Glorious Revolution in America*, 242) find such allegations uncorroborated and are more sceptical. On the swift carrying to North America of the news of the revolution, see Steele, *The English Atlantic*, 94–110.
19 Declaration, 18 April 1689, *Andros Tracts*, 1:11–20; Johnson, *Adjustment to Empire*, 84–91; Lovejoy, *Glorious Revolution in America*, 239–41.
20 Minutes of Council of Safety, 1, 2, 10, 22–4 May 1689, MA, General Court records, 6:11–27; Johnson, *Adjustment to Empire*, 96–107.
21 Randolph to Lords of Trade, 29 May 1689, PRO, CO5/855, no. 8. Although Randolph's letter was dated 29 May (the same date as Phips's arrival in Bos-

ton), the reference to Phips came in a later passage that may have been added at a later date. It seems likely that the letters referred to had been carried on the vessel on which Phips had sailed, perhaps entrusted to his care along with the royal proclamations.

22 Mather, 'Pietas in Patriam,' 295.

23 Minutes of Council of Safety, 23, 24 April 1689, MA, General Court records, 6:7–8; letter to John Usher, 10 July 1689, PRO, CO5/855, no. 16.

24 'A Short Account of the Loss of Pemaquid Fort,' 3 August 1689, PRO, CO5/855, no. 27.

25 See Morrison, The Embattled Northeast, 123–5, and Edwin A. Churchill, 'Introduction: Colonial Pemaquid,' in Camp, Archaeological Excavations at Pemaquid, xiv. While no direct evidence connects Sir William Phips with Wabanaki–New England relations in this period, an obscure episode in later years suggests that he had some involvement. In July 1703, the journal of the Board of Trade recorded that Sir Henry Ashurst had had in his service for some fourteen years a Wabanaki boy brought or sent to London by Phips (letter of Joseph Dudley, 10 May 1703 PRO, CO5/751, no. 48; Board of Trade journal, 13 July 1703, PRO, CO391/16, 178–81).

26 Sewall, Diary, [29 June 1689], 1:222; Increase Mather to Thomas Hinckley, 12 September 1689, in Moody and Simmons, eds., Glorious Revolution in Massachusetts, 442–3.

27 Examples include Randolph to Francis Nicholson, 29 July 1689, PRO, CO5/855, no. 23; Randolph to Lords of Trade, 5 September 1689, ibid., no. 34; Randolph to Lords of Trade, 15 October 1689, ibid., no. 38; Randolph to the Bishop of London, 25 October 1689, ibid., no. 42.

28 Thomas Brinley to Francis Brinley, in Moody and Simmons, eds., Glorious Revolution in Massachusetts, 451–4; journal of the Lords of Trade, 10, 17 April 1690, PRO, CO391/6, 321–4; 'Matters objected against Sir Edmond Andros et al.,' 14 April 1690, PRO, CO5/855, no. 82; order in council, PRO, CO5/905, 188. See also Hall, Edward Randolph and the American Colonies, 1676, 127–30, and The Last American Puritan, 231–3.

29 Mather to John Richards, 1 or 4 May, 4 June 1690, in Moody and Simmons, eds., Glorious Revolution in Massachusetts, 447–8, 455–7.

30 Minutes of Council of Safety, 5 June 1689, declaration of the representatives, 7 June 1689, MA, General Court records, 6:31–5; resolution, 6 December 1689, MA, vol. 35, 104. On Cooke, see Foster, The Long Argument, 247.

31 See bond of Joseph Dudley, 13 July 1689, PRO, CO5/855, no. 21(iii); Simon Bradstreet to Dudley, 16 July 1689, ibid., no. 21(ix).

32 Petition of Boston members of the Church of England [January 1690], PRO, CO5/855, no. 58.

33 Petition of Maine inhabitants, 25 January 1690, PRO, CO5/855, no. 55.
34 Petition of Charlestown inhabitants [January 1690], PRO, CO5/855, no. 59. For further analysis of the circumstances that engendered the petition, see Johnson, *Adjustment to Empire*, 120–1; Breen, *Puritans and Adventurers*, 102–4.
35 Petition of inhabitants of Boston and adjacent places, 25 January 1690, PRO, CO5/855, no. 56. See also Simmons, 'Historical Introduction,' in Moody and Simmons, eds., *Glorious Revolution in Massachusetts*, 11–12; Johnson, *John Nelson*, 56–7.
36 Mather, 'Pietas in Patriam,' 298; Sewall, *Diary*, 22 March 1690, 1:255; journal of Benjamin Bullivant, 18 March 1690 [*sic* for 22 or 23 March], PRO, CO5/855, no. 94. Bullivant was a physician, a Church of England member, and formerly a minor official under the dominion.
37 Mather, 'Pietas in Patriam,' 296–7. See also Cohen, *God's Caress*, 137–61, 201–41.
38 Mather, 'Pietas in Patriam,' 296; Cohen, *God's Caress*, 140–57.
39 General Court minutes, 30 January, MA, General Court records, 6:108; order of deputies, 19 March 1690, MA, vol. 35, 321b.
40 Journal of Benjamin Bullivant, 18 March 1690 [*sic* for a date between 22 and 27 March], PRO, CO5/855, no. 94.
41 *The Book of Possessions*, Second Report of Record Commissioners of the City of Boston, 120; *Turell v. Phips*, 24 April 1677, in Morison, ed., *Records of the Suffolk County Court, 1671–1680*, 2:807; *Suffolk Deeds*, 8:23, 317, 346, 358; Noyes, Libby, and Davis, eds., *Genealogical Dictionary of Maine and New Hampshire*, 426, 700. One of the Turells, in partnership with a John Coney, purchased land on the west bank of the Kennebec in 1678 from a shipwright, John Leighton. This further northeastern connection may also have been connected with the Turells' relationship with Phips.
42 Petition of Daniel Turell Jr, 18 March 1690, MA, vol. 35, 320; Thomas, *Religion and the Decline of Magic*, 236. See also Clark, *Goodwin Wharton*.
43 Articles of agreement, 11 January 1684, MA, vol. 36, 352; bill of sale, 14 January 1684, MA, vol. 37, 159; Richard Wharton to Hezekiah Usher, 29 September 1687, ibid., 160; deposition of Daniel Turell Jr, 29 January 1691, MA, vol. 36, 351–2.
44 Thomas Mitchell v. Joseph Smith, 9 December 1684, MA, Middlesex Court Files; deposition of Daniel Turell Jr, 29 January 1691, MA, vol. 36, 351–2.
45 *Way v. Pease*, 31 October 1676, in Morison, ed., *Records of the Suffolk County Court, 1671–1680*, 2:747; *Way v. Walker*, 30 October 1677, ibid., 855; Savage, *Genealogical Dictionary*, 4:440–1; Daniel Turell Sr and Mary Turell to John Foster, 9 June 1684, *Suffolk Deeds*, 13:134.
46 Hall, *The Last American Puritan*, 71.

47 Cony to Nottingham, 21 October 1684, PRO, CO1/55, no. 53. During the 1680s, John Hornibrook had lived at Tuessic Neck, a short distance from the Phips homestead. His neighbour had been John Bish, an obscure individual of whom virtually nothing is known. The uncommon surname he shared with Henry Bish, however, provides some basis for speculation on possible ties between Phips and radical Protestants (Noyes, Libby, and Davis, eds., *Genealogical Dictionary of Maine and New Hampshire*, 93, 349).

48 Quoted in Andrews, ed., *Narratives of the Insurrections*, 336. See also Randolph to Lords of Trade, 29 May 1689, in Toppan and Goodrick, eds., *Randolph Letters*, 6:280; Lovejoy, *Glorious Revolution in America*, 240, 302.

49 See Moody, 'The Maine Frontier,' 238–46.

50 [King] to Denonville, 20 March 1689, AC, B, vol. 15, 52.

51 Mémoire to Frontenac, 7 June 1689, ibid., 92–9; king to Frontenac and Champigny, 14 July 1690, ibid., 121–3.

52 Original French: 'une diversion qui le puisse empescher d'envahir le Port Royal' (Lagny to the minister, 21 February 1690, AC, C11D, vol. 2, 144–5).

53 Vote of General Court, 16 December 1689, MA, vol. 35, 126.

54 Proposal of John Nelson, 4 January 1690, MA, vol. 35, 161–2; vote of representatives, 4 January 1690, ibid., 160a; minutes of council, 10 January 1690, MA, General Court records, 6:100–1; Petition of inhabitants of Boston and adjacent places, 25 January 1690, PRO, CO5/855, no. 56; Johnson, *John Nelson*, 59–60.

55 Johnson, *John Nelson*, 60–1; Rawlyk, *Nova Scotia's Massachusetts*, 62–5; Sewall, *Diary*, 24 February 1690, 1:251–2.

56 Minutes of General Court, 15, 19 March 1690, MA, General Court records, 6:126–7.

57 Ibid., 18, 20, 22 March 1690, MA, General Court records, 6:126–31; Sewall, *Diary*, 21, 22 March 1690, 1:254–5; journal of Benjamin Bullivant, 18 March 1690 [*sic* for 22 March], PRO, CO5/855, no. 94.

58 Knepp Journal, 14 November 1683, BL, Egerton MSS, 2526, 13; minutes of Expedition Committee, 24 March 1690, in Moody and Simmons, eds., *Glorious Revolution in Massachusetts*, 235.

59 Cotton Mather, *Diary*, 29 April 1692; Massachusetts Historical Society *Collections*, 7th ser. 7:148.

60 Journal of Benjamin Bullivant, 18 March 1690 [*sic* for 22 or 23 March], PRO, CO5/855, no. 94.

5: The Expeditions of 1690

1 Minutes of Expedition Committee, 24 March 1690, in Moody and Simmons, eds., *Glorious Revolution in Massachusetts*, 235; Sewall, *Diary*, 24 March 1690,

1:255; Simon Bradstreet to Shrewsbury, 29 March 1690, PRO, CO5/855, no. 70; Elisha Hutchinson to Elisha Cooke, 31 March 1690, ibid., no. 75.

2 Daniel Allin to Joseph Dudley, 1 April 1690, ibid., no. 77; Journal of Benjamin Bullivant, 18 March [sic for a later date], 3 April 1690, ibid., no. 94; *Journal of the Proceedings in the Late Expedition to Port-Royal* (hereafter *Expedition Journal*), 16; Eames, 'Rustic Warriors,' 326. The Coleman referred to by Bullivant was probably William Coleman, who was listed later in the year as a regimental muster master. See General Court minutes, 20 June 1690, MA, General Court records, 6:145.

3 Letter of Francis Foxcroft (abstract), 2 April 1690, PRO, CO5/855, no. 79.

4 Cotton Mather, *The Present State of New England Considered*, 32–3. The details on the expedition's sailing and its strength are from the *Expedition Journal*, 3, 15–16.

5 Instructions to Sir William Phips, 18 April 1690, MA, vol. 36, 17–18.

6 *Expedition Journal*, 3–5.

7 Original French: 'il a eu comme presque tous les Ingenieurs des veues trop vastes et disproportionnees aux choses qu'il avoit a faire'; 'il a laissé les choses en cet estat, le fort ouvert et par consequent moins en deffence qu'auparavant' (Mémoire, 1690, AC, C11D, vol. 2, 159–62; Baudry, 'Des Friches de Meneval, Louis-Alexandre,' DCB, 2: 182–3).

8 Original French: 'je vous assure qu'a la premiere occasion sans ordre et sans permission je sortirés d'icy quoy qu'il en pust arriver ayman mieux cent fois demeurer trois ans à la bastille qu'une seulle semaine icy' Meneval to [Chevry], 8 September 1689, AC, C11D, vol. 2, 117). See also Reid, *Acadia, Maine, and New Scotland*, 177.

9 Original French: 'ce que j'ay eu sujet d'appréhender tous les jours, depuys que je suis icy, est enfin arrivé'; 'trois frégattes de guerre, de 46 et 30 pièces de canon, cinq ou six moindres bastiments et huict à neuf cens hommes de débarquement' Meneval to the minister, 29 May 1690, *Collection de manuscrits*, 2:10; 'Relation de la prise du Port-Royal ...' (hereafter 'Relation de la prise'), in Doughty, *Report of the Work of the Archives Branch*, app. F, 67–73.

10 *Expedition Journal*, 5, 9–10; 'Relation de la prise,' 67. On the Melansons, see d'Entremont, 'Du nouveau sur les Melanson,' 339–52, and 'Les Melanson d'Acadie sont français de père et anglais de mère,' 416–19.

11 Original French: 'de peur de lirriter' ('Relation de la prise,' 67–8; mémoire of Petit, Trouvé, Dubreuil, and Meneval, 27 May 1690, *Collection de manuscrits*, 2:6–7).

12 *Expedition Journal*, 6.

13 Ibid.

14 Original French: 'qui se mit apres son départ a boire et a piller' ('Relation de la prise,' 68).

15 *Expedition Journal*, 9; original French is 'en gens de guerre avec armes et bag-gages' (Mémoire of Petit, Trouvé, Dubreuil, and Meneval, 27 May 1690, *Collection de manuscrits*, 2:7); 'Relation de la prise,' 68.

16 Original French: 'le Général voyant à son arrivée au Port Royal qu'il n'y avoit point de fort ny aulcunes fortifications ou l'on se put deffendre ainsy qu'il l'avoit crust et que la garnison estoit moins nombreuse qu'il ne se l'estoit imaginé, fut fasché de l'honneste compromis qu'il avoit accordé, et cherchant des prétextes pour le rompre, prit celuy de quelque desordre qui estoit arrivé au Port Royal en l'absence de Monsieur le Gouverneur' (Mémoire of Petit, Trouvé, Dubreuil, and Meneval, 27 May 1690, *Collection de manuscrits*, 2:8).

17 On English anti-Catholicism and its sources in this period, see Bosher, 'The Franco-Catholic Danger, 1660–1715.'

18 Original French: 'Monsieur demeneval estant arrivé a bord dud[it] Commandant fut conduit en sa chambre dans le fond de laquelle jl estoit assis. La arrivant Mr demeneval luy fit une profonde reverence, Ce commandant y repondit en jnclinant la teste a droite et a gauche a la maniere angloise'; 'gens fort irritez dont je n'attends guère grace ny de bons traittemens' ('Relation de la prise,' 68; Meneval to the minister, 29 May 1690, *Collection de manuscrits*, 2:11).

19 'Relation de la prise,' 69; *Expedition Journal*, 7.

20 *Expedition Journal*, 6–7, 11–12, 13–15; C. Bruce Fergusson (in collaboration), 'La Tourasse, Charles,' DCB, 1:426–7. On Saint-Lusson in the Kennebec-Penobscot region, see Reid, 'French Aspirations in the Kennebec-Penobscot Region, 1671,' 85–92.

21 *Expedition Journal*, 12–13; Cyprian Southack to his father and mother, 18 June 1690, MA, vol. 36, 127–9.

22 *Expedition Journal*, 7–8; General Court minutes, 31 May, 5, 14 June 1690, MA, General Court records, 6:136–8, 142–4; deed, Benjamin Davis to Sir William Phips, 13 June 1690, Suffolk Deeds, 15:51–2; Meneval to Seignelay, 6 April 1691, *Collection de manuscrits*, 2:41.

23 Inventory [June 1690], MA, vol. 36, 123–24a.

24 Sewall, *Diary*, 22 May, 16 June 1690, 1:260; [Simon Bradstreet] to Jacob Leisler, 27 May 1690, MA, vol. 36, 83; account of fight between *Rose* and French man-of-war [1690], PRO, CO5/855, no. 96; letter from Falmouth, 10 July 1690, HLBP, BL291; Moody, 'The Maine Frontier,' 249–50.

25 Letter to John Usher, 27 May 1690, PRO, CO5/855, no. 100; letter of Thomas Newton, 26 May 1690, PRO, CO5/1081, no. 138; Francis Nicholson to Lords of Trade, 4 November 1690, PRO, CO5/1305, no. 50.

26 Original French: 'toutte la conduitte de Monsieur de Meneval a esté mauvaise et peu de gens l'ont trouvé bon'; 'malgré ses protestations, il estoit fort

lié avec cette nation qui luy a toujours esté sy chère' (Perrot to Chevry, 2 June
1690, *Collection de manuscrits*, 2:12–13). For more details of the allegations of
the trading relationship of the priests with John Nelson, and the involvement
of Meneval, see 'Mémoire instructif,' 1690, AC, C11D, vol. 2, 147–52, and de
Goutin to the minister, 2 September 1690, ibid., 153–8. See also Johnson, *John
Nelson*, 46, and Daigle, 'Nos amis les ennemis,' 112–16.

27 'Humble Address' [9 April 1691], PRO, CO5/856, no. 143(i). On Byfield, see
Black, 'Nathaniel Byfield, 1653–1733,' 57–105, and Andrews, ed., *Narratives of
the Insurrections*, 168–9.

28 See Villebon to Chevry [1690], in Webster, ed., *Acadia at the End of the Seventeenth Century*, 24; Villebon, 'Journal of Acadia,' December 1692, ibid., 44–5.

29 On the reluctance of New England militia to undertake isolated garrison
duty, see Eames, 'Rustic Warriors,' 210.

30 Letter to John Usher, 27 May 1690, PRO, CO5/855, no. 100.

31 Vote of General Court, 3 June 1690, MA, vol. 36, 105; General Court minutes,
25 May, 12 June 1690, MA, General Court records, 6:132–3, 141.

32 See Johnson, *John Nelson*, 64–5.

33 See Johnson, *Adjustment to Empire*, 193–5.

34 Letter of Joseph Dudley [27 June 1690], PRO, CO5/855, no. 115.

35 Council minutes, 15 July, 1 August 1690, MA, vols. 81, 92, 99; General Court
minutes, 1 August 1690, MA, General Court records, 6:157; Breen, *Puritans
and Adventurers*, 96–7; Myrand, ed., *Sir William Phips devant Québec*, 216,
222. On the soldiers from Sudbury, so many of whom later received veterans' land grants that one of the townships created for this purpose was
named 'Sudbury Canada'(later known as Bethel, Maine), see Lapham, *History of Bethel, Maine*, 19–27, and Hudson, *History of Sudbury, Massachusetts*,
269–72.

36 Myrand, ed., *Sir William Phips devant Québec*, 196–7, 216; Watkins, *Soldiers
in the Expedition to Canada*, 77 and passim.

37 Governor and council to the king, 29 March 1690, PRO, CO5/855, no. 71;
Lords of Trade to the king, 12 June 1690, PRO, CO5/905, 226–7; Johnson,
Adjustment to Empire, 196. On the shortage of ammunition, see Wise 'The
Narrative of Mr. John Wise,' 284.

38 Stephen Van Cortlandt to William Blathwayt, 5 July, 1 August 1690, CWBP,
vol. 9, folder 1.

39 Council minutes, 17 June 1690, MA, vol. 81, 90; General Court minutes, 26
June 1690, MA, General Court Records, 6:147; Thomas Savage to Perez Savage, 2 February 1691, in Myrand, ed., Sir William Phips devant Québec, 49.

40 'Sir William Phips's Account of his Expedition against Canada' [21 April
1691], PRO, CO5/905, 268; narrative of John Walley, 27 November 1690, in

Myrand, ed., *Sir William Phips devant Québec*, 37; Wise, 'The Narrative of Mr. John Wise,' 306–12.

41 Eccles, *Canada under Louis XIV*, 178–80; Revolutionary Government of New York to Shrewsbury, 20 October 1690, PRO, CO5/1081, no. 174; Frontenac to the minister, 12 November 1690, AC, C11A, vol. 11, 89–90; journal of Sylvanus Davis [November 1690], MA, vol. 36, 216.

42 Phips to Frontenac or deputy, 6 October 1690, in Mather, 'Pietas in Patriam,' 302–3. Only when the New England land force captured and interrogated a prisoner on 8 October did Major-General John Walley gain accurate intelligence of the military strength of Quebec (narrative of John Walley, 27 November 1690, in Myrand, ed., *Sir William Phips devant Québec*, 40–1). On the implications of surrender on mercy, see Donagan, 'Atrocity, War Crime, and Treason in the English Civil War,' 1150–1.

43 Original French: 'un homme qui n'a pas gardé la Capitulation qu'il avoit fait avec le gouverneur de Port Royal'; 'je nay point de reponse a faire a vostre general que par la bouche de mes Canons et a Coups de fusil; qu'il apprenne que ce nest pas de la sorte qu'on Envoie sommer un homme Comme Moy; qu'il fasse du mieux qu'il pourra de son Costé, comme je feray du Mien' (letter of James Lloyd (abstract), 8 January 1691, CO5/856, no. 131; relation de Monseignat, AC, C11A, vol. 11, 33–4; relation du Baron de La Hontan, 12 January 1691, in Myrand, ed., Sir William Phips devant Québec, 55–6). Although Lahontan went out of his way to assert that Frontenac had been in deadly earnest in his order that Savage be hanged, it is difficult to avoid seeing the episode as another facet of what was essentially a theatrical production designed to unnerve Savage and those who had sent him.

44 Narrative of John Walley, 27 November 1690, in Myrand, ed., Sir William Phips devant Québec, 38; Frontenac to the minister, 12 November 1690, AC, C11A, vol. 11, 91. See also Stacey, 'Sir William Phips' Attack on Quebec, 1690,' in his *Introduction to the Study of Military History for Canadian Students*, 50–1.

45 Narrative of John Walley, 27 November 1690, in Myrand, ed., Sir William Phips devant Québec, 39–48; Frontenac to the minister, 12 November 1690, AC, C11A, vol. 11, f. 91; Thomas Savage to his brother, 2 February 1691, PRO, CO5/856, no. 139.

46 Phips's account [21 April 1691], PRO, CO5/905, 269. In 1995 and 1996 underwater archaeologists discovered and excavated the remains of one of the four vessels wrecked on the return descent of the St Lawrence. See Marc-André Bernier, 'Épave de l'anse aux Bouleaux,' Intervention d'urgence, Parks Canada, 1995.

47 Letter of Samuel Myles (abstract), 12 December 1690, PRO, CO5/856, no. 127.

48 Ibid.; Myrand, 'Morts et blessés de l'armée anglaise,' in *Sir William Phips devant Québec*, 267–94; Johnson, *Adjustment to Empire*, 197.

49 General Court minutes, 10 December 1690, MA, General Court records, 6:167–9; Bradstreet to Ashurst, Cooke, Mather, and Oakes, 29 November 1690, MA, vol. 36, 227–30.

50 Sewall to Mather, 29 December 1690, 'Letter-Book of Samuel Sewall,' Massachusetts Historical Society *Collections*, 6th serv., 1:115. A similar conclusion was reached by the eyewitness John Wise, a correspondent of Increase Mather, (Wise, 'Narrative of Mr. John Wise,' 283, and [Journal of John Wise], 315).

51 Letter to John Usher [January 1691?], PRO, CO5/856, no. 136; letter from Boston, 31 December 1690, ibid., no. 138; letter of James Lloyd (abstract), 8 January 1691, ibid., no. 131.

52 Letter of James Lloyd (abstract), 8 January 1691, ibid., no. 131; Benjamin Davis to Francis Nicholson, 17 April 1691, CWBP, vol. 4, folder 4; deed, Benjamin Davis to Sir William Phips, 13 June 1690, Suffolk Deeds, 15:51–2; petition of inhabitants of Boston and adjacent places, 25 January 1690, PRO, CO5/855, no. 56; Johnson, *John Nelson*, 22.

53 Narrative of John Walley, 27 November 1690, in Myrand, ed., *Sir William Phips devant Québec*, 48; letter from Boston, 8 December 1690, PRO, CO5/856, no. 138.

54 Original French: 'sont d'une pierre extrêmement dure et qui est à l'épreuve du boulet' (Relation du Baron de La Hontan, 12 January 1691, in Myrand, ed., *Sir William Phips devant Québec*, 59–60).

55 Stacey, 'Sir William Phips' Attack on Quebec,' in his *Introduction to the Study of Military History for Canadian Students*, 55.

56 Eames, 'Rustic Warriors,' 1–29, but for factional disputes within militia companies arising out of the Revolution of 1868–9, see also Breen, *Puritans and Adventurers*, 96–102.

57 See Jean Blain, 'Le Moyne de Sainte-Hélène, Jacques,' DCB, 1:465–7. For an account that confirms the limited success of the New Englanders, though in a context strongly unfavourable to Walley, see Wise, 'Narrative of Mr. John Wise,' 288–9.

58 Narrative of John Walley, 27 November 1690, in Myrand, ed., *Sir William Phips devant Québec*, 41.

59 Journal of Silvanus Davis [November 1690], MA, vol. 36, 215-16. The food shortages were confirmed by the recollections of the superior of Quebec's Hôtel–Dieu and by another English prisoner in Quebec, Richard Smithsend (Relation de Jeanne-Françoise Juchereau de La Ferté, in Myrand, ed., Sir William Phips devant Québec, 90; report of Smithsend [3 December 1691], PRO, CO5/856, no. 209).

60 Revolutionary Government of New York to Shrewsbury, 20 October 1690, PRO, CO5/1081, no. 174; Francis Nicholson to Lords of Trade, 4 November 1690, PRO, CO5/1305, no. 50.

61 Ashurst and Edmund Harrison to Board of Trade, 11 February 1697, PRO, CO5/859, no. 69.

62 On Walley's reluctance to press the attack, see Wise, 'Narrative of Mr. John Wise,' 289–90.

63 Jeremy Black, 'Introduction,' in Black and Woodfine, eds., *The British Navy and the Use of Naval Power in the Eighteenth Century*, 8; J.R. Jones, 'Limitations of British Sea Power in the French Wars, 1689–1815,' ibid., 44.

64 Blathwayt to Nottingham, 6 March 1691, PRO, SP63d/353, no. 55; Blathwayt to George Stepney, 6 August 1703, quoted by Jeremy Black, 'British Naval Power and International Commitments: Political and Strategic Problems, 1688–1770,' in Duffy, ed., *Parameters of British Naval Power, 1650–1850*, 41; Black, 'Naval Power, Strategy, and Foreign Policy, 1775–1791,' ibid., 98; Webb, 'William Blathwayt, Imperial Fixer: Muddling Through to Empire,' 392.

65 Letter of James Lloyd (abstract), 8 January 1691, PRO, CO5/856, no. 131.

66 King to Frontenac and Champigny, 14 July 1690, AC, B, vol. 15, 121; Revolutionary Government of New York to Shrewsbury, 20 October 1690, PRO, CO5/1081, no. 174; Francis Nicholson to Lords of Trade, 4 November 1690, CO5/1305, no. 50.

67 New England agents to Lords of Trade [21 April 1690], PRO, CO5/856, no. 150; agreement, 1 May 1691, ibid., no. 160.

68 Bradstreet to Henry Sloughter, 18 June 1691, PRO, CO5/1037, no. 32; king to Frontenac and Champigny, 7 April 1691, AC, B, vol. 16, 34–5; instructions to Villebon, 7 April 1691, ibid., 46–8; king to Frontenac, 7 April 1691, ibid., 49; [minister] to Frontenac, 30 May 1691, ibid., 63–4.

69 'Humble Address' [9 April 1691], PRO, CO5/856, no. 143(i); Mather, 'Pietas in Patriam,' 307. See also letter of James Lloyd (abstract), 8 January 1691, PRO, CO5/856, no. 131.

70 Council minutes, 5 November 1690, MA, vol. 81, 107; Breen, *Puritans and Adventurers*, 103. For the date of Phips's arrival in Boston, 19 November 1690, see Mather, 'Pietas in Patriam,' 306.

71 General Court minutes, November 1690, MA, General Court records, 6:164; council minutes, 6 November 1690, MA, vol. 81, 108.

72 Order of the General Court, 10 December 1690, MA, General Court records, 6:170–1; Dickson, *The Financial Revolution in England*, 7–11; Joseph A. Ernst, 'Shays's Rebellion in Long Perspective: The Merchants and the "Money Question,"' in Gross, ed., *In Debt to Shays*, 188–9; Davis, ed., *Colonial Currency Reprints*, 1:21–4, 26–7.

73 Letter from Boston, 2 February 1691, PRO, CO5/856, no. 138.

74 Mather, 'Pietas in Patriam,' 307–9; Breen, *Puritans and Adventurers*, 103–4. On the later difficulties experienced in reimbursing public creditors, see *Acts and Resolves of the Province of Massachusetts Bay*, vol. 1, *Province Laws*, 1692–3, C7, 35–6; petition of John Richards et al. [1693], MA, vol. 100, 416.

75 Thomas Savage to Perez Savage, 2 February 1691, PRO, CO5/856, no. 139; Eames, 'Rustic Warriors,' 364–5. Walley was appointed to an artillery command for the planned assault on Quebec in 1709, but the expedition never sailed. See C.P. Stacey, 'Walley, John,' DCB, 2:662.

76 Letter from Boston, 2 February 1691, PRO, CO5/856, no. 138; letter to John Usher [?January 1691], ibid., no. 136.

77 See list of magistrates elected, 18 April 1691, PRO, CO5/856, no. 146.

78 Sewall, *Diary*, 29 November 1690, 1:271; Meneval to Pontchartrain, 6 April 1691, *Collection de Manuscrits*, 2:42; warrant, 6 December 1690, MA, vol. 36, 233. On this entire episode, see also Johnson, *John Nelson*, 65.

79 Original French: 'le fit amener à Baston où, de son authorité particulière et à l'inçu du Gouverneur et du Conseil, il le fit mettre dans la prison' Meneval to Pontchartrain, 6 April 1691, *Collection de manuscrits*, 2:42); warrant, 25 December 1690, MA, vol. 36, 262.

80 Sewall, *Diary*, 29, 30 December 1690, 1:272–3. A search of Massachusetts judicial archives has revealed no writ or other action taken by Meneval. In this regard, we thank Elizabeth C. Bouvier. A question that inevitably arises is whether there ever was such a writ, or whether Sewall referred to an action initiated by Robert Bronson (also in December 1690) in connection with Phips's outstanding debts from the voyage of the *Golden Rose*, which may have been taken to be inspired by Meneval. The Bronson case, however, went to court in January 1691, so the reference to annulment of a writ seems likely to relate to an attempted action by Meneval of which no other direct evidence has survived.

81 Original French: 'qu'il ... ne fist connoistre sa malhoneteté et son manquement de parolle' (Meneval to Pontchartrain, 6 April 1691, *Collection de manuscrits*, 2:42)

82 Original French: 'il estoit dangereux de voir une sédition dans la ville où la canaille est la plus forte' (Meneval to Pontchartrain, 6 April 1691, *Collection de manuscrits*, 2:43). See also Bradstreet to Phips, 7 January 1691, MA, vol. 36, 263a, and mémoire of Meneval [1700], ibid., 339–40. Meneval continued to maintain in 1700 that 4,000 out of 5,000 livres had not been returned by Phips.

83 Sewall, *Diary*, 7 January 1691, 1:274.

84 Warrants, 22 December 1690, MA, vol. 36, 344–5; certificates of John Winch-

combe, marshal, 24 December 1690, ibid., 344a, 345a; warrant [22 December 1690], Suffolk County Court Files, 4062; certificate of John Winchcombe, 24 December 1690, ibid.; deposition of Henry Dickeson, 24 January 1691, MA, vol. 36, 348a; deposition of William Bryant, 29 January 1691, ibid., 349; Noble, ed., *Records of the Court of Assistants of the Colony of the Massachusetts Bay*, 1:337–8.
85 Letter from Boston, 31 December 1690, PRO, CO5/856, no. 138.
86 Mather, 'Pietas in Patriam,' 315.
87 Elisha Cooke to Simon Bradstreet, 9 May 1691, in Moody and Simmons, eds., *The Glorious Revolution in Massachusetts*, 520; Baudry, Des Friches de Meneval, Louise-Alexandre,' DCB, 2:184.
88 Letter to John Usher, [?January 1691], PRO, CO5/856, no. 136.

6: The Charter and Beyond

1 Hall, *The Last American Puritan*, 250–1. See also Johnson, *Adjustment to Empire*, 228–9.
2 Diary of Increase Mather, 4, 5, 6, 7 March 1691, AAS; Elisha Cooke to Simon Bradstreet, 9 May 1691, in Moody and Simmons, eds., *Glorious Revolution in Massachusetts*, 520.
3 See Baxter, *William III*, 292–4.
4 Quoted in Horwitz, *Revolution Politicks*, 123.
5 See ibid., 121–8; DNB, 17:429–31; Webb, 'William Blathwayt, Imperial Fixer: Muddling Through to Empire,' 378–80.
6 Horwitz, *Revolution Politicks*, 128–30; Johnson, *Adjustment to Empire*, 148–9, 216.
7 Instructions, 24 January 1690, MA, vol. 35, 181.
8 Charles Lidget to Francis Foxcroft, 5 November 1690, in Moody and Simmons, eds., *Glorious Revolution in Massachusetts*, 468; Johnson, *Adjustment to Empire*, 178–9; Cotton Mather, *Parentator*, 124.
9 Hall, *The Last American Puritan*, 236–8, 240; Johnson, *Adjustment to Empire*, 179–81.
10 *Paris Gazette*, 5 February 1691, PRO, CO5/856, no. 133.
11 Blathwayt to Nottingham, 6 March 1691, PRO, SP63d/353, no. 55.
12 Nottingham to Blathwayt, 13 March 1691, Great Britain, HMC, *Report on the Manuscripts of Allan George Finch, Esq.*, 3:29.
13 For the pamphlet, see *Andros Tracts*, 2:223–30. Two versions were printed: one relating only to Massachusetts, the other dealing also with other New England charters. On the meetings during March and April 1691, see Diary of Increase Mather, 9 March – 17 April 1691, AAS.

14 *Andros Tracts*, 2:229.

15 Phips's account [21 April 1691], PRO, CO5/905, 267–9.

16 Diary of Increase Mather, 9 April 1691, AAS.

17 Order in council, 9 April 1691, PRO, CO5/856, no. 143; Cooke to Bradstreet, 9 May 1691, in Moody and Simmons, eds., *Glorious Revolution in Massachusetts*, 521.

18 'Humble Address' [9 April 1691], PRO, CO5/856, no. 143(i); order in council, 9 April 1691, ibid., no. 143.

19 'Petition of Several Merchants' [18 April 1691], MA, vol. 37, 7; Diary of Increase Mather, 18 April 1691, AAS; Massachusetts agents to Lords of Trade [21 April 1691], PRO, CO5/856, no. 150; Cooke to Bradstreet, 9 May 1691, in Moody and Simmons, eds., *Glorious Revolution in Massachusetts*, 521. Cooke attributed these events to 20 April, but it seems clear that this is an error for 21 April.

20 This paragraph is based primarily on De Krey, *A Fractured Society*, esp. pp. 21, 52, 62, 78–9, 84, 89–90, 92, 104–6, 114–15, 138–9, 183; Jones, 'London Overseas,' 387–508 passim; Woodhead, *The Rulers of London*, 19, 64–5, 87–8, 105. See also Hall, *The Last American Puritan*, 213; Henning, *The House of Commons, 1660–1690*, 1:558–60; Olson, *Making the Empire Work*, 28; and Steele, *The English Atlantic*, 267. The list of names on the petition even extended to Thomas Phips, who may have been the same Thomas who was the older brother of Constantine Phips and a cousin of Sir William (pedigree of Francis Phipps, 11 March 1664, BODL, Rawlinson MSS, D 865, 86). The names of Richard Merriweather and four other signatories to the petition – William Chambers, Thomas Cuddon, James Pettet, and Thomas Southey – had also appeared a year earlier on a petition headed by Thomas Brinley, which had opposed by implication the charter government of Massachusetts. The February 1691 petition therefore gives evidence of successful recruitment by Mather and Ashurst among merchants not previously sympathetic ('Petition of Severall Merchants, Traders and Inhabitants unto and in New England' [13 February 1690], PRO, CO5/855, no. 65).

21 See Dickson, *Financial Revolution in England*, 46–50.

22 See De Krey, *A Fractured Society*, 61–73; also Horwitz, *Revolution Politicks*, 120–1. The episode also demonstrates, for historians, the extent to which colonial issues could be affected by City politics as well as by party disputes at the parliamentary level.

23 'Petition of Several Merchants' [18 April 1691], MA, vol. 37, 7.

24 Memorandum, 23 April 1691, PRO, CO5/856, no. 152; Cooke to Bradstreet, 9 May 1691, in Moody and Simmons, eds., *Glorious Revolution in Massachusetts*, 521–2; Johnson, *Adjustment to Empire*, 210–11.

25 Diary of Increase Mather, 28 April 1691, AAS.

26 Mémoire of Meneval, 6 April 1691, *Collection de manuscrits*, 2:40–4.
27 Cabinet council minutes, 30 April 1691, Great Britain, HMC, *Report on the Manuscripts of Allan George Finch, Esq.*, 3:389.
28 Original French: 'la mauvaise foy des Anglois.' (Frontenac to the minister, 15 September 1692, AC, C11A, vol. 12, 26).
29 [Increase Mather], 'A Brief Account concerning Several of the Agents of New-England,' 1691, in *Andros Tracts*, 2:280. See also minute of Lords of Trade to Lord Sydney, 22 April 1691, PRO, CO5/856, no. 151; minute of Lords of Trade, 27 April 1691, PRO, CO5/905, 269; Diary of Increase Mather, 28 April 1691, AAS; Cooke to Bradstreet, 9 May 1691, in Moody and Simmons, eds., *Glorious Revolution in Massachusetts*, 522.
30 Order in council, 30 April 1691, PRO, CO5/905, 270–1; [Increase Mather], 'A Brief Account concerning Several of the Agents of New-England,' *Andros Tracts*, 2:280; Johnson, *Adjustment to Empire*, 212.
31 Diary of Increase Mather, 17 June 1691, AAS; Johnson, *Adjustment to Empire*, 212–14; Hall, *The Last American Puritan*, 242–6.
32 Johnson, *Adjustment to Empire*, 213–14; Nottingham to William III, 31 July 1691, in Moody and Simmons, eds., *Glorious Revolution in Massachusetts*, 570.
33 Journal of Lords of Trade, 2 July 1691, PRO, CO391/7, 30–1; petition of Massachusetts agents [n.d.], PRO, CO5/856, no. 169; report of attorney General [29 July 1691], ibid., no. 176; journal of Lords of Trade, 29 July 1691, PRO, CO391/7, 37–9; order in council, 30 July 1691, PRO, CO5/905, 279–81; Johnson, *Adjustment to Empire*, 215–16; Simmons, 'The Massachusetts Charter of 1691,' in Allen and Thompson, eds., *Contrast and Connection*, 77–9.
34 Nottingham to William III, 31 July 1691, in Moody and Simmons, eds., *Glorious Revolution in Massachusetts*, 569–70; Sydney to Nottingham, 10 August 1691, ibid., 570.
35 Diary of Increase Mather, 10, 23, 31 July 1691, AAS; On Paterson, see Armitage, 'The Projecting Age,' 5–10.
36 Diary of Increase Mather, 6–14 August 1691, AAS.
37 [Increase Mather], 'A Brief Account concerning Several of the Agents of New-England,' *Andros Tracts*, 2:283; 'An Account of Mather's Agency in a Reply to Calef,' ibid., 2:319–20. This point was first made in Johnson, *Adjustment to Empire*, 224–5.
38 Nottingham to Sydney, 11 August 1691, in Moody and Simmons, eds., *Glorious Revolution in Massachusetts*, 570–1.
39 Diary of Increase Mather, 19 August 1691, AAS; journal of Lords of Trade, 20 August 1691, PRO, CO391/7, 40–1. Phips and the agents had been summoned to attend this meeting of the Lords of Trade, though it is unclear how many of them (if any) did so (Summons [August 1691], PRO, CO5/924, no. 5).

40 Johnson, *Adjustment to Empire*, 224–5.

41 'An Account of Mather's Agency in a reply to Calef,' *Andros Tracts*, 2:320.

42 [Increase Mather], 'A Brief Account concerning Several of the Agents of New-England,' *Andros Tracts*, 2:283.

43 Diary of Increase Mather, 24 July 1691, AAS.

44 Summons, [August 1691], PRO, CO5/924, no. 5.

45 Newsletter, 7 March 1691, PRO, ADM77/4, no. 1.

46 Petition of Sir William Phips, 30 June 1691, PRO, CO5/856, no. 172; proposal of Sir William Phips [30 June 1691], ibid., no. 171.

47 Phips to Lords of Trade, 21 September 1691, PRO, CO5/856, no. 196; Phips to Lords of Trade, 23 September 1691, ibid., no. 197; journal of Lords of Trade, 28 September 1691, PRO, CO391/7, 53–4. See also P.G.M. Dickson and John Sperling, 'War Finance, 1689–1714,' in Bromley, ed., *The New Cambridge Modern History*, 6:285–6.

48 Proceedings on the petition of Sir William Phips et al., 13 August 1691, PRO, SP44/235, 170; memorial of Phips and Increase Mather, 9 November 1691, PRO, CO5/856, no. 202; instructions, 24 January 1690, MA, vol. 35, 181. On Evance and Lake, see chapter 8 below. The link with the John Smith of 1686–7 is tentatively advanced in Johnson, 'Adjustment to Empire,' 636, although the name is obviously a common one. Another John Smith was a Whig politician and, like Evance, a prominent public creditor of the 1690s (Dickson, *Financial Revolution in England*, 429). On the possible connections of Frith and Porter, see Phillip Madoxe to Sir Robert Southwell, Southwell-Madoxe Letters, BODL, MSS Eng. lett., c 53–4, and DNB, 14:90.

49 Petition of Dudley et al., April 1691, PRO, CO5/857, no. 6(xii); Johnson, *Adjustment to Empire*, 220–1.

50 Journal of Lords of Trade, 2 September 1691, PRO, CO391/7, 42; Phips to Lords of Trade [September 1691], PRO, CO5/856, no. 184; queries concerning naval stores [September 1691], ibid., no. 185; memorandum of Andros, n.d., ibid., no. 186; memorandum of Lidget, n.d., ibid., no. 187. The minute of the Lords of Trade does not make clear whether Phips's written submission was made at the meeting itself on 2 September (as is suggested, but not established, by an obviously later addition of that date to the document) or whether it was made soon thereafter.

51 Petition of Richard Lord Gorges [30 July 1691], PRO, CO5/856, no. 178 (i); petitions of Ferdinando Gorges [July 1691], ibid., nos. 175, 179; petition of Samuel Allen [29 July 1691], PRO, CO5/924, no. 5; petition of New England agents, 27 August 1691, PRO, CO5/856, no. 183; journal of Lords of Trade, 31 August 1691, PRO, CO391/7, 28.

52 Petition of New England agents, 27 August 1691, PRO, CO5/856, no. 183;

Armitage, 'The Projecting Age,' 7. The possibility that Phips may also have been acting in concert with Samuel Allen is suggested by Johnson, *Adjustment to Empire*, 219.

53 *Andros Tracts*, 2:229; Diary of Increase Mather, 31 March 1691, AAS.
54 Phips to Lords of Trade [September 1691], PRO, CO5/856, no. 184.
55 Cooke to Bradstreet, 10 September 1691, in Moody and Simmons, eds., *Glorious Revolution in Massachusetts*, 592.
56 Mather and Ashurst to Lords of Trade, 18 September 1691, PRO, CO5/856, no. 193; Diary of Increase Mather, 18 May 1695, AAS. See also Hall, *The Last American Puritan*, 250–1; Johnson, *Adjustment to Empire*, 227; Simmons, 'Massachusetts Charter of 1691,' in Allen and Thompson, eds., *Contrast and Connection*, 80–1; Sosin, *English America and the Revolution of 1688*, 139–41.
57 Journal of Lords of Trade, 2–3 September 1691, PRO, CO391/7, 42–4. Phips's discussions with the committee, and possibly his written submission, appear to have exerted an influence that led towards its recommendation, the following day, that the charter incorporate restrictions on the cutting of mast trees and a prohibition on the granting of any lands without royal approval from the Kennebec to the St Lawrence and all points northeastward to the ocean.
58 Ashurst to Mather, 3 September 1691, in Hutchinson, *History of the Colony and Province of Massachusetts-Bay*, 1:349; Ashurst to William Stoughton, 22 October 1692, BODL, Ashurst Papers, Letterbook of Sir Henry Ashurst, 84; Massachusetts agents to Lords of Trade, 15 September 1691, PRO, CO5/856, no. 192. Although the last document was in the names of the agents, that designation had been loosely used for some time (in the absence on most occasions of the consent of Cooke and Oakes) for the actions taken by Mather and Ashurst. The document is endorsed 'Received ... from Mr. Mather.'
59 Phips to Nottingham, 12 October 1692, PRO, CO5/751, no. 15; Phips to Nottingham, 28 February 1693, ibid., no. 30.
60 Edward Randolph to William Blathwayt, 27 September 1692, CWBP, vol. 2, folder 3; Cooke to Bradstreet, 4 November 1691, in Moody and Simmons, eds., *Glorious Revolution in Massachusetts*, 593; Diary of Increase Mather, 4 November 1691, AAS; Increase Mather, *Autobiography*, 336–7. See also Johnson, *Adjustment to Empire*, 258–62, 329–38; Labaree, *Royal Government in America*, 37–51; and Murison, 'William Blathwayt's Empire,' 92.
61 Journal of the Lords of Trade, 27 November 1691, PRO, CO391/7, 71; order in council, 27 November 1691, CO5/905, 364; draft commission [27 November 1691], PRO, CO5/856, no. 207. The commission passed the Great Seal on 12 December 1691.
62 Charter of Massachusetts, 7 October 1691, PRO, CO5/905, 298–352; Johnson, *Adjustment to Empire*, 205–6, 219. See also Phips's submission to the Lords of

Trade in November of twelve possible sites for townships in 'East New England and Nova Scotia,' PRO, CO5/856, no. 203.

63 [Increase Mather], 'A Brief Account concerning Several of the Agents of New-England,' *Andros Tracts*, 2:294; Increase Mather, *Autobiography*, 337; Diary of Increase Mather, 26 November 1691, AAS; Cotton Mather, *Diary*, 29 April 1691, Massachusetts Historical Society *Collections*, 7th series, 7:148.

64 Cooke to Bradstreet, 4 November 1691, in Moody and Simmons, eds., *Glorious Revolution in Massachusetts*, 593; Mather to John Richards, 26 October 1691, ibid., 621.

65 Blathwayt to Nicholson, 5 December 1691, CWBP, vol. 15, folder 2.

66 Instructions, 31 December 1691, PRO, CO5/905, 365–94; Labaree, ed., *Royal Instructions to British Colonial Governors*, 1:410, 453, 2:464, 482–3, 719–20, and passim; commission, 12 December 1691, PRO, CO5/856, no. 207. For the allegations against Shrimpton, see deposition of Robert Tufton Mason, 27 January 1692, PRO, CO5/1037, no. 80; Johnson, *John Nelson*, 45.

67 Diary of Increase Mather, 7, 17 December 1691, AAS; Phips to Lords of Trade [11 December 1691], PRO, CO5/856, no. 211; journal of Lords of Trade, 11 December 1691, PRO, CO391/7, 72; order in council, 17 December 1691, PRO, CO5/905, 401–2.

68 Diary of Increase Mather, 19 October 1691, AAS; memorial of Phips and Mather, 9 November 1691, PRO, CO5/856, no. 202; Treasury reference, 12 January 1692, PRO, T4/6, 364; report of the officers of the Mint, 19 January 1692, Treasury Papers, vol. 17, no. 15.

69 Receipt, 22 February 1692, PRO, CO5/857, no. 2; Increase Mather, *Autobiography*, 343–4.

70 PRO, Rowbotham, 'Pepys List of Ships and Officers, 1660–1688,' 85. The frigate *Nonsuch* was not the same vessel as the ketch of the same name that carried Médard Chouart des Groseilliers to winter on James Bay in 1668. See Rich, ed., *Minutes of the Hudson's Bay Company, 1671–1674*, 226, 228.

71 National Maritime Museum, 'Pitcairn-Jones Sea Officers' List, 1660–1815'; Charnock, *Biographica Navalis* 2:403; officer listings, 1689–90, PRO, ADM8/2; ibid., 1692–3, PRO, ADM8/3; Hornstein, *Restoration Navy*, 10–32 passim.

72 Record of Admiralty Court, 27 July 1692, PRO, CO5/858, no. 10(viii); deposition of George Mills, 15 January 1694, ibid., no. 10(xiii); deposition of Benjamin Jackson, 18 January 1694, ibid., no. 10(xvi).

73 Deposition of George Webster, 18 January 1694, ibid., no. 10(xiv).

74 Robert Fairfax to James Sotherne, PRO, CO5/857, no. 22.

75 Sewall, *Diary*, 26 January, 4, 14 May 1692, 1:287, 291; election results, May 1692, in Moody and Simmons, eds., *Glorious Revolution in Massachusetts*, 422; General Court minutes, 4 May 1692, MA, General Court records, 6:214.

76 Sewall, *Diary*, 14 May 1692, 1:291; Joshua Brodbent to Francis Nicholson, 21 June 1692, PRO, CO5/1037, no. 112.

7: Statecraft and Witchcraft, 1692

1   Willard, *The Character of a Good Ruler*, 3; John Pynchon to Isaac Addington, 20 May 1692, MA, vol. 51, 1–2.
2   Baker, 'Trouble to the Eastward,' 178–220.
3   Foster, *The Long Argument*, 220.
4   Bodge, *Soldiers in King Philip's War*, 133–41.
5   William Hubbard, 'A Narrative of the Troubles with the Indians in New England from Piscataqua to Pemaquid,' in Drake, ed., *The Indian Wars in New England*, 235–6; Bodge, *Soldiers in King Philip's War*, 221, 342–7; Kences, 'Some Unexplored Relationships of Essex County Witchcraft to the Indian Wars of 1675 and 1689.'
6   Bodge, *Soldiers in King Philip's War*, 344–5; Axtell, 'The Vengeful Women of Marblehead,' 647.
7   Deposition of Robert Roules, 7 July 1677 [*sic*], ibid., 652.
8   'Refugees at Salem, January 1675/6,' 20, 21, 25; Noyes, Libby, and Davis, eds., *Genealogical Dictionary of Maine and New Hampshire*, 5, 747. Other refugees are scattered in the list of men taking the oath of fidelity in late 1677 and early 1678; see *Records of the Quarterly Courts of Essex County*, 6:398–402. On levels of taxation and the political tensions that resulted, see Breen, 'War, Taxes, and Political Brokers,' in Breen, *Puritans and Adventurers*, 81–90.
9   Petition of Elizabeth Phips, n.d., Maine State Library, Sheepscot Papers.
10 'Order to Hold a Court at Pemaquid,' 22 July 1674, MA, vol. 3, 307ff; grant from Sir Edmund Andros, 6 September 1679, ibid., 336; 'Those Who Took the Oath of Fidelity,' 18 December 1677, *Records of the Quarterly Courts of Essex County*, 6:401; Noyes, Libby, and Davis, eds., *Genealogical Dictionary of Maine and New Hampshire*, 651, 751.
11 Petition of John Spenser, 6 December 1687, *Documentary History of the State of Maine*, 6:308.
12 Baker, *The Clarke & Lake Company*, 10, 14–15; Alice R. Stewart, 'Davis, Silvanus,' DCB, 2:172; Noyes, Libby, and Davis, eds., *Genealogical Dictionary of Maine and New Hampshire*, 187–88, 412.
13 Articles of Peace, 8 September 1685, PRO, CO1/58, no. 51. See also Morrison, *The Embattled Northeast*, 112; Cotton Mather, *Magnalia Christi Americana*, 2:584; deposition of Joseph Lynde, 14 January 1690, *Andros Tracts*, 1:91–2; Johnson, *Adjustment to Empire*, 80–1.
14 Cotton Mather, *Magnalia Christi Americana*, 2:619. For a more general treat-

ment of environmentally related conflicts, see Cronon, *Changes in the Land*, esp. 63, 127–39; Anderson, 'King Philip's Herds,' 601–24; Morrison, *The Embattled Northeast*, 113–17; and Baker, 'Trouble to the Eastward,' 221–30.

15 Eccles, *France in America*, 95–96; Jennings, *The Ambiguous Iroquois Empire*, 195–6.

16 'An Account of Forces Raised in New England, April 1689,' Hutchinson Papers, Massachusetts Historical Society *Collections*, 3rd ser., 1:84–7; Johnston, *A History of Bristol and Bremen*, 161–7; letter of Elisha Andrews, 19 May 1689, *Documentary History of the State of Maine*, 6:480; petition of the inhabitants of Kennebec River, ibid., 480–1.

17 Morrison, *The Embattled Northeast*, 123–5; Cotton Mather, *Magnalia Christi Americana*, 2:586–618; Drake, *Border Wars of New England*, 36–72; Church, *The History of Philip's War*, 210.

18 Massachusetts agents to the Lords of Trade [21 April 1691], PRO, CO5/856, no. 150; 'Account of the Treaty with the Indians,' 1 May 1691, ibid., no. 159; agreement, 1 May 1691, ibid., no. 160; Simon Bradstreet to Henry Sloughter, 18 June 1691, PRO, CO5/1037, no. 32.

19 Cotton Mather, *Magnalia Christi Americana*, 2:611–13.

20 A sample of recent works would include Boyer and Nissenbaum, *Salem Possessed*, Demos, *Entertaining Satan*, Godbeer, *The Devil's Dominion*, and Weisman, *Magic, Witchcraft, and Religion in Seventeenth-Century New England*. For the relationship between witchcraft and the frontier, see Kences, 'Some Unexplored Relationships of Essex County Witchcraft to the Indian Wars of 1675 and 1689,' 181–92, and Karlsen, *The Devil in the Shape of a Woman*, 226–7, 245–6.

21 Boyer and Nissenbaum, *Salem Possessed*, 39–54; Noyes, Libby, and Davis, eds., *Genealogical Dictionary of Maine and New Hampshire*, 122.

22 Boyer and Nissenbaum, *Salem Possessed*, 54–6; Willis, *History of Portland*, 262–3; *Records of the Quarterly Courts of Essex County*, 9:30–2, 47–9.

23 Boyer and Nissenbaum, *Salem Possessed*, 55–9.

24 Corliss, *Old Times*, 195–6, 227–31; Remich, *History of Kennebunk*, 38–9, 48; Konig, *Law and Society in Puritan Massachusetts*, 76–8; Noyes, Libby, and Davis, eds., *Genealogical Dictionary of Maine and New Hampshire*, 318. On the timber trade and Essex County involvement, see Carroll, *The Timber Economy of Puritan New England*, 105–6, 115.

25 Cotton Mather, 'Decennium Luctuosum,' in his *Magnalia Christi Americana*, 2:620; Baker, 'Trouble to the Eastward,' 226–8; Sewall, *Diary*, 26 January 1692, 1:287.

26 On fortune-telling and related practices, see Hall, *Worlds of Wonder, Days of Judgment*, 98–100.

27 Cotton Mather, 'Pietas in Patriam,' 327.

28 See Boyer and Nissenbaum, *Salem Possessed*, 80–132.

29 Richard Wharton to Bartholomew Gedney, 10 March 1688, Massachusetts Historical Society Collections, 6th Serv., 5:11; Dow, *History of Topsfield*, 378; Zerubabel Endicott to John Curtice, 1681, Essex Deeds, 7:325–6; Thomas Putnam Sr to Thomas Putnam Jr, 1685, ibid., 382–6; Thomas Putnam Sr to Edward Putnam, 1685, ibid., 464–9; proceedings on the petition of Sir William Phips et al., 13 August 1691, PRO, SP44/235, 170; Towne, 'The Topsfield Copper Mines,' 73–81. We thank James Kences for bringing the Blind Hole mine to our attention.

30 Cotton Mather, *Magnalia Christi Americana*, 2:620–3; Drake, *Border Wars of New England*, 86, 117–28, 134. Anxiety over the threat of warfare can be further shown by the spread of the witchcraft outbreak to the frontier town of Andover. By the end of 1692, forty residents of Andover had suffered accusations of witchcraft, while only twenty-seven residents of Salem Village were accused (Weisman, *Witchcraft, Magic, and Religion*, 209–16).

31 Kences, 'Some Unexplored Relationships of Essex County Witchcraft to the Indian Wars of 1675 and 1689,' 192 and passim. Subsequent to Kences's work, others have noticed this linkage, including Karlsen (*The Devil in the Shape of a Woman*, 226–7, 245–6) and McWilliams ('Indian John and the Northern Tawnies,' 580–604). See also Cooper and Minkema, eds., *Sermon Notebook of Samuel Parris*, 13–21; Mather, 'Pietas in Patriam,' 327, 337; and Godbeer, *The Devil's Dominion*, 191–3.

32 Kences, 'Some Unexplored Relationships of Essex County Witchcraft to the Indian Wars of 1675 and 1689,' passim; Noyes, Libby, and Davis, eds., *Genealogical Dictionary of Maine and New Hampshire*, 98–9, 142, 430, 627–8.

33 Deposition of Thomas Gage, 20 May 1692, in Boyer and Nissenbaum, eds., *The Salem Witchcraft Papers*, 3:772.

34 Presentment of Bridget Oliver [1679], file papers of the Essex Quarterly Court and County Court, 1636–1692, vol. 34, 114; Konig, *Law and Society in Puritan Massachusetts*, 151; Boyer and Nissenbaum, eds., *The Salem Witchcraft Papers*, 1:295, 2:351, 545–7, 583, and 3:820; Noyes, Libby, and Davis, eds., *Genealogical Dictionary of Maine and New Hampshire*, 98–9, 510; Boyer and Nissenbaum, *Salem Possessed*, 110–52.

35 John Alden's account of his examination, 28 August 1692, in Boyer and Nissenbaum, eds., *The Salem Witchcraft Papers*, 1:52; Complaint vs. Nicholas Frost, 5 September 1692, ibid., 2:345; Noyes, Libby, and Davis, eds., *Genealogical Dictionary of Maine and New Hampshire*, 196, 247–8; York Deeds, 1:157–8.

36 Deposition of Ann Putnam Jr, 20 April 1692, in Boyer and Nissenbaum, eds., *The Salem Witchcraft Papers*, 1:164; deposition of Thomas Greenslade, ibid.,

160; deposition of Willard and William Wormall, 3 August 1692, ibid., 161; deposition of Benjamin Hutchinson, n.d., ibid., 171–2; memorandum in case of George Burroughs, n.d., ibid., 178.

37 Godbeer, *The Devil's Dominion*, 216–21; deposition of Ann Putnam Jr, 3 August 1692, in Boyer and Nissenbaum, eds., *The Salem Witchcraft Papers*, 1:164, 166–7; deposition of Sarah Bibber, 3 August 1692, ibid., 1:167–8; deposition of Mercy Lewis, 3 August 1692, ibid., 1:168–9; Increase Mather, *Cases of conscience Concerning Evil Spirits Impersonating Men*.

38 Phips to Blathwayt, 12 October 1692, PRO, CO5/857, no. 7; minutes of Massachusetts council, 27 May 1692, PRO, CO5/785, 177–8; DAB, 18:113–14; Weisman, *Witchcraft, Magic, and Religion*, 148, 209–16.

39 Deposition of John Bly Sr and William Bly vs. Bridget Bishop, in Boyer and Nissenbaum, eds., *The Salem Witchcraft Papers*, 1:101; Hansen, *Witchcraft at Salem*, 63–6.

40 See Weisman, *Witchcraft, Magic, and Religion*, 136–8, 209–16; Demos, *Entertaining Satan*, 57–94; Karlsen, *The Devil in the Shape of a Woman*, 46–116.

41 Mather to Richards, 31 May 1692, in Silverman, ed., *Selected Letters of Cotton Mather*, 36; Boyer and Nissenbaum, *Salem Possessed*, 9–10; Foster, *The Long Argument*, 254–61; Michael Hall, *The Last American Puritan*, 256–62.

42 Increase Mather, *Cases of Conscience concerning Evil Spirits Impersonating Men*, postscript; Levin, *Cotton Mather*, 208–10.

43 Letter of Thomas Brattle, 8 October 1692, in Burr, ed., *Narratives of the Witchcraft Cases*, 184; Weisman, *Witchcraft, Magic, and Religion*, 149–53.

44 Hale, *A Modest Inquiry into the Nature of Witchcraft*, 38–9. Although Hale wrote his book in 1697, Phillips's illness had to take place before the Salem witchcraft trials, for it occurred at Black Point, Maine, a place abandoned in 1690 and not reoccupied until well after Hale wrote. Therefore, this was an incident of which Phips was doubtless aware in 1692.

45 'A Letter from New England,' 1 November 1694, PRO, CO5/858, no. 41A. This source was later cited in Hutchinson, *History of the Colony and Province of Massachusetts Bay*, 2:46.

46 Calef, *More Wonders of the Invisible World*, 154; Whiting, *Truth and Innocency Defended against Falsehood and Envy*, 140.

47 Karlsen, *The Devil in the Shape of a Woman*, 116; Weisman, *Witchcraft, Magic, and Religion*, 146–7.

48 See Hall, *Worlds of Wonder, Days of Judgment*, 284.

49 'Witchcraft in Maine,' 193–6; *Province and Court Records of Maine*, 2:86; Hale, *A Modest Inquiry Into the Nature of Witchcraft*, 70. Noyes, Libby, and Davis, eds., *Genealogical Dictionary of Maine and New Hampshire*, 72–3, 119, 513, 651, 751.

50 Nathaniel Byfield et al. to Blathwayt, 20 February 1693, CWBP, vol. 4, folder 4; inventory, 9 September 1696, in Goold, 'Sir William Phips,' 65–7. Slaves from the Caribbean (in contrast to those brought directly from Africa) were sometimes referred to as 'Indian servants.' Although we do not know for certain the origins of Phips's slaves, Cotton Mather noted in his diary entry for 12 September 1696 – just three days after the inventorying of Phips's estate – that 'about three years ago, *Sir William Phips*, our Governour, bestowed a *Spanish Indian* for a *Servant* on myself' (Cotton Mather, *Diary*, 1:203). Also possibly a member of the household was Spencer Phips, adopted son of Sir William and Mary Spencer Phips, who was the son of Rebecca Spencer Bully and was thus the grandnephew of the accused Eleanor Bully. However, it is also possible that of his adoption occurred after the Salem outbreak.

51 Jordan, *The White Man's Burden*, 3–25; Hoffer, *The Devil's Disciples*, 115–16.

52 Deposition of John Phillips Jr, 27 July 1736, *York Deeds*, 28:184.

53 Mather, 'Pietas in Patriam,' 344.

54 Wharton to Gedney, 10 March 1688, *Massachusetts Historical Society Collections*, 6th ser., 5:11. See also Kittredge, *Witchcraft in Old and New England*, 204–13; Thomas, *Religion and the Decline of Magic*, 234–7; William R. Jones, 'Hill–Diggers and Hell–Raisers: Treasure Hunting and the Supernatural in Old and New England,' in Benes, ed., *Wonders of the Invisible World*, 97–106; Macfarlane, *Witchcraft in Tudor and Stuart England*, 14–15; Brooke, *The Refiner's Fire*, 54–5.

55 Mather, 'Pietas in Patriam,' 347. For examples of Mather's denunciations of fortune–telling, see ibid., 326; Mather, *The Bostonian Ebenezer*, 191.

56 Mather, 'Pietas in Patriam,' 348.

57 Calef, *More Wonders of the Invisible World*, 154–5.

58 Boyer and Nissenbaum, *Salem Possessed*, 213–14; Bunyan, *Pilgrim's Progress*, 300–3; Innes, *Creating the Commonwealth*, 92–3, 310; OED, 2:607. See also Bowen, *Elites, Enterprise, and the Making of the British Overseas Empire*, 65.

59 Complaint against Legg [1690], file papers of the Essex Quarterly Court and County Court, 1636–92, vol. 50, 5–11; Konig, *Law and Society in Puritan Massachusetts*, 166–7; Myrand, *Sir William Phips devant Québec*, 216–21; Savage, *Genealogical Dictionary*, 1:48.

60 Church, *History of Philip's War*, 207–9; minutes Massachusetts council, 8 July 1692, PRO, CO5/785, 183–4. See also Phips to Blathwayt, 21 July 1692, CWBP, vol. 5, folder 1.

61 Church, *The History of Philip's War*, 209–10. As these reminiscences were written down by Church's son many years after the fall of Fort William Henry, one may wonder if Church actually made such an accurate prediction in 1692.

62 Ibid., 210–15; Cotton Mather, *Magnalia Christi Americana*, 2:620; Phips to Nottingham, 15 February 1693, PRO, CO5/751, no. 19.

63 Boyer and Nissenbaum, *Salem Possessed*, 190; Weisman, *Witchcraft, Magic, and Religion*, 117–18.

64 Warrant, 25 June 1692, MA, vol. 106, 372; Foster, *The Long Argument*, 256–60.

65 Levin, *Cotton Mather*, 213–16; Hansen, *Witchcraft at Salem*, 146–9.

66 Phips to Blathwayt, 12 October 1692, pro, co5/857, no. 7; Sewall, *Diary*, 26–9 October 1692, 1:299–300.

67 Sewall, *Diary of Samuel Sewall*, 6, 22 December 1692, 1:301–2; minutes of Massachusetts council, 7 December 1692, PRO, CO5/785, 364–7; Superior Court of Judicature, Witchcraft Trials, January – May 1693, in Boyer and Nissenbaum, eds., *Salem Witchcraft Papers*, 3:903–44; Weisman, *Witchcraft, Magic, and Religion*, 168–9.

68 Phips to Nottingham, 21 February 1693, PRO, CO5/751, no. 28.

69 Increase Mather, *Cases of Conscience concerning Evil Spirits Impersonating Men*.

70 Cotton Mather, *Wonders of the Invisible World*; Hall, *The Last American Puritan*, 262–3. Wendel Craker's recent interpretation of the proceedings suggests that virtually all of those executed in 1692 did face evidence that they had used non-spectral forms of witchcraft. Regardless, 79 people were charged with witchcraft based entirely on spectral evidence, and this evidence was crucial in the conviction of others, in direct contravention of the advice of the panel of twelve clergymen. Clearly, many citizens believed that the widespread use of spectral evidence had been improper (Craker, 'Spectral Evidence,' 331–58).

71 Phips to Blathwayt, 12 October 1692, PRO, CO5/857, no. 7; Karlsen, *The Devil in the Shape of a Woman*, 41; Weisman, *Witchcraft, Magic, and Religion*, 166–73.

72 Phips to Blathwayt, 12 October 1692, PRO, CO5/857, no. 7. Phips echoed this theme in Phips to Nottingham, 21 February 1693, PRO, CO5/751, no. 28.

73 General Court minutes, 27 June–2 July 1692, PRO, CO5/785, 337–9; minutes of council, 8–25 July 1692, ibid., 183–4, 187–92; Phips to Stoughton, 1 August 1692, MA, vol. 51, 112; Church, *History of Philip's War*, 210–12; Sewall, *Diary*, 29 September 1692, 1:297.

74 See Hall, *The Last American Puritan*, 262–5; Levin, *Cotton Mather*, 218–22.

8: Frontier Governor and Projector, 1692–1694

1 Charter of Massachusetts Bay, 7 October 1691, PRO, CO5/905, 322.

2 Villebon, 'Journal of Acadia,' in Webster, ed., *Acadia at the End of the Seventeenth Century*, 47. See also C. Bruce Fergusson, in collaboration, 'La Tourasse Charles,' DCB, 1:426–7.

3 Information of Mark Emerson, enclosed in Samuel Ravenscroft to Francis Nicholson, 5 November 1691, PRO, CO5/1037, no. 67. See also Johnson, *John Nelson*, 66.

4 Villebon, 'Journal of Acadia,' in Webster, ed., *Acadia at the End of the Seventeenth Century*, 34–5; Emery LeBlanc, in collaboration, 'Robinau de Villebon, Joseph,' DCB, 1:576–8.

5 Agreement, 4 June 1691, MA, vol. 36, 108–9; Samuel Ravenscroft to Francis Nicholson, 5 November 1691, PRO, CO5/1037, no. 67; Johnson, *John Nelson*, 66–9.

6 Villebon to [Governor Bradstreet], 19 October 1691, in Webster, ed., *Acadia at the End of the Seventeenth Century*, 32; commander in chief and council of New York to William Blathwayt, 8 January 1692, PRO, CO5/1037, no. 76.

7 Villebon to Massachusetts governor and council, 10 May 1692, in Webster, ed., *Acadia at the End of the Seventeenth Century*, 39–40. See also Villebon, 'Journal of Acadia,' ibid., 37–8.

8 See W. Austin Squires, 'Maisonnat, Pierre,' DCB, 2:449–50.

9 Villebon, 'Journal of Acadia,' in Webster, ed., *Acadia at the End of the Seventeenth Century*, 40–1. On Short's seeming reluctance, on which we have only the evidence of Phips, see Phips to Nottingham, 15 February 1693, PRO, CO5/751, no. 19.

10 Phips to Blathwayt, 12 October 1692, CWBP, vol. 5, folder 1; Villebon, 'Journal of Acadia,' in Webster, ed., *Acadia at the End of the Seventeenth Century*, 44; Bernard Pothier, 'Le Moyne d'Iberville et d'Ardillières, Pierre,' DCB, 2:391. See also Phips to Nottingham, 12 October 1692, PRO, CO5/751, no. 15.

11 Villebon, 'Journal of Acadia,' in Webster, ed., *Acadia at the End of the Seventeenth Century*, 41.

12 Letter of John Nelson, 26–7 August 1692, in Hutchinson, *History of Massachusetts Bay*, 1:321–2.

13 Frontenac to the minister, 15 September 1692, AC, C11A, vol. 12, 27; d'Iberville to the minister, 16 December 1692, ibid., 110–13; relation de Champigny, 17 August 1693, ibid., 258; memoir, November 1692, AC, C11D, 2, 191–2; journal of *Poly*, 1692, ibid., 201; Mather to Nelson, 20 March 1711, in Johnson, *John Nelson*, 142–5; Clarence J. d'Entremont, 'Serreau de Saint-Aubin, Jean,' DCB, 2:604–5; Bernard Pothier, 'Le Moyne d'Iberville et d'Ardillières, Pierre,' ibid., 2:393. More generally, this paragraph draws on Johnson, *John Nelson*, 73–7. The guides' families were hostages in Boston, where they had been taken after being captured by Benjamin Church's expedition in the summer of 1692.

14 Villebon to Pontchartrain, 1694, in Webster, ed., *Acadia at the End of the Seventeenth Century*, 71.

15 Petition of Jean Martel and Abraham Boudrot, 6 May 1691, MA, vol. 37, 23. For an example of provisions shipped to Port-Royal, see Phips to Lords of Trade, 3 April 1693, PRO, CO5/857, no. 46.
16 Deposition of William Hill and Henry Francklyn, 10 September 1694, PRO, CO5/858, no. 42 (i), 8–15. On Faneuil, see Bosher, 'Huguenot Merchants and the Protestant International in the Seventeenth Century,' 80–1, 90–2. On Martel, see Bernard Pothier, 'Martel de Magos, Jean,' DCB, 2:459–60.
17 Phips to Lords of Trade, 3 April 1693, PRO, CO5/857, no. 46; Daigle, 'Nos amis les ennemis' 139–50; John G. Reid, 'Imperial Intrusions,' in Buckner and Reid, eds., The Atlantic Region to Confederation, 83. Charles Melanson's brother, Pierre, had played a part in Phips's capture of Port-Royal in 1690.
18 See Bernard Pothier, 'Martel de Magos, Jean,' DCB, 2:459–60.
19 Villebon to Pontchartrain, 1694, in Webster, ed., Acadia at the End of the Seventeenth Century, 72; Villebon to Pontchartrain, 20 August 1694, ibid., 68; 'Plan for Attack on Pemaquid, 1694,' AC, C11D, vol. 2, 220.
20 Phips to Lords of Trade, 3 April 1693, PRO, CO5/857, no. 46; Michael Perry to John Usher, 3 May 1693, MHS, Jeffries Papers, 3:76; Villebon, 'Journal of Acadia,' in Webster, ed., Acadia at the End of the Seventeenth Century, 46–7.
21 Church, The History of Philip's War, 210–15; Cotton Mather, Magnalia Christi Americana, 2:620; Phips to Nottingham, 15 February 1693, PRO, CO5/751, no. 19; Nathaniel Byfield et al. to William Blathwayt, 20 February 1693, CWBP, vol. 4, folder 4; Robert Fairfax to the Admiralty, 29 March 1693, PRO, CO5/857, no. 42.
22 Phips to Nottingham, 15 February 1693, PRO, CO5/751, no. 19; minutes of the General Assembly of Massachusetts, 17 October 1692, PRO, CO5/785, 345–6.
23 Cotton Mather, Magnalia Christi Americana, 2:619; Villebon to Pontchartrain, 20 August 1694, in Webster, ed., Acadia at the End of the Seventeenth Century, 68.
24 Phips to Nottingham, 11 September 1693, PRO, CO5/751, no. 37.
25 John Dottin to John Ive, 31 January 1693, PRO, CO5/1038, no. 2.
26 Villebon to Pontchartrain, 20 August 1694, in Webster, ed., Acadia at the End of the Seventeenth Century, 68; Bradley and Camp, The Forts of Pemaquid, 11; Robert L. Bradley, 'Colonel Wolfgang Romer,' in Biographical Dictionary of Architects in Maine, vol. 4, no. 3, 3–4.
27 Answer of House of Representatives, 16 November 1703, MA, vol. 108, 13–14.
28 Mather, 'Pietas in Patriam,' 338; Villebon to Pontchartrain, 20 August 1694, in Webster, ed., Acadia at the End of the Seventeenth Century, 67–71.
29 Cotton Mather, Magnalia Christi Americana, 2:619–20.
30 Usher to William Stoughton, 28 July 1694, PRO, CO5/924, no. 40(i).

31 For a discussion of trade goods, see Baker, 'Trouble to the Eastward,' 132–43. On the Pemaquid fur trade more generally, see DePaoli, 'Beaver, Blankets, Liquor, and Politics.'

32 Gardner to Leverett, 22 September 1675, *Documentary History of the State of Maine*, 6:91–3; letter of Kennebec Sachems, 1 July 1677, ibid., 177–9; information of Mark Emerson [5 November 1691], PRO, CO5/1037, no. 67. See also Dean R. Snow, 'Eastern Abenaki,' in Trigger, ed., *Handbook of North American Indians*, vol. 15, *Northeast*, 142–3; Morrison, 'The Bias of Colonial Law,' 373–7; Will and Cole-Will, 'Preliminary Report on the Anne Hilton Site,' 1–11; Will and Clark, 'Report on the Excavation and Analysis of the Anne Hilton Site.' For a view that rejects the notion of Native dependency on firearms, in a context of war rather than hunting, see Given, *A Most Pernicious Thing*.

33 Truce, 21 July 1693, MA, vol. 30, 333; minutes of Massachusetts council, 25–6 July 1693, PRO, CO5/785, 241–4.

34 Villebon, 'Journal of Acadia,' in Webster, ed., *Acadia at the End of the Seventeenth Century*, 42.

35 Phips to Lords of Trade, 3 April 1693, PRO, CO5/857, no. 46; Morrison, *The Embattled Northeast*, 126–27; Church, *The History of Philip's War*, 207–15.

36 Minutes of Massachusetts council, 16 February 1693, PRO, CO5/785, 217–19; resolution of House of Representatives, 6 December 1693, ma, vol. 70, 217.

37 Usher to Lords of Trade, 14 July 1693, PRO, CO5/924, no. 27. See also James Sotherne to John Povey, 22 June 1693, PRO, CO5/924, nos. 26, 26(i).

38 Chidley Brooke to Benjamin Fletcher, 2 August 1693, PRO, CO5/1038, no. 23; Sir Francis Wheeler to Phips, 8 July 1693, PRO, CO5/857, no. 68; Phips to Wheeler, 12 July 1693, ibid., no. 69; Phips to Wheeler, 27 July 1693, MA, vol. 51, 22–3.

39 Phips to Wheeler, ibid.; Villebon, 'Journal of Acadia,' in Webster, ed., *Acadia at the End of the Seventeenth Century*, 48; Villebon, to Pontchartrain, 1694, ibid., 71; Cotton Mather, *Magnalia Christi Americana*, 2:624; Addington to Blathwayt, 23 October 1693, CWBP, vol. 5, folder 3.

40 Submission and agreements of the eastern Indians, 11 August 1693, PRO, CO5/751, no. 37(i); articles signed by Sir William Phips to the eastern Indians, 11 August 1693, ibid., no. 37(iv).

41 Morrison, *The Embattled Northeast*, 128; Calloway, ed., *Dawnland Encounters*, 100–2; Phips to Nottingham, 11 September 1693, PRO, CO5/751, no. 37.

42 Mather, 'Pietas in Patriam,' 337; petition of Sir William Phips [1693], PRO, CO5/857, no. 95.

43 Original French: 'parmy ... des plus considerables' (Thury to Frontenac, 11 September 1694, in *Collection de manuscrits*, 2:161); Addington to Blathwayt, 23 October 1693, CWBP, vol. 5, folder 3.

44 For further discussion of this point, see Ghere, 'Abenaki Factionalism, Emigration, and Social Continuity,' 7–12, and 'Mistranslations and Misinformation'; Calloway, ed., *Dawnland Encounters*, 93–6, 115–18. The translators at Pemaquid in August 1693 were the English trader John Hornibrook, Ragatawanongan (known to the English as Sheepscot John), and 'Philousakis squaw.' The signature of a woman on the treaty, particularly a Wabanaki woman, is unusual indeed (Submission and agreements of the eastern Indians, 11 August 1693, PRO, CO5/751, no. 37[i]).

45 Phips to Nottingham, 18 January 1694, PRO, CO5/751, no. 40.

46 Submission and agreements of the eastern Indians, 11 August 1693, PRO, CO5/751, no. 37(i).

47 Villebon, 'Journal of Acadia,' in Webster, ed., *Acadia at the End of the Seventeenth Century*, 53–5.

48 Submission and agreements of the eastern Indians, 11 August 1693, PRO, CO5/751, no. 37(i); *Acts and Resolves of Massachusetts*, 1:172–3. On earlier trade problems, see Baker, 'Trouble to the Eastward,' 136, 144–5, 184–5.

49 See Villebon's comment on the English offering trade goods to the Wabanaki 'at the low prices current in Boston' (Villebon to Pontchartrain, 20 August 1694, in Webster, ed., *Acadia at the End of the Seventeenth Century*, 67).

50 Phips to Blathwayt, 11 September 1693, CWBP, vol. 5, folder 1. See also Murison, 'William Blathwayt's Empire,' 216.

51 Phips to Blathwayt, 3 October 1693, CWBP, vol. 5, folder 1; petition of Sir William Phips [3 October 1693], PRO, CO5/857, no. 95.

52 Phips to Nottingham, 18 January 1694, PRO, CO5/751, no. 40; Addington to Blathwayt, 26 May 1694, CWBP, vol. 5, folder 3.

53 *York Deeds*, 10:237.

54 'Account of a Journey Made by Monsieur de Villieu, 8 June 1694,' in Webster, ed., *Acadia at the End of the Seventeenth Century*, 62.

55 Deposition of John Phillips, 2 July 1736, *Documentary History of the State of Maine*, 11:149–50.

56 'Account of a Journey Made by Monsieur de Villieu, 8 June 1694,' in Webster, ed., *Acadia at the End of the Seventeenth Century*, 62; Jennings, *Invasion of America*, 128–45; Baker, 'A Scratch with a Bear's Paw,' 235–56.

57 'Account of a Journey Made by Monsieur de Villieu, 8 June 1694,' in Webster, ed., *Acadia at the End of the Seventeenth Century*, 60–3.

58 Baker, 'A Scratch With a Bear's Paw,' 252–3; Bourque, 'Ethnicity on the Maritime Peninsula,' 266–7, 270. See also Morrison, *The Embattled Northeast*, 129–32.

59 Address of council and assembly to the crown, 31 October 1694, PRO, CO5/858, no. 41.

60 Usher to Nottingham, 30 October 1693, PRO, CO5/751, no. 38; Usher to Lords of Trade, 30 October 1693, CO5/924, no. 29; Usher to Stoughton, 28 July 1694, ibid., no. 40 (i); copy of Sir William Phips's accounts [7 September 1694], ibid., no. 38; 'A Letter from New England,' 1 November 1694, PRO, CO5/858, no. 41A.

61 Original French: 'appaiser les Bastonnais qui luy ont imputé tous les dégats qu'ils [the Wabanaki] ont faicts sur eulx, parce qu'ayant assuré tout le monde que la paix qu'il avoit faicte avecq les sauvages estoit véritable, personne ne se tenoit plus sur ses gardes' (Thury to Frontenac, 11 September 1694, *Collection de manuscrits*, 2:161); minutes of Massachusetts council, 2 August 1694, PRO, CO5/785, 263; declaration of Phips to eastern sachems, 8 August 1694, MA, vol. 30, 351–1a; Phips to Trenchard, 18 September 1694, PRO, CO5/751, no. 44.

62 Names of harbours and places suitable for townships, 10 November 1691, PRO, CO5/856, no. 203. Although the words are somewhat different, there can be little doubt that they represent the same place. Phips lists the locations from west to east, placing Puttdumquoar west of the next location, the Penobscot. Matonquoog is specifically the name of an island at the mouth of the St John. The location appears in the Madockawando to Phips deed (*York Deeds* 10:237; Eckstorm, *Indian Place Names of the Penobscot Valley and the Maine Coast*, 87–8.

63 *York Deeds*, 10: 236, 240. Since the heirs of the late Governor John Leverett included his sons-in-law Elisha Cooke, Paul Dudley, and James Lloyd (all actual or former political opponents of Sir William Phips) the possibility exists that political leverage may have been one of Phips's contributing motives for the purchase. See Savage, *Genealogical Dictionary*, 3:83.

64 *Suffolk Deeds* 9:241; *York Deeds* 17:191.

65 Proceedings on the petition of Sir William Phips et al., 13 August 1691, PRO, SP44/235, 170; *York Deeds*, 1:157–8; ibid., 8:221. John Alden was the same man who traded on the Acadian coast during the 1680s and 1690s; see Charles Bruce Fergusson, 'Alden, John,' DCB, 2:14–15.

66 Record of town meeting, 9 September 1672, in Dexter, ed., *New Haven Town Records*, 306; Baker, *Clarke & Lake Company*, 6–7; Noyes, Libby, and Davis, eds., *Genealogical Dictionary of Maine and New Hampshire*, 408; Savage, *Genealogical Dictionary*, 2:127; Dickson, *Financial Revolution in England*, 252, 343–4, 491.

67 George Turfrey to William Blathwayt, 15 March 1687, CWBP, vol. V, folder 4; Noyes, Libby, and Davis, eds., *Genealogical Dictionary of Maine and New Hampshire*, 699; Varney, *Gazetteer of the State of Maine*, 65; proposals Made by Sir Mathew Dudley et al., 27 January 1694, PRO, CO5/858, no. 12.

68 Phips to Lords of Trade [2 September 1691], PRO, CO5/856, no. 184; Phips to Lords of Trade, 3 April 1693, PRO, CO5/857, no. 46.

69 Sir Henry Ashurst and Sir Steven Evance to Lords of Trade and Plantations, 26 March 1694, PRO, CO323/1, no. 83; 'Reasons why Sir Matthew Dudley et al. should not be delayed' [March 1694], ibid., no. 84; journal of Board of Trade, 24 July 1696, PRO, CO391/9, 22–4; Johnson, *Adjustment to Empire*, 255.

9: Factional Currents, 1692–1694

1 Cotton Mather, 'Political Fables,' in *Andros Tracts*, 2:325–6.

2 Ibid., 327–8.

3 Increase Mather, 'A Brief Account concerning Several of the Agents of New-England,' in *Andros Tracts*, 2:286–95.

4 Phips to Blathwayt, 27 February 1693, CWBP, vol. 5, folder 1; Johnson, *Adjustment to Empire*, 281.

5 Cotton Mather, *Diary*, 1:148.

6 Johnson, *Adjustment to Empire*, 388–9, 640–1; R.C. Simmons, 'The Massachusetts Charter of 1691,' in Allen and Thompson, eds., *Contrast and Connection*, 80–1.

7 Sewall, *Diary*, 4 May 1692, 1:291; General Court minutes, 4 May 1692, MA, General Court records, 6:214.

8 Joshua Broadbent to Francis Nicholson, 21 June 1692, PRO, CO5/1037, no. 112; proclamation, 18 June 1692, *Acts and Resolves of Massachusetts*, 7:9; Mather to Nottingham, PRO, CO5/751, no. 7.

9 Broadbent to Nicholson, 21 June 1692, PRO, CO5/1037, no. 112; John Pynchon to Isaac Addington, 20 May 1692, MA, vol. 51, 1; 'Humble Address' [9 April 1691], PRO, CO5/856, no. 143(i).

10 *Acts and Resolves of Massachusetts*, 1:27, 99–100; Johnson, *Adjustment to Empire*, 276.

11 *Acts and Resolves of Massachusetts*, 1: 90.

12 Ibid., 1:41–2.

13 Ibid., 1:40–1, 94–9.

14 Ibid., 1:37, 63–4, 74–5.

15 Ibid., 1:34–5, 38–9.

16 Sewall, *Diary*, 6 December 1692, 1:301–2.

17 *Acts and Resolves of Massachusetts*, 1:51–3, 56–7, 65–7, 72–6; charter, 7 October 1691, PRO, CO5/905, 328, 337. See also Konig, *Law and Society in Puritan Massachusetts*, 158–65.

18 Phips to Blathwayt, 20 February 1693, CWBP, vol. 5, folder 1.

19 Charter, 7 October 1691, PRO, CO5/905, 343–4; minute of Lords of Trade, 4 June 1695, PRO, CO5/906, 187–94; Palfrey, *History of New England*, 4:160–2.

20 Addington to Blathwayt, 21 February 1693, CWBP, vol. 5, folder 3.

21 Breen, *Character of a the Good Ruler*, 180; Pencak, *War, Politics, and Revolution in Provincial Massachusetts*, 21.

22 *Acts and Resolves of Massachusetts*, 1:109; Phips to Lords of Trade, 3 April 1693, PRO, CO5/857, no. 46; petition [3 April 1693], ibid., no. 47; minutes of Massachusetts council, 29 June 1693, PRO, CO5/785, 240–1. Ironically, the salary question faced by Governor Thomas Hutchinson in 1772 centred on the claim of the House of Representatives to pay the governor's salary as a means of preventing him from becoming unduly independent. See Bailyn, *The Ordeal of Thomas Hutchinson*, 202–3.

23 *Acts and Resolves of Massachusetts*, 1:174, 188. On eighteenth-century controversies over this issue, see Labaree, *Royal Instructions to British Colonial Governors*, 1:256–65, and Bushman, *King and People in Provincial Massachusetts*, 118–20.

24 Phips to Blathwayt, 27 February 1693, CWBP, vol. 5, folder 1.

25 Suffolk County Probate File, no. 2245; Goold, 'Sir William Phips,' 65–7.

26 Olson, *Making the Empire Work*, 79; Nash, *The Urban Crucible*, 399.

27 Diary of Increase Mather, 11 January 1693, 30 June 1693, 9 and 11 November 1693; AAS; Sewall, *Diary*, 19 November 1692, 23 June 1693, 15 November 1694, 1:300–1, 311, 323. Sewall had been entertained at the house at least once before Phips became governor, and he also visited the house for a council meeting in November 1694. For the estate inventory, see Goold, 'Sir William Phips,' 65–7, and Suffolk County Probate File, no. 2245.

28 *Acts and Resolves of Massachusetts*, 1:88–90; Shurtleff, ed., *Records of the Governor and Company of Massachusetts Bay*, vol. 5 passim.

29 *Acts and Resolves of Massachusetts*, 7:5–8.

30 Ibid., 1:88.

31 Ibid., 7:5–8, 19–21.

32 Foster, *The Long Argument*, 256–66; Willard, *The Character of a Good Ruler*.

33 Stoughton to Blathwayt, 24 October 1693, CWBP, vol. 5, folder 4.

34 Ashurst to Mather, 18 October 1692, BODL, Ashurst Papers, Letterbook of Sir Henry Ashurst, 84.

35 Ashurst to Stoughton, 22 October 1692, ibid.

36 Ashurst to Dudley and Allin, 9 April 1684, ibid., 33; Ashurst to Stoughton, 24 July 1684, ibid., 34. By 1695 Ashurst and Dudley would again be opponents, so much so that Ashurst would work effectively to keep Dudley from obtaining the governorship. See Kimball, *Public Life of Joseph Dudley*, 67–8.

37 Ashurst to John Evance, 26 December 1692, BODL, Ashurst Papers, Letterbook of Sir Henry Ashurst, 86.

38 Sewall, *Diary*, 28–9 October 1692, 15 November, 1:299–300. For Shrimpton, see Bailyn, *New England Merchants in the Seventeenth Century*, 192–3; Foster, *The Long Argument*, 367.

39 Increase Mather, *The Great Blessing of Primitive Counsellours*, 19; Diary of Increase Mather, 31 May 1693, AAS. See also Michael Hall, *The Last American Puritan*, 266.

40 *Acts and Resolves of Massachusetts*, 7:19–21; Haffenden, *New England in the English Nation*, 180; Lewis, 'Massachusetts and the Glorious Revolution,' 435–6; petition of Inhabitants of Boston and adjacent places, 25 January 1690, PRO, CO5/855, no. 56; petition of Boston members of the Church of England [January 1690], ibid., no. 58; petition of Charlestown inhabitants [January 1690], ibid., no. 59; 'Humble Address' [9 April 1691], PRO, CO5/856, no. 143(i). On the close ties within the merchant community, see Bailyn, *New England Merchants*, 135–8; Lewis, 'Massachusetts and the Glorious Revolution,' 413–40. On Byfield and his origins, see Black, 'Nathaniel Byfield, 1653–1733,' 57–105. The Short and Brenton affairs are more fully discussed in, respectively, chapters 10 and 11 below.

41 Captain Floyd to governor and council, 27 January 1692, *Documentary History of the State of Maine*, 5:314; Sewall, *Diary*, 31 May 1693, 1:309; Bodge, *Soldiers in King Philip's War*, 158.

42 Sewall, *Diary*, 31 May 1693, 1:309.

43 Council minutes, 1 June 1693, PRO, CO5/785, 396; Sewall, *Diary*, 1, 8 June 1693, 1:309–10.

44 Phips to Blathwayt, 12 October 1692, 27 February 1693, CWBP, vol. 5, folder 1. See also Phips to Nottingham, 12 October 1692, PRO, CO5/751, no. 15; Phips to Lords of Trade, 3 April 1693, PRO, CO5/857, no. 46.

45 Council minutes, 2 June 1693, PRO, CO5/785, 397; Sewall, *Diary*, 2 June 1693, 1:309.

46 Ibid., 3 June 1693, 1:309.

47 Resolution, 7 June 1693, MA, vol. 100, 435.

48 Dudley to Blathwayt, 25 February 1693, CWBP, vol. 4, folder 5; Blathwayt to Dudley, 26 February 1693, ibid.

49 Sewall, *Diary*, 8 June 1693, 1:310.

50 Diary of Increase Mather, 30 June 1693, AAS; Sewall, *Diary*, 11, 15 July 1693, 1:311; bill, 8 July 1693, MA, vol. 100, 443; resolution, 14 July 1693, ibid., 448; minutes of council, 14, 15 July 1693, PRO, CO5/785, 415–16.

51 Address, 16 November 1693, MA, General Court records, 6:305–7.

52 Minute of House of Representatives, 21 November 1693, PRO, CO5/857, no. 86.

53 Ibid.; Sewall, *Diary*, 21 November 1693, 1:314; minutes of General Court, 21–2 November 1693, MA, General Court Records, 6:309–10.

54 *Acts and Resolves of Massachusetts*, 1:147; Sewall, *Diary*, 25, 28 November 1693, 1:314–15; protest, 25 November 1693, MA, vol. 48, 224. Thomas Dudley was not a member of this assembly, although the pro-Dudley group was strengthened by the return of Giles Dyer to represent Little Compton, whose name also appeared on the protest (*Acts and Resolves of Massachusetts*, 7:29–30).

55 Resolution, 6 December 1693, MA, vol. 70, 217.

56 Exceptions to accounts of John Phillips, 22 November 1693, MA, vol. 100, 464; answers of Phillips, n.d., ibid., 465; council minutes, 12, 16 December 1693, MA, General Court records, 6:325–6; Dudley to Blathwayt, 5 December 1693 [*sic*, though the General Court had not yet adjourned by this date], CWBP, vol. 4, folder 5. On the voyage of the *Mary* to Beaubassin, see Michael Perry to John Usher, 3 May 1693, MHS, Jeffries Papers, 3:76.

57 Council minutes, 13, 16 December 1693, 3 March 1694, MA, General Court records, 6:325–6, 337; report, 21 February 1694, MA, vol. 100, 471–2.

58 Council minutes, 30 May 1694, PRO, CO5/785, 422.

59 [Byfield] to Dudley, 12 June 1694, PRO, CO5/858, no. 31.

60 Ibid. For Legge's role in the Canada expedition, see minutes of General Court, 7 June 1690, MA, General Court records, 6:139, and Myrand, *Sir William Phips devant Québec*, 224.

61 'A Letter from New England,' 1 November 1694, PRO, CO5/858, no. 41A. Although anonymous, this pamphlet was either written or heavily influenced by Byfield.

62 On the episode of 1642, see Fletcher, *Outbreak of the English Civil War*, 179–84.

63 Willard, *Character of a Good Ruler*.

64 [Byfield] to Dudley, 12 June 1694, PRO, CO5/858, no. 31; Byfield to Usher, 12 July 1694, ibid., no. 35.

65 Council minutes, 30, 31 May, 2 June 1694, PRO, CO5/785, 423–6.

66 *Acts and Resolves of Massachusetts*, 1:170; council minutes, 7, 8 June 1694, PRO, CO5/785, 429–31.

67 *Acts and Resolves of Massachusetts*, 7:49; council minutes, 19 June 1694, PRO, CO5/785, 438–9.

68 *Acts and Resolves of Massachusetts*, 1:172–3; council minutes, 13, 14 June 1694, PRO, CO5/785, 433–5.

69 Sir William Phips's speech, 14 September 1694, HLBP, BL 245.

70 Mather, 'Pietas in Patriam,' 323–4; 'A Letter from New England,' 1 November 1694, PRO, CO5/858, no. 41A.

71 Address of council and assembly, 31 October 1694, ibid., no. 41.

72 Stoughton to Blathwayt, 14 November 1694, CWBP, vol. 5, folder 4; Chidley Brooke to Benjamin Fletcher, 2 August 1693, PRO, CO5/1038, no. 23.

73 Mather, 'Pietas in Patriam,' 340; *York Deeds*, 10:237; Deposition of John Fos-

ter, 22 August 1694, PRO, CO5/858, no. 42 (i), 33; Sewall, *Diary*, 9 November 1694, 1:323.

74 Increase Mather to Blathwayt, 6 July 1694, CWBP, vol. 5, folder 6; Sir William Phips's speech, 14 September 1694, HLBP, BL 245.

75 Villebon to Pontchartrain, 1694, in Webster, *Acadia at the End of the Seventeenth Century*, 74; Sewall, *Diary*, 5 May 1695, 1:321. On the crowd actions of 1690, see chapters 4 and 5 above. For documents witnessed by Gouverneur, see *York Deeds*, 10:237; Essex County Courthouse, Essex Deeds, 8:51.

76 Suffolk Deeds, 15:1, 51, 211–12, 16:111, 242, and 17:221–4. Details of the arson case involving the Creeks are in MA, vol. 112, 280–310.

10: Imperial Governorship: Conflicts and Clientage, 1692–1693

1 Randolph to Blathwayt, 27 September 1692, CWBP, vol. 2, folder 3.

2 See Dickerson, *American Colonial Government*, 154–7; Labaree, *Royal Government in America*, 123–6; Leamon, 'Governor Fletcher's Recall,' 533–7; Olson, *Making the Empire Work*, 76–80; Steele, *Politics of Colonial Policy*, 49–50.

3 John Higginson to John How, 1 August 1694, in Moody, ed., *Saltonstall Papers*, 1:214.

4 Proposal of Sir William Phips [30 June 1691], PRO, CO5/856, no. 171; memorial of Sir William Phips, 21 September 1691, ibid., no. 196; petition of Sir William Phips, ibid., no. 197.

5 Phips to Blathwayt, 12 October 1692, CWBP, vol. 5, folder 1; Phips to Nottingham, 12 October 1692, PRO, CO5/751, no. 15.

6 Phips to Blathwayt, 12 October 1692, CWBP, vol. 5, folder 1; Blathwayt to Phips, 20 February 1693, ibid.; Blathwayt to Increase Mather, 20 February, ibid., folder 6.

7 Original French: 'Cecy se prouve premierement par le retour du sieur Phips a Baston dont le prince D'Orange la fait Gouverneur et luy a donné deux ou trois vaisseaux de guerre et des soldats pour grossir sa flotte, il a protesté vouloir reparer lhonneur des Anglois et de retirer au peril de sa Vie, l'ancre et les cinq canons qu'il laissa devant Kebec, lors qu'il en leva le siege'; 'de se rendre maitres par la prise de ce poste de toutes l'Amerique septentrionale, des Pesches des Pelleteries et de l'interieur des terres'; 'Phips est toujours dans le dessein de faire ses efforts pour nous venir revoir l'année proschaine, ce qui m'obligera a prendre toutes les precautions que je pourray pour le bien recevoir' (Mémoire des R[évérends] P[ères], [1692], AC, C11A, vol. 12, 133; Frontenac to the minister, 15 September 1692, ibid., 27).

8 Phips to Nottingham, 20 February 1693, PRO, CO5/751, no. 24; Court of Admiralty proceedings, 3 October 1692, PRO, CO5/858, no. 42(i), 47–9.

9 Warrant, 21 June 1692, PRO, CO5/858, no. 42(i), 50; complaint of Peter Wood-
   bery, 4 July 1692, PRO, CO5/751, no. 8; complaint of John Tomson, 4 July 1692,
   ibid., no. 12.
10 Nathaniel Byfield et al. to Blathwayt, 20 February 1693, CWBP, vol. 4, folder 4;
   Phips to Nottingham, 20 February 1693, PRO, CO5/751, no. 24.
11 Deposition of Timothy Clarke, 31 August 1694, PRO, CO5/858, no. 42(i), 54–5;
   deposition of Nathaniel Oliver, 22 August 1694, ibid., 56; deposition of
   Andrew Belcher, 4 September 1694, ibid., 57; Deposition of William N.
   Snowton, 17 August 1694, ibid., 52. On the related impressment of guns, see
   Deposition of Edward Sinkler, 4 September 1694, ibid., 53. See also Bailyn,
   New England Merchants, 195–7.
12 Randolph to Blathwayt, 27 September 1692, CWBP, vol. 2, folder 3; Hall,
   Edward Randolph and the American Colonies, 138–42.
13 Petition of Salem merchants, n.d., MA, vol. 70, 194; petition of eleven subjects,
   n.d., MA, vol. 100, 416; petition of seven subjects [14 July 1693], ibid., 452. On
   the relationship of governors with commercial interests in this period, see
   Olson, *Making the Empire Work*, 41–2, 76–81.
14 Short to James Sotherne, 20 April 1693, PRO, CO5/857, no. 54; Fletcher to Nottingham, 8 March 1693, PRO, CO5/1082, no. 31. On Phips's presence at the
   Exchange tavern, see deposition of Nathaniel Byfield [1694], MA, vol. 61, 474.
15 Minute of New York council, 12 August 1692, MA, vol. 2, 385a; Richard
   Ingoldesby to Mayhew, 18 August 1692, ibid., 386; Baines Coffin and William Worth to Capt. Gardner, 13 October 1692, ibid., 386b; Phips to Fletcher,
   26 October 1692, ibid., 387; minutes of Massachusetts council, 1 November
   1692, PRO, CO5/785, 198.
16 Minutes of New York council, 16 January, 13 February 1693, PRO, CO5/1183,
   367, 373; Fletcher to [Blathwayt], 14 February 1693, PRO, CO5/1038, no. 6;
   Phips to Nottingham, 20 February 1693, PRO, CO5/751, no. 21. See also
   Fletcher to Nottingham, 14 February 1693, PRO, CO5/1082, no. 27; Phips to
   Blathwayt, 20 February 1693, CWBP, vol. 5, folder 1. For examples of continuing developments over Martha's Vineyard and Nantucket, see the actions of
   the Massachusetts General Court in June 1693 to validate land titles and
   facilitate tax collection (minutes of General Court, 12–17 June 1693, PRO,
   CO5/785, 402–8).
17 Phips to Nottingham, 20 February 1693, PRO, CO5/751, no. 23; governor and
   company of Rhode Island to the king and queen, 2 August 1692, PRO, CO5/
   857, no. 73 (ii); governor and company of Rhode Island to the king, 22
   November 1692, ibid., no. 73(iii); credentials of Christopher Almy, 22
   November 1692, ibid., no. 73 (iv); letter from Boston [24 March 1693], ibid.,
   no. 41; minutes of New York council, 11 May 1693, PRO, CO5/1183, 422. On

factional disputes centring on the Narragansett country, see Daniels, *Dissent and Conformity on Narragansett Bay*, 26–30, and Bailyn, *New England Merchants*, 171–2.

18 Daniel Wilcok, Henry Head, and David Lake to governor and council of Rhode Island, 26 October 1692, MA, vol. 2, 60; Easton to [Phips], 26 October 1692, ibid., 61; Easton to [Phips], 9 November 1692, ibid., 61a; Phips to governor and council of Rhode Island, 28 November 1692, ibid., 62; letter of Easton et al., 3 December 1692, ibid., 62a. On the background to this dispute, see Demos, *A Little Commonwealth*, 11; Daniels, *Dissent and Conformity on Narragansett Bay*, 41–5; Langdon, *Pilgrim Colony*, 226–34, 245.

19 Samuel Gookin to Phips, 3 December 1692, ibid., 63; John Walley to Phips, 4 December 1692, ibid., 64; [Isaac Addington] to Gookin, 8 December 1692, ibid., 65; Walley to Addington, 15 December 1692, ibid., 68a; 'Petition of Sundrey Inhabitants of Little Compton,' 27 February 1693, ibid., 69; minutes of Massachusetts council, 2, 11, 26 November, 6, 8 December 1692, PRO, CO5/785, 198–9, 201, 203–8; minutes of General Court, 11 February, 13 March 1693, ibid., 376–7, 385; Phips to Blathwayt, CWBP, vol. 5, folder 1. On the political state of Rhode Island and the political significance of Bristol County, see Johnson, *Adjustment to Empire*, 287–8, 298–301; Black, 'Nathaniel Byfield, 1653–1733,' 70.

20 Commission of Samuel Allen, 1 March 1693, PRO, CO5/940, 193; see also Johnson, *Adjustment to Empire*, 217–20.

21 Usher to Phips, 15 October 1692, with endorsements, PRO, CO5/857, no. 8; Phips to Usher, 18 October 1692, PRO, CO5/924, no. 18(i); Phips to Blathwayt, 12 October 1692, CWBP, vol. 5, folder 1.

22 See Usher to Lords of Trade, 31 January 1693, PRO, CO5/924, no. 19; Usher to Nottingham, 31 January 1693, PRO, CO5/751, no. 18.

23 Usher to Lords of Trade, 31 January 1693, PRO, CO5/924, no. 19; Phips to Usher, 14 March 1693, and reply, 18 March 1693, PRO, CO5/857, no. 39; Usher to Lords of Trade, 11 April 1693, PRO, CO5/924, no. 23.

24 Isaac Addington to governor and council of Connecticut, 30 July 1692, MA, vol. 2, 211; Phips to governor and council of Connecticut, 24 February 1693, ibid., 212; Addington to John Pynchon et al., 24 February 1693, MA, vol. 51, 15–16; Pynchon to Phips, 8 March 1693, ibid., 17–18; John Allyn to Phips, 24 May 1693, MA, vol. 2, 214; [Addington to governor and council of Connecticut], 1 March 1694, ibid., 215–15a. See also Melvoin, *New England Outpost*, 196–7.

25 Blathwayt to Fletcher, 26 February 1693, CWBP, vol. 8, folder 3; commission to Fletcher, 1 May 1693, PRO, CO5/1114, 29–32; Leamon, 'Governor Fletcher's Recall,' 528.

26 Benjamin Fletcher to Nottingham, 14 February 1693, PRO, CO5/1082, no. 27; Fletcher to [Blathwayt], 8 March 1693, PRO, CO5/1038, no. 7; Jennings, *The Ambiguous Iroquois Empire*, 203–4.

27 Phips to Fletcher, 13 July 1693, MA, vol. 30, 330a; Phips to Fletcher, 24 August 1693, ibid., 342.

28 Fletcher to Phips, 31 August 1693, PRO, CO5/1038, no. 30(i).

29 Abraham Gouverneur to his parents, 12 October 1692, PRO, CO5/1037, no. 133. See also Kammen, *Colonial New York*, 140–1.

30 Minutes of New York council, 5 January 1693, PRO, CO5/1183, 364; Fletcher to Phips, 6 January 1693, PRO, CO5/751, no. 18(i); Fletcher to Dudley, 7 January 1693, PRO, CO5/1038, no. 1.

31 Messenger's account [January 1693], PRO, CO5/751, no. 18(i).

32 Phips to Fletcher, 27 January 1693, ibid., no. 18(iii); Gouverneur to Fletcher, 20 January 1693, ibid., no. 17. For later references to Gouverneur in Phips's company, see deposition of Abraham Gouverneur, 4 September 1694, PRO, CO5/858, no. 42(i), 76; *York Deeds*, 10:237.

33 Phips to Nottingham, 20 February 1693, ibid., no. 21; Phips to Blathwayt, 20 February 1693, CWBP, vol. 5, folder 1; Fletcher to [Blathwayt], 14 February 1693, PRO, CO5/1038, no. 6; Fletcher to Nottingham, 14 February 1693, PRO, CO5/1082, no. 27; Usher to Nottingham, 31 January 1693, PRO, CO5/751, no. 18; Dudley to Blathwayt, 25 February 1693, CWBP, vol. 4, folder 5; Graham to Blathwayt, 8 February 1693, CWBP, vol. 10, folder 6; Van Cortlandt to Blathwayt, 6 March 1693, CWBP, vol. 9, folder 2. Both Dudley and Graham indicated that Phips intended to send Gouverneur to England to plead the Leislerians' case, in company with William Milborne and one James Barry. What substance this suggestion had is unclear, especially as Phips had issued a warrant for Milborne's arrest in the preceding June, in the context of the Salem trials, for circulating 'a Scandalous and Seditious paper' regarding the government of Massachusetts (warrant, 25 June 1692, MA, vol. 106, 372).

34 Deposition of Joseph Short [25 March 1693], ibid., no. 57 (i); Phips to Nottingham, 15 February 1693, PRO, CO5/751, no. 19.

35 Deposition of John March and Nathaniel Hatch, 4 January 1693, PRO, CO5/857, no. 18; letter from Boston [24 March 1693], ibid., no. 41; Short to the Admiralty, 24 April 1693, ibid., no. 57; Fairfax to the Admiralty, 29 March 1693, ibid., no. 42; warrant, 4 January 1693, PRO, CO5/858, no. 10(iii). Short, in his letter of 24 April, attributed the weakness of his right hand to an injury some nine months earlier.

36 Order of Phips, 16 September 1692, with statement of Benjamin Jackson, 15 November 1694, MA, vol. 61, 331–2; Phips to Nottingham, 15 February 1693, PRO, CO5/751, no. 19.

37 Fairfax to the Admiralty, 29 March 1693, PRO, CO5/857, no. 42; Short to the Admiralty [March 1692], ibid., no. 44.

38 Deposition of Benjamin Jackson, 18 January 1694, PRO, CO5/858, no. 10(xvi); deposition of Henry Short, 17 August 1694, ibid., no. 42(i), 84; copy of Sir William Phips's accounts [7 September 1694], PRO, CO5/924, no. 38. See also Nathaniel Byfield to Joseph Dudley, 12 June 1694, PRO, CO5/858, no. 31.

39 Deposition of Jackson, 18 January 1694, ibid., no. 10(xvi); letter from Boston [24 March 1693], PRO, CO5/857, no. 41; Fairfax to the Admiralty, 29 March 1693, ibid., no. 42. On the contemporary sense of 'bigot' as one obstinately or unreasonably attached to another person, see OED, 2:185.

40 Deposition of Thomas Dobbins, 4 September 1694, PRO, CO5/858, no. 42(i), 82.

41 Deposition of John Halsey, 25 April 1693, PRO, CO5/858, no. 10(vi); deposition of David Thomas, 25 April 1693, ibid., no. 10(vii). Sir William's sister Margaret was married at this time to a Halsey. His full name is unknown, but Halsey was such an unusual surname in Boston and in New England as a whole that all of that name were probably related. Margaret and her two daughters were particularly close to Lady Phips, who remembered them in her will (Noyes, Libby, and Davis, *Genealogical Dictionary of Maine and New Hampshire*, 302, 550; will of Dame Mary Sergeant, 19 February 1705, Suffolk County Probate Files).

42 Deposition of Benjamin Eames, 17 August 1694, PRO, CO5/858, no. 42(i), 85–6; Nathaniel Byfield et al. to Blathwayt, CWBP, vol. 4, folder 4.

43 Graves, *A Memorial or Short Account*, 7–8. On the location of Tortuga Salada (referred to by English contemporaries, with numerous variants, as 'Salt Tertudos') off the coast of the modern Venezuela, see Newton, *Colonising Activities of the English Puritans*, 225, and Pares, *War and Trade in the West Indies*, 276–7. Salt was also harvested from the Turks Islands (Craton, *History of the Bahamas*, 94–5). On the duration of the voyage and the cargo, see deposition of Benjamin Eames, 17 August 1694, PRO, CO5/858, no. 42(i), 85–6; deposition of William Hill and Henry Francklyn, 10 September 1694, ibid., 10. See also Mather, 'Pietas in Patriam,' 352. Brazilletta was a form of dye-wood.

44 Receipt, 9 June 1693, PRO, CO5/858, no. 42(i), 86; deposition of Francis Foxcroft, 10 September 1694, ibid., 87; Byfield et al. to Blathwayt, 20 February 1693, CWBP, vol. 4, folder 4.

45 Deposition of John March, 17 September 1694, PRO, CO5/858, no. 42(i), 66; deposition of Robert Smith, 4 September 1694, ibid., 67.

46 Fairfax to the Admiralty, 29 March 1693, PRO, CO5/857, no. 42; letter from Boston [24 March 1693], PRO, CO5/857, no. 41. The acute class sensibilities of, for example, Villebon led him to describe Short as 'merely a sailor,' while

Fairfax was 'a gentleman of quality' (Villebon, 'Journal of Acadia,' 4 July
1692, in Webster, ed., *Acadia at the End of the Seventeenth Century*, 40; Villebon
to Pontchartrain, 1694, ibid., 74). On the practice of hiring out seamen, and
more general consideration of sources of personal profit for naval captains,
see Davies, *Gentlemen and Tarpaulins*, 50–2, and Haffenden, *New England in
the English Nation, 1689–1713*, 98.

47 Byfield et al. to Blathwayt, 20 February 1693, CWBP, vol. 4, folder 4; warrant,
21 January 1693, PRO, CO5/857, no. 20.
48 Warrant, 1 March 1693, PRO, CO5/858, no. 42(i), 63; deposition of Alexander
Mitchell, 4 September 1694, ibid., 75; order of Phips to militia officers, 26 July
1692, with endorsement, PRO, CO5/857, no. 4. Byfield and Mico had also been
the previous tenants of a Boston warehouse bought by Phips from Benjamin
Davis in 1690 (deed [extract], 13 June 1690, MHS, Jeffries Papers, vol. 5, 13).
49 Deposition of Nathaniel Byfield [1694], MA, vol. 61, 474; Deposition of Alexander Mitchell and John Raines, 24 March 1693, PRO, CO5/858, no. 10(xviii);
warrant, 6 March 1693, MHS, Miscellaneous Bound Manuscripts, 1689–94.
50 Deposition of Byfield [1694], MA, vol. 61, 474; Byfield to Usher, 13 March
1693, MHS, Jeffries Papers, vol. 3, 81; Deposition of Jeremiah Tay, 22 August
1694, PRO, CO5/858, no. 42 (i), 71; deposition of William Goddard, 4 September 1694, ibid., 72.
51 Phips to Nottingham, 6 April 1693, PRO, CO5/751, no. 34; Usher to Lords of
Trade, 11 April 1693, PRO, CO5/924, no. 23; Thomas Davis to Usher, 31 March
1693, ibid., no. 23(vii); Short to the Admiralty, 24 April 1693, PRO, CO5/857,
no. 57; Short to Sotherne, 22 June 1693, ibid., no. 67.
52 Short to Sotherne, ibid.; deposition of Ralph Carter, 11 October 1694, PRO,
CO5/858, no. 42 (i), 89; service record of Richard Short, PRO, ADM6/424. Charnock, *Biographia Navalis*, 2:403, and NMM, 'Pitcairn-Jones Sea Officers' List,
1660–1815,' 835, contain contradictory accounts of Short's later career. Charnock has his naval career ending with his quitting the *Nonsuch* and his death
in 1702, while Pitcairn-Jones had him serving on three more vessels, including one beyond that date. Either is possible, though Pitcairn-Jones, who
incorrectly attributed Short's service in 1678 to another officer of the same
name, may also have been inaccurate for the later years.
53 Phips to Nottingham, 15 February 1693, PRO, CO5/751, no. 19; Short to Admiralty, 24 April 1693, PRO, CO5/857, no. 57; Dobbins to Sotherne, 27 February
1693, PRO, CO5/857, no. 30; Hore to Sotherne, 4 April 1693, ibid., no. 48;
Naval List, 1 December 1693, PRO, ADM8/3; deposition of Thomas Dobbins, 4
September 1694, PRO, CO5/858, no. 42(i), 82.
54 Phips to the Lords of Trade, 3 April 1693, PRO, CO5/857, no. 46; Phips to the
Admiralty, ibid., no. 49; Povey to Sotherne, 12 June 1693, PRO, CO5/905, 435–

6; probate inventory of Sir William Phips, 9 September 1696, Suffolk County Probate Files.

55 Nottingham to Blathwayt, 17 June 1692, bl, Add. mss, vol. 37,991, 96. For fuller discussion of the expedition, its origins, and the strategic background, see Webb, 'William Blathwayt, Imperial Fixer: Muddling Through to Empire,' 383–94; Murison, 'William Blathwayt's Empire,' 128–30; and J.R. Jones, 'Limitations of British Sea Power in the French Wars, 1689–1815,' in Black and Woodfine, eds., *The British Navy and the Use of Naval Power in the Eighteenth Century*, 44–5.

56 Sewall, *Diary*, 13, 23 June 1693, 1:310–11; Blathwayt to Nottingham, 31 July 1692, BL, Add. mss, vol. 37,991, 123; Webb, 'William Blathwayt, Imperial Fixer: Muddling Through to Empire,' 392–3; Guttridge, *The Colonial Policy of William III in America and the West Indies*, 65–8. On the epidemic, see Mather, *Magnalia Christi Americana*, ed. Murdock, 426; Steele, *The English Atlantic*, 257–8.

57 Blathwayt to Nottingham, 31 July 1692, BL, Add. mss, vol. 37,991, 123; Lords of the Treasury to Phips, 20 September 1692, pro, co5/905, 437–8; Phips to Lords of the Treasury, 20 March 1693, pro, co5/857, no. 40.

58 King to Phips, 2 February 1693, pro, co5/905, 454–8; Blathwayt to Phips, 20 February 1693, cwbp, vol. 5, folder 1; Nottingham to Blathwayt, 7 April 1693, nmm, Southwell Papers, sou/14; Blathwayt to Nottingham, 14 April 1693, bl, Add. mss, vol. 37,992, 4–5; Blathwayt to Nottingham, 12 June 1693, ibid., 13; Phips to Lords of Trade, 25 September 1693, pro, co5/857, no. 82.

59 Letter from Boston [24 March 1693], pro, co5/857, no. 41; 'Relation de ce qui s'est passé en Canada depuis le mois de Septembre 1692 jusques au départ des Vaisseaux en 1693,' ac, c11a, vol. 12, 199; minutes of New York council, 17 July 1693, pro, co5/1183, 439–41.

60 Wheeler to Phips, 8 July 1693, pro, co5/857, no. 68; minutes of General Court, 11–12 July 1693, pro, co5/785, 412–13; Phips to Wheeler, 12 July 1693, pro, co5/857, no. 69; Phips to Wheeler, 27 July 1693, ibid., no. 72.

61 Nottingham to Blathwayt, 17 October 1693, nmm, Southwell Papers, sou/14; Frontenac and Champigny to the minister, 5 November 1694, ac, c11a, vol. 13, 4.

62 Phips to Blathwayt, 26 September 1693, cwbp, vol. 5, folder 1 (emphasis added); Phips to Nottingham, 11 September 1693, pro, co5/751, no. 37. See also Phips to Lords of Trade, 25 September 1693, pro, co5/857, no. 82; Phips to the king, 30 September 1693, cwbp, vol. 5, folder 1.

63 Van Cortlandt to Blathwayt, 18 August 1693, cwbp, vol. 9, folder 2; Fletcher to Nottingham, 5 October 1693, pro, co5/1082, no. 36. A decision had been taken in London in mid-July to recall Wheeler and his fleet, although it was

clearly too late to affect decisions already being made in New England (Blathwayt to Nottingham, 17 July 1693, BL, Add. MSS, vol. 37,992, 17–18).

64 Chidley Brooke to Benjamin Fletcher, 2 August 1693, PRO, CO5/1038, no. 23.

65 Villebon to Pontchartrain, 1694, in Webster, ed., *Acadia at the End of the Seventeenth Century*, 74; minutes of New York council, 24 August 1693, PRO, CO5/1183, 453; Brooke to Fletcher, 2 August 1693, endorsement, PRO, CO5/1038, no. 23.

66 Dudley to Blathwayt, 25 February 1693, CWBP, vol. 4, folder 5.

67 Letter from Boston [24 March 1693], PRO, CO5/857, no. 41. See also Phips to Nottingham, 15, 20 (four letters), 21, 28 February 1693, PRO, CO5/751, nos. 19, 21, 23, 24, 26, 28, 30; Phips to Blathwayt, 20 (four letters), 21, 27 (two letters), CWBP, vol. 5, folder 1.

68 Byfield to Usher, 12 July 1694, PRO, CO5/858, no. 35.

69 Phips to Blathwayt, 12 October 1692, 27 February, 11 September 1693, CWBP, vol. 5, folder 1; Blathwayt to Phips [June 1693], ibid.; Addington to Blathwayt, 21 February 1693, ibid., folder 3.

70 Nathaniel Byfield et al. to Blathwayt, 20 February 1693, endorsement, CWBP, vol. 4, folder 4; Dudley to Blathwayt, ibid., folder 5.

11: Imperial Governorship: Recall, 1693–1694

1 King to Phips, 15 February 1694, PRO, CO5/858, no. 16; Phips to Nottingham, 12 July 1694, PRO, CO5/751, no. 41. Why Phips chose to address his letter to Nottingham, who had been out of office for several months, is unclear.

2 Petition of Jahleel Brenton to the Lords of the Treasury [20 July 1693], PRO, CO5/857, no. 87(i). Brenton's petition was undated, but the customs commissioners, in forwarding it to the Treasury, referred to his 'letter' of 20 July 1693 (customs commissioners to Treasury, 22 November 1693, ibid., no. 87). 'Fustick' was a dye-wood originating in Jamaica; see OED, 6:293.

3 Customs commissioners to Treasury, 22 November 1693, PRO, CO5/857, no. 87. Where the customs commissioners obtained the additional details is unclear, though they were at least partly (and probably wholly) accurate; see deposition of David Edwards, 14 August 1694, PRO, CO5/858, no. 42(i), 31; deposition of John Foster, 22 August 1694, ibid., 32–3. Brenton did have an agent acting in England, who is mentioned but not named in the journal of the Lords of Trade, 15 January 1694, PRO, CO391/7, 257. The date of the original incident is established in the deposition of Nathaniel Byfield, 31 August 1694, PRO, CO5/858, no. 42(i), 41.

4 Journal of the Lords of Trade, 15 January 1694, PRO, CO391/7, 257.

5 Brenton to Phips, 8 September 1692, MA, vol. 61, 326–7; Randolph to Blath-

wayt, 29 September 1692, CWBP, vol. 2, folder 3. See also Hall, *Edward Randolph and the American Colonies*, 133–4, 142. On the possible involvement of Mather in Brenton's appointment, see Johnson, *Adjustment to Empire*, 184.

6 Phips to Blathwayt, 12 October 1692, CWBP, vol. 5, folder 1; Privy Council records, 22 December 1692, in Grant and Munro, eds., *Acts of the Privy Council of England: Colonial Series*, 2:237–41.

7 Barrow, *Trade and Empire*, 32–3; Bailyn, *New England Merchants*, 162–77. The more general observations in this paragraph are based on Barrow, *Trade and Empire*, 4–19; Bailyn, *New England Merchants*, 143–67; Hall, *Edward Randolph and the American Colonies*, 21–52; Harper, *The English Navigation Laws*, 9–62; and McCusker and Menard, *Economy of British America*, 46–50.

8 Massachusetts Province Laws, 1692–3, c 6; petition of Benjamin Jackson [1692], MA, vol. 61, 323; minutes of Massachusetts council, 14 October 1692, PRO, CO5/785, 194–5.

9 *Acts and Resolves, Public and Private, of the Province of Massachusetts Bay*, 1:34–5; Barrow, *Trade and Empire*, 53–9; Phips to commissioners of customs, 19 January 1693, MA, vol. 51, 12–13.

10 Petition of Brenton [20 July 1693], PRO, CO5/857, no. 87(i); Privy Council records, 22 December 1692, in Grant and Munro, eds., *Acts of the Privy Council of England: Colonial Series*, 2:237–41. For other evidence of Shrimpton's continental trade in this period, see the deposition of Robert Tufton Mason, 27 January 1692, PRO, CO5/1037, no. 80.

11 Deposition of Henry Graven, 15 August 1692, MA, vol. 61, 322; deposition of Jeremiah Tay, 17 August 1694, PRO, CO5/858, no. 42(i), 7. On the term 'waiter,' denoting a customs official, see OED, 19:822.

12 Court of Admiralty proceedings, 27 July 1692, PRO, CO5/858, no. 10(viii); Phips to Blathwayt, 27 February 1693, CWBP, vol. 5, folder 1; depositions of Henry Francklyn and William Hill, 10 September 1694, PRO, CO5/858, no. 42(i), 9–10; Edward Randolph to John Usher, 4 October 1692, MHS, 1689–94. Only one reference has been discovered for Jackson before 1692: on 4 January 1690, he witnessed Phips's purchase of a property in the North End of Boston (Suffolk Deeds, 16:111–12).

13 Deposition of Thomas Cobbitt, 11 January 1693, MA, vol. 61, 353–4.

14 Depositions of Hill and Francklyn, 10 September 1694, PRO, CO5/858, no. 42(i), 12–13, 14. On La Tour, see deposition of Hill and Francklyn, 10 September 1694, ibid., 15; Daigle, 'Les relations commerciales de l'Acadie avec le Massachusetts,' 53–61.

15 Deposition of James Leblond, 4 September 1694, PRO, CO5/858, no. 42(i), 22.

16 Memorial of Lidget, February 1693, PRO, CO5/857, no. 27; Bailyn, *New England Merchants*, 190–3; Johnson, *Adjustment to Empire*, 209–11.

17 Usher to Lords of Trade, 31 January 1693, PRO, CO5/924, no. 19; Usher to Nottingham, 31 January 1693, PRO, CO5/751, no. 18; Usher to Lords of Trade, 30 October 1693, PRO, CO5/924, no. 29; Fletcher to [Blathwayt], 14 February 1693, PRO, CO5/1038, no. 6.

18 Articles of Jahleel Brenton [November 1694], PRO, CO5/858, no. 44.

19 Declaration of Thomas Wake, 27 May 1693, ibid., no. 42(i), 23; entry certificate, 26 May 1693, ibid., 24; deposition of Daniel Freith, 22 August 1694, ibid., 30; deposition of David Edwards, 14 August 1694, ibid., 31; deposition of John Foster, 22 August 1694, ibid., 33; deposition of Benjamin Jackson, 15 November 1694, ibid., no. 42(ii), 5. Wake later gave his arrival date as 28 May, but 25th May is in accord with other evidence (deposition of Thomas Wake, 17 July 1694, ibid., no. 42(i), 28).

20 Deposition of Thomas Wake, 17 July 1694, ibid., 28–9; deposition of Daniel Freith, 22 August 1694, ibid., 30; deposition of Sampson Sheafe, 17 July 1694, ibid., 23.

21 Deposition of John Foster, 22 August 1694, ibid., 32–3; Deposition of William Hill and Henry Francklyn, 17 July 1694, ibid., 34–5; Fairfax to Sotherne, 31 January 1693, PRO, CO5/857, no. 22.

22 Deposition of Thomas Wake, 17 July 1694, PRO, CO5/858, no. 42 (i), 28–9; deposition of John Foster, 22 August 1694, ibid., 32–3; petition of Jahleel Brenton to the Lords of the Treasury [20 July 1693], PRO, CO5/857, no. 87(i). On 'stob' as a contemporary synonym for 'stab,' see OED, 16:730.

23 'A letter from New England,' 1 November 1694, PRO, CO5/858, no. 41A.

24 Deposition of Timothy Clarke, 31 August 1694, ibid., no. 42 (i), 54–5; deposition of Andrew Belcher, 4 September 1694, ibid., 57; proceedings of Court of Admiralty, 3 October 1692, ibid., 47–9; attestation of Sampson Sheafe, 14 August 1694, ibid., 49.

25 'A letter from New England,' 1 November 1694, PRO, CO5/858, no. 41A; memorial of Edward Randolph, 25 August 1696, PRO, CO323/2, no. 7; Phips to Blathwayt, 12 October 1692, CWBP, vol. 5, folder 1; petition of Thomas Newton [23 November 1693], PRO, CO5/857, no. 89; DAB, 7:476–7; proceedings of Court of Admiralty, 27 July 1692, PRO, CO5/858, no. 10(viii). On Checkley's earlier appointment, see General Court records, 14 June 1689, MA, General Court records, 6:40.

26 See Johnson, *John Nelson*, 45.

27 Byfield to Dudley, 12 June 1693, PRO, CO5/858, no. 31; deposition of David Bassett, 30 June 1694, MA, vol. 61, 446–7; deposition of William Hews, 30 June 1694, ibid., 448–9.

28 Accounts of Sir William Phips [July 1694], PRO, CO5/924, no. 38. On the taking of the *Trempeuse*, see Phips to Nottingham, 11 September 1693, PRO, CO5/

751, no. 37. It is possible also that Phips's defences against charges of associating with pirates may have been complicated by memories of the brief pirate careers of Richard Phips and William Bennett five years earlier. After deserting in August 1689 from the garrison at Fort Loyal, Casco Bay, both had sailed with the pirate Thomas Pound until captured two months later. While neither of these otherwise obscure individuals can be identified with certainty, Phips was a rare surname in New England, and the name of William Bennett suggests in a Maine context a possible connection with Mary Spencer Phips's brother-in-law David Bennett. It is tempting also to identify another of Pound's crew, Thomas Johnson (or Johnston), with the man of the same name who had been a crew member in Phips's first treasure-seeking expedition. See Dow, *Pirates of the New England Coast*, 54–72, and deposition of Thomas Johnston, 15 June 1682, in Noble, *Records of the Court of Assistants*, 1:211.

29 Commissioners of customs to Lords of the Treasury, 22 November 1693, PRO, CO5/857, no. 87; order in council, 30 November 1693, ibid., no. 90; journal of Lords of Trade, 6 December 1693, PRO, CO391/7, 234; minute of Lords of Trade, 6 December 1693, PRO, CO5/906, 69–72; minutes of Privy Council, 7 December 1693, in Grant and Munro, eds., *Acts of the Privy Council of England: Colonial Series*, 2:257; order in council, 7 December 1693, PRO, CO5/857, no. 92; petition of Richard Short [7 December 1693], ibid., no. 92 (i).

30 Phips to Lords of Trade, 25 September 1693, ibid., no. 82; Johnson, *Adjustment to Empire*, 308.

31 Stoughton to Blathwayt, 24 October 1693, CWBP, vol. 5, folder 4.

32 Dudley to Blathwayt, 5 December 1693, CWBP, vol. 4, folder 5.

33 Address to the crown, 16 November 1693, MA, General Court records, 6305–7; 'A Letter from New England,' 1 November 1694, PRO, CO5/858, no. 41A. The anonymous letter's contents and terminology can be compared with Byfield to Dudley, 12 June 1694, ibid., no. 31.

34 Dudley to Blathwayt, 5 December 1693, CWBP, vol. 4, folder 5.

35 Commissioners of customs to Lords of Trade, 4 January 1694, PRO, CO5/858, no. 1; protest, 22 November 1693, PRO, CO5/857, no. 86.

36 Petition of Benjamin Jackson, 5 January 1694, PRO, CO5/858, no. 2; journal of Lords of Trade, 8, 12 January 1694, PRO, CO391/7, 246–7, 254; Povey to Sotherne, 12 January 1694, PRO, CO5/858, no. 5.

37 Journal of Lords of Trade, 15, 19 January 1694, PRO, CO391/7, 257–9; minute of Lords of Trade, 15 January 1694, PRO, CO5/858, no. 6; minute of Lords of Trade, and evidence, 19 January 1694, ibid., nos. 10, 10(i)–(xix).

38 Petition of Benjamin Jackson [25 January 1694], ibid., no. 11; minute of Lords of Trade, 19 January 1694, endorsement [1 February 1694], ibid., no. 10.

39 Journal of Lords of Trade, 2 February 1694, PRO, CO391/7, 259–60; minute of Lords of Trade, 2 February 1694, PRO, CO5/858, no. 15; king to Phips, 15 February 1694, ibid., no. 16. On the delivery of the order, see receipt of Robert Maxwell, 3 April 1694, ibid., no. 25; Sewall, *Diary*, 4, 5 July 1694, 1:319.

40 Phips to Nottingham, 12 July 1694, PRO, CO5/751, no. 41; Byfield to Dudley, 12 June 1694, PRO, CO5/858, no. 31. The circumstances in which the investigating committee recommended by the customs commissioners was abandoned are not clear from surviving evidence. Cotton Mather identified only vaguely what he portrayed as the unwillingness of the king and Privy Council to have Phips's fate rest with 'a *Committee* of Persons nominated by his Enemies' (Mather, 'Pietas in Patriam,' 350). On the difficulties attending efforts to remove governors, see Burns, *Controversies between Royal Governors and Their Assemblies*, 22–3.

41 Mather to Blathwayt, 6 July 1694, CWBP, vol. 5, folder 6; Stoughton to Sir John Trenchard, 17 September 1694, PRO, CO5/751, no. 42; Stoughton to Blathwayt, 14 November 1694, CWBP, vol. 5, folder 4. The minister John Higginson had made similar comments some weeks earlier (Higginson to John How, 1 August 1694, in Moody, ed., *The Saltonstall Papers*, 1:214–15; Higginson to Dudley, 2 August 1694, ibid., 216–17).

42 Villebon to Pontchartrain, 1694, in Webster, ed., *Acadia at the End of the Seventeenth Century*, 74.

43 Usher to Phips, 18, 21, 23, 30 July 1694, PRO, CO5/924, no. 40 (i); Phips to Usher, 19 July 1694, ibid.; Stoughton to Usher, 22, 26 July 1694, ibid.; Usher to Stoughton, 28 July 1694, ibid.; Stoughton to Usher, 3 August 1694, ibid., no. 40(iii); Usher to Lords of Trade [September 1694], ibid., no. 40.

44 Stoughton to John Allyn, 23, 25, 30 July 1694, MA, vol. 2, 221–3; Fletcher to Nottingham, 10 December 1693, PRO, CO5/1082, no. 38.

45 Phips to Fletcher, 29 June 1694, MA, vol. 2, 394; minutes of New York council, 9 July, 13 August 1694, PRO, CO5/1183, 534, 551–3; minutes of Massachusetts council, 4 August 1694, PRO, CO5/785, 264.

46 Graham to Randolph, 11 October 1693, in Toppan and Goodrick, eds., *Randolph Letters*, 7:450–1. In the letter, the words 'a woodden sword' had been inserted in place of the deleted words, 'whipping post.'

47 Order, 5 July 1694, MA, vol. 61, 441; minutes of Massachusetts council, 5, 17 July, 14, 22, 31 August, 4, 10, 17 September, 17, 20 October 1694, PRO, CO5/785, 255–6, 260, 266, 269, 270, 273–4, 276.

48 Sewall, *Diary*, 15 November 1694, 1:323; minutes of Massachusetts council, 15 November 1694, PRO, CO5/785, 489–90; certificate of William Stoughton, 16 November 1694, PRO, CO5/858, no. 42(ii). See also Stoughton to Trenchard, 15 November 1694, ibid., no. 42.

49 Phips to Trenchard, 18 September 1694, PRO, CO5/751, no. 44; Addington to
   Blathwayt, 13 November 1694, CWBP, vol. 5, folder 3.
50 Articles of Jahleel Brenton [November 1694], PRO, CO5/858, no. 44.
51 Deposition of Francis Foxcroft, 17 August 1694, ibid., no. 42 (i), 60; deposition of William Goddard, 4 September 1694, ibid., 72; deposition of Ralph
   Carter, 11 October 1694, ibid., 89; deposition of Matthew Cary, 4 September
   1694, ibid., 77–8.
52 Deposition of Walter Willett, 4 September 1694, ibid., 88; deposition of Benjamin Eames, 17 August 1694, ibid., 85–6; depositions of John Halsey and
   David Thomas, 25 April 1693, attested by Benjamin Jackson, 15 November
   1694, ibid., 9–10.
53 Deposition of Andrew Belcher, 4 September 1694, ibid., 57; deposition of
   Timothy Clarke, 31 August 1694, ibid., 54–5; deposition of Nathaniel Oliver,
   22 August 1694, ibid., 56; deposition of William N. Snowton, 17 August 1694,
   ibid., 52; deposition of Edward Sinkler, 4 September 1694, ibid., 53; Court of
   Admiralty proceedings, 3 October 1692, and attestation of Sampson Sheafe
   [14 August 1694], ibid., 47–9; Depositions of Benjamin Jackson, 15 November
   1694, ibid., no. 42(ii), 6–8.
54 Depositions of Hill and Francklyn, 10 September 1694, ibid., no. 42(i), 8–15.
55 Deposition of Hill and Francklyn, 17 July 1694, ibid., 34–5; deposition of Timothy Clarke, 14 August 1694, ibid., 36; protest of dissenting members, 25
   November 1693, MA, vol. 48, 224; deposition of William Rous, 17 July 1694,
   PRO, CO5/858, no. 42(i), 37.
56 Deposition of Hill and Francklyn, 17 July 1694, ibid., 34–5; deposition of John
   Barnard, 17 July 1694, ibid., 38; deposition of Robert Gibbs, 22 August 1694,
   ibid., 42; deposition of William Crow, 22 August 1694, ibid., 44.
57 Deposition of Hill and Francklyn, 17 July 1694, ibid., 34–5; deposition of
   Nathaniel Byfield, 31 August 1694, ibid., 41; deposition of John Barnard, 17
   July 1694, ibid., 38; deposition of Thomas Wake, 17 July 1694, ibid., 28–9;
   deposition of Timothy Clarke, 14 August 1694, ibid., 36.
58 Deposition of John Barnard, 17 July 1694, ibid., 38.
59 Deposition of Joshua Winsor [22 August 1694], ibid., 39; 'Humble Address'
   [9 April 1691], PRO, CO5/856, no. 143(i); Byfield et al. to Blathwayt, 20 February 1693, CWBP, vol. 4, folder 4. Waterhouse, with other merchants such as
   Foster, Shrimpton, and Nelson, had also been among those signing the crucial declaration of 18 April 1689 (declaration, 18 April 1689, *Andros Tracts*,
   1:11–20). He and Foster had been accused at that time, by a critic of the revolution, of illicitly trading supplies and munitions to the Wabanaki (Andrews,
   ed., *Narratives of the Insurrections*, 198).
60 Black, 'Nathaniel Byfield, 1653–1733,' 58, 70.

61 Byfield to Usher, 12 July 1694, PRO, CO5/858, no. 35; deposition of Hill and Francklyn, 17 July 1694, ibid., no. 42(i), 34–5. On the backgrounds of Brenton and Byfield, see Johnson, *Adjustment to Empire*, 184, 287–9, 357–8.
62 Addington to Blathwayt, 13 November 1694, CWBP, vol. 5, folder 3.
63 Sewall, *Diary*, 1, 7, 9 November 1694, 1:322–3.
64 ibid., 9 November 1694, 1:323; *Tay vs. Dobbins*, 1694, MA, records of the Superior Court of Judicature, 1:136–7.
65 Ibid., 17 November 1694, 1:323; minutes of Massachusetts council, 15, 17 November 1694, PRO, CO5/785, 489–90; Mather 'Pietas in Patriam,' 350. According to John Pynchon, Phips sailed first for the Piscataqua River to join up with a convoy of mast ships for the transatlantic crossing (Pynchon to Isaac Addington, 3 December 1694, in Bridenbaugh, ed., *The Pynchon Papers*, 1:287).

12: Endings

1 Newsletter to the earl of Derwentwater, 14 December 1694, PRO, ADM77/4, no. 57; Ashurst to Mather, 5 May 1695, in Hutchinson, *History of the Colony and Province of Massachusetts Bay*, 2:64. Hutchinson identified the other accuser as Brenton, but without citing any evidence other than a reference to 'Mr. B.' in Ashurst's letter.
2 Petition of Sir William Phips [31 January 1695], PRO, CO5/859, no. 1(i); order in council, 31 January 1695, ibid., no. 1; journal of Lords of Trade, 12, 13 February 1695, PRO, CO391/7, 401, 406.
3 Fitz–John Winthrop to Wait Winthrop, 6 March 1695, Winthrop Papers, Massachusetts Historical Society *Collections*, 5th ser., 5:326; Mather, 'Pietas in Patriam,' 351–3. It is possible that Fitz-John Winthrop mistook the date of his and Phips's attendance at Whitehall, for the relevant meeting of the Lords of Trade took place on the thirteenth. However, his letter did specify that this took place on the Tuesday prior to Phips's death, which was the twelfth.
4 Mather, 'Pietas in Patriam,' 352–3; Fitz-John Winthrop to Wait Winthrop, 6 March 1695, Winthrop Papers, Massachusetts Historical Society *Collections*, 5th ser., 5:326. For St Mary Woolnoth, see Stow, *Stow's Survey of London*, 179, 184.
5 Sewall, *Diary*, 5–8 May 1695, 1:331–2. For a detailed description of the monument, see 'Monument of Sir William Phipps in London,' *New England Historical and Genealogical Register*, 4 (1850), 290. The church crypt was cleared out when an underground railway was built through it in the late nineteenth century. All human remains were removed and re-interred in Surrey. The monument does not survive.

6 Mather, 'Pietas in Patriam,' 355–6; newsletter to the earl of Derwentwater, 21
   February 1695, PRO, ADM77/4, no. 65; Stephen Wesendonck to John Usher, 15
   March 1695, MHS, Jeffries Papers, vol. 3, 116; Sewall, *Diary*, 5 May 1695, 1:331;
   Fitz-John Winthrop to Wait Winthrop, 13 July 1695, Winthrop Papers, Massachusetts Historical Society *Collections*, 5th ser., 5:324; Johnson, *Adjustment
   to Empire*, 258–9, 263–4.
7 Inventory, 9 September 1696, in Goold, 'Sir William Phips,' 65–7. For a
   detailed analysis of wealth holding in Boston, see Nash, *The Urban Crucible*,
   20–4, 387–401. Phips's major transactions included the following: Daniel
   Turell and Samuel Wakefield to Phips, 27 November 1687, Suffolk Deeds,
   17:221; Daniel Turell to Phips, 7 January 1688, ibid., 17:223; Benjamin Davis
   to Phips, 13 June 1690, ibid., 15:51–2; Phips to William Green, 7 October 1692,
   ibid., 15:210; Francis Whitmore to Phips, 28 June 1693, ibid., 16:242.
8 Mary Phips to Thomas Adkins, 30 November 1695, Suffolk Deeds, 17:190;
   Phips to William Colman, 22 February 1696, ibid., 17:202; Phips to Richard
   Keats, 18 March 1696, ibid., 17:205; Phips to Mary Henchman, 28 May 1696,
   ibid., 17:267; Phips to Samuel Clough, 18 August 1699, ibid., 19:182; 'Vessels
   Built in New England, 1697–1714,' MA, vol. 7, 89, 97, 116, 145. On Sargeant,
   see Bailyn, *New England Merchants*, 176, 183.
9 Sibley and Shipton, *Biographical Sketches of Those Who Attended Harvard College*, 5:224–34.
10 Ibid., 5:225–6, 233, 8: 457–9, and 11:53–6; Stark, *Loyalists of Massachusetts*, 420–1.
11 Minute of Lords of Trade, 4 June 1695, PRO, CO5/906, 187–94; 'Documents
   Presented by Sir Henry Ashurst,' 31 July 1696, PRO, CO5/859, no. 17(i)-(iii);
   Barrow, *Trade and Empire*, 53–9; Steele, *Politics of Colonial Policy*, 16–19.
12 Memorial of John Nelson [23 September 1696], PRO, CO323/2, no. 10; petition
   of John Usher, 28 June 1697, PRO, CO5/859, no. 112; mémoire of Meneval,
   1700, *Collection de manuscrits*, 2:339–40.
13 Mather, 'Pietas in Patriam,' 359.
14 Ibid., 352; Defoe, *Essay upon Projects*, 27; Diary of Increase Mather, 31 July
   1691, AAS.
15 Blathwayt to Nottingham, 6 March 1691, PRO, SP63d/353, no. 55; Diary of
   Increase Mather, 6 August 1691, AAS.
16 On the importance of entertaining, see Olson, *Making the Empire Work*, 79–80.
17 Ibid., 79.
18 Brewer, *Sinews of Power*, esp. 137–54; Cain and Hopkins, *British Imperialism:
   Innovation and Expansion*, esp. 22–9, 58–64. The term 'financial revolution'
   comes, of course, from Dickson, *Financial Revolution in England*. On imperial
   expansion, see also Bowen, *Elites, Enterprise, and the Making of the British
   Overseas Empire*, 126–30.

Bibliography

Primary Sources

MANUSCRIPT SOURCES

France
Archives nationales. Archives des colonies. Series B, C11A; C11D

Great Britain
Bodleian Library, Oxford University. Ashurst Papers; Rawlinson MSS, A171, A300; Sloane MSS, A179, A189; Southwell-Povey Papers
Bristol Record Office, Bristol Apprenticeship Registers, 1532–1658
British Library. Additional mss, 9313, 25374, 37991, 37992; Egerton MSS, 2526, 9336; Naval Listings, 1546–1714; Sloane MSS, 45, 50, 3984
Guildhall Library. MSS 1525
Kent Archives Office, Centre for Kentish Studies. U515/03, U515/09, U515/010
National Maritime Museum. Letterbook of Sir John Narbrough; Lieutenant's Journal of *Foresight*; Pitcairn-Jones Sea Officers' List; Southwell Papers
Northamptonshire Record Office. Albemarle Papers
Public Record Office. Series ADM1, ADM2, ADM8, ADM10, ADM35, ADM51, ADM77, ADM106, C8, C10, C41, C66, CO1, CO5, CO138, CO389, CO391, SP44, SP63d, SP94, T4, T11, T27, T52, T54, T61, T64; Rowbotham, W.B., 'Pepys List of Ships and Officers, 1660–1688'
University of Nottingham. Portland MSS

United States
American Antiquarian Society. Diary of Increase Mather
Colonial Williamsburg Foundation. Blathwayt Papers, vols.1, 2, 4, 5, 8, 9, 10, 15, 25

324   Bibliography

Essex County, Massachusetts. Essex County Court Files, Essex County Deeds
Huntington Library. Blathwayt Papers
Lincoln County, Maine. Lincoln Deeds
Maine Historical Society. Kennebec Proprietors Papers
Maine State Library. Sheepscot Papers
Massachusetts Historical Society. Gay Transcripts; Jeffries Papers; Miscellaneous Bound Manuscripts, 1689–1694
Massachusetts State Archives. Massachusetts Archives, 2, 3, 6, 7, 30, 35, 36, 37, 48, 51, 61, 69, 70, 81, 100, 106, 108, 129; Records of the General Court, vol. 6; Records of the Superior Court of Judicature, vol. 1
Middlesex County, Massachusetts. Middlesex Deeds; Middlesex Court Files
Suffolk County, Massachusetts. Suffolk Deeds; Suffolk Court Files
York County, Maine. York Deeds

PRINTED SOURCES

'An Account of Forces Raised in New England, April 1689.' Hutchinson Papers, *Collections of the Massachusetts Historical Society*, 3rd ser., 3. Boston, 1825
Acts and Resolves, Public and Private, of the Province of the Massachusetts Bay, ed. Abner C. Goodell and Melville M. Bigelow. 21 vols. Boston: Published by the State, 1869–1922
American Husbandry. 1775. Revised edn., ed. Harry J. Carman, New York: Columbia University Press, 1939
Andrews, Charles M., ed. *Narratives of the Insurrections, 1675–1690*. New York: Barnes and Noble, 1915
The Andros Tracts: Being a Collection of Pamphlets and Official Papers, Issued During the Period Between the Overthrow of the Andros Government and the Establishment of the Second Charter of Massachusetts, ed. William H. Whitmore. 3 vols. Boston: Prince Society, 1868–74
The Autobiography of Sir John Bramston, K.B. London: Camden Society, 1845
Baker, Thomas. *Piracy and Diplomacy in Seventeenth-Century North Africa: The Journal of Thomas Baker, English Consul in Tripoli, 1677–1685*, ed. C.R. Pennell. Rutherford, N.J.: Fairleigh Dickinson University Press, 1989.
Baxter, James Phinney, ed. *Sir Ferdinando Gorges and His Province of Maine*. 3 vols. Boston: Prince Society, 1890
Berwick, Edward, ed. *The Rawdon Papers, Consisting of Letters on Various Subjects, Literary, Political, and Ecclesiastical, to and from Dr. John Bramhall, Primate of Ireland*. London: John Nichols and Son, 1819
The Book of Possessions. Second Report of Record Commissioners of the City of Boston. Boston: Rockwell and Churchill, 1881

Boyer, Paul, and Stephen Nissenbaum, eds. *The Salem Witchcraft Papers: Verbatim Transcripts of the Legal Documents of the Salem Witchcraft Outbreak of 1692.* 3 vols. New York: Da Capo Press, 1977

Bridenbaugh, Carl, ed. *The Pynchon Papers.* Vol. 1, *Letters of John Pynchon, 1654–1700.* Boston: Colonial Society of Massachusetts, 1982

Brigham, Clarence S., ed. *British Royal Proclamations Relating to America, 1603–1787.* Transactions and Proceedings of the American Antiquarian Society, 12. Cambridge, Mass.: 1911

Bunyan, John. *The Pilgrim's Progress from This World to That Which Is to Come*, ed. Roger Sharrock. New York: Oxford University Press, 1960

Burr, G. Lincoln, ed. *Narratives of the Witchcraft Cases, 1648–1706.* New York: Barnes and Noble, 1914

Calef, Robert. *More Wonders of the Invisible World.* London: N. Hillar and J. Collyer, 1700

Calloway, Colin G., ed. *Dawnland Encounters: Indians and Europeans in Northern New England.* Hanover and London: University Press of New England, 1991

Church, Thomas. *The History of Philip's War, Commonly Called the Great Indian War, of 1675 and 1676*, ed. Samuel G. Drake. 2nd ed. Exeter, N.H.: J. & B. Williams, 1829

Collection de manuscrits contenant lettres, mémoires, et autres documents historiques relatifs à la Nouvelle-France recueillis aux Archives de la province de Québec ou copiés a l'étranger. 4 vols. Quebec: A. Côté, 1883–5

Cooper, James F., Jr, and Kenneth P. Minkema. *The Sermon Notebook of Samuel Parris, 1689–1694.* Boston: Colonial Society of Massachusetts, 1993

Crokat, Gilbert. *A Consolatory Letter, Written to Lady Shovell on the Surprising and Calamitous Loss of Her Husband and Two Only-Sons.* London: George Strahan, 1708

Davis, Andrew M., ed. *Colonial Currency Reprints, 1682–1751.* 4 vols. Boston: Prince Society, 1910–11

Defoe, Daniel. *An Essay upon Projects.* London: Thomas Cockerill, 1697

A General History of the Pyrates; From Their First Rise and Settlement in the Island of Providence to the Present Time. 2nd ed. London: T. Warren, 1724

Dexter, Franklin B., ed. *New Haven Town Records, 1662–1684.* New Haven: New Haven Colony Historical Society, 1919

Documentary History of the State of Maine, ed. William Willis et al. Maine Historical Society *Collections*, 2nd ser. 24 vols. Portland and Cambridge, Mass., 1869–1916

Doughty, Arthur G., ed. *Report of the Work of the Archives Branch for the Year 1912.* Ottawa: King's Printer, 1913

Drake, Samuel E., ed. *The Witchcraft Delusion in New England.* 3 vols. Roxbury, Mass.: Eliot Woodward, 1866

Ellis, George Agar., ed. *The Ellis Correspondence*. 2 vols. London: Henry Colburn, 1829

Esquemeling, John. *The Buccaneers of America*. 1685. Reprint, London: Routledge, n.d.

Evelyn, John. *The Diary of John Evelyn*. ed. E.S. de Beer. 6 vols. Oxford: Clarendon Press, 1955

An Exact and Perfect Relation of the Arrival of the Ship the James and Mary Captain Phipps Commander. [London, 1687]

Grant, W.L. and James Munro, eds. *Acts of the Privy Council of England: Colonial Series*. 6 vols. London: HMSO, 1908–12

Graves, John. *A Memorial or Short Account*. London, 1708

Great Britain, Historical Manuscripts Commission. *Seventh Report of the Royal Commission on Historical Manuscripts*. Part 1, *Report and Appendix*. London: HMSO, 1879

– *Eleventh Report, Appendix*. Part 5, *The Manuscripts of the Earl of Dartmouth*. London: HMSO, 1887

– *Twelfth Report, Appendix*. Part 5, *The Manuscripts of the Duke of Rutland, K.G., Preserved at Belvoir Castle*. Vol. 2. London: HMSO, 1889

– *Twelfth Report, Appendix*. Part 9, *The Manuscripts of the Duke of Beaufort, K.G., the Earl of Donoughmore, and Others*. London: HMSO, 1891

– *Report on the Manuscripts of Allan George Finch, Esq., of Burley-on-the-Hill, Rutland*. 3 vols. London: HMSO, 1913–57

– *Report on the Manuscripts of the Marquess of Downshire, Preserved at Easthampstead Park, Berks*. 4 vols. London: HMSO, 1924–40

Hale, John. *A Modest Inquiry into the Nature of Witchcraft and How Persons Guilty of that Crime May Be Convicted; and the Means Used for Their Discovery Discussed, Both Negatively and Affirmatively, According to Scripture and Experience. By John Hale, Pastor of the Church of Christ in Beverly, Anno Domini, 1697*. Boston: B. Green and J. Allen, 1702

Hough, Franklin B., ed. 'Papers Relating to Pemaquid.' Maine Historical Society, *Collections*, 1st ser., 5 (1857), 1–136

House of Lords Manuscripts, Vol. 6 (New Series), The Manuscripts of the House of Lords, 1704–1706. London: HMSO, 1912

Hubbard, William. *The History of the Indian Wars in New England*. 1677, ed. by Samuel G. Drake, 1865. Reprint, New York: Burt Franklin, 1971

Josselyn, John. *John Josselyn, Colonial Traveler: A Critical Edition* of Two Voyages to New England, ed. Paul J. Lindholdt. Hanover: University Press of New England, 1988

A Journal of the Proceedings in the Late Expedition to Port-Royal, On Board Their Maj-

esties Ship, the Six Friends, *The Honourable Sir William Phipps Knight, Commander in Chief, etc.* Boston: Benjamin Harris, 1690

Labaree, Leonard Woods, ed. *Royal Instructions to British Colonial Governors, 1670–1776.* 2 vols. Reprint, New York: Octagon Books, 1967

Lefroy, J.H. *Memorials of the Discovery and Early Settlement of the Bermudas or Somers Islands, 1515–1685. Compiled from the Colonial Records and Other Written Sources.* 1887. 2 vols. Reprint, Bermuda: Bermuda Historical Society and Bermuda National Trust, 1981

London Gazette, 1681, 1687

Luttrell, Narcissus. *A Brief Historical Relation of State Affairs from September 1678 to April 1714.* 6 vols. Oxford: Oxford University Press, 1857

Maine Historical and Genealogical Register. Portland: S.M. Watson, 1884–94

Massachusetts Historical Society. *Collections.* Boston, 1792–

– *Proceedings.* Boston, 1879–

Mather, Cotton. *The Bostonian Ebenezer. Some Historical Remarks on the State of Boston, the Chief Town of New-England, and of the English America.* Boston: B. Green and J. Allen, for Samuel Phillips, 1698

– *Diary of Cotton Mather.* 2 vols. New York: Frederick Ungar, 1957

– *Magnalia Christi Americana: Books I and II,* ed., by Kenneth B. Murdock with Elizabeth W. Miller. Cambridge, Mass.: Harvard University Press, 1977

– *Magnalia Christi Americana; Or the History of New-England.* 1701. 2 vols. Reprint, New York: Russell and Russell, 1867

– *Parentator: Memoirs of Remarkables in the Life and the Death of the Ever-Memorable Dr. Increase Mather.* Boston: B. Green, 1724

– *The Present State of New England Considered in a Discourse on the Necessities and Advantages of a Public Spirit In Every Man; Especially at Such a Time as This.* Boston: Samuel Green, 1690

– *The Wonders of the Invisible World.* Boston: Benjamin Harris, 1693

Mather, Increase. *Autobiography of Increase Mather,* ed. Michael G. Hall. American Antiquarian Society, *Proceedings.* New ser., 71 (1961), 271–360

– *Cases of Conscience concerning Evil Spirits Impersonating Men.* Boston, 1693

– *The Great Blessing of Primitive Counsellours.* Boston: Benjamin Harris, 1693.

Mitchell, B.R., and Phyllis Deane. *Abstract of British Historical Statistics.* Cambridge: Cambridge University Press, 1962

Moody, Robert E., ed. *The Letters of Thomas Gorges.* Portland: Maine Historical Society, 1978

– ed. *The Saltonstall Papers, 1607–1815.* Vol. 1, *1607–1789.* Boston: Massachusetts Historical Society, 1972. Massachusetts Historical Society *Collections* 80

Moody, Robert E., and Richard C. Simmons, eds. *The Glorious Revolution in Mas-*

sachusetts, 1689–1692: Selected Documents. Boston: Colonial Society of Massachusetts, 1988

Morison, Samuel E., ed. *Records of the Suffolk County Court, 1671–1680*. Boston: Colonial Society of Massachusetts, 1933. Colonial Society of Massachusetts *Publications* 29–30

Myrand, Ernest, ed. *Sir William Phips devant Québec: Histoire d'un siège*. Quebec: Demers, 1893

Noble, John, ed. *Records of the Court of Assistants of the Colony of the Massachusetts Bay*. Vol. 1, *1630–1692*. Boston: County of Suffolk, 1901

O'Callaghan, E.B. and B. Fernow, eds. *Documents Relative to the Colonial History of the State of New York*. 15 vols. Albany: Weed, Parsons & Co., 1853–87.

Province and Court Records of Maine, ed. Charles Thornton Libby, Robert E. Moody, and Neal W. Allen Jr. 6 vols. Portland: Maine Historical Society, 1928–75

Records and Files of the Quarterly Courts of Essex County, Massachusetts. 9 vols. Salem: Essex Institute, 1911–75

'Refugees at Salem, January 1675/6.' *Essex Institute Historical Collections* 48 (1912), 20–5

Rich, E.E., ed. *Minutes of the Hudson's Bay Company, 1671–1674*. Toronto: Champlain Society, 1942

Sewall, Samuel. *Diary of Samuel Sewall*, ed. M. Halsey Thomas. 2 vols. New York: Farrar, Straus, and Giroux, 1973

– 'Letter-Book of Samuel Sewall.' *Massachusetts Historical Society Collections*, 6th ser., vol. 1. Boston, 1886

Shurtleff, Nathaniel B., ed. *Records of the Colony of New Plymouth in New England*. 10 vols. in 11 books. Boston: Press of William White, 1855

– *Records of the Governor and Company of the Massachusetts Bay in New England*. 5 vols. Boston: Press of William White, 1853–4

Silverman, Kenneth, ed. *Selected Letters of Cotton Mather*. Baton Rouge: Louisiana State University Press, 1971

Stow, John. *Stow's Survey of London*. 1598. Revd. ed., London: Dent, 1956

Suffolk Deeds. 14 vols. Boston: Rockwell and Churchill, 1880–1906

Tanner, J.R., ed. *A Descriptive Catalogue of the Naval Manuscripts in the Pepysian Library at Magdalen College, Cambridge*. London: Navy Records Society, 1903

Thompson, Edward Maunde, ed. *Correspondence of the Family of Hatton, Being Chiefly Letters Addressed to Christopher, First Viscount Hatton, A.D. 1601–1704*. 2 vols. London: Camden Society, 1878

Thwaites, Reuben G., ed. *The Jesuit Relations and Allied Documents*. 73 vols. Cleveland: Burrows Brothers, 1896–1901

Toppan, Robert Noxon, ed. 'Andros Records.' *American Antiquarian Society, Proceedings* 8 (1900), 237–68, 463–99

Toppan, Robert Noxon, and Alfred Thomas Scrope Goodrick, eds., *Edward Randolph; Including His Letters and Official Papers from the New England, Middle, and Southern Colonies in America, with Other Documents Relating Chiefly to the Vacating of the Royal Charter of the Colony of Massachusetts Bay, 1676–1703*. 7 vols. Boston: Prince Society, 1898–1909

Webster, John Clarence, ed. *Acadia at the End of the Seventeenth Century: Letters, Journals, and Memoirs of Joseph Robineau de Villebon, Commandant in Acadia, 1690–1700, and Other Contemporary Documents*. Saint John, N.B.: New Brunswick Museum, 1934

Whiting, John. *Truth and Innocency Defended: Against Falsehood and Envy: and the Martyrs of Jesus, and Sufferers for His Sake, Vindicated. In Answer to Cotton Mather (a Priest of Boston) His Calumnies, Lyes and Abuses of the People Called Quakers, in his Late Church-History of New-England*. London: T. Sowle, 1702

Willard, Samuel. *The Character of a Good Ruler*. Boston: M. Perry, 1694

Winship, George P., ed. *Sailors' Narratives of Voyages Along the New England Coast, 1524–1624*. 1905. Reprint, New York: Burt Franklin, 1968. New York: Burt Franklin, 1968

Wise, John. 'Narrative of Mr. John Wise, Minister of God's Word at Chebacco,' and '[Journal of John Wise].' *Proceedings of the Massachusetts Historical Society*, 2nd ser., 15 (Boston, 1902): 283–319

York Deeds. 18 vols. Portland: Maine Historical Society, 1887–1911

Secondary Sources

BOOKS

Allen, H.C., and Roger Thompson, eds. *Contrast and Connection: Bicentennial Essays in Anglo-American History*. Athens: Ohio University Press, 1976

Bailyn, Bernard. *The New England Merchants in the Seventeenth Century*. Cambridge: Harvard University Press, 1955

– *The Ordeal of Thomas Hutchinson*. Cambridge: Belknap Press of Harvard University Press, 1974

Bailyn, Bernard, and Philip Morgan, eds. *Strangers within the Realm: Cultural Margins of the First British Empire*. Chapel Hill: University of North Carolina Press, 1991

Baker, Emerson W. *The Clarke & Lake Company: The Historical Archaeology of a Seventeenth-Century Maine Settlement*. Occasional Publications in Maine Archaeology, 4. Augusta: Maine Historic Preservation Commission, 1985

Baker, William A. *Colonial Vessels: Some Seventeenth-Century Sailing Craft*. Barre, Mass.: Barre Publishing Co., 1962

– *A Maritime History of Bath, Maine and the Kennebec Region.* Bath, Maine: Marine Research Society of Bath, 1973

Banks, Charles E. *History of York, Maine.* 2 vols. Boston: The Calkins Press, 1931

Barnes, Viola Florence. *The Dominion of New England: A Study of British Colonial Policy.* New Haven: Yale University Press, 1923

Barrow, Thomas C. *Trade and Empire: The British Customs Service in Colonial America, 1660–1775.* Cambridge: Harvard University Press, 1967

Baxter, Stephen B. *William III.* London: Longmans, 1966

Beebe, William. *Half Mile Down.* New York: Duell, Sloan, and Pearce, 1934

Benes, Peter, ed. *Wonders of the Invisible World: Proceedings of the Dublin Seminar of New England Folklife.* Boston: Boston University, 1992

Black, Jeremy, and Philip Woodfine, eds. *The British Navy and the Use of Naval Power in the Eighteenth Century.* Leicester: Leicester University Press, 1988

Bliss, Robert M. *Revolution and Empire: English Politics and American Colonies in the Seventeenth Century.* Manchester: Manchester University Press, 1990

Bodge, George M. *Soldiers in King Philip's War.* 1906. Reprint, Baltimore: Genealogical Publishing Company, 1976

Bowen, H.V. *Elites, Enterprise and the Making of the British Overseas Empire, 1688–1775.* London: Macmillan, 1996

Boyer, Paul, and Stephen Nissenbaum. *Salem Possessed: The Social Origins of Witchcraft.* Cambridge: Harvard University Press, 1974

Bradley, Robert L. *Maine's First Buildings, The Architecture of Settlement, 1604–1700.* Augusta: Maine Historic Preservation Commission, 1978

Bradley, Robert L., and Helen B. Camp. *The Forts of Pemaquid, Maine: An Archaeological and Historical Study.* Augusta: Maine Historic Preservation Commission, 1994

Breen, T.H. *The Character of the Good Ruler: A Study of Puritan Political Ideas in New England, 1630–1730.* New Haven: Yale University Press, 1970

– *Puritans and Adventurers: Resistance and Change in Early America.* New York: Oxford University Press, 1980

Bremer, Francis J. *Congregational Communion: Clerical Friendship in the Anglo-American Puritan Community, 1610–1692.* Boston: Northeastern University Press, 1994

Breslaw, Elaine G. *Tituba, Reluctant Witch of Salem: Devilish Indians and Puritan Fantasies.* New York: New York University Press, 1996

Brewer, John. *The Sinews of Power: War, Money, and the English State, 1688–1783.* New York: Knopf, 1989

Bromley, J.S. *Corsairs and Navies, 1660 to 1760.* London: Hambledon Press, 1987

– ed. *The New Cambridge Modern History, Vol. 6, The Rise of Great Britain and Russia, 1688–1715/1725.* Cambridge: Cambridge University Press, 1970

Brooke, John L. *The Refiner's Fire: The Making of Mormon Cosmology, 1644-1844.* Cambridge: Cambridge University Press, 1994

Buckner, Phillip A., and John G. Reid, eds. *The Atlantic Region to Confederation: A History.* Toronto: University of Toronto Press, 1994

Burns, John F. *Controversies Between Royal Governors and Their Assemblies in the Northern American Colonies.* New York: Russell and Russell, 1923

Burrage, Henry S. *The Beginnings of Colonial Maine, 1602–1658.* Portland: Marks Printing House, 1914

Bushman, Richard L. *King and People in Provincial Massachusetts.* Chapel Hill: University of North Carolina Press, 1985

Cain, P.J., and A.G. Hopkins. *British Imperialism: Innovation and Expansion, 1688–1914.* London: Longman, 1993

Camp, Helen B. *Archaeological Excavations at Pemaquid, Maine, 1965–1974.* Augusta: Maine State Museum, 1975

Canup, John. *Out of the Wilderness: The Emergence of an American Identity in Colonial New England.* Middletown, Conn.: Wesleyan University Press, 1990

Carroll, Charles F. *The Timber Economy of Puritan New England.* Providence, R.I.: Brown University Press, 1973

Charnock, John. *Biographica Navalis.* 6 vols. London: R. Faulder, 1794–8

Clapham, Sir John. *The Bank of England: A History.* 2 vols. Cambridge: Cambridge University Press, 1944

Clark, Charles E. *The Eastern Frontier: The Settlement of Northern New England, 1610–1763.* New York: Knopf, 1970

Clark, J. Kent. *Goodwin Wharton.* New York: Oxford University Press, 1984

Cohen, Charles Lloyd. *God's Caress: The Psychology of Puritan Religious Experience.* New York: Oxford University Press, 1986

Corliss, Augustus W. *Old Times: North Yarmouth, Maine, 1877–1884.* Somersworth, N.H.: New Hampshire Publishing Company, 1977

Cranmer, Leon. *Cushnoc: The History and Archaeology of Plymouth Colony Traders on the Kennebec.* Augusta: Maine Historic Preservation Commission, 1990

Craton, Michael. *A History of the Bahamas.* 2nd ed. London: Collins, 1968

Cressy, David. *Coming Over: Migration and Communication between England and New England in the Seventeenth Century.* New York: Cambridge University Press, 1987

– *Literacy and the Social Order: Reading and Writing in Tudor and Stuart England.* Cambridge: Cambridge University Press, 1980

Cronon, William. *Changes in the Land: Indians, Colonists, and the Ecology of New England.* New York: Hill and Wang, 1983

Daniels, Bruce C. *Dissent and Conformity on Narragansett Bay: The Colonial Rhode Island Town.* Middletown, Conn.: Wesleyan University Press, 1983

Davies, J.D. *Gentlemen and Tarpaulins: The Officers and Men of the Restoration Navy*. Oxford: Clarendon Press, 1991

De Krey, Gary Stuart. *A Fractured Society: The Politics of London in the First Age of Party, 1688–1715*. Oxford: Clarendon Press, 1985

Demos, John P. *Entertaining Satan: Witchcraft and the Culture of Early New England*. New York: Oxford University Press, 1982

- *A Little Commonwealth: Family Life in Plymouth Colony*. New York: Oxford University Press, 1970

Dickerson, Oliver Morton. *American Colonial Government, 1696–1765: A Study of the British Board of Trade in Its Relation to the American Colonies, Political, Industrial, Administrative*. 2nd ed. New York: Russell and Russell 1962

Dickson, P.G.M. *The Financial Revolution in England: A Study in the Development of Public Credit, 1688–1756*. London: Macmillan, 1967. 2nd ed. Aldershot: Gregg Revivals, 1993

Dictionary of American Biography, ed. Allen Johnson and Dumas Malone. 20 vols. New York: Charles Scribner's Sons, 1928–37

Dictionary of Canadian Biography, ed. George W. Brown et al. 13 vols. to date. Toronto: University of Toronto Press, 1966–

Dictionary of National Biography: From the Earliest Times to 1900, ed. Sir Stephen Leslie and Sir Sidney Lee. 22 vols. London: Oxford University Press, 1885–1901

Dow, George F. *History of Topsfield, Massachusetts*. Topsfield: Topsfield Historical Society, 1940

- *Pirates of the New England Coast, 1630-1730*. Salem: Marine Research Society, 1923

Drake, Samuel Adams. *The Border Wars of New England*. 1897. Reprint, Williamstown, Mass.: Corner House Publishers, 1973

Drake, Samuel G. *The Book of the Indians*. 9th ed. Boston: Benjamin B. Mussey, 1845

Duffy, Michael, ed. *Parameters of British Naval Power, 1650–1850*. Exeter: University of Exeter Press, 1992

Dunn, Richard S. *Sugar and Slaves: The Rise of the Planter Class in the English West Indies, 1624–1713*. Chapel Hill: University of North Carolina Press, 1972

Dyer, Florence E. *The Life of Sir John Narbrough: 'That Great Commander and Able Seaman.'* London: Philip Allan, 1931

Earle, Peter. *The Treasure of the* Concepción: *The Wreck of the Almiranta*. New York: Viking Press, 1980. (First published as *The Wreck of the Almiranta: Sir William Phips and the Hispaniola Treasure*. London: Macmillan 1979)

Eccles, W.J. *Canada under Louis XIV, 1663–1701*. Toronto: McClelland and Stewart, 1964

– *France in America*. New York: Harper and Row, 1972

Eckstorm, Fannie Hardy. *Indian Place Names of the Penobscot Valley and the Maine Coast*. Orono: University of Maine Press, 1941

Faulkner, Alaric, and Gretchen F. Faulkner. *The French at Pentagoet, 1635–1674: An Archaeological Portrait of the Acadian Frontier*. Augusta: Maine Historic Preservation Commission, 1987

Fletcher, Anthony. *The Outbreak of the English Civil War*. New York: New York University Press, 1981

Foster, Stephen. *The Long Argument: English Puritanism and the Shaping of New England Culture, 1570–1700*. Chapel Hill. University of North Carolina Press, 1991

Gallay, Alan, ed. *Colonial Wars of North America, 1512–1763: An Encyclopedia*. New York: Garland Publishing, 1996

Given, Brian J. *A Most Pernicious Thing: Gun Trading and Native Warfare in the Early Contact Period*. Ottawa: Carleton University Press, 1994

Godbeer, Richard. *The Devil's Dominion: Magic and Religion in Early New England*. New York: Cambridge University Press, 1992

Godfrey, William G. *Pursuit of Profit and Preferment in Colonial North America: John Bradstreet's Quest*. Waterloo: Wilfrid Laurier University Press, 1982

Greene, Jack P. *Pursuits of Happiness: The Social Development of Early Modern British Colonies and the Formation of American Culture*. Chapel Hill: University of North Carolina Press, 1988

Greven, Philip J. *Four Generations: Population, Land, and Family in Colonial Andover, Massachusetts*. Ithaca: Cornell University Press, 1970

Gross, Robert A. *The Minutemen and Their World*. New York: Hill and Wang, 1976

– ed. *In Debt to Shays: The Bicentennial of an Agrarian Rebellion*. Charlottesville: University Press of Virginia, 1993

Grumet, Robert S., ed. *Northeastern Indian Lives, 1632-1816*. Amherst: University of Massachusetts Press, 1996

Guttridge, G.H. *The Colonial Policy of William III in America and the West Indies*. 1922. Reprint, London: Frank Cass, 1966

Haffenden, Philip S. *New England in the English Nation, 1689–1713*. Oxford: Clarendon Press, 1974

Hall, David D. *Worlds of Wonder, Days of Judgment: Popular Religious Belief in Early New England*. New York: Knopf, 1989

Hall, Michael G. *Edward Randolph and the American Colonies, 1676–1703*. Chapel Hill: University of North Carolina Press, 1960

– *The Last American Puritan: The Life of Increase Mather, 1609–1723*. Middletown, Conn.: Wesleyan University Press, 1988

Hansen, Chadwick. *Witchcraft at Salem*. New York: George Braziller, 1969

Harper, Lawrence A. *The English Navigation Laws: A Seventeenth-Century Experiment in Social Engineering.* New York: Columbia University Press, 1939

Henning, Basil Duke. *The House of Commons, 1660–1690.* 3 vols. London: Secker and Warburg for the History of Parliament Trust, 1983

Hoffer, Peter C. *The Devil's Disciples: Makers of the Salem Witchcraft Trials.* Baltimore: Johns Hopkins University Press, 1996

Holifield, E. Brooks. *Era of Persuasion: American Thought and Letters, 1521–1680.* Boston: Twayne Publishers, 1989

Hornstein, Sari R. *The Restoration Navy and English Foreign Trade, 1674–1688: A Study in the Peacetime Use of Sea Power.* Aldershot: Scolar Press, 1991

Horwitz, Henry. *Revolution Politicks: The Career of Daniel Finch, Second Earl of Nottingham, 1647–1730.* Cambridge: Cambridge University Press, 1968

Howell, Roger, Jr, and Emerson W. Baker. *Maine in the Age of Discovery.* Portland: Maine Historical Society, 1988

Hudson, Alfred S. *The History of Sudbury, Massachusetts, 1638-1889.* Sudbury: Town of Sudbury, 1889

Hulme, Peter. *Colonial Encounters: Europe and the Native Caribbean, 1492–1797.* London: Routledge, 1986

Hutchinson, Thomas. *The History of the Colony and Province of Massachusetts Bay.* 1796. Reprint, ed. Lawrence Shaw Mayo. 3 vols. Cambridge: Harvard University Press, 1936

Innes, Stephen. *Creating the Commonwealth: The Economic Culture of Puritan New England.* New York: Norton, 1995

– *Labor in a New Land: Economy and Society in Seventeenth-Century Springfield.* Princeton: Princeton University Press, 1983

Israel, Jonathan I. *The Anglo-Dutch Moment: Essays on the Glorious Revolution and Its World Impact.* Cambridge: Cambridge University Press, 1991

James, Sydney V., ed. *Three Visitors to Early Plymouth.* Plymouth, Mass., 1963

Jennings, Francis. *The Ambiguous Iroquois Empire: The Covenant Chain Confederation of Indian Tribes with English Colonies from Its Beginnings to the Lancaster Treaty of 1744.* New York: Norton, 1984

– *The Invasion of America: Indians, Colonialism, and the Cant of Conquest.* Chapel Hill: University of North Carolina Press, 1975

Johnson, Richard R. *Adjustment to Empire: The New England Colonies, 1675–1715.* New Brunswick, N.J.: Rutgers University Press, 1981

– *John Nelson, Merchant Adventurer: A Life between Empires.* New York: Oxford University Press, 1991

Johnston, John. *A History of Bristol and Bremen, Including the Pemaquid Settlement.* Albany: Joel Munsell, 1873

Jones, D.W. *War and Economy in the Age of William III and Marlborough.* Oxford: Basil Blackwell, 1988

Jones, J.R. *The Revolution of 1688 in England*. New York: W.W. Norton, 1972

Jordan, Winthrop D. *The White Man's Burden: Historical Origins of Racism in the United States*. New York: Oxford University Press, 1974

Kammen, Michael. *Colonial New York: A History*. New York: Charles Scribner's Sons, 1975

Karlsen, Carol F. *The Devil in the Shape of a Woman: Witchcraft in Colonial New England*. New York: Norton, 1987

Karraker, Cyrus H. *The Hispaniola Treasure*. Philadelphia: University of Pennsylvania Press, 1934

Kennedy, Jean. *Isle of Devils: Bermuda under the Somers Island Company, 1609–1685*. London: Collins, 1971

Keynes, John Maynard. *A Treatise on Money*. 2 vols. London: Macmillan, 1930

Kimball, Everett. *The Public Life of Joseph Dudley: A Study of the Colonial Policy of the Stuarts in New England, 1660–1715*. London: Longmans, Green, 1911

Kittredge, George Lyman. *Witchcraft in Old and New England*. New York: Russell and Russell, 1929

Konig, David Thomas. *Law and Society in Puritan Massachusetts: Essex County, 1629–1692*. Chapel Hill: University of North Carolina Press, 1979

Labaree, Leonard Woods. *Royal Government in America: A Study of the British Colonial System Before 1783*. New Haven: Yale University Press, 1930

Langdon, George D., Jr. *Pilgrim Colony: A History of New Plymouth, 1620–1691*. New Haven: Yale University Press, 1966

Lapham, William B. *History of Bethel, Maine*. Augusta: Press of *The Maine Farmer*, 1891.

Lawson, Philip. *The East India Company: A History*. London: Longman, 1993

Lethbridge, Peter. *Here Lies Gold: Stories of the World's Lost Treasure*. London: Peter Lunn, 1947

Levin, David. *Cotton Mather: The Young Life of the Lord's Remembrancer, 1663–1703*. Cambridge: Harvard University Press, 1978

Lockridge, Kenneth A. *Literacy in Colonial New England: An Inquiry into the Social Context of Literacy in the Early Modern West*. New York: W.W. Norton, 1974

– *A New England Town: The First Hundred Years*. New York: W.W. Norton, 1970

Lounsberry, Alice. *Sir William Phips: Treasure Fisherman and Governor of the Massachusetts Bay Colony*. New York: Charles Scribner's Sons, 1941

Lovejoy, David. *The Glorious Revolution in America*. New York: Harper and Row, 1972

McCusker, John J., and Russell R. Menard. *The Economy of British America, 1607–1789*. Chapel Hill: University of North Carolina Press, 1985

Macfarlane, Alan. *Witchcraft in Tudor and Stuart England: A Regional and Comparative Study*. London: Routledge, 1970

Melvoin, Richard I. *New England Outpost: War and Society in Colonial Deerfield*. New York: W.W. Norton, 1989

Miller, Perry. *The New England Mind: From Colony to Province*. Cambridge: Harvard University Press, 1953

Morley, Henry, ed. *The Earlier Life and the Chief Earlier Works of Daniel Defoe*. London: Routledge, 1889

Morrison, Kenneth M. *The Embattled Northeast: The Elusive Ideal of Alliance in Abenaki-Euramerican Relations*. Los Angeles: University of California Press, 1985

Nash, Gary B. *The Urban Crucible: Social Change, Political Consciousness, and the Origins of the American Revolution*. Cambridge: Harvard University Press, 1979

Newton, Arthur Percival, *The Colonising Activities of the English Puritans: The Last Phase of the Elizabethan Struggle with Spain*. New Haven: Yale University Press, 1914

Noyes, Sybil, Charles T. Libby, and Walter G. Davis. *Genealogical Dictionary of Maine and New Hampshire*. 1928–1939. Reprint, Baltimore: Genealogical Publishing Company, 1979

Ollard, Richard. *Man of War: Sir Robert Holmes and the Restoration Navy*. London: Hodder and Stoughton, 1969

Olson, Alison Gilbert. *Making the Empire Work: London and American Interest Groups, 1690–1790*. Cambridge: Harvard University Press, 1992

Owen, Henry W. *History of Bath, Maine*. Brunswick, Maine: The Times Company, 1936

Oxford English Dictionary. 2nd ed. 20 vols. Oxford: Clarendon Press, 1989

Palfrey, John G. *History of New England*. 5 vols. Boston: Little, Brown and Company, 1858–90

Pares, Richard. *War and Trade in the West Indies, 1739-1763*. Reprint, London: Frank Cass, 1963

Pencak, William. *War, Politics, and Revolution in Provincial Massachusetts*. Boston: Northeastern University Press, 1981

Powell, Sumner Chilton. *Puritan Village: The Formation of a New England Town*. Middletown, Conn.: Wesleyan University Press, 1963

Rawlyk, George A. *Nova Scotia's Massachusetts: A Study of Massachusetts–Nova Scotia Relations, 1630 to 1784*. Montreal and London: McGill-Queen's University Press, 1973

Rediker, Marcus. *Between the Devil and the Deep Blue Sea: Merchant Seamen, Pirates, and the Anglo-American Maritime World, 1700–1750*. Cambridge: Cambridge University Press, 1987

Reid, John G. *Acadia, Maine and New Scotland: Marginal Colonies in the Seventeenth Century*. Toronto: University of Toronto Press, 1981

‒ *Maine, Charles II, and Massachusetts: Governmental Relations in Early Northern New England*. Portland: Maine Historical Society, 1977

Remich, Daniel. *History of Kennebunk from Its Earliest Settlement until 1890*. Kennebunk: Published by the Author, 1911

Ritchie, Robert C. *Captain Kidd and the War against the Pirates*. Cambridge: Harvard University Press, 1986

Rosenthal, Bernard. *Salem Story: Reading the Witch Trials of 1692*. New York: Cambridge University Press, 1993

Rutman, Darrett B. *Winthrop's Boston: Portrait of a Puritan Town*. Chapel Hill: University of North Carolina Press, 1965

Sacks, David Harris. *The Widening Gate: Bristol and the Atlantic Economy, 1450‒1700*. Berkeley: University of California Press, 1991

Salisbury, Neal. *Manitou and Providence: Indians, Europeans, and the Making of New England, 1500‒1643*. New York: Oxford University Press, 1982

Savage, James. *Genealogical Dictionary of the First Settlers of New England*. 4 vols. 1860‒2. Reprint, Baltimore: Genealogical Publishing Company, 1981

Scott, William Robert. *The Constitution and Finance of English, Scottish, and Irish Joint Stock Companies to 1720*. 3 vols. Cambridge: Cambridge University Press, 1912

Shields, David S. *Oracles of Empire: Poetry, Politics, and Commerce in British America, 1690‒1750*. Chicago: University of Chicago Press, 1990

Sibley, John L., and Clifford K. Shipton, eds. *Biographical Sketches of Those Who Attended Harvard College*. 17 vols. Boston: Massachusetts Historical Society, 1873‒1975

Sosin, J.M. *English America and the Revolution of 1688: Royal Administration and the Structure of Provincial Government*. Lincoln: University of Nebraska Press, 1982

Spencer, Wilbur D. *Pioneers on Maine Rivers*. 1930. Reprint, Baltimore: Genealogical Publishing Co., 1973

Stacey, C.P. *Introduction to the Study of Military History for Canadian Students*. 6th ed., 3rd revision. Ottawa: Information Canada, 1973

Stark, James Henry. *The Loyalists of Massachusetts and the Other Side of the American Revolution*. Boston: J.H. Stark, 1910

Steele, I.K. *The English Atlantic, 1675‒1740: An Exploration of Communication and Community*. New York: Oxford University Press, 1986

‒ *Politics of Colonial Policy: The Board of Trade in Colonial Administration, 1696‒1720*. Oxford: Clarendon Press, 1968

Stone, Lawrence, ed. *An Imperial State at War: Britain from 1689 to 1815*. London: Routledge, 1994

Sullivan, James. *History of the District of Maine*. 1795. Reprint, Portland: Maine Historical Society, 1978

Thayer, Henry O. *Sir William Phips, Adventurer and Statesman: A Study in Colonial Biography*. Portland: Maine Historical Society, 1927

Thomas, Keith. *Religion and the Decline of Magic*. New York: Charles Scribner's Sons, 1971

Thornton, A.P. *West-India Policy under the Restoration*. Oxford: Clarendon Press, 1956

Trigger, Bruce G., ed. *Handbook of North American Indians*, Vol. 15, *Northeast*. Washington, D.C.: Smithsonian Institution, 1978

Ulrich, Laurel Thatcher. *Good Wives: Images and Reality in the Lives of Women in Northern New England, 1650–1750*. New York: Knopf, 1982

Van Deventer, David E. *The Emergence of Provincial New Hampshire, 1623–1741*. Baltimore: Johns Hopkins University Press, 1976

Varney, George. *A Gazetteer of the State of Maine*. Boston: B.B. Russell, 1882

Vaughan, Alden T. *New England Frontier: Puritans and Indians, 1620–1675*. 2nd ed. Boston: Little, Brown, 1979

Vickers, Daniel. *Farmers and Fishermen: Two Centuries of Work in Essex County, Massachusetts, 1630–1850*. Chapel Hill: University of North Carolina Press, 1994

Ward, Estelle Frances. *Christopher Monck, Duke of Albemarle*. London: John Murray, 1915

Watkins, Walter Kendall. *Soldiers in the Expedition to Canada in 1690 and Grantees of the Canada Townships*. Boston: Privately published, 1898

Weisman, Richard. *Magic, Witchcraft, and Religion in Seventeenth-Century New England*. Amherst: University of Massachusetts Press, 1984

Wilkinson, Henry. *The Adventurers of Bermuda: A History of the Island from Its Discovery until the Dissolution of the Somers Island Company in 1684*. 2nd ed. Oxford: Clarendon Press, 1958

Williamson, William D. *The History of the State of Maine; From Its First Discovery, A.D. 1602, to the Separation, A.D. 1820*. 2 vols. Hallowell, Maine: Glazier and Masters, 1832

Willis, William D. *The History of Portland, from 1632 to 1864*. 2nd ed. Portland: Bailey and Noyes, 1865

Woodhead, J.R. *The Rulers of London, 1660–1689: A Biographical Record of the Aldermen and Common Councilmen of the City of London*. London: London and Middlesex Archaeological Society, 1965

ARTICLES

Alsop, J.D. 'The Age of the Projectors: British Imperial Strategy in the North Atlantic in the War of the Spanish Succession.' *Acadiensis* 21, no. 1 (Autumn 1991), 30–53

Anderson, Virginia DeJohn. 'King Philip's Herds: Indians, Colonists, and the Problem of Livestock in Early New England.' *William and Mary Quarterly*, 3rd ser., 51 (1994), 601–24

Armitage, David. '"The Projecting Age": William Paterson and the Bank of England.' *History Today* 44, no. 6 (June 1994), 5–10

Axtell, James. 'The Vengeful Women of Marblehead: Robert Roules's Deposition of 1677.' *William and Mary Quarterly*, 3rd ser., 31 (1974), 647–52

Baker, Emerson W. '"A Scratch with a Bear's Paw": Anglo–Indian Land Deeds in Early Maine.' *Ethnohistory* 36 (1989), 235–56

Barnes, Viola Florence. 'Phippus Maximus.' *New England Quarterly* 1 (1928), 532–53

– 'The Rise of William Phips.' *New England Quarterly* 1 (1928), 271–94

Black, Barbara A. 'Nathaniel Byfield, 1653–1733.' *Law in Colonial Massachusetts, 1630–1800: A Conference Held 6 and 7 November 1981 by the Colonial Society of Massachusetts*. Colonial Society of Massachusetts *Publications* 62. Boston: Colonial Society of Massachusetts, 1984

Bosher, J.F. 'The Franco-Catholic Danger, 1660–1715.' *History* 79 (1994), 5–30

– 'Huguenot Merchants and the Protestant International in the Seventeenth Century.' *William and Mary Quarterly*, 3rd ser., 52 (1995), 77–92

Bourque, Bruce J. 'Ethnicity on the Maritime Peninsula, 1600–1759.' *Ethnohistory* 36 (1989), 257–84

Bowden, Tracy. 'Gleaning Treasure from the Silver Bank.' *National Geographic* 190, no. 1 (1996), 90–105

Bowen, Francis. 'Sir William Phips.' In Jared Sparks, ed., *American Biography* 10 (1902), 3–100

Braddick, M.J. 'An English Military Revolution?' *Historical Journal* 36 (1993): 965–75

Bradley, Robert L. 'Colonel Wolfgang Romer.' *Biographical Dictionary of Architects in Maine* 10, no. 3 (1987), 1–6

– 'Was the Plantation Despicable? The Archaeology of the Phips Site, ca. 1646–1676.' *The Kennebec Proprietor* 6, no. 2 (1990), 11–17

Chard, Donald F. 'Lack of a Consensus: New England's Attitude to Acadia, 1689–1713.' *Nova Scotia Historical Society Collections* 38 (1973), 5–25

Churchill, Edwin A. 'The Founding of Maine, 1600–1640: A Revisionist Interpretation.' *Maine Historical Society Quarterly* 18 (1978), 21–54

Clark, Charles, E. 'The Founding of Maine, 1600–1640: A Comment.' *Maine Historical Society Quarterly* 18 (1978), 55–62

Craker, Wendel D. 'Spectral Evidence, Non-Spectral Acts of Witchcraft, and Confession at Salem in 1692.' *Historical Journal* 40 (1997), 331–58

Daigle, Jean. 'Les relations commerciales de l'Acadie avec le Massachusetts: Le cas de Charles-Amador de Saint-Etienne de La Tour, 1695–1697.' *Revue de l'Université de Moncton* 9 (1976), 53–61

d'Entremont, Clarence-J. 'Les Melanson d'Acadie sont français de père et anglais de mère.' *La Société historique acadienne: Les cahiers* 4, no. 10 (1973), 416–19

– 'Du nouveau sur les Melanson.' *La Société historique acadienne: Les cahiers* 3, no. 8 (1970), 339–52

DePaoli, Neill. 'Beaver, Blankets, Liquor, and Politics: Pemaquid's Fur Trade, 1614–1760.' *Maine Historical Society Quarterly* 33 (1993–4), 166–201

Donagan, Barbara. 'Atrocity, War Crime, and Treason in the English Civil War.' *American Historical Review* 99 (1994), 1137–51

Eccles, W.J. 'Sovereignty-Association, 1500–1783.' *Canadian Historical Review* 65 (1984), 475–510

George, Robert H. 'The Treasure Trove of William Phips.' *New England Quarterly* 6 (1933), 294–318

Ghere, David. 'Mistranslations and Misinformation: Diplomacy on the Maine Frontier, 1725 to 1755.' *American Indian Culture and Research Journal* 8, no. 4 (1984), 3–26

Goggin, Jacqueline. 'Challenging Sexual Discrimination in the Historical Profession: Women Historians and the American Historical Association, 1890–1940.' *American Historical Review* 97 (1992), 769–802

Goold, William. 'Sir William Phips.' *Maine Historical Society Collections* 9 (1887), 1–72

Gough, Barry M. '"The Adventurers of England Trading into Hudson's Bay": A Study of the Founding Members of the Hudson's Bay Company, 1665–1670.' *Albion* 2 (1970), 35–47

Gura, Philip F. 'Cotton Mather's *Life of Phips*: "A Vice with the Vizard of Vertue upon It."' *New England Quarterly* 50 (1977), 440–57

Johnson, Richard R. 'Charles McLean Andrews and the Invention of American Colonial History.' *William and Mary Quarterly* 3rd ser., 43 (1986), 519–41

Karraker, Cyrus H. 'Spanish Treasure, Casual Revenue of the Crown.' *Journal of Modern History* 5 (1933), 301–18

– 'The Treasure Expedition of Captain William Phips to the Bahama Banks.' *New England Quarterly* 5 (1932), 731–52

Kences, James. 'Some Unexplored Relationships of Essex County Witchcraft to the Indian Wars of 1675 and 1689.' *Essex Institute Historical Collections* 120 (1984), 181–211

Leamon, James. 'Governor Fletcher's Recall.' *William and Mary Quarterly* 3rd ser., 20 (1963): 527–42

McCully, Bruce Tiebout. 'The New England–Acadia Fishery Dispute and the Nicholson Mission of August 1686.' *Essex Institute Historical Collections* 96 (1960), 277–90

McWilliams, John. 'Indian John and the Northern Tawnies.' *New England Quarterly* 69 (1996), 580–604

Monaghan, E. Jennifer. 'Family Literacy in Early Eighteenth-Century Boston: Cotton Mather and His Children.' *Reading Research Quarterly* 26 (1991), 342–70

Morrison, Kenneth M. 'The Bias of Colonial Law: English Paranoia and the Abenaki Arena of King Philip's War, 1675–1678.' *New England Quarterly* 53 (1980), 363–378

Reid, John G. 'French Aspirations in the Kennebec-Penobscot Region, 1671.' *Maine Historical Society Quarterly* 23 (1983–4), 85–92

Sprague's Journal of Maine History. Dover-Foxcroft: Sprague's Journal of Maine History, Inc., 1913–25

Towne, Mrs G. Warren. 'The Topsfield Copper Mines.' *The Historical Collections of the Topsfield Historical Society* 2 (1896), 73–81

Webb, Stephen Saunders. 'William Blathwayt, Imperial Fixer: Muddling through to Empire, 1689–1717.' *William and Mary Quarterly*, 3rd ser., 26 (1969), 373–92

– 'William Blathwayt, Imperial Fixer: From Popish Plot to Glorious Revolution.' *William and Mary Quarterly*, 3rd ser., 25 (1968), 3–21

Will, Richard T., and Rebecca Cole-Will. 'A Preliminary Report on the Anne Hilton Site.' *Maine Archaeological Society Bulletin* 15 (1990), 1–11

'Witchcraft in Maine.' *New England Historical and Genealogical Register* 13 (1859), 193–6

Zahedieh, Nuala. '"A Frugal, Prudential and Hopeful Trade": Privateering in Jamaica, 1655–89.' *Journal of Imperial and Commonwealth History* 18 (1990), 145–68

UNPUBLISHED WORKS

Baker, Emerson Woods. 'Settlement Patterns and Site Location Characteristics in Early Maine.' Paper presented at the Council for Northeast Historical Archaeology annual meeting, 1993

– 'Trouble to the Eastward: The Failure of Anglo-Indian Relations in Early Maine.' PhD dissertation, College of William and Mary, 1986

Baker, Emerson Woods, and John G. Reid. 'Sir William Phips, Violence, and the Historians: Verbal and Physical Abuse in the Behaviour of "the Best Conditioned Gentleman in the World."' Paper presented at American Historical Society (Pacific Coast Branch), August 1996

Baker, Emerson Woods, et al. 'Earthfast Architecture in Early Maine.' Paper presented at Vernacular Architecture Forum annual meeting, 1993

Cass, Edward. 'Settlement on the Kennebec, 1600–1650.' MA thesis, University of Maine, 1970

Churchill, Edwin A. 'Too Great the Challenge: The Birth and Death of Falmouth, Maine, 1624–1676.' PhD dissertation, University of Maine, 1979

Daigle, Jean. 'Nos amis les ennemis: Relations commerciales de l'Acadie avec le Massachusetts, 1670–1711.' PhD dissertation, University of Maine, 1975

Eames, Steven C. 'Rustic Warriors: Warfare and the Provincial Soldier on the Northern Frontier, 1689–1748.' PhD dissertation, University of New Hampshire, 1989

Ghere, David Lynn. 'Abenaki Factionalism, Emigration, and Social Continuity: Indian Society in Northern New England, 1725 to 1765.' PhD dissertation, University of Maine, 1988

Johnson, Richard Rigby. 'Adjustment to Empire: War, New England, and British Colonial Policy in the Late Seventeenth Century.' PhD dissertation, University of California at Berkeley, 1972

Jones, D.W. 'London Overseas: Merchant Groups at the End of the Seventeenth Century and the Moves against the East India Company.' D Phil. thesis, Oxford University, 1970

Lewis, Theodore B., Jr. 'Massachusetts and the Glorious Revolution, 1660–1692.' PhD dissertation, University of Wisconsin, 1967

Moody, Robert Earle. 'The Maine Frontier, 1607 to 1763.' PhD dissertation, Yale University, 1933

Murison, Barbara Cresswell. 'William Blathwayt's Empire: Politics and Administration in England and the Atlantic Colonies, 1668–1710.' PhD dissertation, University of Western Ontario, 1981

Will, Richard T., and James Clark. 'A Report on the Excavation and Analysis of the Anne Hilton Site.' Manuscript report on file at the Maine Historic Preservation Commission, 1991

Index